WORDSWORTH AND THE ART OF PHILOSOPHICAL TRAVEL

At the heart of Wordsworth's concerns is the question of how travel – both foreign and everyday – might also become an adventure into philosophy itself. This is an art of travel both as an approach to experience, one that draws on habits in order to revise them in the shock of the new, and as a poetic approach that gives voice to the singular and foreign through the unique shapes of verse. Close readings of Wordsworth's 'pictures of Nature, Man, and Society' show how the natural is entangled with – and not simply opposed to, as many critics have suggested – the social, the political and the historical in this verse. The book draws both on eighteenth-century anthropology and travel literature, and on debates in modern critical theory, to highlight Wordsworth's remarkable originality and his ongoing ability to transform our theoretical prejudgements in the unknown territory of the travel encounter.

MARK OFFORD teaches at the University of Cambridge.

CAMBRIDGE STUDIES IN ROMANTICISM

This series aims to foster the best new work in one of the most challenging fields within English literary studies. From the early 1780s to the early 1830s a formidable array of talented men and women took to literary composition, not just in poetry, which some of them famously transformed, but in many modes of writing. The expansion of publishing created new opportunities for writers, and the political stakes of what they wrote were raised again by what Wordsworth called those 'great national events' that were 'almost daily taking place': the French Revolution, the Napoleonic and American wars, urbanization, industrialization, religious revival, an expanded empire abroad and the reform movement at home. This was an enormous ambition, even when it pretended otherwise. The relations between science, philosophy, religion and literature were reworked in texts such as *Frankenstein* and *Biographia Literaria*; gender relations in *A Vindication of the Rights of Woman* and *Don Juan*; journalism by Cobbett and Hazlitt; poetic form, content and style by the Lake School and the Cockney School. Outside Shakespeare studies, probably no body of writing has produced such a wealth of comment or done so much to shape the responses of modern criticism. This indeed is the period that saw the emergence of those notions of 'literature' and of literary history, especially national literary history, on which modern scholarship in English has been founded.

The categories produced by Romanticism have also been challenged by recent historicist arguments. The task of the series is to engage both with a challenging corpus of Romantic writings and with the changing field of criticism they have helped to shape. As with other literary series published by Cambridge, this one will represent the work of both younger and more established scholars, on either side of the Atlantic and elsewhere.

For a complete list of titles published see end of book.

WORDSWORTH AND THE ART OF PHILOSOPHICAL TRAVEL

MARK OFFORD

CAMBRIDGE
UNIVERSITY PRESS

CAMBRIDGE
UNIVERSITY PRESS

University Printing House, Cambridge CB2 8BS, United Kingdom

Cambridge University Press is part of the University of Cambridge.

It furthers the University's mission by disseminating knowledge in the pursuit of education, learning and research at the highest international levels of excellence.

www.cambridge.org
Information on this title: www.cambridge.org/9781107155589

First published 2016

Printed in the United States of America by Sheridan Books, Inc.

A catalogue record for this publication is available from the British Library

ISBN 978-1-107-15558-9 Hardback

For Rosemary, in remembrance

'For the tragic transport is actually empty, and the least restrained.– Thereby, in the rhythmic sequence of the representations wherein the transport presents itself, there becomes necessary what in poetic metre is called caesura, the pure word, the counter-rhythmic rupture.'

Friedrich Hölderlin, 'Annotations to Oedipus'

Contents

Acknowledgements

This study began as a Ph.D. thesis at Cambridge University entitled 'Wordsworth, Enlightenment Anthropology and the Literature of Travel', which has since been comprehensively rewritten. It is inevitable that, through such a long period of gestation, I should have incurred too many debts to list everyone who has helped in some capacity. But along with all my family, friends, colleagues and teachers, I would like to thank the following individuals in particular: Nandi and Åsa Eriksson Ahuja, Jane Alexander, the late John Chancellor, Cynthia Chase, Siobhán Ní Chonaill, Charles Cornish-Dale, Adam Coutts, Farah Dakhlallah, Chris Eastland, Daniel Eggers, the late John Field, Christian Goeschel, the late Jack Goody, Paul Hamilton, Ceri Hiles, Stefan Hoesel-Uhlig, Mary Jacobus, Carol Long, Beatriz Martinez-Gatell, Alexander Masters, Taren McCallan Moore, Juliet Mitchell, Nicholas Murgatroyd, Simon Norton, Nigel Offord, Vivienne Offord, John Offord, Simon Offord, Sophie Offord, Kate Offord, Simon and Dani Redhead, Quentin Tannock and Manuela Wedgwood. I would also like to thank the Arts and Humanities Research Council (AHRC) for funding the thesis research, and Darwin College and Jesus College, Cambridge University, along with the English Faculty at Cambridge, for their assistance during the period of writing. The two anonymous readers for Cambridge University Press were illuminating in their generous comments and suggestions. I would also like to thank the series General Editor, Jim Chandler, for his very helpful and encouraging report, and everyone at Cambridge University Press who assisted so much in the preparation and production of this book: above all, Linda Bree and her team, Anna Bond, Sarah Starkey and Frances Brown. Alexander Dougherty's erudite and thoughtful responses to the manuscript proved an invaluable resource. Catriona Gray also read the chapter drafts and her astute comments were a great help and encouragement. The early stages of this project benefited hugely from the learning and judgement of Nigel Leask, my initial thesis supervisor prior to his departure for Glasgow University. My greatest debt, however, is to the thesis' subsequent supervisor, Simon Jarvis, who has been a never-failing source of encouragement, inspiration and brilliance of insight.

Abbreviations (of Wordsworth Editions Cited)

B	*The Borderers*, ed. Robert Osborn (Ithaca: Cornell University Press, 1982).
DS	*Descriptive Sketches*, ed. Eric Birdsall (Ithaca: Cornell University Press, 1984). References will be to the first draft of the poem (1791–2), unless indicated.
EW	*An Evening Walk*, ed. James Averill (Ithaca: Cornell University Press, 1984).
Exc.	*The Excursion*, ed. Sally Bushell, James A. Butler and Michael C. Jaye (Ithaca: Cornell University Press, 2007).
EY	*The Letters of William and Dorothy Wordsworth, Early Years 1787–1805*, ed. Ernest de Selincourt, revised by Chester L. Shaver (Oxford: Clarendon Press, 1967).
14BkPr.	*The Fourteen-Book Prelude*, ed. W. J. B. Owen (Ithaca: Cornell University Press, 1985).
HG	*Home at Grasmere, Part First, Book First, of The Recluse*, ed. Beth Darlington (Ithaca: Cornell University Press, 1977).
LB	*Lyrical Ballads, and Other Poems, 1797–1800*, ed. James Butler and Karen Green (Ithaca: Cornell University Press, 1992).
LP	*Last Poems, 1821–1850*, ed. Jared Curtis (Ithaca: Cornell University Press, 1999).
LY	*The Letters of William and Dorothy Wordsworth, Later Years*, 4 vols., ed. Ernest de Selincourt, revised Alan G. Hill (Oxford: Clarendon Press, 1979).
MY	*The Letters of William and Dorothy Wordsworth, Middle Years*, 2 vols., ed. Ernest de Selincourt, revised Mary Moorman (Oxford: Clarendon Press, 1970).
PB	*Peter Bell*, ed. John E. Jordan (Ithaca: Cornell University Press, 1985).

Pr.	*The Thirteen-Book Prelude*, vol. I, ed. Mark L. Reed (Ithaca: Cornell University Press, 1991). References will be to the 'A-B Reading Text' of the poem in 1805.
Pr2	*The Thirteen-Book Prelude*, vol. II, ed. Mark L. Reed (Ithaca: Cornell University Press, 1991).
P2V	*Poems, in Two Volumes, and Other Poems, 1800–1807*, ed. Jared Curtis (Ithaca: Cornell University Press, 1983).
PW	*The Prose Works of William Wordsworth*, ed. W. J. B. Owen and Jane Worthington Smyser, 3 vols. (Oxford: Clarendon Press, 1974).
RC	*The Ruined Cottage and The Pedlar*, ed. James Butler (Ithaca: Cornell University Press, 1979).
SP	*The Salisbury Plain Poems of William Wordsworth*, ed. Stephen Gill (Ithaca: Cornell University Press, 1975). References will be to the first draft (1793–4) unless otherwise indicated in the text.
SSI	*Sonnet Series and Itinerary Poems, 1820–1845*, ed. Geoffrey Jackson (Ithaca: Cornell University Press, 2004).
TP	*The Tuft of Primroses with Other Late Poems for The Recluse*, ed. Joseph F. Kishel (Ithaca: Cornell University Press, 1986).

Introduction

Wordsworth's earliest conception of *The Recluse* – the overarching project that he hoped would provide a structure for all his poetry – had an art of philosophical travel as its objective. It was first announced in a letter to James Tobin on 6 March 1798:

> I have written 1300 lines of a poem in which I contrive to convey most of the knowledge of which I am possessed. My object is to give pictures of Nature, Man, and Society. Indeed, I know not anything which will not come within the scope of my plan . . . *If you could collect for me any books of travels you would render me an essential service, as without much of such reading my present labours cannot be brought to a conclusion.*[1] (my emphasis)

An encyclopaedic range is to be conveyed through individual pictures alone. At this stage, Wordsworth's single long poem was paradoxically composed of four self-contained vignettes: 'The Discharged Soldier', 'A Night-Piece', 'The Ruined Cottage' and 'The Old Cumberland Beggar'. Descriptive poems about encounters with the poor and their rural environment, they largely eschew discursive philosophy. Yet they possess nearly the maximum of knowledge for Wordsworth.

As Alan Bewell has observed in a pioneering study,[2] Wordsworth sought to overcome a widespread eighteenth-century division of labour between the 'moral philosopher' – the writer of systematic treatises on the 'natural history of man', the philosophical and historical anthropology of a universal human nature – and the travel writer out in the field, the ethnographer of scattered observations and anecdotes ('pictures') concerning 'savage' or foreign modes of life. Across the distance of social class, and an estranged nature itself, Wordsworth's exploration of a Lakeland landscape of the working and vagrant poor was also a mode of foreign travel. But this project, centred on the 'picture' more than systematic exposition – 'spots of time' that were to remain the nodal points of his longer and more discursive later writings for *The Recluse*, as with *The Prelude* and even *The Excursion* – was in a state of critical tension with moral philosophy.

The task was surely indebted to Coleridge who had announced almost a year earlier, in early April 1797, a long poem he would never write, for he had projected no less than 'ten years' of research into 'the *mind of man* – then the *minds of men* – in all Travels, Voyages, and Histories'.[3] It testified to the daunting challenge in reconciling an indivisible human nature with the vast archive of cultural diversity. It is instructive to compare Wordsworth's attempted solution to this problem with that of an innovative, though characteristic, 'moral philosopher'. In 1771, John Millar had argued that demonstrating the 'similarity' of anthropological 'wants', and the 'remarkable uniformity' of their world-historical development, required a comparative synthesis of travel accounts. From the 'agreement or disagreement' of descriptions, the anthropologist might arrive at a composite view, and 'ascertain the credit' to be given to the notoriously uncertain 'veracity of the relater'.[4] As Edmund Burke wrote on 9 June 1777 to William Robertson, the historian of 'savage' America: 'now the Great Map of Mankind is unrolled at once; and there is no state or Gradation of barbarism, and no mode of refinement which we have not at the same instant under our View'.[5] The spatializing effect of these hierarchical structures of knowledge had an alternative, flattening result, depicted by Millar as the unrolling of an aesthetic pluralism: 'the most wonderful variety of appearances . . . the greatest diversity of manners and customs'.[6] Surveying the map from an elevated prospect, knowledge might yield to contemplative enjoyment. The cognitive and aesthetic spheres are distinct, viewed from different angles.

Outlining 'The Design' of his *Essay on Man* (1734), the most successful and influential work of the eighteenth-century genre that would both culminate and disintegrate in *The Recluse*, the versification of philosophical anthropology in the didactic long poem, Alexander Pope had characterized it as 'a *general map* of MAN, marking out no more than the *greater parts*, their *extent*, their *limits*, and their *connection*, but leaving out the particular to be more fully delineated in the charts which are to follow'.[7] For Wordsworth, however, there is no map, only the frontal scrutiny of a series of 'pictures'. Or charts of the particular: subsequent characterizations of *The Recluse* would refer both to 'pictures' and to '*views*'[8] – the image must open up a prospect. There is no space for aesthetic wonder to detach itself from cognitive appraisal: it is the very medium of knowledge.

Yet Thomas De Quincey's 1823 antithesis of a 'literature of knowledge' and 'literature of power' was credited as stemming from 'many years' conversations with Mr. Wordsworth'.[9] The literature of power specializes in 'emotions which ordinary life rarely or never supplies occasions for exciting' – dormant until a poet is able 'to organize' these 'inert and sleeping forms'.[10] The contrasting literature of knowledge includes even the 'higher pretensions' of 'books of voyages and travels, and generally all books in which the matter to be communicated is paramount to the manner or form of its communication'.[11] Wordsworth's 1798 poem, it seems, can offer no generally valid knowledge, only exceptions to the formal rule.

In *The Prelude*, a schooling in travel as the literature of knowledge would epitomize the indifferent learning of the precocious child: 'He knows the policies of foreign Lands; / Can string you names of districts, cities, towns, / The whole world over' (*Pr.* v.334–6). Opposed to this was the education of travel as experience, the child's exploration of his native environment, a genuine

> knowledge, rightly honor'd with that name,
> Knowledge not purchas'd with the loss of power!
> (448–9)

In Book II, childhood is a time when 'all knowledge is delight' (306). It is to experience

> that universal power
> And fitness in the latent qualities
> And essences of things
> (343–5)

Here 'power' has usurped the attribute of knowledge: it is 'universal'. As with secular theodicies of the 'chain of being' or progress, the great map is one of global 'fitness'. Yet this is not quite to say with the *Essay on Man* that 'Whatever is, is right.' Things are as they should be – at a level that is only 'latent'. Or in De Quincey's words, 'inert and sleeping'. Descriptive knowledge is haunted by a power of prescription for what has yet to become fully manifest. A traditional distinction of essence and appearance has become slippery and ungraspable.

We are both near and far from the 'wonderful variety' of appearances for Millar, a panorama of variegated and curious data, organized and hierarchized into the progressive stages of universal history. The literature of manifest quantities, it seems, would be the cognition of things in their exile from fitness. The aesthetic *is* moving towards its autonomy – through a refusal to countenance it as an insulated sphere. In Kojin Karatani's phrase, the aesthetic has opened up a 'parallax view', a radical change in the object when seen from a different position – as a physiognomic reading of latent qualities, a head-on picture rather than a mapped co-ordinate.

For Karatani, it is the 'parallax view' of travel that necessitates the task of philosophy, the 'transcritique' by which it traverses and negotiates rival positions.[12] Karatani gives three examples: Descartes, who stated explicitly that the *cogito* was an attempt to locate a secure ground of knowledge following the shock that travel had given him, its relativizing of custom and tradition as a reliable authority; Kant, who refused to travel beyond the commercial seaport of Königsberg in order to maintain his anthropology from a cosmopolitan point of view; and Marx, whose residences in Germany, France and Britain were to inform a critical transposition of idealism, rationalism and empiricism within a new materialist dialectic. Travel was notoriously destabilizing in its threat to received opinion and the *sensus communis*. Jonathan Lamb has cited Samuel Johnson's disorientation in *A Journey to the Western Isles of Scotland*: 'He who has not made the experiment . . . will scarcely believe how much a few hours take from the certainty of knowledge, and distinctness of imagery.'[13] Lamb accounts for the enormous popularity of travel literature in the eighteenth century in terms of its dramatization of individual 'self-preservation' as it struggled to survive amidst the foreign.[14]

The most serious cruxes of philosophy were at stake. In a picture of 'Nature, Man, and Society' in South-East America, William Bartram described a mysterious incident in which an Indian on horseback, a noted thief, murderer and renegade from his tribe, pursued Bartram and fixed him with his rifle, only to draw it away and take Bartram's extended hand in friendship. Bartram is led to remark: 'Can it be denied, but that the moral principle which directs the savages to virtuous and praiseworthy actions, is natural and innate?'[15] Bartram had been schooled at the Philadelphia Academy, whose curriculum was modelled on Francis Hutcheson's theory of the benevolent 'moral sense'.[16] By contrast for Locke, as Ann Talbot has shown,[17] travel literature abundantly vindicated his conviction that there were no innate ideas or moral principles, while confirming the prejudices of a literate European superiority: 'But alas, amongst *children*, *idiots*, and *savages*, and the grossly *illiterate*, what general maxims are to be found?'[18] The so-called 'savage', it seems, was all too empiricist. In their polar contrast, Locke and Bartram were equally trapped in a hermeneutic circle.

Soon after Wordsworth's announcement of *The Recluse*, Novalis would famously diagnose philosophy as a 'homesickness', a drive (*Trieb*) to be everywhere at home.[19] The Enlightenment system, with its staking out of the first principles from which all of world history and its ethnic diversity could be gathered together and reclaimed, brought back home to the philosopher's fireside, was an unwitting testament to this pathos of distance. With youthful confidence, Wordsworth could state in 1798, 'I know not anything which will not come within the scope of my plan.' For Rousseau, the philosopher's laborious homecoming merely converted the world into their own mirror-image. European philosophy displayed a fundamental inability to travel:

> Although the inhabitants of Europe have for the past three or four hundred years overrun the other parts of the world and are constantly publishing new collections of travels and reports, I am convinced that the only men we know are the Europeans; what is more, it would seem that, judging by the ridiculous prejudices that have not died out even among Men of Letters, very nearly all anyone does under the pompous heading of the study of man is to study the men of his country. Regardless of how much individuals may come and go, it would seem that Philosophy does not travel.[20]

But it is tempting to respond at this point with Stephen Greenblatt (on Columbus' first contact with the inhabitants of the Americas):

> We can demonstrate that, in the face of the unknown, Europeans used their conventional intellectual and organizational structures, fashioned over centuries of mediated contact with other cultures, and that these structures greatly impeded a clear grasp of the radical otherness of the American lands and peoples. What else would we expect?[21]

Greenblatt's important argument is that we must not 'efface the incommensurability, the astonishing singularity' of 12 October 1492.[22] Even in the universal context of European effacements of the singular in favour of the global structure, we have an utterly singular instance of such an effacement – and one that we must not efface ourselves through systematic and global interpretation. But while that truly epochal singularity is obviously not in dispute, nor the strangeness and imaginary quality of Columbus' routine and ritual gestures of land possession in such an 'unprecedented situation' (as Greenblatt observes eloquently and acutely), do not the paradoxes here suggest that the 'otherness', on every side of the encounter, might not be quite so radically absolute? Yet there is a crucial awareness here that such episodes have their own unique differences as well as similarities, that it is necessary to assemble, as Wordsworth indicated to Tobin, a wide range of 'pictures'.

The period in which Wordsworth was writing had started to experiment formally with new ways to think through the singular and the global. Clifford Siskin has observed that in 1798, 'the Year of the System', a troubled relationship between the particular and the universal was to characterize its intellectual production: 'embedding systems as parts within adventurously incomplete wholes' or 'unsystematic' genres (the short poem, for example).[23] It is because Wordsworth was unable fully to make the transition from the picture to the system – *The Recluse* was eventually abandoned – yet also unable to settle for a nominalistic and absolute metaphysics of the singular, that his travels in *terra incognita*, his willingness to articulate the strange and foreign even among 'the men of his country', were perhaps the first adventure in philosophical travel ever to be angled at a genuine 'parallax'.

The Rights of Nature

The great shortcoming of Wordsworth's 'pictures', the absence of an overarching and structural analysis of 'Nature, Man, and Society', is also their greatest asset: an ability to uncover the most minute points of resistance in the face of such a totality. But this search for an individual autonomy in the 'essences of things' – all the way down to the minuscule detail or latent quality – took its initial rise from another universalizing discourse of the Enlightenment: the deduction of principles of natural law and the 'rights of man'. It was the quest for individual pictures of the universal heart of rights, voiced through impoverished suffering, which drove sentimental journeys in verse like that of John Thelwall's *The Peripatetic, or Sketches of the Heart, Nature and Society* (1793), which points to a strong influence on *The Recluse* through its title alone. Kenneth Johnston has argued that the early *Recluse* was conceived not as a 'vast nebulous scheme', but within the conventions of 'loco-descriptive-meditative poetry'.[24] But the peripatetic philosophy of *The Recluse* went off in search of 'pictures of Man', an infinitely more vast and nebulous prospect than sketches of the heart alone.

Sentimental literature left home to explore a *topos* that Wordsworth was radically to reclaim as his own. The state of nature, the primordial condition before social classes and culture, in which 'liberty, equality and fraternity' were transparently evident as humanity's natural birthright, was now located through its anguished expression in the contemporary world. Travel was bound up with politics and the question of rights as it searched for a philosophical anthropology. Wordsworth's earliest critics quite clearly perceived his poetry's indebtedness to the discourse of natural rights, as proclaimed by the American and French Revolutions and inspired by thinkers such as Tom Paine and Rousseau.[25] As Mary Jacobus has recently observed, this was drastically extended by Wordsworth to include even the 'rights of nature' itself.[26]

But there is a major problem here, one that points to this verse's status as art and its difficult relation to that *sine qua non* of philosophy, the concept. Such 'rights' are almost never explicitly mentioned at all.[27] For Maureen McLane, Wordsworth rejects the historiographies of the primitive, the fountain of natural rights, in favour of the uniquely situated and historically particular. Wordsworth's versions of 'natural man', his rustics and so-called primitives, are 'No longer objects of representation in conjectural histories . . . [but] emerge, however problematical, as subjects with voices, situations, histories.'[28] Alan Bewell has likewise proposed that in Wordsworth's 1798 poem 'The Discharged Soldier', the truly 'human status' of its vagrant subject emerges only when Wordsworth realizes the falsehood of 'divesting the man of cultural attributes in order to increase his conformity with an anthropological idea of primitive man'.[29] Such a definition of the human would seem to preclude absolute rights, shifting to positive rather than natural law, for if they are purely cultural and historical – rather than 'primitive' to the embodied condition – then they have been posited rather than universally grounded. How can Wordsworth seem to gesture not only to the human rights of the somatic and affective self, to its personal independence and equality, but also even to the 'rights of nature', the rights of matter itself?

David Bromwich, by sharp contrast, proposes that Wordsworth's figures of a 'radical humanity' tear apart 'a social context with intelligible meanings'. Bromwich, like McLane and Bewell, discerns a new particularism in this verse, only now this is directly opposed to the historical and cultural: Wordsworth's 'particulars are natural . . . merely everything that culture is not'.[30] Wordsworth is somehow locatable on both sides of an either/or proposition. The 'human' is either purely cultural or exclusively natural. How might Wordsworth's pictures of 'Man' in the contexts of both 'Nature' *and* 'Society' appear in the light of Walter Benjamin's 'axiom of the way to avoid mythic thinking': 'No historical category without natural substance; no natural substance without its historical filter'?[31] Can poems like 'The Discharged Soldier' show a way to avoid both cultural idealism *and* a dogmatic naturalism?

James Chandler has argued that such a dense entanglement of nature and history was to register a change in Wordsworth's conception of rights. For Chandler, Wordsworth's 1798 poems move away from Rousseau, abandon the notion of a state of nature,[32] and turn to an exploration of what Edmund Burke deemed a 'second nature'. In Burke's version of positive law, the 'natural rights' affirmed by the French Revolution were no longer relevant amid the complexity of a stratified society, its welter of unequal and inherited rights. For Burke, on 'entering into common life, like rays of light which pierce into a dense medium', all 'primitive rights' get 'refracted from their straight line'.[33] The opposition between culture and nature has been resolved by history into the second-order necessity (the 'second nature') of habits and social conventions.

In the year of the 1832 Reform Bill, Wordsworth wrote an encomium to the 'Genius of Burke' for *The Prelude* that celebrated his denunciation of 'all systems built on abstract rights' (*14BkPr.* VII.524). But in 1798, Wordsworth's odyssey of the 1790s across political theory had not quite found a secure resting-place.[34] He seems to have read Paine's *The Rights of Man* soon after it appeared in 1791,[35] while an unfinished essay of the same year, his 'Letter to the Bishop of Llandaff', had affirmed the Rousseauan principle of a 'social contract' founded in the 'general will'. Following the Terror, this youthful enthusiasm for 'abstract rights' was mitigated not by Burke but by the radically progressive and anarchic, if not revolutionary, thought of William Godwin, whose *Enquiry into Political Justice* (1793) had opened with a polemic against natural rights as subversive of social duty. In 1826, Godwin recalled that in the mid-1790s he had 'had the honour, in the talk of one evening to convert Wordsworth, from the doctrine of self-love to that of benevolence – ask him . . . that is perhaps my powerful topic'.[36] Godwinian benevolence was rational, not a natural instinct elevated to a law as with Rousseau's *amour de soi-même*. Faced with an impossible choice between rival first principles, it is understandable that Wordsworth's Godwinian phase would end, as he recounts in *The Prelude*, in a state of aporetic exhaustion: 'wearied out with contrarieties', he 'Yielded up moral questions in despair' (*Pr.* x.899–900).

Wordsworth came to view Godwin's rejection of nature as a pseudo-rationality in which 'passions had the privilege to work' unconsciously (*Pr.* x.812). Godwin's alternative to abstract right was what Wordsworth would call 'the immediate law' in his 1795–6 play *The Borderers* (*B* III.4.31). In words partly transferred later to his Godwinian phase in *The Prelude*, that law was said to emerge from 'the light of circumstances, flashed / Upon an independent intellect' (*ibid.*, 32–3; *Pr.* x.828–9). In terms indeed reminiscent of Burke, this was no less abstract for Wordsworth than the rights tradition in its 'shaking off . . . The accidents of nature, time, and place' in local and historical development (*Pr.* x.821–3). The corrupted Godwinianism of Rivers, the central figure in *The Borderers*, laid claim to the 'immediate law' in order to justify a gratuitous murder. Godwin's law of unique circumstances was readily convertible into an arbitrary decisionism. Rivers, however, makes appeal to the natural as well as immediate law: according to the 'institutes of nature', humans have a right to 'destroy' each other with 'licence', just as they do with the animal kingdom (*B* III.5.95–102). The natural law of 'whatever is, is right', collapsing the moral into the given, was also a licence to kill. But the positive law was equally violent as an arbitrary, though historically sanctified, imposition – and its difference from an immediate law that flashed out from a singular context, to strike with its own violence, risked falling into undecidability.

Against the aporias of law, political failure and moral despair, Wordsworth had only 'the accidents of nature, time, and place' as a bulwark. As opposed to a univocal light of circumstances, immediately self-evident, what were both historical *and* natural particulars or 'accidents' had to be painstakingly *read* within an individual configuration. In a 1798–9 prose fragment now titled the 'Essay on Morals', Wordsworth would indeed, like Burke, call upon the force of habit or 'second nature' within the dense medium of moral-political law. Here he rails indiscriminately against the 'whole tribe' of moral philosophers (naming Godwin) for being 'impotent over our habits' in their merely abstract prescriptions.[37] Wordsworth was writing under circumstances that are perhaps not unfamiliar: a failed revolution coinciding with a proliferation of normative 'theory' (largely identified with a French predilection for the abstract). In 1832, Wordsworth commended Burke for 'exploding upstart Theory' (*14BkPr.* VII.529). As David Simpson observes, figures like Burke, and the traveller and rural surveyor Arthur Young – who had scorned the 'ideal and visionary rights of nature' on a journey through France just a month before the fall of the Bastille[38] – had appealed to a British national character identified with empiricism, custom and practical common sense as their mainstay against 'French' theory.[39] Simpson argues that Wordsworth attempted 'a synthesis of the otherwise antagonist principles of Burke and Paine' by endorsing the 'habitual conventions' of rural manners as 'an image of democratic social life'.[40] Wordsworth's 'democratic universalism' of the countryside was one of 'feeling, or thought-in-feeling', not the 'rationalist radicalism' of 'setting forth the rights of man in propositional form'.[41]

The 'Essay on Morals' argued that poetry's 'thought-in-feeling' must reach into the whole inner body of the reader in order to engage its habitual responses. It must go deeper than sentiment to 'incorporate itself with the blood and vital juices of our minds' and 'melt into our affection'.[42] What moral-political theories lacked were precisely 'pictures of Nature, Man, and Society' capable of mimetically laying hold of the reader. Philosophy's 'lifeless words, & abstract propositions . . . contain no picture of human life; they describe nothing'.[43] Though Wordsworth's critics have been right to insist on the centrality of habit in his verse, the explicit aim here is not to reaffirm habits – not even the 'second nature' of rural custom – but to *change* them. For Wordsworth, it was folly to expect that 'an old habit will be foregone, or a new one formed, by a series of propositions, which, presenting no image to the [?mind] can convey no feeling which has any connection with the supposed archetype or fountain of the proposition existing in human life'.[44] Normative thought is empty unless it can describe the contexts from which it arises with its own necessity. Wordsworth does not tell us that such a moment of 'human life' is identical with the abstract proposition – only that there is a 'connection'. The archetype contains, but the fountain overflows.

Travel was the search for such pictures. Wordsworth's argument can be traced back to the rhetorical tradition of Renaissance and Classical Humanism. Ernesto Grassi characterized the role of the poetic in this tradition as a demonstration of the *archai* – archetypal images that cannot be obtained rationally, for they are the givens from which deduction unfolds: 'Such speech is immediately a "showing" – and for this reason "figurative" or "imaginative," and thus in the original sense theoretical [*theorein* – i.e., to see].'[45] But like Thelwall, Wordsworth also inherited a more recent search for the *archai*. Lynn Hunt has argued that the mid-eighteenth-century novel of 'sensibility' was a key source for the nascent discourse of human rights.[46] As the reader sympathized with the agonies of the marginalized, so the equal rights to bodily integrity and the human universality of feeling were established as 'self-evident'. Hunt points out that Jean-Jacques Burlamaqui's (1747) *The Principles of Natural Law* (a major influence on his fellow Genevan, Rousseau), which revived and synthesized seventeenth-century theories of natural law, had 'updated the concept' by linking it to Francis Hutcheson's notion of an 'internal moral sense'.[47] In his *Elements of Criticism* (1762), Lord Kames had famously argued for such an immediately moral aesthetic by way of literature's 'ideal presence' for the reader.

Wordsworth's attack on the 'lifeless words' of moral philosophy was by implication a call for vitally engaging and persuasive speech. But this could take a markedly subdued, rather than exhortatory form. Wordsworth's emphasis on words rather than propositions lent a 'peculiar force' to 'the most inconspicuous words',[48] as Simon Jarvis has put it, so that they become 'fundamental words'[49] – a language of implication that cannot be easily assimilated either to an 'ideal presence' of the archetype or to a transparent reason and sentiment. This was not, Jarvis observes, an exhaustive rendering of particular detail, but rather a 'stripping down of poetry, the removal of everything that is adventitious to a description . . . [forcing] us right up against that in language which will not be made absolutely literal: the way in which under the steadiest description still sounds a prescription, the way in which a norm, or a value, or a meaning, echoes in what is apparently the most naked and simple'.[50] The rights of nature are pared down to an echo that sounds even in bare life.

In *The Prelude*, there was a time when natural right had seemed visibly the immediate law. As a young traveller in France, Wordsworth recalls troops of soldiers, 'Even files of Strangers merely' (IX.281) – filing down that image to its barest evocation – as they marched past him in revolutionary Paris:

> Even by these passing spectacles my heart
> Was oftentimes uplifted, and they seem'd
> Like arguments from Heaven that 'twas a cause
> Good
>
> (IX.287–90)

This secular revelation has the force of 'arguments'[51] rather than *archai*. It is only 'Like' something dropped down 'from Heaven'. No timeless archetype, it disturbs as an image of history at its most violent and revolutionary. Wordsworth was soon to be thrown into a moral turmoil of divided loyalty when the Pitt government declared war on France. It remains an 'argument' rather than a self-evident truth – the spectacle demands reflection and appraisal. For no less than a war is at stake. But there is a salutary parallax in the image, a sidelong perspective that uncovers what is irreducible to the passing spectacle, the marching boots that rise and fall in revolutionary unity. Twice in the passage, Wordsworth emphasizes that these are 'strangers', a repetition that underscores this as a fundamental word. They are 'mere' strangers, bare life, in their uniform equality as simple 'files'. Yet what makes them strange is also the capacity for 'a face / Or person' at times to be 'singled out among the rest', a survival of the individual in conditions of extreme levelling – 'Yet still a stranger and beloved as such' (284–6). In that most alien, blank or frightening of words, 'stranger', a norm and value can still resonate, and even become something worth fighting for: an autonomous life that is worthy of love precisely because it is hidden from us.

The value of the stranger 'as such' was simply inconceivable to the literature of sensibility in its merging of identical sentiments. As a trend in ethnography, Pierre Bourdieu called versions of the latter an 'intuitionism' that 'fictitiously denies the distance between the observer and the observed'.[52] By contrast, theory is characterized by social distance for Bourdieu: a contemplation of structures at a privileged remove. He points out that *theoria* connoted not only 'seeing' but also 'spectacle' or 'procession' for the Greeks.[53] Theory circumvents individual agency and practice as it sees only structures or systems of relationships.[54] Working between subjectivism and objectivism is what Bourdieu termed the *habitus*, the 'structuring dispositions' that guide practice,[55] habitually ingrained by past experience. These are 'incorporated structures' derived from, yet also in 'dialectic' with, objective social structures.[56] The sphere of *habitus* is regulated, and involves judgements, without obeying explicit rules (or laws and rights). It takes 'the form of schemes of perception, thought and action'.[57] A 'relation to the body is a fundamental dimension of the *habitus* that is inseparable from a relation to language';[58] it involves 'deep-rooted linguistic and muscular patterns of behaviour . . . reactivating them to function mimetically' through associative links to the past.[59] When, in the 'Essay on Morals', Wordsworth enjoins a bodily immersion in the language of the text through its invocation of 'habits', this is to enter the domain of *habitus*. It is what connects the parallax of travel, an observation or phenomenology of individual practice, to a broader and internalized social structure. Unlike the 'passing spectacles' of *theoria* in the revolutionary situation of 1792, this is Burke's dense prism, a realm of refracted not primitive rights: the pressure of a norm for fulfilment was unlikely to issue in a 'moral' or programme of action.

Bourdieu's notion of *habitus* has been understandably criticized as 'totalizing'.[60] How might this generative matrix be exceeded or challenged or broken down? Can the *habitus* perceive anything foreign to its structures, let alone the stranger 'as such'? Yet it is easier to negate such totalizing frameworks in the abstract than it is to break out of them in practice. For the 'Essay on Morals', the reader must first be led into that 'dense medium' for there to be any hope of finding the way out. Habit was to be enlisted in order to draw on its force and turn it in the direction of the new. When Wordsworth was praised in 1802 for his accuracy in portraying human nature, he replied by insisting that 'a great Poet ought to do more than this': he must 'travel before men occasionally as well as at their sides'. The poet must 'rectify men's feelings, to give them new compositions of feeling'.[61] The 'literature of power' for De Quincey also had to 'organize' such 'inert and sleeping forms' of charged emotion. This was why, in contrast to the literature of knowledge and travel, 'the manner or form of its communication' was pre-eminent above 'the matter to be communicated'. In Wordsworth's poetics of philosophical travel, an aesthetic form *is* the matter to be communicated. The *habitus* as a 'scheme of perception, thought and action' is to unravel and recombine as 'new *compositions* of feeling': alternative structures of perception which the plasticity of verse can model in advance. To be an avant-garde traveller through the *terra incognita* of human feeling is to discover new configurations of poetic technique, new ways of organizing its material. A moral or propositional value has migrated into an elaboration of the poem's form as a new mode of sight and experience.

Terra Incognita

The travel metaphor was not just a passing fancy: the explorer in unknown territory, habitually recoiling from the alien, but gradually arriving at understanding, was a key figure in the background of Wordsworth's verse. In a recent essay, Jonathan Lamb has traced how seventeenth- and eighteenth-century voyages and travels in *terra incognita* and the crises or raptures that attended them – sensory intensifications, exaggerations and hallucinations, with all their epistemological breakthroughs and quandaries – became a potent trope for scientific discourses.[62] For Robert Hooke, the discovery of 'new Worlds and Terra-Incognita's' became an explicit model for the experimental scientist in new dimensions of matter, as supplied in his *Micrographia* (1665) by the microscope; Coleridge was fascinated by the implications of Addison's observation that sight could become a 'diffusive' kind of touch, and developed his own notion of the 'double touch' of sight, while the skin itself seemed a medical *terra incognita* for him.[63] The effects of his (and Wordsworth's) friend Humphrey Davy's experiments with nitrous oxide at the Pneumatic Institute in 1799, and his confessed inability to articulate the experience, bore marked resemblances to the traveller's diseased or infatuated transports.[64] As Lamb observes, that capacity of the distorted or enlarged senses to transfigure the world – as with the voyager's hyperaesthesia as a symptom of scurvy – was to risk a confirmation of Locke's argument that our embodied sensations were as arbitrary a representation of objects as the linguistic sign. The crisis of *terra incognita* as a new state of nature might be as vacuous as Davy's inhaled gas.

Wordsworth would at times take refuge in more subtly questioning forms of the traveller's empty rhetoric of ineffability, the *je ne sais quoi*. He was certainly fascinated by the hallucinatory potential of imaginative projection, as in the sailor's 'calenture' or transposed imagery of home onto the canvas of tropical seas ('The Brothers'), the delusional visions of the socially alienated expatriate ('The Mad Mother'), or the power of auto-suggestion within a supposed 'witchcraft' as in 'Goody Blake and Harry Gill', whose story he drew from Erasmus Darwin's *Zoonomia*.[65] Naturalists like Darwin, George Cheyne and Thomas Beddoes treated such distortions of the world as diseases of the nerves, highlighting the mediated uncertainty of the senses. The 'double touch' of sight in Coleridge's notebooks was not just a tactility of sense but an apperception of mind that included our habitual evaluations of phenomena as real or false, one that fell away in the 'single touch' of dream. Troubled by the new discoveries of science, the questioning of sense by mechanical philosophy, and the new worlds reported by the possibly deluded or falsifying traveller, the whole wide empire of the *habitus*, the familiar and reliable world of indubitable sense-certainty, had fallen into estrangement and *terra incognita*.

While Francis Bacon's *New Atlantis* had been a glorious utopia, like Thomas More's island, crowned by scientific discoveries, David Hume's sceptical undermining of common sense, scientific law and causality was a 'voyage . . . compassing the globe' in a 'leaky weather-beaten vessel' which had only 'narrowly escap'd shipwreck'.[66] His 'wretched condition, weakness, and disorder of the faculties' made him more inclined 'to perish on the barren rock' than 'venture myself upon that boundless ocean, which runs out into immensity'.[67] For Kant, the 'land of truth' was not the barren rock of Hume's sceptical empiricism but was constituted by the a priori categories of rational understanding, the condition of possibility for that experience without which there could be no empiricism: 'This land, however, is an island . . . surrounded by a broad and stormy ocean, the true seat of illusion . . . ceaselessly deceiving with empty hopes the voyager looking around for new discoveries . . . adventures from which he can never escape.'[68] That treacherous ocean was the *terra incognita* of metaphysics. Hegel, however, was to follow the concept as it left the island and travelled through history, the phenomena of the mind or *Phenomenology of Spirit*, which (predictably by now) he called his 'voyage of discovery'.[69]

Wordsworth's phenomenology was interested in a truth of *personal* experience – 'A Traveller I am / And all my Tale is of myself' (*Pr.* III.196–7) – prior to its interpretation as real or illusion by the *habitus* or 'natural attitude'.[70] Even at its most reduced, the faintest touch, it was 'A Presence which is not to be put by' ('Ode', 119), however traversed by absence, for our sense of life depends on it. The whole intervening machinery of post-Lockean metaphysics – a proliferating middle ground of vibrating nerves, effluvia, animal spirits, categories and chains of association – was much easier to put by. Imagination is offset by 'impulses' that seem to break through from outside – in 'The Mad Mother', it is the double touch of an affect of the body, breast-feeding, that gives respite from hallucinations. Wordsworth sought a *sensus communis* that might be more than Thomas Reid's 'common sense'. His wish was for the text of experience, as much as the literary text of the 'Essay on Morals', to 'incorporate itself with the blood and vital juices of our minds' and 'melt into our affection'. Even David Hartley's association of ideas – following Locke's and Hume's distinction between what the latter called 'impression' and a subsequent 'idea' – in a state of excitement or vivid sensation might operate directly rather than gradually arise from repeated experience. A 'wild secluded scene' might *directly* 'impress / Thoughts of more deep seclusion' ('Tintern Abbey', 6–7) – just as a 'felt . . . presence' might 'disturb', immediately and directly shake us with 'the joy / Of elevated thoughts' (94–6) we are not told, a 'thought-feeling' irreducible to words. Thought and intuition, when feeling is involved, might not be so separable in analysis and time after all.

Wordsworth was convinced of a possible truth in appearances just as they are. In 'A Night-Piece', one of the 'pictures' announced to Tobin in 1798, we are simply told that the moon and stars are wondrously driving across the sky, no less than a 'vision' (20), not an optical illusion created by the moving clouds. It is a naïveté that cannot be put aside, for we are constantly falling into it. Wordsworth's project might even be called the redemption of illusion. *Something* has been communicated by such a movement, an elevation of thought that can be neither interpreted nor put by – in 'A Night-Piece' Wordsworth is simply 'left to muse upon the solemn scene' (23) – and which thereby acquires an enigmatic sign-character, akin to allegory or the poetic ideogram, while remaining the most concrete and directly felt experience. It is the subjective distortion that registers the pressure or impact of an objectivity. Such experiences, so private and illusory and dream-like, yet of 'widest commonalty', might even be the truest of all, what is most real and definitive of the self – precisely insofar as they exceed the subjective intentionality that they disturb. 'Points have we all of us within our souls, / Where all stand single' – or made to stand by the singular. What the self owns is not what it commands, but what it cannot put by.

This was also a phenomenology of questioning doubt, or at least 'musing', as much as rapturous immediacy. In 'Tintern Abbey', a seeing into 'the life of things' is directly after exposed as a potentially 'vain belief'.

Both moments had to be recorded to stay true to the experience in its unfolding. To locate the universal condition of possibility for such experiences, Wordsworth had to find a strikingly new and alternative *habitus* of 'thought-feeling', an unrecognized *terra incognita* amid the categories of understanding, or schemata of habit, and one which remains unexplored in contemporary phenomenology. It is neither conscious nor unconscious. Wordsworth was forced to devise a new lexicon to express it, above all in compound formations: that of an 'under-sense', 'under-agents', the 'half-consciousness' of what is 'not unfelt', an 'underpresence'. In a 22 May 1815 letter to Coleridge, Wordsworth wrote that his aim was 'to remind men of their knowledge, as it lurks inoperative and unvalued in their own minds'.[71] It is perhaps the greater part of sentient life, beyond even the direct intentionality that holds centre stage. This sensible registration or understanding – in interplay or not with the linguistic *habitus* – is the basis for a sense of phenomena in their *language*.

The whole wager of this poetry is staked on an affective cognition within a 'language of the sense' ('Tintern Abbey', 109). At the basis of Locke's arbitrary sign of identity – what makes it possible for the strange as such to be forced into commensurate value through sentimental, linguistic and commercial exchange – is a singular speaking that cannot be identified or exchanged with any other, even as it articulates a not fully identifiable surplus or resonance beyond itself which allows it to communicate with other phenomena. We can read or hear it only as it is registered within affect. All the resources of language and poetic form were to be brought to bear – strained and fractured – under the pressure or longing not only to reach *terra incognita* as a transport 'evermore about to be' beyond the pedestrian subject, but to give substance to the gleam of its accidents and particulars. That very exertion, however, was also insistently to pose 'Obstinate questionings / Of sense and outward things' ('Ode', 145).

'New compositions'

Wordsworth's journey into 'unknown modes of being' perhaps also alerts us to how we should, or should not, read him. We must travel through the text as it unwinds, not just paraphrase it, in search of *terra incognita*. There is no way to get there other than through its 'accidents'. This must include those of the time and place that situate it, the *habitus* of the discourses through which it speaks. But this is not our terminus. In the reshaping of that *habitus* is a strangeness that might still leap out at us to engage with the concerns of the present. Wordsworth's poetry of vanguard travel was ambiguously suspended between its own moment in history and an unknown future. A truly historical reading must look towards that afterlife. The approach is that of an immanent criticism – one that tries not to judge the work by criteria imported from abroad, like the prejudiced traveller, but whose terms are uncovered in the fundamental words of the text itself. It demands the closest reading, even participant observation, a 'free and indirect style', in its effort to articulate or translate the foreign. So this remains a critical investigation, attentive to the verse's inner contradictions and moments of hermeneutic breakdown. As the 'Essay on Morals' makes clear, this is a poetry that both points to the abstract proposition – a moral, social or cognitive value – and resists that conceptual enclosure. In his major period from 1798, Wordsworth was not writing *against* theory, but *for the sake of* theory, to rescue or redeem its tenuous actuality, at once concretely tangible and latent. As we approach the text through our own *habitus*, including that of previous scholarship, so theories of our own time must also be marshalled in the effort of understanding – precisely to expose them to revision in the parallax of the travel encounter. As his letter to Tobin implied, Wordsworth impossibly wanted both the picture *and* the global 'view'. His 'pictures of Nature, Man, and Society' must be constellated and organized into the shape of a 'new composition' – a configuration of equally pivotal moments, often contradictory, fragmented or anomalous – as a dense medium through which the proposition or idea has been refracted.

A travel towards the new might also have to turn back to the most ancient. Wordsworth's 'pictures of Nature, Man, and Society' habitually turn on the image of humanity in a *contemporary* state of nature. Whether conscious or not, such an estranged perspective became a *habitus* at least in part instilled by the overt and explicit attempts of his youthful verse directly to image the original state of nature. Even in this early verse, the traces of a natural state were also to be read in the present. What is uncovered is not a single and definitive state of nature, but a plurality of conflicting and changing *states* – prefigured in the contrast between the violently hostile and blank nature of *Salisbury Plain* and the Arcadian pastoral of *Descriptive Sketches*. This study's focus is on these early long poems and Wordsworth's major work towards *The Recluse*. Wordsworth's earliest drafts or published versions have generally been preferred as the closest in aspiration to this project. But to follow Wordsworth's subsequent revisions – a mode of travel as revisitation that also risked domestication – is often illuminating in diagnosing the problems that afflicted it. *The Prelude* opens up a new perspective as childhood and adolescence rehearse ontogenetic rather than phylogenetic versions of the primal scene. As *Lyrical Ballads* and its prefaces and appendices show, many of Wordsworth's shorter lyrics of the late 1790s and early 1800s can also be situated in an effort to translate a lost poetics of the primitive or archaic within the contexts of a disenchanted modernity.[72]

The return of a repressed nature will summon even the materiality of language itself. As Wordsworth's emphasis on 'compositions' suggests, this includes structures of rhetoric and syntax in tandem or at odds with poetic form. This poetry is emphatically an *art* of philosophical travel, an artifice or making of verse. The poetry itself resists what has been a damaging bifurcation into aesthetic formalism on the one hand, and thematic extrapolation or contextualization (theoretical or historical) on the other. While formalistic approaches have treated aspects of Wordsworth's prosody and poetic metre, they have yet to gauge not only its key significance in the philosophical anthropology of the period, but also its crucial role in Wordsworth's passionate labour of translation. Prosody can acquire an almost ontological status in this work, embodying key structures of experience – wavering between the descriptive and the prescriptive – that are more than just a travelling set of footsteps. The shapes of verse offer a hidden and largely unrecognized key to much of his major poetry. Wordsworth seems almost to have wanted to make prosody his form of life, the fundamental *habitus*. In its contrapuntal flexibility, its capacity for interruption, it displays an openness of comportment that might indeed be oriented to the 'stranger as such'.

What keeps it from ontology is that another, stranger utterance speaks through it. There is no first principle in Wordsworth, not even 'nature' – but at key moments we can read or hear the echoes and traces of what might be called a *linguistic* materialism. Remarkably, this has been quickly passed over in the critical literature – as though merely an outdated trope or rhetoric, a cliché even, heir to a long and now discounted theology of the Word in nature. But Wordsworth marks a crisis in this tradition. This is not a 'pan-linguisticism' of the semantic sign; its materiality is not interpretable. On the contrary, as it bypasses the sign to work directly on the eye and ear, it is that which breaks through human language and discourse – that to which Wordsworth's struggles with language seek access. It is the enigma that prohibits a secure ontology – for it is 'a language of the ancient earth' whose referent has been withheld from us, that may not even exist. Like a foreign tongue that we do not know, its articulate patterns or murmuring rhythms are heard as immediately meaningful yet unintelligible. But it remains a 'fountain' of the proposition itself, uncanny in its 'universal power' of meaning.

This is the place to look for Wordsworth's real politics. For in Wordsworth's 'pictures of Nature, Man, and Society' that haunting and encrypted speech has also been filtered through history. While it would not be true to say that Wordsworth's poems are moral-political in import, it would be equally untrue to say that they are not. A 'strange meaning' is what takes the place of declarations of rights in Wordsworth's verse, as natural law gives way to a language of nature in history. This is why Wordsworth's pictures resemble the dense nexus of 'second nature' – and intertwine the particulars of nature with the historically and culturally immediate – even as they come to shatter its *habitus*. And it is on arrival at the *ultima Thule* of travel that this language is most likely to be heard. What is pressed down by the habitual identifications of human discourse re-emerges in a state of estrangement. It is the way in which things speak, 'as if a voice were in them', when they lose their identity. What happens to philosophy when it can no longer speak in rational propositions, but only through indecipherable sounds and characters?

CHAPTER I

Salisbury Plain

It is in *Salisbury Plain*, rather than the earlier *Descriptive Sketches*, that we find the young Wordsworth's most extensive attempt to image the state of nature. The poem belongs to the 1790s genre of politicized sentimental literature, being largely formed of a string of encounters between the rural poor, and the ensuing narratives of social distress by which they explain their present destitution. Although that social criticism is at times distorted into fashionably Gothic or sentimental exaggerations, with an attendant clumsiness of diction and rhyme, the poem is worth close study for its embryonic and simplified anticipation of powerful motifs in Wordsworth's mature verse. Most importantly, the poem opens with a direct presentation of the state of nature, a *topos* that would appear only at an oblique angle in the later work.

In *Salisbury Plain*, the entirety of modern life hangs as a pendant to the 'natural condition', for the state of nature has here become largely a *critical* concept. The poem uncovers a milieu, supposedly exited by humanity aeons back in time, which remains imbricated in our social environment. While *Salisbury Plain*'s verbal echoes of Rousseau's account of the state of nature have been itemized by scholars, its darker vision, reminiscent of Hobbes, has gone largely unremarked. Wordsworth may or may not have been thinking of Hobbes; he was certainly opposing a kind of Leviathan. This was an engagement less with the arguments of Rousseau and Hobbes than a reworking of their rhetoric, their *figures*, their own 'pictures of Nature, Man, and Society'.

The state of nature was a necessary postulate for these thinkers, as it supplied the concrete ground for natural rights and the governing principles of the social contract. Here was a place in which they could be seen in their full clarity and transparency, as a fundamental given in the natural order of things. But as that state preceded history, there was no access to it other than through figures of imagination, quasi-literary fantasy, and rhetorical operations by which the clothing of modernity was drastically stripped away. But if the state of nature, as its theory presupposes, survives into modernity at the level of principle, might it not therefore enter into experience? In Wordsworth, this remains possible above all through the disorientations of travel. The state of nature, that seemingly most outmoded and mythical of Enlightenment concepts, might still retain some purchase on our contemporary experience.

Hobbes and Rousseau

The 'natural condition of mankind' prior to the formation of societies was prohibitively hard to represent for an obvious reason – as Hobbes was quite prepared to confess: 'It may peradventure be thought, there was never such a time . . . as this; and I believe it was never generally so, over all the world.'[1] Rousseau warned that deductions of the state of nature 'ought not to be taken for historical truths, but only for hypothetical and conditional reasonings; better suited to elucidate the Nature of things than to show their genuine origin'.[2] It was a kind of thought-experiment. For Hobbes, the answer to this representational dilemma was to locate a proto-rational principle at the heart of human nature. In his 1651 treatise *Leviathan*, one single principle flourished wildly in the absence of contractual restraint: naked self-interest. The rhetorical *archai* for that state were correspondingly lapidary, allusive and metaphorical formulae – a 'war of all against all' in which 'man is a wolf to men' (*homo homini lupus*). The tremor provoked was to instill the reader's consent to the natural state's final denouement: the universal sacrifice of the right to kill to a single ruler and their government, thus guaranteeing the safety of all in civil society.[3] To picture the aboriginal state of violence in tandem with modernity could be achieved only by resorting to the shock-effects of a negative inventory: 'In such condition, there is no place for Industry; because the fruit thereof is uncertain', and hence there is no agriculture, 'no commodious Building', no transport, no knowledge, and so, finally: 'no Arts; no Letters; no Society'.[4]

There was one way, however, to fill this vast blank in the map of mankind. The armchair anthropologist could draw on the reportage of travellers once the so-called 'savage' was deemed to be only minimally advanced beyond the 'natural condition'. Hobbes went so far as to assert that 'the savage people in many places of America, except the government of small Families, the concord whereof dependeth on naturall lust, have no government at all; and live at this day in that brutish manner, as I said before'.[5] This American savage was no less of a conceptual persona than its lupine ancestors, an abstraction born of a European underestimation of customary law in place of contractual government. In subsequent decades, *Leviathan* in turn may well have influenced a similar rhetoric in ethnographic travel description, as studied by Jonathan Lamb. Such tropes, Lamb discerns, have the 'ghostly specificity' of litotes – not in the familiar sense of an understatement ('not bad'), but as the apophatic definition of something by stating what it is not.[6] Lamb cites William Dampier's first impression of the Native Australians in 1688: here there were 'no Houses, and skin Garments, Sheep, Poultry, and Fruits of the Earth, Ostrich-eggs' – and so the list goes on until Dampier concludes, ambiguously evoking an Horatian or Stoic *nil admirari* and rejection of luxury as much as an apathetic ignorance, 'Neither did they seem to admire any thing that we had.'[7] As Lamb observes, 'emptiness fills up with its own particularization'; litotes introduces a 'peculiarity of wants' (say, ostrich eggs) in which the 'language of specification becomes the language of passion'.[8] Yet all this detail is heaped upon blankness.

The state of nature, however, was not merely a privative condition now wholly superseded. It was, rather, the pristine origin of a first principle still fully active in modernity as the basis of the social contract. Might one not look on 'civilization' – like the traveller before the so-called 'savage state' – and see it likewise fall into a universal blank? Giorgio Agamben has suggested that 'the Hobbesian mythologeme of the state of nature . . . is not a real epoch chronologically prior to the foundation of the City but a principle internal to the City, which appears at the moment the City is considered *tanquam dissoluta*, "as if it were dissolved" (in this sense, therefore, the state of nature is something like a state of exception)'.[9] For Agamben, the basis of political and social life cannot be 'citizen's rights, free will, and social contracts' so long as the Hobbesian sovereign retains his 'natural right to do anything to anyone, which now appears as the right to punish' – above all, by declaring the suspension of legal rights in a state of emergency or 'exception'.[10] Sovereign power has never left a state of nature that might at any moment break out for its citizens in a violence that reduces them to 'bare life'.

For Agamben, the human body has in this way become '*the bearer both of subjection to sovereign power and of individual liberties*'.[11] It is 'precisely bare natural life', Agamben claims of the 1789 *Déclaration des droits de l'homme et du citoyen*, that 'appears here as the source and bearer of rights'.[12] Jean-Jacques Rousseau, of course, had been a tutelary spirit behind that far-reaching statement. Yet looking back over nearly one hundred and fifty years of rival conjectural histories – including those of Grotius, Pufendorf, Locke and Condillac – Rousseau had dismissed the entire tradition for having 'transferred to the state of Nature ideas they had taken from society; They spoke of Savage Man and depicted Civil man'.[13] That did not prevent Rousseau from drawing up his own version of 'bare life'. If, as Paul Hamilton argues perceptively, Rousseau's state of nature was not simply nostalgic but aimed 'to recover our natural state in a contemporary form', to find 'new ways of communicating the obligations of natural law' in modernity,[14] it was also a picture of isolation set within a darker state of subjection.

Rousseau, as much as Hobbes, naturalized the principle of self-interest: a healthy *amour de soi-même* prevails in the state of nature which later degenerates into the civilized vanity of *amour propre*.[15] The primeval human beings are forest-dwelling solitaries, with no social impulses, and who meet only under the imperative of mating.[16] To regain such *archai* in the modern world necessitated a rhetorically violent reduction to 'bare natural life'. Only by forcibly removing all social and other attributes from the human person, like layer upon layer of clothing, might one arrive at a picture of natural humanity: 'By stripping this Being' of 'supernatural gifts' and 'artificial faculties', Rousseau claimed, 'I see an animal . . . finding his bed at the foot of the same tree that supplied his meal.'[17] The paucity of that end-result made a turn to litotes inevitable: the human animal is 'without industry, without speech, without settled abode, without war, and without tie, without any need of others'.[18] As Jean Starobinski observed: 'Rousseau is concerned with formulating a negative anthropology: natural man is defined by the absence of every specific property of civilized man.'[19] But Rousseau's epochal boldness was to insist that privation itself was fullness: 'To go naked, to be without habitation, and to be deprived of all the useless things we believe so necessary is, then, not such a great misfortune for these first men.'[20] While Hobbes and Dampier projected an endless catalogue of absent things onto a supposedly blank nature, Rousseau was to turn that sense of loss into a paradoxical passion for apathy. The primal creature's toughness both anticipated and negated a Spartan, Stoic or republican *vertu*, for it had no need of society: 'Accustomed from childhood to the inclemencies of the weather, and the rigor of the seasons, hardened to fatigue, and forced to defend naked and unarmed their life and their Prey against the other ferocious Beasts or to escape them by running, Men develop a robust and almost unalterable temperament.'[21] But Rousseau's nostalgia harboured a more fundamental ambivalence, raising the suspicion that he too had transferred to the natural state an idea formed in his social experience. The idyll takes place, like Rousseau's own harried social life, in a state of persecution.

As critics have observed, Rousseau's vision of the primeval solitary fending off an enemy world was a direct influence on Wordsworth's portrayal of the state of nature at the very beginning of *Salisbury Plain*.[22] Little attention, however, has been paid to how Wordsworth's account differs.[23] The ambivalence hiding in Rousseau's picture, its proximity to the Hobbesian *archai* of the 'nasty, brutish, and short', is here made fully explicit:

> Hard is the life when naked and unhouzed
> And wasted by the long day's fruitless pains,
> The hungry savage, 'mid deep forests, roused
> By storms, lies down at night on unknown plains
> And lifts his head in fear, while famished trains
> Of boars along the crashing forests prowl,
> And heard in darkness, as the rushing rains
> Put out his watch-fire, bears contending growl
> And round his fenceless bed gaunt wolves in armies howl.
> (*SP* 1–9)

The 'ferocious Beasts' of Rousseau's wilderness have been enlarged into the 'armies' of a state of war. A piling up of gerunds sustains the threat of continuous yet indeterminate violence in bare natural life: 'crashing', 'rushing', 'contending'. That obscure danger finds its correlate in an almost featureless landscape of 'darkness', the 'deep' and the 'unknown'. Again the paradox of a tangible void seeks refuge in litotes: the state of nature's 'fenceless' and 'unhouzed' condition is the negative image of true civilization – the secure peace of protective dwelling.

The next stanza, however, swings back from Hobbesian ferocity to Rousseau's celebration of a natural ataraxia: 'Yet is he strong to suffer, and his mind / Encounters all his evils unsubdued', for he has never known 'happier days' (10–12). Stoic indifference is the affect, or rather deadening of affect, which corresponds to the state of nature in its blankness. Ignorance shelters the man from the very perspective that elicits Wordsworth and Rousseau's envy: the comparative eye of the anthropologist and traveller. In *Salisbury Plain*, comparison is the source not only of sympathy but also of the greatest misery: an ability to perceive differing social states, like the 'couch of Affluence' viewed from 'Penury's iron breast' (21–7), now hardened into the allegoric forms of eighteenth-century poetic diction. For the poor, modernity is not only just as bad as the state of nature – comparison makes it *worse*.

With a considerable jolt, however, we next learn that Wordsworth's 'savage' is not Rousseau's primeval solitary at all – for he does have knowledge of society. If he lacks the comparative vision, it is because the state of culture he has fallen out of, or fled from, is no different in its Hobbesian violence to a blindly antagonistic nature:

> and when by foes pursued
> With life he scarce has reached the fortress rude,
> While with the war-song's peal the valleys shake,
> What in those wild assemblies has he viewed
> But men who all of his hard lot partake,
> Repose in the same fear, to the same toil awake?
> (13–18)

The forest modulates into the near anagram of 'fortress' in this universal state of war. Far from being an a priori condition, the state of nature has become a perspective that we gain only a posteriori. As with *Salisbury Plain*'s 'hungry savage', we reach that vision as we stumble out of, or run away from – yet also project – the *habitus* of our immersion in society. It is characterized by an inability to distinguish culture from nature. The 'savage' escapes from society to a protective nature, only to see it congeal into an image of the social. A state of nature is that aspect of the environment which a particular society has cultivated, nature as that society has determined it. Hunted by warrior 'assemblies', nature becomes an image of persecuting violence for this man in a condition of bare life.

The Contemporary State of Nature

Despite *Salisbury Plain*'s at times gauche simplicity of tone, it is in its radically contemporary vision of the state of nature that we find the key, if anywhere, to what made so 'unusual an impression' on the young Coleridge in the poem's 'union of deep feeling with profound thought'.[24] This has been easy to overlook, given an inevitable bias towards the fuller drafts of the 1795 *Adventures on Salisbury Plain* (copied and revised in 1799), and the final published version of 1842 (renamed *Guilt and Sorrow*[25]). For in the 1795 draft – presumably due to Wordsworth's shift by 1795 from Paine's and Rousseau's influence to that of Godwin, who disregarded natural origins – the opening picture of a state of nature was simply edited out. This, however, served only to reinforce the original purpose of that evocation: to focus attention on the state of nature as a contemporary locus. As such, *Salisbury Plain* takes its place in a largely overlooked literary tradition: one that includes Lear on the heath and Timon on the beach, Crusoe's island and that of the Yahoos and Houyhnhnms, while looking forwards to Frankenstein's creature, Conrad's imperial hinterland, and the landscapes of Samuel Beckett.[26]

Wordsworth's contribution to this genre was distinctive. Like the 'savage' on the run from the warrior tribe in *Salisbury Plain*'s opening, an individual enters the latter-day state of nature as they slip from or fall out of society. They begin to see it everywhere. The state of nature stands for the materiality through which a culture articulates itself, a layer constantly poised to obtrude. It is the 'bare matter' that goes missing in Agamben's account of 'bare life'. To capture that moment in all its foreignness as well as familiarity, as Wordsworth recalled of Coleridge's praise for the poem in November 1795, was to present a 'tone', an 'image' and a 'character' that had been 'by books not hitherto / Reflected' (*Pr.* XII.358–60). But as more than just a reflection of Hobbes and Rousseau, it did show what it might mean to live through some of their pictures.

A gateway to the state of nature in modernity is opened through the dislocations of travel. The 1793–4 draft had immediately jumped forward from the prehistoric state to a modern 'traveller' on Salisbury Plain (*SP* 38) – the opening scene of the 1795 *Adventures on Salisbury Plain.* An initiatory process begins into the state of nature as a state of deepening estrangement. Right at its outset, it is characterized by a failure of the *sign*, the withdrawal of a geographical and social point of orientation: 'the distant spire / That fixed at every turn his backward eye / Was lost' (39–41). Moving forwards can no longer be distinguished from turning wrongly or circling back, as the traveller falls from society into a place without compass points and of infinite extension. On the bleak wastes of Salisbury Plain, that disorientation is intensified by the anxiety of physical need: 'By thirst and hunger pressed', the traveller 'gazed around' (42) desperate for social warmth and assistance. What meets his eye directly plunges him into the latter-day state of nature:

> And scarce could any trace of man descry,
> Save wastes of corn that stretched without a bound,
> But where the sower dwelt was nowhere to be found.
>
> (43–5)

Agriculture regresses to the limitless wasteland, deliberately evoking the 'unknown plains' of the first draft's opening.

It is an image in negative of the *transparence* extolled by Rousseau as the social ideal:[27] the face-to-face act of charity, the traditional hospitality of the individual owner-labourer of a small plot of land (the 'sower'), sharing out a frugal surplus with the stranger. The state of nature is here an experience not of the origin, but of an opacity that has arisen *historically*: the decline of the independent or tenant farmer and the rise of absentee ownership and large-scale holdings.[28] Wordsworth does not immediately present that distancing of social relations; we are thrown into an aesthetic that forms its expression. In the withdrawal of social care, the sign reverts to a blank materiality.

In the 1795 draft, that semiotic breakdown is overt. Here the state of estrangement begins not with the loss of the church spire as a landmark, but with

> One lonely inn upon the wilder moor.
> But entrance none was there for such as they,
> No board inscribed the needy to allure,
> The grapes hung glittering at the gilded door.
>
> (29–32)

The transparency of the sign – advertising entry to its referent – is withheld from those too poor to engage in social exchange. This inaugural moment is echoed later on in *Adventures*:

> No swinging sign creak'd from its cottage elm
> To bid his weary limbs new force assume;
> 'Twas dark and void as ocean's watry realm
> Roaring with storms beneath night's starless gloom.
>
> (172–5)

Through the rest of the stanza, the 'void' is fleshed out by the familiar trope of litotes, an eclipse of social care in the absence of the most elementary signs of warmth and light, tending and dwelling: there is 'No gypsey' with a fire, 'No labourer' with a 'kiln', and 'No taper' from a 'sick man's room' (176–8). The tactile and visual blank has its auditory equivalent in a 'Roaring' wind. In lines that appear in both 1790s drafts following the vision of the dehumanized cornfield, the traveller cries out to a shepherd in the distance – and only a mere 'whistling' alleviates the echo chamber of litotes: 'No sound replies but winds that whistling near / Sweep the thin grass and passing wildly plain' (*Adventures* 62–3). The wild nature of this complaint distinguishes it from the cry for sympathy with which it reverberates – even as it puns on its equivocal referent as a sign, 'passing' back into the visual plainness of the desolate tract.

The sign of natural sympathy or social care is no longer able to communicate – or can speak only as a cipher of potential complaint. An expressive materiality which the sign has subordinated to an index, a mere vehicle of purpose – the sheer stuff from which the sign is made – can return only as bare matter when that meaning fails. In the 1805 *Prelude*, at the very opposite end to the archaic on the scale of progress, in the heart of the great metropolis itself, a state of nature opens up in a thoroughfare overwhelmed with the signs of advertising and property. It is a wilderness through which the traveller wanders in *terra incognita* – or like a nomad, as Wordsworth characterizes his London residence, having 'pitch'd my vagrant tent . . . among / The unfenced regions of society' (VII.60–2), just as the 'hungry savage' roams the 'fenceless' woods at the beginning of *Salisbury Plain*. In London, the 'face to face' gives way to the 'face after face – the string of dazzling wares / Shop after shop, with symbols, blazoned names'. Presenting only the signs of individual ownership, and without exchange to enliven its images, the cityscape is converted into a meaningless script: into names that remain anonymous, 'allegoric shapes' that mean nothing to the observer, the 'fronts of houses, like a title-page / With letters huge inscribed from top to toe'. What cannot be read can however be heard: 'Meanwhile the roar continues' (VII.172–84). The man of leisure can 'lie and listen' to the city in its state of nature, hear the echo in its traffic of 'the mountain flood / Murmuring from Glaramara's inmost caves' ('Yew Trees', 32–3) – even through its distorted amplification.

What is experienced as dazzling, as well as disorientating, by the young Wordsworth in London, takes the form of panic for the destitute traveller on Salisbury Plain. The rural wasteland discloses what Walter Benjamin perceived as a key to the modern city-dweller's experience: 'To his horror, the melancholy man sees the earth revert to a mere state of nature. No breath of prehistory surrounds it: there is no aura.'[29] In the same essay on Baudelaire's Paris, Benjamin goes on to quote Paul Valéry's (Rousseauan) vision of the city: 'The inhabitant of the great urban centres reverts to a state of savagery – that is, of isolation. The feeling of being dependent on others, which used to be kept alive by need, is gradually blunted by the smooth functioning of the social mechanism.'[30] But in *Salisbury Plain*, it is that mechanism's malfunctioning, a state of need and dependence, which defines the breath of prehistory through litotes:

> No shade was there, no meads of pleasant green,
> No brook to wet his lip or soothe his ear
>
> (46–7)

Litotes no longer elaborates an inventory of civilization, but an alternative state of nature: the bounteous hospitality of a richly varied landscape prior to human beings,[31] a rhapsodic state that *Salisbury Plain* can define only in the negative.[32] Yet the marks of prehistory as a state of war are also embedded in this landscape:

> He stands beholding with astonished gaze,
> Frequent upon the deep entrenched ground,
> Strange marks of mighty arms of former days.
>
> (74–6)

It is as impossible to decipher the historical signs of violence as it had been to participate in the economic or natural sign. The man's perspectival dizziness and estrangement, coupled with an impassable historical distance, leads to figural distortions and misrecognition: Stonehenge at a distance is mistaken for an 'antique castle' (78), a giddy conflation of Hobbesian prehistory with the feudal signs of war and power. The 'mighty arms' of Sarum's original inhabitants conjure 'warrior spectres of gigantic bones' (97). Yet such ghostly misreadings aim at a figurative truth: modernity is made spectral as it is haunted by a persistence of the archaic.

The State of Sacrifice

Even as late as 1842, in the 'Advertisement' to *Guilt and Sorrow*, Wordsworth would single out a persisting atavism within modernity as *Salisbury Plain*'s essential theme. Here he recounted the poem's inception on a 1793 hike through Salisbury Plain, after seeing the naval fleet docked at the Isle of Wight in readiness for Britain's imminent war with France: 'The monuments and traces of antiquity, scattered in abundance over that region, led me unavoidably to compare what we know or guess of those remote times with certain aspects of modern society, and with calamities, principally those consequent upon war, to which, more than other classes of men, the poor are subject.'[33] It was from this comparative perspective that Wordsworth's use of archaic diction and the Spenserian stanza for their feudal-chivalric associations – though as stiffly artificial as the poem's historical conflations may seem tendentiously over-simplified – aimed to estrange the present by showing it as the past.

Wordsworth took his place here within a widespread radical discourse. The 'warrior spectres' of prehistory are companions to the Druidic priests of human sacrifice, whose victims, 'the sacrificial altar fed with living men' (185), are luridly hallucinated in the 'Giant wicker' of classical legend in the poem (and later, of course, in Book XII of *The Prelude*). The Druids not only were celebrated erroneously as the founders of Stonehenge by eighteenth-century antiquarians such as William Stukeley,[34] but were also the target of a deistic and radical tradition stemming from John Toland's *A Critical History of the Druids* (1723), and taken up in varying guises by figures such as Paine, Constantin Volney, William Blake and the young Coleridge.[35] This trend aligned the establishment of a class of priests with idol-worship and human sacrifice; such were the archaic origins of social rank, state religion and the idolatry of power (such as monarchy). Aristocracy and priesthood were said to emerge in the historical transition from an egalitarian 'savage state' to a 'barbarian' stage. While Wordsworth was clearly not alone, then, in determining the sociopolitical correlates of religious practices like sacrifice, *Salisbury Plain* was unique in identifying the very earliest society with human sacrifice.[36] In a 1794 draft for the poem's opening account of the state of nature, the 'wild assemblies' from which the 'hungry savage' has fled are here shown feeding a pyre with 'living captives' in the name of an 'idol God of war'.[37] Wordsworth's disquiet persisted long into his career. In a sonnet composed in 1818 for the early part of the River Duddon sonnet sequence, Wordsworth imagines an ancient Briton stumbling onto a dell near the river's source (symbolizing the state of nature, while the river is that of 'progress'), having 'roved or fled' from his 'tribe' – like the 'savage' on the run in *Salisbury Plain.* Wordsworth asks: 'Was the intruder nursed / In hideous usages, and rites accursed / That thinned the living and disturbed the dead?' But 'No voice replies' (*SSI* VIII.4–9). The silence of an unanswerable question now holds the place once occupied by pictures of the state of nature.

Wordsworth was haunted by the possibility that human sacrifice might be the fundamental datum of a social anthropology – all the way down to the sacrifice of the poor in a contemporary state of warfare. Society was maintained by the sacrifice of the individual on behalf of the collective. As Lynn Hunt writes of the torture and capital punishment opposed by 'the rights of man': 'the offender served as a kind of sacrificial victim whose suffering would restore wholeness to the community and order to the state'.[38] Yet sacrifice was also implied in the liberal tradition: the partial surrender of individual rights upon forming the 'social contract'. As Henri Hubert and Marcel Mauss noted in their classic account of religious sacrifice in 1898: 'Fundamentally there is perhaps no sacrifice that has not some contractual element.'[39] In *Violence and the Sacred,* René Girard would argue that the rationality of judicial punishment overcomes ritual sacrifice and its expulsion of the scapegoat from the community.[40] Yet Wordsworth's intertwining of the ancient and modern highlights an archaic residue in apparently enlightened practices. In Wordsworth's medieval drama of 1797, *The Borderers,* the aged Herbert, whom Rivers is plotting to have killed, is presented as a sacrificial victim to nothing more than Rivers' self-proclaimed right, arbitrarily, to decide the law: 'We recognize in this old man a victim / Prepared already for the sacrifice' (II.iii.400–1). There is a link between sacrifice and the reduction to 'bare natural life', even if, as Agamben points out, the latter is denied a sacrificial aura.[41] Wordsworth pointedly keeps to the same figure of sacrifice when Rivers' machinations line up Herbert for judicial execution; that legal killing is identified by a soldier, Lacy, with the symbolic affirmation of the community itself: 'He shall be led, and there, the country round / All gathered to the spot, in open day / He shall be sacrificed' (II.iii.426–8). Sacrifice remains inherent within what Benjamin called 'law-preserving' as much as (Rivers') 'law-making' violence.[42]

Agamben's focus on international politics, and his neglect of political economy in *Homo Sacer*, leads to a privileging of the refugee as the modern figure of 'bare life', without any reference to that conspicuous version of bare life both inside and outside the local community: the homeless. The central character of the 1793–4 *Salisbury Plain*, the 'female vagrant', whom the traveller meets when he seeks shelter in a ruined 'Spital', recounts a narrative of circumstances that show the link between the social forces of sacrifice, however accidental rather than planned, and the reduction to bare life in a contemporary state of nature. Her weaver husband, having fallen out of work, was driven to join the military, taking his family with him to the American Wars. Just how the whole family, apart from the woman, perishes in that conflict is left unclear – they fall victim both 'by sword / And scourge of fiery fever' (321–2) – just as we are not told whether the rural disaster that forces her husband to enlist is a product of natural or economic conditions ('the children's meal began to fail', 294). Social catastrophes strike the poor with the blindness and contingency of natural forces. Her estrangement from social life grows wider until, as the woman says of her return by sea from America: 'Some mighty gulf of separation passed / I seemed transported to another world' (370–1). That gulf then opens up within the modern city itself, recalling the claim in the poem's opening section that a state of comparison in 'Penury' is even worse than the prehistoric state of nature: 'And homeless near a thousand tables I stood / And near a thousand tables pined, and wanted food' (386–7).

In the traveller's account of his own fall into vagrancy, added to the 1795 version, the emphasis is on a state of sacrifice that makes social pressure indistinguishable from natural instinct as a behavioural motivation. Rousseau and Godwin, the rival inspirations of the 1793–4 and 1795 drafts of *Salisbury Plain* respectively, were both agreed that the Hobbesian wolf-man was a social product. For Rousseau, the Hobbesian 'war of all against all' did not occur in the state of nature, but followed 'the breakdown of equality' into 'the usurpations of the rich, the Banditry of the poor' – 'Nascent society gave way to the most horrible state of war.'[43] Internecine warfare ends only when the rich draw up laws of property and seduce the poor into accepting them.[44] For Godwin, that war was ongoing. The greed, cruelty and injustice of the rich 'must inevitably expose them to reprisals; and the poor man will be induced to regard the state of society as a state of war'.[45] So in the Godwinian *Adventures*, when the traveller confesses to the female vagrant that he is a criminal on the run, having robbed and murdered a passer-by shortly after leaving the military, such Hobbesian rapine is presented as an internalization of his experience of the state. The man had been press-ganged, passively forced to become 'Death's minister' in war (83), and returns home only to have his discharge pay unfairly withheld. Just as Godwin argued that crime was socially conditioned, so the man acts out a social theft and murder. As agency is made indeterminate, so guilt and innocence fall into ambiguity. The opposition slides into what became the poem's final title: *Guilt and Sorrow*.

The title evokes a double bind that is the awareness in sorrow of a guilt both wholly social and ineradicably personal: for both spheres are governed by self-interest. Guilt and sorrow drive the individual to seek out oblivion as the physical state of nature, the outlaw wilderness, becomes both a refuge and a compulsion. This is why the former soldier is wandering Salisbury Plain. So Marmaduke at the end of *The Borderers*, in his guilt and sorrow on discovering that Rivers had tricked him into leading an innocent man to his death, can define only by litotes what is both a place and a state of mind:

> I will go forth a wanderer on the earth,
> A shadowy thing, and as I wander on
> No human ear shall ever hear my voice,
> No human dwelling ever give me food
> Or sleep or rest, and all the uncertain way
> Shall be as darkness to me, as a waste
> Unnamed by man!
>
> (*B* v.3.265–71)

The postlapsarian Miltonic grandeur of this 'uncertain way' is made both humbler and more credibly desperate in the to-and-fro of flight that occurs in a revision to Wordsworth's lyrical ballad 'The Last of the Flock'. Here a shepherd, obliged by economic pressures to sell off his beloved livestock, becomes progressively alienated from his family and dwelling. In his rage, bitterness and guilt

> crazily and wearily
> I went my work about;
> And oft was moved to flee from home,
> And hide my head where wild beasts roam.
>
> (76–80)

More plausibly still, in the original 1798 version the man simply recalls that 'Oft-times I thought to run away' (*LB* 79). The 'mighty gulf of separation' invades even the home and workplace.

In the shepherd's state of second nature, there is no distinction between a 'natural' bond of family and an 'artificial' identification with property. 'The Last of the Flock' retrospectively undermines the *Salisbury Plain* traveller's contrast between a Hobbesian self-interest, a 'war of all against all' that is now the 'world's law' itself – on seeing a father strike the head of his own child in anger – and the natural law of domestic and familial sympathy:

> 'Tis a bad world, and hard is the world's law;
> Each prowls to strip his brother of his fleece;
> Much need have ye that time more closely draw
> The bond of nature, all unkindness cease.
> (*SP* 658–61)

Richard Gravil writes intriguingly of this passage: 'At the time Wordsworth wrote *Salisbury Plain* he was still trying to persuade himself that the bonds of nature were of more account than the abstract rights of man.'[46] Such bonds, however, were not meant to be incompatible with legal rights for Condillac and Rousseau; sympathy extended from self-interest, at least in natural origin, as it sprang from self-identification with another's pain. But in *Salisbury Plain*, even the sympathetic 'bond of nature' has been invaded by the 'world's law'. The traveller's sorrow on seeing the child's head-wound cannot be separated from his own guilt feelings: the blood 'Flow'd from the spot where he that deadly wound / Had fix'd on him he murder'd' (644–5). That remorse intensifies to a crisis point when the traveller (through a somewhat contrived plot device) meets the wife he had abandoned; she has subsequently also become an itinerant, and is now dying. The socially impelled death-drive, expressed through aggression and internalized as guilt, now seeks a public absolution: the traveller decides to give himself up to the authorities and confess.

The universal context of guilt and sorrow has only one way out: the introversion of sacrifice into *self-sacrifice*. This alone can escape the 'world's law' of self-preservation in both the individual and the state. The traveller's self-surrender does not betray the Godwinian critique that Wordsworth intended for *Adventures*: 'to expose the vices of the penal law and the calamities of war as they affect individuals'.[47] As the man's executed body is hung up on a gibbet 'in iron case' – the sacrifice of the individual to the community in full ritual display – so 'festive booths' are set up for families to enjoy the carnival atmosphere (820–4).[48] But Wordsworth imagines 'some kindred sufferer' who will 'drop . . . in miserable trance' at this prospect of guilt and sorrow (826–8), just as the traveller himself, earlier in the poem, had passed out before an ancient gibbet that recalled his former crime. To hold up suffering as a spectacle for popular consumption was the guilt and sorrow of sentimental literature itself – including *Salisbury Plain*. Attempts to enforce sympathy through images of violence and extreme misery, always liable to stray into Gothic, also encouraged a more surreptitious voyeurism. The appropriate response to social suffering – compassion entwined with the guilt of complicity – was impossible to sustain without falling into unconsciousness or estrangement.

Splendour in the Grass

What carries *Salisbury Plain* beyond its moral-philosophical sources is both its serious weakness and its greatest strength: a rigorous attention to social conditions only insofar 'as they affect individuals'. The poem's allusions to agrarian crisis and the loss of small-scale land tenure contain no account of the increasing Enclosure Acts, the challenge of factories to cottage industry, and the strain of rising population, let alone more contingent factors such as wartime scarcity, bad harvests and high grain costs[49] – such things just happen to the poor, with a long-range causality too remote to be felt directly. By targeting the later poems, critical attacks on Wordsworth's distancing of historical context have overlooked the irony that this had its origins in the explicitly social-critical agenda of his early work. Only a focus on individual experience as a social phenomenology, the blind spot of theory – on the aesthetic at its primitive base (*aisthetikos*, the perceptual) – might unveil the social production of new manifestations of nature. Wordsworth was perhaps the first to bear witness to a second nature, a 'mighty gulf of separation', that has since become so commonplace that it is barely noticed. As a French traveller in 1980s America was to observe: 'The natural deserts tell me what I need to know about the deserts of the sign.'[50] Wordsworth was even able to give the experience a homely motto:

> life is like this desart broad,
> Where all the happiest find is but a shed
> And a green spot 'mid wastes interminably spread.
> (421–3)

The domestic idyll of sheds and lawns seems rather pitiful when encircled by that illimitable desert.

Coleridge, however, in famous words of praise rarely acknowledged as specific to this poem, was impressed not by the withering of aura that spreads through *Salisbury Plain*, but by its very opposite: '[Wordsworth's] original gift of spreading the tone, the *atmosphere*, and with it the depth and height of the ideal world around forms, incidents, and situations, of which, for the common view, custom had be-dimmed all the lustre, had dried up the sparkle and the dew drops.'[51] Only a hair's breadth divides the bare matter of *Salisbury Plain* from the 'visionary dreariness' of the 'bare Common' and 'naked Pool' at Penrith Beacon in *The Prelude*. At its centre stands an image of poverty recorded without sentiment, a girl who holds a pitcher to her head struggling against the wind (XI.303–11). But it is merely a common view: 'It was, in truth / An ordinary sight' (308–9). Yet Wordsworth's 'levelling muse' – a projection of Jacobin equality for Hazlitt – has enacted a wholesale reversal: a customary indifference to the bare and common has at last woken up. No longer blank, that 'dreariness' is at once dull, frightening and compelling. An enigma of the material universe, and of social distance from both girl and scene, it is a unique moment in a specific place that is also an imageless and expressionless vision: 'I should need / Colours and words that are unknown to man' to 'paint' that tone and atmosphere (309–11).

This celebrated prospect, a childhood experience, is conditioned by the uncanny state of estrangement – an entwined image of nature and society – that briefly precedes it. Once more we encounter Wordsworth's obsessive fascination with sacrifice, the gibbet and public execution,[52] only now with a strikingly fresh emphasis. And again we are taken through an initiatory process that leads to a state of estrangement: the small-scale rite of passage of a child's first horse ride. That step towards socialization is not affirmed, but interrupted. The child, like the traveller, enters into the uncertain negotiation of an alien cultural world. As with the wanderer on *Salisbury Plain*, the process begins as the child gets lost. The servant who had been his guide disappears from view, leading the child to dismount 'through fear' (286). Immediately he finds himself at an ancient execution ground, an unintelligible sight for the child, now denuded of Gothic or sentimental pathos. Indeed, no response is given at all:

> The gibbet-mast was moulder'd down, the bones
> And iron case were gone; but on the turf
> Hard by, soon after that fell deed was wrought
> Some unknown hand had carved the Murderer's name.
> The monumental writing was engraven
> In times long past, and still, from year to year

By superstition of the neighbourhood
The grass is clear'd away; and to this hour
The letters are all fresh and visible.

(291–9)

The gibbet disappears as we look on at a conspicuous detail, a trace of its prehistory, like those 'strange marks' engraved on Salisbury Plain. Here too, the marks of violence, mere 'letters', are indecipherable. Wordsworth observes only that this 'monumental writing' is annually renewed. The absorption of an instant expands into the compulsion of a whole community to keep looking.

For Jonathan Wordsworth, the insertion of this scene as a prelude to the Penrith Beacon episode, first drafted in 1799, was the regrettable intrusion of 'a versified guidebook entry . . . oddly trivial in its associations'.[53] But it is the very lack of tourist information that confines its reader to 'associations'. There is a quality of unknowing in the child's attentiveness. For although these engraved characters may contain *in nuce* a whole library of ethnographic behaviours – the warding off of an evil spirit, the supplication of a crime, a warning to the beholder, the celebration of a sacrifice that vindicates and restores community, or merely the commemoration of an event – it is none of these at the same time as it is all of them.

What has survived is the record of a name we do not know, the material trace of an individuation. Carrying most significance in Wordsworth's description is not the custom or its meaning, but a physical quality of its writing: the 'freshness' visible of the letters in the grass. In the River Duddon sonnets, the fount of the river, an emblem here of the state of nature, is surrounded by 'brilliant moss, instinct with freshness rare' (*SSI* III.13). The name-giving power of language is inscribed within nature's freshness itself. Neither good nor evil, it returns 'year after year' like the slain god of spring. It is the magnification of a sense of individual life. The murderer's name is the stubborn remainder of what should be cancelled out in revenge or reciprocity – '*the great Law of Nature, Who so sheddeth Mans Blood, by Man shall his Blood be shed*' –[54] in a state of sacrifice that has trivialized the individual.[55] Caught by the flash of a name, the child stands riveted at the 'fountain' of a moral proposition.

CHAPTER 2

Building, Dwelling, Embodying

The freshness of Book XI's letters in the grass, under a mouldered gibbet, is an image of the dissolution of natural law into a language embedded in nature. Its correlate in human language would be the uniqueness of a person or place as embodied in the proper name. Drawing the observer out of a blank state of estrangement, this linguistic experience joins with the redemptive counter-forces of *Salisbury Plain*, an independence of home, livelihood and body, and the act of sympathy or social care. But how might they stand together? A clue is offered by a short and neglected lyric, written and published in 1800. It has all the appearance of being one of Wordsworth's most inconsequential and doggerel pieces of versifying. But the seriousness hidden within the (at times excessive) whimsy of poems like *Peter Bell*, 'The Idiot Boy' and 'To the Spade of a Friend' suggests that for Wordsworth the test of truth is to survive a change of register or scale – when certain significances have been forgotten or denigrated, they might take refuge in the silly or absurd.

The poem in question concerns three 'rosy-cheeked School-boys' who, climbing Great How in Grasmere, 'built up without mortar or lime / A Man on the peak of the crag' (*LB* 2–6). A few days later, however, the wind 'blew the Giant away'. Yet like the annual renewal of the name in the grass, though with a more boisterous sense of playful repetition, 'The very next day / They went and they built up another' (16–18). The Giant is pagan – the Primal or Archetypal Man, the *Anthropos* of innumerable myths, often identified with the cosmos – yet also Christian or Christ-like (the boys 'christen'd him', 8), and is further compared to the 'Magog' of the Old Testament (12). At the same time the figure is none of these; it displays the materials from which myth is constructed, as a building upon the creative and mimetic instincts of childhood. To demythologize here is not to blow myth and ritual away in a violent gesture, but to see them in their analogue as a carefree game. To what meaning, and its fragility, does that game mimetically pay honour? To the stature of the human figure in its independence at the peak of nature? To an endless cycle of standing and falling, rising above nature only to be ruined by its greater force? And why the reference to a prototype of house building, 'without mortar or lime'? The Giant is pregnant with a creative language that at once summons mythic archetypes and refuses them. The poem's enigma is concentrated in the tongue-in-cheek pomposity of its incongruous title, which stands above it like a motto at the head of a rebus: 'Rural Architecture'.

Descriptive Sketches

'Rural Architecture' is Wordsworth's most explicit yoking of the primitive building to the upright body as outstanding figures of independence. This view of the human *physis* as an archetype can be traced back to *Descriptive Sketches* (1791–2), a loco-descriptive account of a Swiss tour that was Wordsworth's most ambitious long poem prior to *Salisbury Plain*. Here the individual body as Primal Man is an avowed image of humanity in the state of nature. *Descriptive Sketches*, written at a more hopeful stage of the French Revolution than *Salisbury Plain*, by contrast evokes the state of nature in a rhapsodic and Arcadian key. The portrait has its roots in a Cynic and Stoic tradition that fed into later Christianity, as noted by Ernst Bloch and Norman Cohn, in which the state of nature (Eden for Christian natural law[1]) was a paradise without labour or inequality.[2] For Bloch, this was natural law as 'maternal law', an egalitarian happiness in the lap of a bounteous nature, the 'social utopia' or 'land of Cockaigne'. Bloch also insisted, however, upon its counterbalance, natural right's emphasis on non-servitude and dignity as 'the problem of the upright carriage [*aufrechter Gang*]'.[3] The natural rights tradition, apparently so rule-bound and conceptual, had also implied a figure of bodily comportment in its vision of a freestanding independence in which 'the cause of human rights . . . is beyond all forms of contracts and contractors'.[4] But if that rigidly upstanding posture invites its own satirical tripping up or falling over, this might also point to a real contradiction in the interplay of so-called 'maternal' and 'patriarchal' law. By grouping together Wordsworth's varied representations of the 'Life, Liberty, and Estate' identified by Locke with the natural right to possess our own body and its dwelling or property,[5] we can more fully gauge such a historical tension between domination and freedom, the upright and prone, and its competing gendered values.

In *Descriptive Sketches*, the 'land of Cockaigne' and the ideal state of natural law are nearly identified by their contiguity in the text. The legendary 'Golden Age' appears as a Swiss folk 'tradition' (474), a time of perpetual summer in which hunger was unknown, honey flowed from the rocks, fountains watered the plains, and now-poisonous plants were wholesome (476–89). This pastoral myth soon modulates into a dithyrambic vision of Rousseau's primeval solitary, walking with the 'upright carriage' of natural law:

> Once Man entirely free, alone and wild,
> Was bless'd as free – for he was Nature's child.
> He, all superior but his God disdain'd,
> Walk'd none restraining, and by none restrain'd,
> Confess'd no law but what his reason taught,
> Did all he wish'd, and wish'd but what he ought.
> (*DS* 520–5)

The cluster of negative definitions is close to litotes. Yet negative and positive liberties meet: 'virtue' is not social, but 'alone, and wild' – a sphere of unimpeded freedom in nature. But we are given no picture of that wish-fulfilment or the law to which it corresponds[6] – the state of nature remains blank.

Hence Wordsworth must immediately turn to a latter-day state of nature – still accessible to the modern traveller-explorer within the supposedly archaic habitat of the Alpine shepherd – but one in which we find only 'traces' from which the past can be inferred. Wordsworth stands before the law as a vision of the upright body:

> by vestal Nature guarded, here
> The traces of primæval Man appear.
> The native dignity no forms debase,
> The eye-sublime, and surly lion-grace.
> The slave of none, of beasts alone the lord,
> He marches with his flute, his book, and sword,
> Well taught by that to feel his rights, prepar'd
> With this 'the blessings he enjoys to guard.'
> (528–35)

The shepherd is more an emblem than a man, a textual figure as much as an immediate 'trace' of nature's law. The archetype refers back not only to Rousseau's solitary but also – 'The image of his glorious sire display'd' (527) – to *Paradise Lost* and the original Adam: the divine image of humanity. In Book IV the 'shape' of Milton's Adam is 'erect and tall / God-like erect' (287–9) with 'native honour' and 'native majesty' (289–90); in his 'looks divine' shines the 'image' of the 'glorious Maker' (291–2).[7] An 'eye-sublime' is lodged here too (300), one that 'declared / Absolute rule' (300–1) over a nature that here includes women (simply absent in Wordsworth's image) as well as animals. Wordsworth's patriarch is also Lord of the Beasts in this Puritan mode.[8] While there is a concrete hierarchy in the man's subordination to God and lordship over animals, it seems that social equality in this isolated context is merely the absence of other people – a state in which, as Knud Haakonssen observes drily of natural jurisprudence, the 'primary duty to others is simply to leave them alone'.[9] But despite the proclaimed absence of debasing social 'forms', the man possesses a flute, book and sword that are the Protestant and republican insignia of social and religious independence, the safeguarding of which extends to the Swiss militia invoked in the subsequent verse paragraph (the victories of the outnumbered Swiss against invading Austrian armies). The man is not quite so alone and wild, after all. More crucially here for Wordsworth's later verse, however, is an understanding of perception as a form of *reading* – to read that which extends through the social or intertextual sign. What is absent as well as present in the image is conveyed by a body *language*: a 'lion-grace' of comportment and an inscrutable 'eye-sublime'. For all the exaggeration and cliché, what takes subtler forms in the mature Wordsworth is here given its first articulation: an independent power that is not expressed through domination but inaccessibly held in reserve.

The Arcadian image is riven with the tensions that inhabit any affirmation of the individual. On the one hand, against all the compromise formations of contract theory, Wordsworth is lucid enough to present the genuine wish-image of individual rights: an untrammelled freedom of milieu, an independent strength of mind, and a firm resistance to control. But at the same time, the figure exposes the dangers that have reinforced the now familiar attacks on the 'subject' and its 'autonomy'. An extreme version of that critique was advanced by Michel Foucault: 'Do not demand of politics that it restores the "rights" of the individual, as philosophy has defined them', he exhorts, for 'The individual is a product of power.'[10] Drawing on the work of Deleuze and Guattari, Foucault instead calls for a 'group' that is not 'an organic bond' – a 'body politic' corresponding to the individual body in its unity – but rather 'a constant generator of de-individualization' through 'multiplication and displacement, diverse combinations'.[11] But to 'de-individualize' is to sacrifice on behalf of a collective as totalizing as any organic bond, only now without individual points of resistance. Yet to individualize itself is to sacrifice or subordinate the 'diverse' to an overall identity or body-image.

While Wordsworth (like Rousseau) was drawn equally to the organic community and the self-sufficient isolate, his attempts to envisage both together are often not quite reducible to either pole. Embedded in such forms is also the potential for a free co-ordination of the individual and the multiple. From this perspective, an innocent Alpine vista glimpsed briefly in *The Prelude* is also a force-field of cross-currents within the community of individuals. As 'aboriginal', it harks back directly to the Arcadian Swiss of *Descriptive Sketches*:

> A green recess, an aboriginal vale
> Quiet, and lorded over and possess'd
> By naked huts, wood-built, and sown like tents
> Or Indian cabins over the fresh lawns,
> And by the river side.
>
> (VI.448–52)[12]

The 'naked hut' stands for the independent body as a picture of dominion over nature: the vale is 'lorded over and possess'd'. Yet in its 'Quiet' is also a vision of peace, of equilibrium between the states of nature and civil society, an interplay of 'naked' simplicity and the freshness of cultivated 'lawns'. The 'wood-built' cabins rescue a bare matter – Aristotle had used the word *hyle* or 'wood' as a term for primal matter, which did not exist in the Greek lexicon – by giving it a visible shape and expression, a minimal hylozoism. Here too is an unplanned, randomly profuse, yet providentially 'sown' disposition of social life, a scattering of individuals that nevertheless coheres. While the Swiss settlement evokes the American Indian tribe, the latter's communal property – stressed in the anthropologies of Rousseau and Adam Ferguson[13] – has been replaced by private holdings, echoing a republican emphasis on small-scale property as the basis of independent virtue, a mainstay against political corruption. It is a vision of the community as a non-coercive manifold, a free association of independent and equal individuals in unregulated habitation. But unlike the communal and nomadic Indian 'cabins' whose image it conjures, sown too are the germs of individual domination and settlement as forcible possession. The dream-image of reconciliation is only a momentary prospect between mountains: the traveller must move on.

The Idea of the Primitive Hut

As the 'wood-built' chalets of the 'aboriginal vale' suggest, Wordsworth was keenly susceptible to a long-standing obsession in the historiography of architecture: the effort to find or represent what Joseph Rykwert has called 'the idea of the primitive hut' – or 'Adam's House in Paradise'.[14] In a wide-ranging essay on both primitive and latter-day 'huts',[15] J. H. Prynne has linked Wordsworth's use of the word 'hut' in 'The Ruined Cottage' and 'Incipient Madness' to this tradition, while showing how he might have discovered its archetypes in poems such as James Thomson's *The Seasons* (1730) or William Collins' 'Ode to Evening' (1747) – Augustan works that lean towards the primitivist strain in sentimental literature. Prynne's focus is on 'huts rather than issues . . . because what is close to nature can only be recognised through the form of what is distanced from knowledge'.[16] But 'issues' of the most pressing concern haunt these ramshackle structures: the 'hut' was not only held to display the elementary principles of architecture, but also deemed a material embodiment of natural law and the foundations of human nature. In Henri Lefebvre's words: 'Habitation is an anthropological fact . . . the dwelling, the fact of settling on the ground (or detaching oneself from it) . . . the fact of living here or there . . . are inherent in what it is to be human.'[17] But while natural law reduced the 'hut' to its rational or geometrical dimensions, the 'primitive' dwelling in Wordsworth marks out the intermediate ground between such canons of order and the singular, irregular object. Against an overwhelming historical tendency to efface a resistant nature through simplifying conventions of architectural form, Wordsworth latched on to the archaic as the only extant paradigm – in distorted, warped or crumbling shapes – of a building no more at odds with its materials.

To articulate, read or respond to such a material language would be the 'fountain', rather than natural law, of a potential ethic. Martin Heidegger – whose self-styled 'hut' at Todtnauberg in the Black Forest[18] is viewed by Prynne as a late exemplar of the tradition – suggestively rendered (and reified) the Greek *ethos* as 'abode, dwelling place'.[19] Jonathan Bate has argued that Wordsworth 'remains the founding father for a thinking of poetry in relation to place, to our dwelling on the earth'.[20] He associates this project with 'a Rousseauesque story about imagining a state of nature prior to the fall into property, into inequality and into the city'.[21] At the same time, Bate explicitly ties this 'eco-poetics', a 'making . . . of the dwelling place',[22] to Heidegger's sense of 'poetic dwelling' as a measuring out of the space between earth and sky, a primal orientation within 'Being'.[23] There is indeed a clear analogy between an a priori natural law traced back to the primitive condition and the quasi-transcendental structures of fundamental ontology, even if in the latter 'nature' gives way to 'Being', and the temporal origin is replaced by what is 'primordial' or presupposed in all 'ontic' or empirical instances: the 'building of buildings'.[24] But in Wordsworth, a potential ethos of dwelling is most characteristically a stance towards the habitation of *another*. While, as Prynne observes, the physical 'hut' was often a 'temporary shelter' for the modern poet, a place of retreat at intervals,[25] Wordsworth was more frequently drawn to the primitive building as a place in which someone or something else *lives* – even that 'Whose dwelling is the light of setting suns' ('Tintern Abbey', *LB* 98).

Wordsworth's poetics attends to dwellings rather than a unified 'dwelling' for it is a form of *travel* more than shelter: multiple and experiential, roaming and open to change, not exclusively transcendental. And so he can be stopped short in the face of anomalies like the eponymous figure of 'The Old Cumberland Beggar' who, far from dwelling between earth and sky, kept 'his eyes for ever on the ground': 'Instead of common and habitual sight / Of fields with rural works, of hill and dale, / And the blue sky, one little span of earth / Is all his prospect' (48–52). The homeless state of estrangement that conditions the man's stooped frame is a clear warning not to separate dwelling, as Heidegger tried, from its social vicissitudes.[26] The 'naked hut', as an individual body, also had 'traces' to be read. The primal is the impoverished. An ethical challenge inhabited the 'primitive hut' and drew out a range of conflicting responses from Wordsworth.

Constellations of the primitive dwelling, language, the body and natural law had a long prehistory in theories of architecture. In his *De Architectura* (first century CE), Vitruvius, the seminal theorist of the 'primitive hut' in Antiquity, and a major influence on the Renaissance, had overtly conjoined architecture and the body. Vitruvius claimed that the Greek temple had translated into stone the original structure of the primitive wooden hut, a triangle mounted upon a square, while its symmetries derived from the relationship of part and whole in the human body.[27] This was best witnessed by the 'orders', with their arrangement of foot, trunk and head in the column.[28] Rykwert discerns the influence of Stoics like Zeno upon Vitruvius – and hence, by extension, of Stoic natural law, which stressed a harmonious adjustment to an ordered cosmos, as well as natural equality and the autonomous will. Likewise, Rykwert detects the presence of Locke and Condillac in a text that had a corresponding impact on the eighteenth century, Marc-Antoine Laugier's *Essai sur l'architecture* (1753). For Laugier, opposed to luxurious 'caprice' was a geometrical ideality and a functional necessity that, as with natural law, identified nature itself with rational principle, and again linked the 'hut' to the Greek temple: 'The upright pieces of wood suggest the idea of columns, the horizontal pieces . . . entablatures . . . [while] the roof provide[s] the idea of a pediment.'[29] 'Let us never lose sight of our little hut', he entreats, for it is the 'type on which all the magnificences of architecture are elaborated'.[30] In his discussion of Laugier's inevitably mythical and conjectural story of origins, Karsten Harries has made explicit the parallel to natural law: 'The primitive hut has played in architectural theory much the same part that the social contract has played in social theory.'[31] Rykwert notes the analogies between Laugier and Rousseau – who refers to the primitive hut in his *Discourse on the Sciences and Arts* (1751) and in the *Essay on the Origin of Languages* (posthumously published in 1781). As Rykwert indicates, however, Rousseau's vision 'stands . . . not for an architectural principle, but for a moral one'.[32] In Wordsworth, however, that dichotomy is open to question, above all through the relationship between architecture and the body.

In recent decades what has been probably the most influential philosophy of architecture, the phenomenological, hermeneutic and post-Heideggerean approach of the late Dalibor Vesely, has aimed to revive this humanist tradition. Vesely articulated the body and building as an ethos which no longer divorces figure and ground or freedom and nature: 'The verticality of upright posture removes us from the ground and thus contributes to development, which requires freedom; at the same time, it points toward the earth that pulls us downward to the ground that carries and gives support to everything achieved in the fulfillment of our freedom.'[33] Heidegger's co-ordination of earth and sky has been given an upright body. This 'articulation and embodiment'[34] of 'a physiognomy through which the structure points beyond itself'[35] was for Vesely the representation of our 'communicative space' – our 'latent' and pre-rational sense of bodily orientation within the world. Vesely contrasted these shared understandings with Jean-François Blondel's late eighteenth-century emphasis on the history of architecture insofar as it 'distinctly presents a style, an expression, a particular character'.[36] But it is precisely that obdurate materiality to which Wordsworth was hypnotically drawn, the language of an embodiment or 'physiognomy' within history – necessarily in part an *individual* character or expression – that must be sacrificed, ultimately, to the generality of Vesely's *sensus communis*. Vesely argued that 'In character we clearly see a tendency to move toward the surface of a building . . . toward the experience of appearances' in place of the 'depth' and 'order' of an 'ethos'.[37] In Wordsworth it is precisely a receptiveness to the individual façade – to the *face* or surface as the articulation of a body or building – that is the very fountain of our moral experience. It is the language of a depth and power that has been held in reserve.

Any reference to the 'face' in a moral context must inevitably recall the 'fundamental ethics' of Emmanuel Levinas. Wordsworth's 'speaking face of earth and heaven' (*Pr.* V.12) – in which Heidegger's measuring of earth and sky is confronted by a radical individuation – has been identified by David P. Haney with Levinas' stress on the 'nontotalizable alterity of another's face'.[38] For Levinas that 'face' can be any body part; it is the 'discourse' which communicates an individual's presence, a revelation of the 'other' which is 'a coinciding of the expressed with him who expresses'.[39] The ethical challenge of another's face, the call to respond in a manner that does justice to its specificity, is what establishes 'the right of the unique, the original right of man'.[40] But as Haney acknowledges, there is an 'obvious difference' between Levinas and Wordsworth insofar as, for the latter, 'the "other" can be, almost interchangeably, a humanized natural form . . . or a human form responded to in natural terms', while for Levinas the 'ethical' is exclusive to persons.[41] And in contrast to Levinas' residual idealism, it might be added, Wordsworth does not present the 'discourse' of another as immediately expressive of self-identity. The façade of a body or building is not transparent, but is necessarily articulated through the opaqueness of nature's materiality within history – the only vehicle of a genuinely singular physiognomy. In sight of the bare matter of modern history, Levinas' 'face to face' encounter, supposedly transcendent as a structure to the empirical, might deteriorate to blankness in a state of second nature: the dying fall of 'face to face / Face after face' in the London book of *The Prelude* (VII.172–3).

Levinas argued that Heidegger's 'foundation of the site' was merely secondary before the 'primacy of the ethical, that is, of the relationship of man to man' as the 'irreducible structure upon which all other structures rest'.[42] By contrast for Harries, following Heidegger, the 'ethical function of architecture' rests on the articulation of a 'common ethos' as 'the way human beings exist in the world: their way of dwelling'.[43] Hence Laugier's 'speculation about the origin of building' remains 'exemplary' for Harries 'as the source of regulative ideals' for an architecture of 'representation'.[44] But when a human quality is made visible in the natural, and a material nature observed within the human, an ethos of dwelling and the ethical relation between persons become mutually inextricable. In Wordsworth's poetry such fixed or regulative structures – the 'common ethos', or latent bodily understanding, the measure of earth and sky, encounters with 'transcendence' through the 'face' – unfold into changing and plural *relationships*. This is to challenge as much as establish the 'common': to be struck by the uncanny and disorientating.

Heidegger drew attention to that estrangement and in the same gesture disallowed it. Humanity takes its 'measure' from the 'unknown God' in the 'sky's manifestness', representing the 'invisible' and 'the alien' in 'familiar appearances' – which somehow equips us to build a 'ground plan . . . within which human dwelling has its security'.[45] 'Building, Dwelling, Thinking' concludes with an equally idealist leap out of alienation: 'as soon as man *gives thought* to his homelessness, it is a misery no longer . . . it is the sole summons that *calls* mortals into their dwelling'.[46] But it is hard to take one's measure when there are 'torrents shooting from the clear blue sky' (*Pr.* VI.561). At moments of greatest intensity, there is no secure dwelling between earth and sky: 'the sky seem'd not a sky / Of earth' (I.350–1), just as the 'surface of the universal earth', in the flux of passion, began to 'Work like a sea' (I.500–2). For Geoffrey Hartman, Wordsworth was unable to dwell on such moments, for 'apocalypse is not habitable'. But such 'a new heaven and a new earth' (Revelation 21:1) was a raising of the veil simply by lifting the 'film of familiarity' – Wordsworth's self-appointed task according to Coleridge.[47] In Wordsworth's images of the rustic, 'primitive' or ruined building, that apocalyptics of the ordinary dwells in the most humble, inconspicuous and dilapidated settings. Here the 'transcendental' is not a fixed ethical or ontological structure, but a *habitus* that is shaken and transformed by experience – as the singular and momentary experiences of travel build up into an orientation towards the strange, the non-human and the abjectly fallen.

Huts, Bowers, Ruins

In Vitruvius' rational architecture of the body, each part justified its place solely within a vertical hierarchy, with no independent validity of its own. Yet a seemingly trivial and merely descriptive moment in Wordsworth's poem 'Michael' shows how such a detail – the purely functional component of a building, a farmhouse chimney – might not only form a synecdoche of the whole, but also overshadow it:

> Down from the ceiling by the chimney's edge,
> Which in our antient uncouth country style
> Did with a huge Projection overbrow
> Large space beneath, as duly as the light
> Of day grew dim, the Housewife hung a Lamp
> (*LB* 112–16)

The protrusion is so 'huge' that it impresses itself over the 'Large space beneath' of the house – a description ambiguous enough to suggest not only the cottage's spacious interior, but also, when viewed from outside, the pastoral lands of its shepherd owner, Michael. There is no sense here of the 'primitive' construction as a proto-classical order of geometrical proportion: the chimney is unshapely, 'uncouth' and outsized, with a rough-hewn peasant ('country') bluntness that seems as 'antient' a style as that of the temple or hut.

The verb Wordsworth chooses to evoke its rude and quasi-active presence, 'overbrows', has a peculiar doubleness when viewed, like the chimney, in close-up. On the one hand, to 'overbrow' is just a figure of speech: this most basic of domestic fixtures is merely hanging or jutting forward over its environment. Yet it resembles not only the brow of a face leaning over, but also an upright body pendant over its space, just as the house itself 'Stood single, with large prospect' (140). Again an image of mental as well as physical independence is tied to a mastery of nature: the chimney is lord of all it surveys, like the patriarch Michael at the head of the household. Its 'Large space beneath' recalls the abyssal view from Snowdon in *The Prelude*: 'The perfect image of a mighty Mind, / Of one that feeds upon infinity' (XIII.69–70). Yet in that space is nothing for the mind to consume or exercise power upon. The chimney projects merely a brooding upon vacancy. It is a perpetual vigilance without object, as if in needful waiting for its space to be fulfilled, just as Michael sits at his sheepfold knowing that the son for whom it was to be built will never return – having been forced to leave to seek money because Michael's property (that 'large space') is not owned by him but heavily mortgaged. The ambiguity of 'overbrows' enables the word to summon such analogues and to resist them, through what is not an interchangeability of the human and natural in the chimney, but a body language all of its own. It is the 'fountain' of a moral dimension in building precisely through its sharp ambivalence, both exemplary and cautionary: its rugged independence and its hollow isolation.

Wordsworth's fascination with the 'ancient uncouth country style' was by 1810 to acquire a polemical edge. First drafted that year, his *Guide through the District of the Lakes* inveighed against recent architectural fashions that recalled the *clara et distincta* of post-Cartesian philosophy: 'distinct ideas . . . order, regularity, and contrivance' had produced 'gross transgressions' of the Lakeland's character.[48] The tenuous independence of Michael's farmhouse, under pressure from long-distance creditors, was another symptom of the large-scale economical-historical forces eroding rural architecture and agglomerating the individual – as with the engulfing of tenancies and freeholds by large estates that forms the background to *Salisbury Plain*. In the *Guide*, Wordsworth observed that shepherd or woodlander tenements had been increasingly bought up by the possessors of 'substantial and comfortable buildings', with the result that the 'aboriginal houses, probably little better than hovels, like the kraels of savages, or the huts of the Highlanders of Scotland, would fall into decay'.[49] Unlike Wordsworth's poetry of the 1790s, the *Guide* celebrated the 'ancient mansions' of the Lakes and 'the happy manner in which they harmonise with the forms of nature'[50] as much as the humble tenement, and reserved its ire for the new buildings appearing in-between, constructions of the industrial or urban *nouveau riche*. Strongly influencing the young John Ruskin's *The Poetry of Architecture* (1837–8) – and perhaps even his later celebration of quasi-natural forms in Gothic style – the *Guide*'s proto-ecological awareness of situation was ambivalently also, as Michael Wheeler observes, 'a picturesque discourse of traditionalism which naturalised the hereditary power that enforced it'.[51]

In his earlier poetry, however, Wordsworth's sympathy for the archaic reached further into an objective stratum: to trace the mechanisms of a return of the repressed within history. In 1815, Wordsworth would ignore Coleridge's suggestion that *The Recluse* should enact world history as a sequence of buildings along a river: 'Savage – Barbarian – Civilized – the lonely cot, or Borderer's Wigwam – the Village – the Manufacturing Town – Sea-port – City – Universities'.[52] While Wordsworth would indeed, not long after this letter, represent a thoroughly ambivalent *telos* in his River Duddon sonnets inspired by Coleridge's unwritten 'The Brook' – in which Coleridge's river was to pass a 'turf barn', a 'sheepfold', a 'lonely cottage', and then 'villages' and 'manufactories'[53] – in this sequence the architectural scheme had been dropped. The younger Wordsworth's more characteristic tendency was to rupture the linear narratives of history to show an implication of past and present. 'The Brook' was to follow the course of a river in Somerset, probably that of the Tone, at whose 'spouts and fountains wild' (*LB* 219) would sit the eponymous heroine of Wordsworth's poem 'Ruth'. The fountains are iconic of Ruth's own latter-day state of nature, the vagabond life to which she has been reduced through the madness of jilted bereavement, and where she toys absent-mindedly with the 'small machinery' of 'little water-mills' she has made (218–20). In a state of estrangement, the 'manufactories' at the apex of progress have reverted to a mere child's play. Like Rousseau's solitary in the *Discourse on Inequality*, hers is a shelter yet more primitive than the hut, 'Under the greenwood tree' (192), beneath which, in contrast to the chartered river of progress, the 'master-current of her brain / Ran permanent and free' (188–9). Wordsworth's concern for the *disjecta membra* of society and progress, for their madness and poverty, their squalor and isolation, was coupled with the vision of a regained freedom in nature – as its only available, though violently distorted, image.

The tree, arbour and bower give the lie to the supposed natural law – rather than social provenance – of the proto-geometrical 'hut'. In 'The Mad Mother', a (presumably) American Indian woman, abandoned by her English husband, is driven into a latter-day state of nature with her child in the West Country forests; she responds to her fate defiantly: 'I'll build an Indian bower; I know / The leaves that make the softest bed' (*LB* 55–6). Her 'savage' and maternal proximity to the wilderness is not only a tendency to soft repose in the lap of nature; her practical wisdom evinces a care and discernment for nature's materials, their nuances and qualities, the 'leaves that make the softest bed'. An alternative picture of independence to that of the upright body as lord and master of nature, this is the recumbent idyll of Bloch's 'maternal law'. Architecture has a horizontal, as well as vertical, plane.

Wordsworth's varied evocations of the 'Indian bower', more easefully intimate with nature, more oriented to pleasure, than the functional and rigid 'idea of the hut', had their Edenic origin in Milton's version of the first ever building: the 'blissful bower' of Adam and Eve, constructed by no less an architect than God himself. The first ever dwelling on earth had a roof made of leaves, walls formed by bushes, and a carpet of 'violet, / Crocus and hyacinth' (*Paradise Lost* IV.690–703). In 1804, Wordsworth built a bower at the head of his garden, lined with moss and coated with heath shrub on its outer walls, where he and Dorothy read to each other in what was surely a more humbly rustic, less luxurious invocation of Milton.[54] In Wordsworth's 1802 poem, 'A Farewell', Dove Cottage itself had been celebrated as 'this Bower, this Indian shed' (*P2V* 26). But while the Indian bower of 'The Mad Mother' harked back to a lost American community, the affirmation of independence in 'A Farewell' – 'These narrow bounds contain our private store' (14) – was also to confess to the narrowness and hoarding of such a retreat from public life. Such a withdrawal might resemble less an Arcadian state of free individuality than the blank estrangement of *Salisbury Plain*. In another poem of 1802, 'Stanzas Written in My Pocket-Copy of Thomson's Castle of Indolence', a Dove Cottage house-guest (an anonymous Coleridge) lies constantly prone under its garden 'bower' – and, 'like a naked Indian, slept himself away' (*P2V* 25–7). While Coleridge (possibly opiated) evokes imperialist myths of the lazy native basking in the sun, the description is neutral enough to inspire a momentary longing for such recumbent leisure – the relaxed posture of a 'maternal law' no longer gendered as feminine. But the figure is haunted by an enigmatic guilt, 'like a sinful creature' (21). As with the discharged soldier of *Salisbury Plain*, Coleridge seeks a refuge from public shame in private oblivion – in a second state of nature.

'Coleridge's ruin, in both life and work, is, I suggest,' wrote Thomas McFarland, 'the true human fact.'[55] McFarland's study of Romanticism and the ruin – though nowhere treating of actual buildings – has shown how the period's drive for organic wholeness, or the total system, inevitably led to forms of breakdown that provoked an equal attention to the fragment.[56] The broken masses of *The Recluse* were famously projected, in the Preface to *The Excursion*, not as Coleridge's riverain progress of buildings, but as no less a structure than the Gothic cathedral – to which *The Prelude* was to be subordinated as an 'ante-chapel'. The isolated cottage or private 'bower' stood as much for the ruin of *The Recluse* as for its unattainable public and cosmic architecture. While in Rousseau and sentimental literature, the cottage hearth was the abode of 'domestic affection' and sympathetic inwardness, Wordsworth drew attention to the historical forces that were leading to its disintegration and exposure: the bare 'human fact' as a latter-day – socially entwined – state of nature. In 'The Ruined Cottage', when Margaret's weaver husband is driven to enlist by rural unemployment, her distracted grief falls into apathy, and her 'poor hut / Sunk to decay' (*RC* 476–7). Like Michael at his unfinished sheepfold, she spends years in fruitless waiting, seated in a 'broken arbour' (450). Rain and wind enter the cottage through fissures in the wall and roof, while sheep nestle at the 'threshold' (336) between nature and culture. In an age of the damaged interior, it is not the 'hut' but the ruin that is architecture in a state of nature.

Yet the 'rank spear-grass' (108) at the beginning of 'The Ruined Cottage', a grossly uncultivated proliferation, has risen by the poem's end from an unweeded garden of base matter to the most upright, elevated status: 'the high spear-grass on that wall', silvered by drops of mist (514–18), is now 'an image of tranquillity' and the 'beautiful'. A wild spontaneity held back or repressed has been allowed to manifest, while a 'secret spirit of humanity' (503), a genius of cultivation, dwelling and building, still haunts the dilapidated tenement. The shocking and almost callous 'happiness' (525) that relieves the narrator's 'sorrow and despair' (520) is that of being able to 'read / The forms of things' (510–11) that outlive the ruin of the individual. But this forced happy ending – inserted as an after-thought for supposedly philosophic uplift – is to read that which has nothing to say. The 'silent walls' (536) of the once humanly expressive building, the 'silent overgrowings' (506) of the garden, and the 'silent rain-drops' on its plumes of grass (515), gather to form an image of the expressionless. If this be more than bare matter or blankness, if there is a still beauty and 'happiness' in 'the calm oblivious tendencies / Of nature' (504–5) and the 'passing shews of being' (522), it is because for an impossible moment we have passed beyond architecture and the anthropomorphic, beyond even the fear of death, to see through inhuman eyes. A slumber has stolen our spirit, yet with a felt resistance, an under-sense, of that 'secret spirit of humanity' which must revive. What the 'primitive hut' sought to bring together – nature's wildness and the spirit of human building[57] – have here been split asunder.

To read the forms of silence is to reach the zero point of natural law. There are no rational axioms deducible from a language that communicates nothing, only an aesthetic or contemplative 'happiness' seemingly irreconcilable with any ethical response to the un-poetic dwelling. In *The Prelude* Wordsworth would recall how, as an adolescent, he had imaginatively transformed an afflicted habitation – that of a 'woodman languish'd with disease / From sleeping night by night among the woods / Within his sod-built Cabin, Indian-wise' (VIII.611–13) – into the contemplative distance of a more poetically acceptable suffering: that of 'the pangs of disappointed love', with 'all the long Etcetera' of exoticized sentimentality (614–15). To aestheticize the primitive was to draw back from a confrontation with real poverty. Nevertheless, at 'The Ruined Cottage' the mutually conditioning poles into which aesthetic idealizations and denigrations of the 'hut' tended to split – Edenic splendour and squalid immiseration – have become as entangled as the 'matted' overgrowth (55) and 'bindweed' (314) that spread through its garden. As a counter-aesthetic, if there is an ethos here, it is that of a defiance of a middle-class conventionality – a *habitus* itself hiding a moral aesthetic – that was liable to react with phobic aversion as the state of nature turned into a state of squalor.

William and Dorothy were certainly not immune to such prejudices: on 26 August 1803, at a boatman's house in Tarbet near Loch Lomond, Dorothy wrote in the journal of her Highlands tour: 'I never saw anything so miserable from dirt, and dirt alone: it reminded one of the house of a decayed weaver in the suburbs of a large town, with a sickly wife and a large family; but Wm. says it was far worse, that it was quite Hottentotish.'[58] An apparently remote 'savagery' leaps out from the poverty-stricken underbelly of Europe. Dorothy is reminded of the 'decayed weaver' in the suburb, evoking the steam-driven textile mills in the industrial cities that were reducing such independent artisans to a merely auxiliary status,[59] or at worst to unemployment (as with Robert in 'The Ruined Cottage'). But her disgust is that of an *aesthetic* of clean surfaces, and a 'civilized' morality of domestic propriety. Likewise, it is an aesthetic of conventional shape or form, associated with rectitude, which underlies Dorothy's recoil from the 'shapeless' dwellings of the 'miserably poor' Dorset peasantry at Racedown in 1795: '[they are] not at all beyond what might be expected in savage life'.[60] Stephen Gill has linked Dorothy's reaction here with Wordsworth's note to 'The Ruined Cottage' as told to Isabella Fenwick: 'All that relates to Margaret and the ruined cottage etc., was taken from observations made in the South-West of England.'[61] But the contrast in responses is equally instructive. In the poem itself, it is because the building is seen not as 'shapeless' but as a ruined individuation that it retains its 'secret spirit of humanity'. If it has become hard to sympathize with Gaston Bachelard's 'poetic image' of the dwelling as a 'pure sublimation'[62] – exemplified by 'a *feeling for the hut* in me' as an icon of 'shelter', '*fortifying*' through 'all the *security* that *simplicity* gives'[63] – we might still respond to its deformation as an expression of suffering individuality.

As it falls into ruin, the upright body collapses and any degree of mastery and possession over nature disintegrates. As Lord Kames wrote of the 'Gothic' or feudal ruin, it is 'the triumph of time over strength, a melancholy but not unpleasant thought'.[64] In a great but neglected passage of *The Prelude*, a Catholic version of the Gothic ruin, that of Furness Abbey, is evocative of the wastes of *Salisbury Plain*: 'from recent showers / The earth was comfortless' (II.127–8). But the child Wordsworth arrives at a broken individuation that speaks through its fragments all the more powerfully. In tears, sighs and tremors, it has the language of a body in pain:

> touch'd by faint
> Internal breezes, sobbings of the place,
> And respirations, from the roofless walls
> The shuddering ivy dripp'd large drops
> (128–31)

Distorting traditional images of the human body as a microcosm in its architecture – which Vitruvius' ideas reinvigorated in the Renaissance – within the abbey we look from both inside and outside at a body. Enfolding the child's space, it resembles both the individual and a whole universe in mourning. A faint inspiration swells into a 'shuddering' discharge of grief. Yet the quasi-human and expressive is at each point in interplay with an expressionless matter: 'respirations' exhale from inner 'breezes', while its 'sobbings' decline into flatly monosyllabic 'drops'. As it shudders at the edge of life, or simply dying, while keeping its inhumanity, there is an uncanny quality to this pathos of the building: a kind of *objective* affect as much as a 'pathetic fallacy', a feeling articulated by the material itself as it configures an individual presence.

This is what distinguishes the ruined abbey from that 'dismembering of the corporeal figure in building' which Anthony Vidler sees as a modern version of 'the architectural uncanny' that emerged in the late eighteenth century from 'the aesthetic of the sublime to its full exploitation in the numerous "haunted houses" of the romantic period'.[65] And the haunted abbey brings into question a key distinction of Michel Henry, a philosopher who has been linked to Wordsworth's recognition of inward affect or the 'subjective body':[66] that he who wants to embody power 'will represent a column, the heavy blocks of stone of the pediment and the roof – *he will represent the temple, represent the world*... [as opposed to the] force of music, the original force of Suffering and Life' which represents '*nothing*'.[67] More than the post-Tudor ruin of the Catholic *logos* and the turn to a Protestant inwardness, the abbey is a new 'world' or macrocosm that is no longer an image of power and fortification, a secure architecture, but an individual face turned towards us in its vulnerability, need and exposure.

It is with a shock that we turn from this passage to the *Guide To the Lakes*' account of the abbey's erstwhile temporal as well as sacred power, at a historical moment of surrender that anticipates its later collapse: '"When the Abbots of Furness", says an author before cited, "enfranchised their villains, and raised them to the dignity of customary tenants, the lands, which they had cultivated for their lord, were divided into whole tenements."'[68] The sense or 'plight' of cosmological dwelling at the ruined abbey is not wholly unaffected by material changes in land-development and housing: 'The enfranchised shepherd, or woodlander, having chosen there his place of residence, builds it of sods, or of the mountain-stone, and, with the permission of his lord, encloses, like Robinson Crusoe, a small croft or two immediately at his door for such animals as he wishes to protect.'[69] The helpless wish of the later Wordsworth, with his uneasy hybrid of Tory republicanism, was to stop history at this fateful juncture – in which the isolation as well as the independence of the Robinsonade might still be offset by a 'mellowed feudality' that connected part with whole.[70] So at Furness Abbey, the child Wordsworth wishes to freeze the moment while listening to the song of a 'single Wren' (125–6) – an individual expression that seems to compensate for the loss of cosmos, while also a ghostly remnant of its bare ruined choirs:

> So sweetly 'mid the gloom the invisible Bird
> Sang to itself, that there I could have made
> My dwelling-place, and liv'd for ever there
> To hear such music.
>
> (132–5)

A singular music animates the ruin and makes it even seem inhabitable – as if the cornerstone, or keynote, of true dwelling itself. And from the abbey, the verse moves on to the recollection of a 'Dwelling... worthy of a Poet's love, a Hut' – with 'rhymes... inscrib'd' on 'The threshold' (153–7).

Wordsworth's emphasis on the individual and the ruin might seem to disavow any representational content in architecture at the level of wider structures beyond the body. Vesely, alluding to Rykwert's association of eighteenth-century attempts to reconstruct the Temple of Solomon with the 'idea of the primitive hut', deemed both a 'search for the origins of representation',[71] albeit through 'reified precedents'.[72] But in Wordsworth we find an alternative picture of the 'origins of representation', one that takes the multiple forms of latter-day states of nature rather than a primordial beginning or reified *logos*. It is what Wordsworth, in 'Yew Trees' (1803), would call the 'natural Temple' (*P2Y* 30). While in the ruin an architectural microcosm breaks down into a state of nature, within the natural temple such constructions are uncannily prefigured – through a gathering of enigmatic forms that creates a sense of *place*. Rather than conduct an anthropological survey of the varieties of temple-building and ritual dwelling, Wordsworth looks to the partially chaotic shapes of nature that anticipate them.[73] The natural temple is both uniquely local and of broader significance; it is close in structure to De Quincey's notion of the 'involute' which, as Hugh Sykes Davies observed, was probably inspired by Wordsworth's 'spots of time' in *The Prelude*.[74] 'Often I have been struck with the important truth', De Quincey claimed, 'that far more of our deepest thoughts and feelings pass to us through perplexed combinations of *concrete* objects, pass to us as *involutes* (if I may coin that word) in compound experiences incapable of being disentangled, than ever reach us *directly*, and in their own abstract shapes.'[75]

To stage a transition from the individual to a group structure, the 'perplexed combination' of 'Yew Trees' follows on from an invocation of the solitary individual, strongly resembling that of 'Michael': a tree at Lorton

Vale that 'stands single in the midst / Of its own darkness' (2–3). The subsequent image of a group of yew trees is explicitly figured as social, a 'Fraternal four' (15) in a grove at Borrowdale, a brotherhood that may indeed be an 'involute' of the 'abstract shapes' directly affirmed in the French Revolution. If the trees are '*Yew*nited', as Geoffrey Hartman puns in his well-known reading,[76] this is not a synthesis but the wish-image of freestanding individuals able to reach out and interrelate with their neighbours. And so, despite the grove's 'pillared shade' (21) and 'sable roof / Of boughs' (24–5), this anticipation of the primitive hut or classical temple resembles less a geometry of squares and triangles than an intertwining that hints at such an order while remaining free: a canopy whose language is that of a knotted chiasmus of polysyllables – 'a growth / Of intertwisted fibres serpentine / Up-coiling, and inveterately convolved' (17–19). But for all the freedom – sensuality even – of its vital growth, this image too is 'incapable of being disentangled'. The trees are a shape as much of nature's fixedness and perplexity as of liberty and equality. As a natural emblem as well as a temple, an object for repeated meditation, the hard knot that it forms is both inexhaustible and uninterpretable – the language of a singular resonance.

Just as yew trees were traditionally associated with ghosts, so too this natural temple appears haunted by an absent suffering and life. It is surrounded by 'ghostly Shapes' that 'meet at noontide – Fear and trembling Hope, / Silence and Foresight – Death the Skeleton / And Time the Shadow', who 'worship' at 'altars undisturbed of mossy stone' (26–31). It resembles the parade of allegorical figures around a cathedral clock at midday. But the natural temple is a theatre of immanence, not redemption: no decision is made between 'Fear and trembling Hope'. The grove maps out a *theatrum mundi*: a microcosm that emphasizes temporality ('Time the Shadow') and history (the ghosts of both pagan and medieval worship) as they emerge within a latter-day state of nature and its apparently timeless immobility. It makes conspicuous the setting or background against which the figures of human pathos are played out. And it forms an arena for the material basis of sounding language, a semi-musical, semi-linguistic rhythm of nature: 'Yew Trees' ends as its ghosts recumbently 'lie' and listen to the 'Murmuring' of a nearby 'mountain flood' (33–4). To hear that murmur, or to read nature's silent forms, is not to deduce a moral norm or natural law but to respond to an enigmatic physiognomy.

On an island near Loch Lomond, in Dorothy's journal of her 1803 Highland tour with William, such a murmuring of nature was to echo in correspondence to 'irregular knots' like those of 'Yew Trees', and a 'forked bough' suspended from a hut's roof like the pendant chimney in 'Michael':

> There were several woodmen's huts, which, with some scattered fir-trees, and others in irregular knots, that made a delicious murmuring in the wind, added greatly to the romantic effect of the scene. They were built in the form of a cone from the ground, like savage's huts, the door being just large enough for a man to enter without stooping. Straw beds were raised on logs of wood, tools lying about, and a forked bough of a tree was generally suspended from the roof in the middle to hang a kettle upon. It was a place that might have been just visited by new settlers. I thought of Ruth and her dreams of romantic love.[77]

If there is a morality of the hut here, it is that of a forked irregularity, and its music, which cannot be assimilated to the faceless and reductive functionalism of those buildings Prynne identifies as latter-day primitive huts: the 'armed surveillance post' at Guantanamo Bay, a 'prototype hut-structure, not unlike the raised watchtowers at the Birkenau death-camp', and disturbingly rhymed by 'the innocent simplicities of beach huts and sheds on allotments and tree-houses for kids'.[78] For all the nostalgia evinced by Dorothy, we might speak of the woodman's dwelling as Heidegger writes of his appeal to 'the Black Forest farm': it 'in no way means that we should or could go back to building such houses; rather, it illustrates by a dwelling that *has been* how it was able to build'.[79]

Dorothy's fantasy is that of a conditional recent past as a vision of the future: 'It was a place that might have been just visited by new settlers.' It is the wish for an unimaginable new building at the edge of a New World – suspending a moment wide open to the foreign, as in Keats' 'On First Looking into Chapman's Homer', just prior to the horror of colonization. The seductive illusion of Ruth's 'dreams of romantic love' was that of an imaginary American wilderness. She and her Cherokee-raised lover would wander like Adam and Eve after their dismissal from the enclosed and protected cosmos of Eden, now transformed into the paradise regained of an unbounded *terra incognita*: 'wandering with an easy mind' and 'A home in every glade' (*LB* 70–2). The unprotectedness of the post-Columbian and Copernican universe, an expulsion from secure dwelling between earth and sky, has here become a dream of the infinitely open and foreign. As the sign, rather than prototype, of such an orientation in building, the Highlands hut ironically correlates to T. W. Adorno's vehement attack on the 'backwardness' and 'provincialism' of a philosophy that acts 'as if we confused a comfortably furnished cottage with the Pentagon' from which the thinker believes 'he can comprehend the universe':

> It is impossible to ignore the smell of the stale atmosphere pervading that 'philosophical cottage'. And if philosophy aspires to anything at all, it must tear down that cottage as fast as possible, and the very last thing it must do is to confuse it with the old shelteredness, to say nothing of a new one.[80]

'Imaginative form'

The 'primitive hut' was more than just a marginal theme in Wordsworth's authorship. The issues it raised were central to Wordsworth's *habitus* towards the alien in other human beings – above all, in terms of the body's own architecture and material language. That approach cannot be termed, in any straightforward sense, a revival of the humanist tradition in figures of the body and building; as at Furness Abbey, the human and the inhuman are mutually unfolding. To return to the body – to its image among the Lakeland shepherds of Wordsworth's childhood in Book VIII of *The Prelude* – is also, then, to treat of nature and architecture.

The English shepherd mediated the patriarchal Swiss for the domestic reader, just as the Swiss had mediated the American Indian at the 'aboriginal vale'. In a transition often observed when we follow cognate imagery from Wordsworth's early to mature verse, the explicitly philosophical or allegorical image – the Swiss herdsman as figure of the state of nature – reappears more immediately and concretely in *The Prelude*, without that abstract characterization, while still retaining the nimbus of an allegory or symbolism it is now impossible to determine. Only a reference to Chartreuse, a station on *Descriptive Sketches*' Alpine tour, recalls the textual origin of these Cumberland shepherds. We are expressly told that they are '*Not* such as in Arcadian Fastnesses / Sequester'd' and do not belong to a pastoral 'golden Age' (183–5; my italics). But they retain an aura or 'power' for the schoolboy traveller that is not entirely their own:

> A rambling School-boy, thus
> Have I beheld him, without knowing why
> Have felt his presence in his own domain
> As of a Lord and Master; or a Power
> Or Genius, under Nature, under God,
> Presiding
>
> (390–5)

Despite this rounding assertion of patriarchal mastery, Wordsworth's awe at the shepherd's physiognomy is not quite as confident as it seems. There is a hint of absence; or rather, of a presence in the image that is not transparent, not wholly available, but felt – 'without knowing why'. If there is a power here, then like that of the Arcadian Swiss, it has been very much held in reserve. For the shepherd is only 'As' or *like* a 'Lord and Master', a qualification, so the syntax implies, that also refers to his being a 'Power', and then in turn to his 'Genius' – all of which are in some sense differentiated. For all the man's presidential power, Wordsworth cannot decide whether it descends from nature or God. And unlike the simple harmonizing of nature and mansion in the *Guide to the Lakes*, the figure stands out from his surrounding environment, and yet is also the embodiment of its character, its 'Genius' – a word that also suggests an interplay between such an incarnation and a uniquely individual and creative expression. Here, then, is the bare lineament of a Wordsworthian theory of true architecture.

When Wordsworth turns to represent the shepherd visually, we are given no more than a material form:

> Mine eyes have glanced upon him, few steps off,
> In size a Giant, stalking through the fog,
> His Sheep like Greenland Bears: at other times
> When round some shady promontory turning,
> His Form hath flash'd upon me, glorified
> By the deep radiance of the setting sun:
> Or him have I descried in distant sky,
> A solitary object and sublime,
> Above all height! like an aerial Cross,
> As it is station'd on some spiry Rock
> Of the Chartreuse, for worship.
>
> (400–10)

These are clearly tricks of the light, angle and perspective – with an immediate shock of the sudden turn, propelled forward by the colons at lines 403 and 406. But they facilitate the creation of what Wordsworth calls an 'imaginative form' (419). The shepherd is a symbol, resembling that of architecture, like the spires or crosses at Chartreuse. The figure seems charged with meaning, almost Christ-like. Yet there is no difference between the symbol and the truth that it symbolizes. The figures are no more and no less than singular manifestations of the individual. But like metaphor, they also have a power to *transport*: to a monastery in the Alps, even to the polar bears of the Arctic. They have a being here, and a being elsewhere.

Architecture must not simply be grounded in an environment and its human orientation, as in the phenomenological or 'humanist' ideal, though it must do this also. Its imaginative singularity must transport us in an unknown direction beyond it. This is also to recognize the ethos that its façade holds in reserve. Through what exceeds the image, the shepherd's physiognomy holds its own moral language: the imaginative 'form' is an 'index of delight, / Of grace and honour, power and worthiness' (414–16). Rather than a deducible natural law, this is the ostensive 'index' of a constellation of moral attributes, experienced through aesthetic pleasure or 'delight' – the building's interiority. It leads the child Wordsworth to 'an unconscious love and reverence / Of human nature' (413–14). The moral effect is not conscious but subliminal and involuntary. It is a reorientation of the *habitus* that might even extend to that of the reader: the 'love of nature leading to love of mankind' that forms the title of Book VIII. But it is some testament to the depth of estrangement behind that aspiration – the 'face after face' of the city – that Wordsworth could only hope to inspire love for the stranger through an appeal to their sheer materiality. The concrete proportions of the human, shared with rocks and trees, the very bones of form, embody a state of nature that has never been left. The building must give voice to its materials.

With an acknowledged debt to Heidegger, this sense of the body in Wordsworth has been cast by Paul Fry in ontological, rather than natural or material, terms: 'The nonhuman in the human, the thinghood human being has in common with all being . . . the somatic zero-degree where life and death intersect.'[81] Nevertheless, Wordsworth is quick to point out that the shepherd is also

> a Man
> With the most common; Husband, Father; learn'd,
> Could teach, admonish, suffer'd with the rest
> From vice and folly, wretchedness and fear:
> Of this I little saw, cared less for it;
> But something must have felt.
>
> (423–8)

As with the child's 'love and reverence' for the figure, or the sentiment of presence 'without knowing why', this social awareness is an unconscious or transcendental feeling (rather than structure) in physiognomic experience. While it may or may not be attributable to childhood, it might certainly be brought to consciousness in the adult reader. Wordsworth goes on to defend the child's vision of 'thinghood' by arguing that it is the very opposite:

> Call ye these appearances
> Which I beheld of Shepherds in my youth,

> This sanctity of nature given to man
> A shadow, a delusion, ye who are fed
> By the dead letter, not the spirit of things,
> Whose truth is not a motion or a shape
> Instinct with vital functions, but a Block
> Or waxen Image which yourselves have made,
> And ye adore.
>
> (428–36)

It is not a vision of the 'dead letter', the degree-zero, but of the 'spirit of things'. It is 'vital', not a material 'Block'. And far from being an aesthetic 'delusion' belied by the man's social circumstances, it is nothing less than the 'truth'. It is the reduction to bare matter, the 'Block' or 'thinghood', which fabricates an idol. Yet Wordsworth employs the most flatly reified and abstract terms imaginable – 'vital functions' – for what we might think of as expressively alive. The body or building is not oppressively mythic, but has a fully operative human functionality – with the key distinction that this is *vital* in all its registers. Fry has argued for Wordsworth's 'insistently *medical*' view of inner life.[82] But while life here has been reduced to its barest, most functional expression, it has not yet reached the degree-zero itself – as if that minimal difference between life and death might make all the difference as it expands. The word 'Instinct', used adjectivally, suggests being passively imbued with, rather than prompted by, a potential vitality – this is what suggests, but also withholds, its identification with the anthropomorphic myth or 'idol'. There is something genuinely pregnant in the non-living, in the inorganic 'motion' or 'shape'. This is what constitutes the 'imaginative form' or face of a building – as opposed to the featureless 'Block'.

Yet while the vision of the shepherd invokes a depth of inwardness by withholding it in sheer externality, its cost is to be placed at a distance from all interrelation. How might the 'love of nature leading to love of mankind' be possible at close quarters or in a prospect of adversity? How might it occur within social exchange itself? The vision of the shepherd is that of an overall whole, an individual form, a *Gestalt*. Might there be a way of seeing the human that does justice to its involution of singularities, its 'perplexed combination'? This is the challenge of 'The Discharged Soldier'.

CHAPTER 3

'The Discharged Soldier'

In 'The Discharged Soldier', the rival evaluations of nature that had been split across *Descriptive Sketches* and *Salisbury Plain* – between a natural liberty and goodness and the estrangement of a violently antagonistic nature – are now with great subtlety intertwined. The poem does this by unravelling, from within, the normal structure for resolving the contradiction between natural generosity and natural egoism: the harmonization of public and private interests through contractual exchange. Individual exchanges corresponded to, and were legally underwritten by, a social contract with the state held to be grounded in natural law. 'The Discharged Soldier', however, is inspired less by a conscious philosophical ambition than by an aesthetic drive to overturn the banal exchanges of sympathy in sentimental literature – whose apparent spontaneity tended rather in its mechanisms to follow the *quid pro quo* of the contract. The poem is implicitly animated by a moral question and paradox: how can an independent life be preserved, 'beyond all forms of contracts' (in Bloch's phrase), even while it remains within a framework of sympathy and exchange?

Primitive Encounters

Alan Bewell has argued that 'The Discharged Soldier' is grounded in what he calls the 'primitive encounter' in Etienne Bonnot de Condillac's theory of language acquisition in the state of nature.[1] Bewell has opened up an illuminating context here, one that is worth exploring further, both in its wider philosophical implications, and in relation to the more immediate influence of sentimental literature. Condillac's conjectures regarding the earliest forms of language were a seminal source for what became a veritable Enlightenment obsession: similar treatises were composed, most famously, by Rousseau and Herder, and theories of 'primitive' language were assessed by a very large proportion of thinkers in the period, notably including Vico, Monboddo, Hamann, Diderot and, ultimately, the comparative linguistics of Wilhelm von Humboldt. This lively speculation on the origins of language did not fully die down until the more positivist temper of the early twentieth century; as late as 1930, Henri Delacroix felt the need to pronounce that 'Discussion of the problem . . . must be shelved.'[2]

Some of the rudiments of that debate, however, might be worth reanimating; for Wordsworth, the 'archaic' was to be found less in some remote past than as an active force in the present. While there is no evidence that Wordsworth read Condillac's *Essay on the Origin of Knowledge* (1746), its 'picture of nature, man and society' had made sufficient headway in British philosophical circles to be reworked by Hugh Blair, whose *Lectures on Rhetoric and Belles Lettres* were a probable influence on Coleridge (and Wordsworth), who borrowed them from Bristol library in 1798. Blair's version was subsequently quoted by Richard Payne Knight in his *An Analytical Inquiry into the Principles of Taste*, in a passage directly annotated by Wordsworth (almost certainly at Coleridge's dictation, while the latter was unwell) in spring 1808. Condillac's picture is summoned up by Blair in a performative invocation: '"Let us figure to ourselves a savage, who beholds some object, such as fruit, which raises his desire, and who requests another to give it to him."'[3] In Condillac's version, the 'savages' are two children, sole survivors of the biblical Flood, and too young to have acquired language. The 'request' for aid in procuring the fruit is what Condillac terms a 'natural sign', an expressive cry of passion, accompanied by the 'language of action': a 'movement, gesture or action that made the expression more striking'.[4] Expression becomes a common sign insofar as it is interpreted through the medium of sympathy: 'Moved by this display, the other fixed the eyes on the same object, and feeling his soul suffused with sentiments he was not yet able to account for to himself, he suffered by seeing the other suffer so miserably' – and prompted by 'instinct' rather than 'reflection', he leaps forward to help.[5] The communicative efficacy of such natural signs leads, in time, to the production of the arbitrary signs of conventional language. In Blair's rendition, this narrative provoked an irritable response from Coleridge (and/or possibly Wordsworth): 'What means all this parade about the Savage when the deduction as far as just may be made at our own firesides, from the sounds words gesticulations looks &c which a child makes use of when learning to talk.'[6] Coleridge and Wordsworth alike saw childhood as a contemporary state of nature.

Although Locke's empiricism was the major influence on Condillac, Hans Aarsleff has observed that the latter differed in his *rhetorical* conception of language.[7] While Locke, like Descartes, had attacked the distortion of pre-linguistic mental contents by emotive language, for Condillac not only do words determine our thinking, but their basis, like that of all social agreement, lies in the expression of shared feelings.[8] But the natural law of sympathy – often counterposed in the eighteenth century, most notably by Hume and Adam Smith, to Hobbes' and Mandeville's self-interest – was also grounded in the ego: the identification with another's suffering as one's own. Sympathy was formed from the self-interest that lay also at the basis of contractual exchange. Condillac, it has been observed, frequently used the word 'commerce' for social and linguistic, as well as mercantile, exchange.[9]

For Locke, the contract was grounded in the state of nature as a condition of sublime equity. In his *Two Treatises on Government* (1690), Locke declared that the American Indian 'knows no Inclosure, and is still a Tenant in common'[10] – and 'In the beginning all the World was America.'[11] But the contemporary American Indian is in no less of a state of nature when he enters into colonial exchange: 'The Promises and Bargains for Truck . . . between a Swiss and an Indian, in the Woods of America, are binding to them, though they are perfectly in a State of Nature, in reference to one another.'[12] Locke's statement may even have inspired Adam Smith's famous claim that the 'propensity to truck, barter and exchange' was a distinguishing anthropological characteristic, 'common to all men, and to be found in no other race of animals', and probably stemmed from 'the faculties of reason and speech'.[13] This implied that the origins of commercial exchange were bound up with the origins of language. For Locke, the 'primitive encounter' remains in the contemporary travel encounter, and for the first time in theories of natural law, the state of nature was proposed by Locke as a fully *latter-day* phenomenon; it occurs simply in the absence of government or formal law. The state of nature is an implicit juridical norm that has, as Leo Strauss observed of Locke, to be *read* out of appearances.[14] This is what enables Locke to challenge Hobbesian self-interest with his own antithetical principle of the state of nature – it is a 'State of Peace, Good Will, Mutual Assistance, and Preservation'[15] – in the midst of all evidence to the contrary. It is to be guaranteed in civil society by contract law. But as the transactions of the American indigene and European traveller make clear, a quantifiable equivalence hid not only inequalities of power and property, a Hobbesian rapaciousness, but discrepancies of cultural form: as an Indian gift economy was absorbed into commodity exchange.[16]

Condillac's rationalization of sentiment or sentimentalization of reason – a mutation of the 'rational animal' into the 'emotional animal' – had a major influence on Rousseau, and thereby on the literature of sensibility. As Mary Jacobus has suggested,[17] an episode in Henry Mackenzie's hugely popular sentimental novel *The Man of Feeling* (1771) was probably the most immediate precursor for 'The Discharged Soldier'. In Mackenzie's novel, homologies between the trafficking of sentiments and commerce are made troublingly evident. The social and class differences between Harley, a disaffected young bourgeois, and the vagabonds and unfortunates he encounters, are blissfully overcome when the victim's tale of woe culminates in mutual tears and embracing. A breakthrough into sentimental identity is in each case followed by Harley's slipping a coin into the indigent's palm: an inadequate relief that is all too close to a payment for emotional services rendered. Wordsworth almost never mentions giving money to the desperate leech-gatherers, out-of-work soldiers, rural labourers and beggars who cross his path as a traveller; in the light of *The Man of Feeling*, that negligence (or reticence) is perhaps best seen less as a subjective failing than as the objective exposure of a morally impossible situation.[18] At the opposite pole of the exchange, the afflicted in Wordsworth tend to show little or no gratitude when some kind of help is extended (as in 'The Old Cumberland Beggar') – or if they do, their gushing accents leave Wordsworth 'mourning' rather than gratified ('Simon Lee', 104). As David Bromwich has suggested, this was also to undermine Adam Smith's argument, in his *Theory of Moral Sentiments* (1759), that the gift of sympathy is legitimately motivated by gratitude as a reward, turning it into a reciprocal exchange: 'Wordsworth hated this prudent commercial morality.'[19]

As the disparities of status and wealth in the sentimental encounter make glaringly apparent, the establishment of identity through exchange was built upon a suppression of prior difference. Even in Condillac's 'primitive encounter', an identification with the other's universal need – hunger – rests upon an initial experience that is far more cryptic: 'feeling his soul suffused with sentiments he was not yet able to account for to himself, he suffered by seeing the other suffer so miserably'.[20] At this stage, sympathy has ruptured self-identity and is unaccountable and unidentifiable; auto-affection has been usurped by a suffering of 'the other'. Only by repeated experience is that shudder resolved into the identification of a universal sentiment: it becomes 'a habit to recognize, by those signs, the sentiment which the other felt at the moment'.[21] But earlier in Condillac's *Essay*, prior to this solidification of the 'natural sign', the expressive cry or gesticulation, into a conventional or 'instituted' sign of feeling, was instead an effect of 'causing others to feel something similar'[22] – 'similar' and not identical emotions, even in the case of physical need. Similarity is felt through a mimetic sympathy with the sign, while identity is the habitual recognition of something that the sign creates.

Such differences were those of the external, as well as internal, body. In the late 1790s, the period in which Wordsworth was drafting the 'The Discharged Soldier', the idea of a sympathetic identity, a universal emotional human nature, had migrated from the literature of sensibility to that of travel. Differences in ethnic physiognomy, as well as culture, might also be transcended by the sympathetic eye. In a text Wordsworth came to know well, Mungo Park's *Travels in the Interior of Africa* (1799), an account of an expedition in 1795, the explorer observed of an emotional reunion between a West African mother and son: 'From this interview I was fully convinced that whatever difference there is between the Negro and the European in the conformation of the nose and the colour of the skin, there is none in the genuine sympathies and characteristic feelings of our nature.'[23] Sentiments like these were a powerful motor of the abolitionist movement. But Park draws attention to the body differentials of ethnocentric prejudice – associated with moral weakness in Linnaeus' bizarre 1758 taxonomy of the human races[24] – even as he tries to bypass them. An intervening distance was required, that of an onlooker, for sympathetic identity to be projected into the interior – as it pushed, rather than read, through appearances. But if Park avoids the flagrant arbitrariness of Linnaeus' moral physiognomy, he too effaces the 'natural signs' of the body into a generalized and homogenous identity, an expressivism of voice and gesture *à la* Condillac.

Sound and Sense

For Condillac, the gestural sign of nature modulated not only into speech, but also into dance and poetry. So exclusive is Condillac's focus on expression that it becomes his sole criterion of value: 'the different genres of dance . . . are all good, provided they express something'.[25] For this reason, an ostensibly artificial convention of verse – metre – is held to develop from the *prosodic* character of the earliest language: 'Everyone knows that it is natural for the voice to vary its inflections in conformity with gestural variation.'[26] For Lord Kames too, along with Rousseau and so many other Enlightenment philosophers of language, the 'music of verse' or metre was right at the centre of what it means to be human: 'The subject is intimately connected with human nature; and to explain it thoroughly, several nice and delicate feelings must be employed.'[27] When, roughly during the period of writing 'The Discharged Soldier' in late January 1798, and six weeks prior to announcing *The Recluse*, Wordsworth made just one notebook entry from Richard Payne Knight's *The Progress of Civil Society* (1796), a didactic long poem of moral philosophy, this was indeed with reference to prosody. His transcription of a footnote citation of Samuel Johnson on blank verse, then, was not necessarily the mark of an insular aestheticism. In the passage, Johnson had himself challenged an arbitrary aesthetic: the violation of English word order in unrhymed verse's attempts to distinguish itself from prose. Within *The Progress*, Payne Knight had outlined a conjectural history of prosody that was strikingly close to Condillac. For Payne Knight, 'social life began' on discovering how 'sound and sentiment accord' through an 'Instinctive mimicry' of the emotional noises made by others.[28] As Payne Knight follows the difficult transition from a gesture to what is strange, or in need, to a language of social identity, an anticipation of poetic metre is the major staging post:

> Long unsuccessful did the savage try,
> In measured notes, to articulate his cry;
> And e'en when some enlighten'd mind had taught
> To join the measured sound with measured thought.
> (219–23)

The couplets have a 'measured' balance even in their visual length. A prosody or metric of quantity gives shape to an equivalence of sound and thought. Everything must be in 'accord'.

It is not surprising, then, that Payne Knight had written in his preface to the poem that if an image were 'too minutely and accurately displayed', this would be rather inelegantly '*spotty*... instead of concentrating the attention to one general combination of parts, subordinate to each other'.[29] In *The Progress of Civil Society*, each chapter or 'part' represented a stage or theme connected with the Scottish Enlightenment's 'four-stage' theory of progress, with each subordinated to the forward vector of time; it was an image of the hypotactic dependency of subordinate to main clause in Payne Knight's syntax. His preface insisted that the 'web or substance' of a long poem was to be comprised of systematic and discursive material 'in which the flowers of poetry are inwrought' only as decoration.[30] Each detail gains its meaning solely from the overarching whole.

Wordsworth's flowers, by contrast, have been uprooted. For Coleridge in the *Biographia Literaria*, Wordsworth's poetry suffered from the prosaisms of 'a laborious minuteness and fidelity in the representations of objects'.[31] But there were other ways in which Wordsworth could distinguish blank verse from prose, while respecting Johnson's insistence on 'natural' word order. Elsewhere in the *Biographia*, Wordsworth would be praised for his flouting of hypotactic convention in favour of paratactical turns, through 'modes of connections' foreign to 'ordinary intercourse', and strange 'breaks and transitions'.[32] There is 'even' a 'peculiar' disruption of the logic of 'grammatical connection', frequent 'omission of the connective particle', and a widespread use of appositional clauses, as though adjectives defining a word.[33] The minute is now affirmed by Coleridge insofar as it conveys 'all the different marks and circumstances . . . of a living and acting power'.[34] This would be the minuteness of an individually material – not ethnic or sentimental – physiognomy. Its breaks, transitions and disjunctive particulars are those of the enigmatic (rather than expressive) marks and torsions of the living body.

But is this really anthropology, the 'Science of Man', at all? Is it not simply an aestheticization of the individual? With its disruption of grammar and logic through serial parataxis, its obtrusive detail and peculiar connections, could such a poetics really have a bearing on the rational norms of any discourse, let alone those of exchange? Coleridge's account of Wordsworth's eccentricities does indeed anticipate some of the features that delineate an 'aesthetic autonomy' in an impressive study by Christoph Menke.[35] For Menke, there can be no 'interplay' between rigorous art and non-aesthetic discourses, only 'a relationship of interminable crisis'.[36] Art would pose a critical threat to a discourse promoting equal exchange, for example, for it undermines the mechanisms that impose a rational identity.

Menke's argument is based, primarily, on a highly formalistic development of themes in Adorno's *Aesthetic Theory*. Menke's aesthetics could be epitomized as the total inverse of Payne Knight's in *The Progress of Civil Society*. Already this points to an art-historical context that remains unaddressed in Menke's ontology of art. What makes a poem like 'The Discharged Soldier' so interesting is that while it marks a stage en route to *l'art pour l'art* poetics, for Wordsworth the cognitive demands made on art by the Enlightenment long poem at the level of discursive content are here no less binding. But here they are to be fulfilled non-discursively within the forms of aesthetic experience itself. For Adorno, who did acknowledge historical changes in art's relationship to meaning, the 'historico-philosophical' truth of modern (and Romantic) art was bound up with its 'negativity', and it is Adorno's formal account of this destructive character that Menke takes over. This is based on the 'processual' or paratactic nature of aesthetic experience, a temporal flow in which detail yields to detail.[37] No particular can be understood in isolation; each must be revised in turn from the perspective of the developing whole, without the latter ever gaining a full intelligibility, for it is always in tension with the singularities from which it is composed. The structure of the artwork is what Menke calls a 'configurative discontinuity'. Drawing on Valéry's theory of prosody as 'a prolonged hesitation between sound and sense'[38] – in contrast to their 'accord' for Payne Knight – Menke argues that matter and meaning are both suspended in a perpetual vacillation that hovers between them.[39] It is this semiotic failure, this breakdown of the 'automatic repetition' of identity we habitually impose upon phenomena, that transforms the non-aesthetic phenomenon into an aesthetic cipher.

Wordsworth would write of a decorative flower in *Peter Bell*: 'A primrose by a river's brim / A yellow primrose was to him / And it was nothing more' (*PB* 218–20). To experience something 'more' than such an automatic identity, for Menke, is not to go beyond meaning, but to seek and fail to establish an identification: 'experience of the genesis of meaning as the experience of the other in understanding is always, at the same time, an experience against understanding'.[40] Is not this experience of the other *in* rather than *to* understanding that of the initial stage in Condillac's 'primitive encounter' – the struggle to identify a wholly new sensation, an alien suffering that is felt as one's own? At a moment just prior to the establishment of sympathetic identity, another's suffering is experienced precisely as that of another. But this is to raise moral, as well as aesthetic, claims that Menke's formalism seems to disallow. Yet a moral dimension is surely implicit when Menke suggests of the object that 'its aesthetic transfiguration frees it of its "worldly" identity and makes it "similar" to itself'. This is nothing less, for Menke, than 'the redemption of the material' as it is rescued from both the semiotic and a 'pure thingness'.[41] Implicitly then, and through a highly artificial, mediated and negative process, the artwork speaks a language of nature.

And while Menke rejects Adorno's claim that aesthetic negativity is social-critical, which would translate art back into a non-aesthetic discourse with which it is radically incompatible for Menke, there can be no gainsaying Adorno's observation that the material content of art is historical. For Menke, art has a 'deictic' or 'showing' character, attained by estranging the contexts of practice that enable 'automatic understanding'.[42] Such contexts are distantly 'quoted' rather than directly presented; the figure is irreducible to its ground.[43] But that distanced and estranged foundation is inevitably historical. Might not the negation of such contexts bear its own critical force? And what for Adorno is the artwork's 'immanent law of form' – not quite the same as what Menke calls its 'kaleidoscopic' structure – might be not without repercussions in the contexts of natural law. Adorno called for a music that 'should constitute itself in an objectively compelling way, in the musical substance itself, and not in terms of external laws'.[44] It was a reading of Wordsworth in 1940 that led Bertolt Brecht, ostensibly that most militant of politically engaged ('heteronomous') artists, to commit to his notebook what has been called the 'most Adornian'[45] of all aesthetic dicta: 'art *is* an autonomous sphere, though by no means an autarchic one'.[46] Art may not have its own ground (*arkhe*), but it does have its own law (*nomos*).

To trace such an individuation, as it obeys and unfolds only its own internal criteria, would be far more subtly inflected than that absolute singularity which immediately strikes the observer in Levinas' ethics of the 'face'. Levinas' structure of the intersubjective was, like the 'I–Thou' relation of Martin Buber, a twentieth-century avatar of Condillac's 'primitive encounter'. Once again, the principles of natural law are converted into an ontological or existential 'primordial' structure. In Levinas, however, there is no exchange, only an asymmetrical obligation. Levinas' disjunction between, on the one hand, the infinite ethical demands of the other in the 'face-to-face' situation, and, on the other, the measured, calculated and distributive justice of society, is precisely the 'diremption of law and ethics' that for Gillian Rose has marked a crisis in modernity.[47] In Condillac's 'primitive encounter', as the archaic form of exchange and ground of the social contract, the law and ethics are one and the same. For Rose, however, we must attend to the 'broken middle' of law and ethics – the relationship of the singular to the universal and particular – without trying idealistically to 'mend' it. In its quotation and distancing of contexts, 'The Discharged Soldier' might be said to enact the drama of that broken middle. For here, the processual character of a singular aesthetic experience will irrupt within the contexts of history and a moral structure of exchange.

'A sudden turning of the road'

If Wordsworth's local 'ethnography' hinges on micro-observation, then its calibration must be equally minute. For the detail or 'letter' in this poetry is rarely simply concrete or literal – it too is a citation of context. Wordsworth's poetry in general, let alone 'The Discharged Soldier', has yet to receive a sustained historical and philosophical close reading that tries to square up to the challenge laid by Menke's ontology of art, its insistence on the 'sovereign' autonomy of an aesthetic negativity. But can Wordsworth's poetry really bear the weight of such philosophical abstraction? This is a question that must be kept open rather than closed. Wordsworth himself, however, was to claim that the poem's significance was to be found in a regulating aesthetic – and also in a philosophy of language. When 'The Discharged Soldier' found its eventual home, in abbreviated form, at the end of Book IV of *The Prelude*, Wordsworth chose to frame the poem, at its beginning and end, with alternative keys to its interpretation.

The first of these introduces the narrative as one of a number of episodes that were

> a store
> Of primitive hours, when, by these hindrances
> Unthwarted – I experienc'd in myself
> Conformity as just as that of old
> To the end and written spirit of God's works,
> Whether held forth in Nature or in Man.
>
> (354–9)

On the student Wordworth's return to the Lakes during his summer vacation from the 'hindrances' of Cambridge, the 'primitive hours' of his childhood, of an ontogenetic (rather than phylogenetic) state of nature, suddenly come back to life. 'The Discharged Soldier' is the most exemplary of these moments. What a 'primitive hour' entails in this passage is no less than the exegesis of a sacred text. But the language of revelation has been conflated with the natural sign. The relationship between the two languages had been a characteristic tension throughout the eighteenth century. Vico and Condillac had sought to appease religious orthodoxy by staging the natural origins of language after the Flood – a second start for language after the supernatural fiat of creation, and Adam's divinely inspired naming of the creatures in Eden. But the issue was surprisingly difficult to resolve. It has been said even of J. G. Herder, whose famous essay, *On the Origin of Language* (1772), had argued for an exclusively natural source, that he 'never shook himself free of the enigma' of a possibly divine origin: 'the gap between spontaneous, mimetic speech-sounds and the wonder of mature language seemed too great'.[48] That 'wonder' was the logic of grammar, syntax and identity. The miracle of a human creativity *ex nihilo* might be cognitive of a divine language of structures and essences. Jonathan Bate has claimed of Wordsworth's 'Poems on the Naming of Places' that they arrogate 'a God-given function, for the ultimate precedent for the poet's act of naming is Adam's'.[49] But Wordsworth's 'primitive hours' are not characterized by the performative imposition of a name, nor by a pantheist consubstantiation; instead, at least here for Wordsworth, they both read and listen to the created and creaturely: 'God's works'.

Against the prioritization of the oral, of 'expressive substance' over material letter, of spoken presence against the distance and interpretive uncertainty of written language – famously reversed by Derrida in his 'deconstruction' of Rousseau's *Essay on the Origin of Languages*[50] – here neither the written nor the spoken is granted the rights of primogeniture.[51] What 'holds forth' has a 'written spirit'. The spirit of the law cannot be disengaged from its 'written' character or letter. It is to be read or heard through 'Conformity' to that textual spirit. Wordsworth (as in the 'Essay on Morals') must read through an experience of the internal body – 'I experienced in myself' – reminiscent of the mimetic sympathy with the sign in Condillac's 'primitive hour'. The long tradition of mystical theories of language, and of its basis in a divine 'Book of Nature',[52] has been given an anthropological turn. The purportedly divine is a strictly material language, both inscribed and expressive 'in man' as well as 'Nature'. But this physiognomic language is somehow more than nakedly concrete: it has a potential *telos* or moral 'end'.

Wordsworth's second commentary on 'The Discharged Soldier', written across its conclusion like a *mene tekel* for the casual reader, binds up the episode's 'end' with the 'rules', the immanent law, of its poetic composition:

> This passed, and he who deigns to mark with care
> By what rules governed, with what end in view,
> This work proceeds, *he* will not wish for more.
> (*14BkPr.* IV.470–2)

Much as a travel writer would, Wordsworth asserts the mimetic authenticity of his eyewitness narration[53] – leaving it ambiguous as to whether the regulatory 'work' brought to bear is that of the artist shaping his material, or something emergent from the plasticity of the experience it recounts. Indeed, far from following some classical canon of the rules of verse, or the imposition of an external framework, the poem's formal character seems to be latent within the content itself – for otherwise there would be no need for the reader to 'mark with care'. If the work's processual form is its own moral 'end', then it cannot issue in a simple result, a culminating maxim or 'moral proposition'. And so the reader must not 'wish for more'. As opposed to the anthropological system laid out extensively in Payne Knight's discursive long poem, here the *intensive* dimensions of a single picture 'of Nature, Man, and Society' must somehow *contain everything* – or at least, as Wordsworth wrote to Tobin of 'The Discharged Soldier' and his other first sketches for *The Recluse*, 'most of the knowledge of which I am possessed'.[54] But if we should not 'wish for more', it is implied that this would be a natural, though mistaken, inclination. Something more than an easy moral is glaringly absent or missing. The poem is encyclopaedic not in terms of what it puts in, but in the form of what it has *left out*.

Nevertheless, the poem begins as though its form were as simple as that of Payne Knight's *Progress of Civil Society* – following the straight, but ascending line of global history. Each of its details evokes and withholds such an identification; Wordsworth's journey is both pedestrianly quotidian and world-historically resonant. He is strolling along 'the public Way' (*LB* 2), up a 'sharp rising' (8), looking 'not round' (26) but 'step by step led on' (36) – as if by Providence. The road's 'watery surface' (7) after rainfall is said to look as though it were rising to join a 'brook' in the distance (10) – perhaps even Coleridge's 'The Brook'. But Wordsworth is simply ambling through a damp landscape at night. He is in a mimetically receptive mood, 'Quiescent, and disposed to sympathy' (16) and with 'A consciousness of animal delight' (33). The body has returned to its Arcadian state of nature: open to the world, yet with a 'self-possession' felt in the intervals of movement (34–5).

Yet in an instant, he is knocked off balance. As the blank verse suddenly turns, in the direction of the new, he is confronted by an unsympathetic object:

> It chanced a sudden turning of the road
> Presented to my view an uncouth shape
> (37–8)

At a corresponding stage in Harley's encounter with a discharged soldier in *The Man of Feeling*, he too is walking 'when, turning round, his notice was attracted by an object, which the fixture of his eye on the spot he walked had before prevented him from observing'.[55] In Mackenzie's novel, the narrative's progress from here is a move from pure object to pure subject: the common humanity exchanged in floods of tears. Wordsworth's object, however, is not an empiricist imprint upon a blank slate, but has been unconsciously turned through a formative and evaluative process – he recoils from an 'uncouth shape'. We are given a first glimpse of just how differently this poem's rules operate.

The shape recalls the 'ancient uncouth country style' of the protuberant chimney in 'Michael'. The adjective 'uncouth' was a key word in Wordsworth's specific idiom. If there is, in Simon Jarvis' phrase, a 'materialism of the beautiful' in Wordsworth,[56] then how might this accommodate the seemingly ugly or 'uncouth'? In 'The Ruined Cottage', the weaver Robert, in aimless unemployment, 'Carved uncouth figures on the heads of sticks' (*RC* 217). In this latter-day state of savagery, the fetish is an 'uncouth' expression of no more than an estranged and frustrated violence (soon displaced, Wordsworth tells us, onto Robert's family). In another poem, 'A Narrow Girdle of Rough Stones' (1800), Wordsworth commemorates a local spot with the name 'Point Rash-Judgment', while admitting that it is 'a memorial name, uncouth indeed / As e'er by Mariner was giv'n to Bay / Or Foreland, on a new-discovered coast' (*LB* 83–6). The uncouth name records an act of disfiguring prejudice in this *terra incognita*: Wordsworth's misrecognition of the bare livelihood of a cripple – fishing – as the pleasant angling of a truant farm worker. David Simpson has noted the ironic overlap of contrite acknowledgement and a blind superimposition of European names onto exotic places in travel literature.[57] The Adamic name is here recalled only through its negative converse. The 'uncouth' stands for what is projected wrongly, or blankly, onto the perceptually foreign. In the 1850 *Prelude*, Wordsworth pointedly added the word in a revision to the Arab dream that immediately follows the discharged soldier episode at the beginning of Book v. At first sight, the Arab-Quixote, both Oriental and European, is also an 'uncouth Shape' (*14BkPr.* 75). The judgement of the uncouth is a default response to what exceeds a framework of understanding or value. It had been Wordsworth's own recoil from the 'Hottentotish' dwelling in the Highlands. A single lexical item has its own fountain in experience.

For Coleridge, Wordsworth's ability to read beyond the evaluative norms of discourse was no less than a breakthrough into the language of Eden: 'The superscription and the image of the Creator still remain legible to *him* under the dark lines, with which guilt or calamity had cancelled or cross-barred it.'[58] But if that lacuna in the palimpsest reveals the 'lines' of a 'superscription' for Coleridge, for Wordsworth it is a materiality that communicates from below. Words like 'the uncouth' were not to be eliminated, but distended through a new referential base. In his 7 June 1802 letter to John Wilson, Wordsworth would state that the uncouth term 'Idiot' could unfortunately not be avoided (in 'The Idiot Boy'), for there was no alternative '*to which we had attached passion*'.[59] Wordsworth aimed at the semantic reorientation of a word. Through a turning or redirection of the passion of instinctive habit, a word can be made indeterminate enough to communicate dignity as well as abjection. What Coleridge noticed as Wordsworth's paratactic tendency to juxtapose clauses, 'in the construction of words by apposition',[60] was exemplary. 'Uncouth' does not reappear as a word in 'The Discharged Soldier' – its redefinition unfolds as each transition of the poem adds new qualifications.

But Wordsworth's first response to the 'uncouth shape' is to leap back. He does so in a manner remarkably close to Swift's parody, in *Gulliver's Travels*, of Dampier's first contact with the Australian aborigines. When Gulliver first spots the Yahoos, he is unable to recognize them as human: 'Their Shape was very singular, and deformed, which a little discomposed me, so that I lay down behind a Thicket to observe them better.'[61] But in Wordsworth's poem, the deformed shape quickly gains a masculine pronoun, as it looms

> So near, that, stepping back into the shade
> Of a thick hawthorn, I could mark him well,
> Myself unseen.
>
> (39–41)

Wordsworth is now at the necessary distance to project a sympathetic identification. Instead, however, he starts to 'mark him well' – just as the reader will be told to 'mark with care'.

Yet what emerges is an immediate challenge to this effort at close reading. The discomposed object may not be human at all:

> He was in stature tall,
> A foot above man's common measure tall,
> And lank, and upright.
>
> (41–3)

Gigantism had been a link between the contrasting states of nature: the 'giant' Edenic shepherds for the child Wordsworth, yet also the 'gigantic bones' of *Salisbury Plain*, figures of a spectral prehistory of violence. For Vico, it was giants who wandered through the primal forests of the state of nature; the origins of language at that time were an effect not of need, but of passionate wonder, most notably through an identification of the 'sky god' in lightning. Vico's confidence in his giants' literal existence in prehistory ironically manifested the very trait he associated with early humanity: a figurative language deemed literal truth, and a poetic thinking that anticipated rational concepts through personified archetypes or 'imaginative universals' (*generi fantastici*).[62] Bewell also detects a parallel here with Rousseau's *Essay on the Origin of Languages*. For Rousseau, the first time one of his solitaries glimpsed another human being in the state of nature, that figure was immediately aggrandized by terror; as with Vico, the original language was figuratively expressive and distorting, and 'Giant' became the very first word.[63] Only on growing accustomed to the sight was a common humanity recognized, as the 'giant' shrunk down to the literal word (and first concept): 'Man'.[64] In his 1809 essay 'Reply to Mathetes', Wordsworth invoked a traveller in America who, on discovering huge bones at a burial mound, had thereby concluded that 'all men were Giants' in prehistory.[65] A 'second and wiser thought' would realize that the man 'had been selected as a Chieftain or Ruler for the very reason that he surpassed the rest of his Tribe in stature'.[66] As much as the 'uncouth', the gargantuan is a parable of colonial or cross-cultural misrecognition; to the same degree as the supposedly 'archaic' or infant, the modern traveller falls into an entanglement of the literal and the figurative. But in 'The Discharged Soldier', the giant has been marked with a literal soberness. He has even been measured.

Associations fall away in a fixation upon the object. The figure holds an internal tension; it has been sharpened to the point of pain:

> There was in his form
> A meagre stiffness. You might almost think
> That his bones wounded him.
>
> (43–5)

For the first time, prompted by a singular form, Wordsworth tries to read into the man's feelings. He does not *feel* the man's suffering, but must 'think' through his responses. The man is no longer purely identified with his outer body. Yet the bones only 'almost' hold an antagonistic independence. There may not be any painful wound at all; the man may feel nothing. But as observation continues, so the limbs suddenly detach:

> His legs were long,
> So long and shapeless that I looked at them
> Forgetful of the body they sustained.
>
> (45–7)[67]

In this 'primitive hour', Wordsworth has returned to his 'conjectures' (237) of infancy in Book II of *The Prelude*, to the original 'primitive hour'. There, he had imagined the new-born child gazing at its mother

> eager to combine
> In one appearance, all the elements
> And parts of the same object, else detach'd
> And loth to coalesce.
>
> (247–50)

Wordsworth has been thrown back to a primal state of dissociation. As coherence dissolves and parts fall loose, he is absorbed in a single detail – as 'incorporated' as the reader in an ideal text for the 'Essay on Morals'. If, in the forgetfulness of a magnetic strangeness, Wordsworth has murdered to dissect, this is more than just an indulgence in 'dehumanizing fictions', as Bewell characterizes the early stages of the poem.[68] The elongated and distended limbs, seen with a visionary focus not astigmatism – as though, like Lear, they have been 'stretched' on 'the rack of this tough world' (v.iii.313–14) or projected at the parallax of another world – are a portent of something genuinely singular about the man. While recalling the shapeless shape of Milton's Death,[69] the figure thwarts all attempts at identification. How can a leg be shapeless?

As Wordsworth now struggles to repair that figure as a whole, particulars continue to spark off from their origin: 'his mouth / Shewed ghastly in the moonlight' (50–1). In this half-light, an oscillation between part and whole has reduced all substance to ghostliness (the meaning of 'ghastly' in the period, but here turning towards its current sense). Signs of a cultural background, quoted from a remote distance, now emerge with their own spectral quality. Cut off from all means of support, the trope of litotes signals the man's passage from an archaic to a contemporary state of nature:

I could mark
That he was clad in military garb,
Though faded yet entire . . .
. . . He was alone
Had no attendant, neither dog, nor staff,
Nor knapsack; – in his very dress appear'd
A desolation, a simplicity
That [appertain'd] to solitude.

(53–64)

In *Adventures on Salisbury Plain*, the traveller's 'ragged coat scarce showed the Soldier's faded red' (9).[70] But unlike that earlier discharged soldier lost within the wastes, now the material blank that follows the withdrawal of personal care is gazed upon with apathy rather than panic: 'His face was turn'd / Towards the road, yet not as if he sought / For any living object' (55–7). It is a gaze too absent and withdrawn to be identified with the ataraxia of the 'savage' in *Salisbury Plain*. And Wordsworth himself has fallen into a state of estrangement. It is he who sees the man as blank and inhuman: even a 'glove' would have 'made him more akin to man' (65–6). But the soldier is perhaps not wholly without affect, for 'He appeared / Forlorn and desolate' (57–8). He is both 'turn'd', and yet not turned, towards the human. The independence affirmed in *Descriptive Sketches*, and the isolate misery of *Salisbury Plain*, have here been superimposed: the man seems both to need, and not to need, a human context.

In this 'ghastly' indeterminacy, a greater effort to read the man's inner state has become paramount. In 'fear and sorrow', the literatures of Gothic and sensibility are uneasily commingled:

> Long time I scann'd him with a mingled sense
> Of fear and sorrow. From his lips, meanwhile,
> There issued murmuring sounds, as if of pain
> Or of uneasy thought, – yet still his form
> Kept the same fearful steadiness. His shadow
> Lay at his feet and moved not.
>
> (67–72)

To scan this physiognomy is also to follow the prosody of its 'murmuring sounds'. Unlike Condillac and Payne Knight, here the 'natural sign' vacillates undecidably between sound and sense, the expressive and the expressionless: the man may be in 'pain', or may be in 'uneasy thought' – or may not be suffering at all. The man's form appears only 'as if' an object of sympathy, while fleeting signs of life bring him back from the undead. But the unmoving shadow is as literal a perception as his 'giant' stature earlier. This is no 'ghastly' hologram, but the 'fearful' solid-state of a living death.

As Wordsworth's reading builds in intensity, so all its details begin to waver at the edge of signification. When we are told that a nearby village is 'an arrow's flight away' (75), an archaic image of war flashes out and recedes from the contingent figure of rural speech. A 'chained mastiff' in that village is ceaselessly howling (73), a contiguous detail that is barely held back in its potential symbolism. In *Descriptive Sketches*, the 'Grison gypsey' heard in the valley beneath her 'The death-dog, howling loud and long, below' (226) in a passage that anticipates the dark state of nature in *Salisbury Plain*. Here only a chain withstands *Salisbury Plain*'s predatorial state of nature, with its endlessly baying wolves. The cumulative effect is that of a suspended animation. This extends even to the 'silent doors' of the inaccessible village below them (73) – opaque signs that might speak when open to the stranger. Just as the inanimate threshold is somehow 'silent', so the man's 'murmuring voice' issues an oxymoronic 'dead complaint' (78). The generalized state of estrangement is 'instinct with vital functions'. The poem is beginning to turn as it seeks for a 'living object'. A 'dead complaint' is not the same as a 'dead letter'.

The potential for meaning is the potential for independent life. As this sense grows stronger through the failure of both Gothic and sentimental identifications, so 'fear and sorrow' turn into *guilt* and sorrow. Wordsworth has been guilty of a voyeuristic lingering:

> Not without reproach
> Had I prolonged my watch, and now confirm'd
> And my heart's specious cowardice subdued,
> I left the shady nook where I had stood,
> And hailed the Stranger.
>
> (82–6)

We are made to feel the forward impulse. As Wordsworth moves (in Condillac's terms) from the 'natural sign' through a 'language of action' to the 'instituted sign', he must begin with that most basic social gesture: a salutation. An urge to make the 'ghastly' human once again, like the infant's effort to restore its mother's face, seems to have surged back. So Wordsworth now inquires into the man's autobiographical and social background: 'I asked his history' (94). From an initial asymmetry – taken hostage, fixated, challenged to respond by the Stranger – Wordsworth lays down the opening gambit of a sympathetic exchange.

At a corresponding stage in Mackenzie's *Man of Feeling*, the former soldier's tale of woe in colonial India had been recounted at exhaustive length. But here we are given only 'a simple fact' (99) without expression, the barest outline of a narrative: he has served in the 'Tropic islands' and, having been discharged, is now returning home (98–103). The man who had evoked first contact with the 'savage' indigene has now become a colonial traveller. What links the two, as with the traveller in *Salisbury Plain*, is that he too is the victim more than the perpetrator of imperial war, enlisted from the lower classes, and reduced to the most primitive misery. The discharged veteran of colonial wars had become a recognizable literary type. Robert Burns' alehouse 'cantata' of 1785, 'Love and Liberty', opened with a former soldier, in 'auld red rags' (15), singing exuberantly of his martial glory. He now 'must beg with a wooden arm and leg' (13), in winter dwelling 'Beneath the woods and rocks oftentimes for a home' (18).[71] Even the officer Lismahago, in Tobias Smollett's satirical novel *Humphrey Clinker* (1771), had returned from the Seven Years' War in America maimed in body to find his family reduced to weaving; his first impulse is to go back and live among the Indians. But in the *Prelude* version of 'The Discharged Soldier', the narrative is a mere 'Soldier's Tale' (IV.445), interchangeable with any other – this, the poem seems to be saying, *is* its historical truth.

Wordsworth obdurately persists in dwelling on the aesthetic exterior. His focus is not on *what* the man tells him, but on *how* that narrative is delivered.[72] The man who had murmured a 'dead complaint' now speaks 'with a quiet, uncomplaining voice' (96). He is acquiring a human quality. While before, an absence of the most ordinarily humanizing props of material culture had extended even to a pair of gloves, the man now picks up 'a Traveller's Staff', 'unobserved' earlier as it lay on the ground (115–16). It seems that the disfigured limbs of the man are able to travel with some assistance. Wordsworth now offers concrete help – with no gesture of pathos or expressive sympathy, just an appropriate reflex action given the visual and aural prompts – and begins to walk the man to a cottage where he will obtain food and shelter.

But a feeling of strangeness persists. For what had seemed a movement 'as if of pain' now appears (but only appears) to indicate pain's absence. The stranger is still 'ghostly':

> He appeared,
> To travel without pain, and I beheld
> With ill-suppress'd astonishment his tall
> And ghostly figure moving at my side;
>
> (121–4)

Despite or because of the walking staff, Wordsworth cannot hold back his astonishment that what is more a 'ghostly figure' (perhaps no longer a giant but still markedly 'tall') than a literal fellow man is not only in his company but even 'moving' – let alone able to match his pace so apparently effortlessly and fluently. There is even a hint of supernatural motion.[73]

As if to resolve all the aporias of a merely perceptual reading, Wordsworth resumes his questioning of the man. The emphasis is now on the past as a key to what had seemed to be the man's present suffering: 'what he had endured / From war, and battle, and the pestilence' (136–7). These were the very afflictions that destroyed the female vagrant's family in *Salisbury Plain*, bringing about the 'mighty gulf of separation' of her homelessness. But in contrast to her elaborate tale of misery, the man's reply, in its content, is now completely withheld. Again, it is the *tone* of his response that bears its significance for Wordsworth:

> solemn and sublime
> He might have seemed, but that in all he said
> There was a strange half-absence, and a tone
> Of weakness and indifference, as of one
> Remembering the importance of his theme
> But feeling it no longer.
>
> (139–44)

The historical subject remains 'ghastly'.

Understandably, this distancing of context has been attacked as just one example of a general suppression of political history in Wordsworth's major period. Nothing less than imperial warfare has been elided through an 'ideology of transcendence'.[74] Yet that guilt seems unavoidable if, as Menke claims, an aesthetic transcendence, its 'redemption of the material', hinges on that obliquity of context. Art with a good conscience would not be art at all. The material it redeems must itself be redeemed through interpretation. To break out of the sphere of art, then, is not possible merely by supplying a more ample quotation of faraway historical data; we go beyond the text only insofar as we do justice to its transfigurations. If historicist criticism attempts, as Hartman wryly notes, to 'load every rift with glue',[75] then a historical approach true to its object must remain ever mindful of that gap. And in 'The Discharged Soldier', it must start by perceiving that it is history itself that has aestheticized or sacrificed – 'discharged' – the man. A historical suffering, effected by causes of no personal 'importance' to its conscripts, has subsided into 'weakness and indifference'. This is what dissociates the figure from context. The lapse registers a historical *experience*. The passage displays the same rigour – or *tact* – that the poem has evinced through all its turnings. Wordsworth remains within the bounds of what we can know by direct perception alone: a surface that is marked. As Bewell has emphasized, that the man is unable even to identify himself with his own past has the effect of conveying, with a greater representational power than historical detail, the horror that has induced an 'alienation almost beyond imagining'.[76] History has moulded itself into a hostile and encompassing background, an arbitrary yet determining environment: a state of second nature.

This is the nature that speaks through the man's 'murmuring sounds', not a primitive materiality. History intervenes between nature and the supernatural, as the aesthetic is tantalizingly held out and pulled back: 'solemn and sublime / He *might* have seemed'. The man is *not* sublime. Yet he might indeed be so, were another atmosphere to pervade his communication. The sublime is present, but in the conditional tense. His identity is in some sense open-ended. Through a grief abated by 'langour' (118), and as sorrow declines into 'mild indifference' (97), he has half-absented himself from history.

By the very mark of his subjection, an estrangement from all context, the man has preserved an infinitesimal self-reliance. Even in bare life, he is a faint afterimage of that 'lion-grace' of the Alpine shepherd in *Descriptive Sketches*. He has a 'stately air' (97) of bodily comportment, and together with the 'measur'd gesture lifted to his head' (88) that returned

Wordsworth's initial greeting – *not* the prompt briskness of a military salute – this is also a form of metrical or prosodic behaviour. Just as Wordsworth had marked or scanned the man with care, through all the breaks and transitions of the verse's prosodic turns, so now both of them 'measure back / The way' (109). They 'shaped' their 'course' (120–1) as they 'advanced / Slowly' (144–5) – no longer quite so painlessly – in the direction of the cottage. This proto-poetic behaviour finds its acoustic analogue in the man's 'murmuring sounds'. There the prosodic gesture – Payne Knight's harmony of 'measured sound and measured thought' – had given way to 'uneasy thought', 'pain', 'indifference' and a 'half-absence' all at once. Language acquires its own independence, while bearing the traces of an individual voice. Affect and thought become latent qualities in sound and rhythm, as though the echo of a language pregnant within nature itself. In that hollow murmuring – the brook at the poem's outset had also 'murmured in the valley' (11) – is the fountain of a poetic communication: between the human and the natural in their interchange, not state of identity. As a 'dead complaint', another nature murmurs within the 'state of war'.[77]

This language now speaks against the muteness of 'every silent window' (107) in the village below them, corresponding to its earlier 'silent doors', in which all the lights are now said to have gone out. The village was a social space closed off to the vagabond soldier, who had sat by the open road. So, walking away, they pass through its opaque silence's correlate in nature, a 'wood' with 'shades gloomy and dark' (145–7). Once again, an accident of narrative bears a quasi-allegorical force – the aura of a primitive habitat, a forest like the state of nature at the beginning of *Salisbury Plain* – while remaining just a concrete, though atmospheric detail.[78] But it is perhaps no coincidence, when they emerge out into the open, that they arrive at a scene of cultivation: a solitary cottage in a field where the man will receive shelter.[79]

With the restoration of social care, the blank is finally able to speak. As Wordsworth brings his companion to the cottage door, the man 'seem'd / To speak with a reviving interest' (167) – at the threshold of a new life. But what such a life might entail is withheld from us right to the end.[80] Only this bare semblance of life inflects the man's token of gratitude: 'he thanked me' (170). It is perhaps the only moment approaching a real exchange, at its most minimal, in the whole poem. Just before, as Wordsworth knocked at the door, he had appealed to the cottager not only in hope of charity, but 'if need be' as a partner in equal exchange: '"This night let him find rest, and give him food – / This service if need be I will requite"' (154–5).[81] So far is the poem's end from a merging of sympathies that Wordsworth now issues the man with a 'reproof' (162). Given the former soldier's condition, he should sit by an inn or cottage to seek help, not on the public highway; or better, he should actively 'Demand the succour' he needs from parish relief or the almshouse. He should snap out of his apathy and be a bit more go-getting – he deserves it. But as the man answers – the only moment, right at the end, that we hear him speak in *The Prelude* – with the 'ghastly mildness' (163) of a returning spectrality, so Wordsworth is rebuked in turn: '"My trust is in the God of heaven, / And in the eye of him that passes me"' (162–3). In a state of estrangement, all trust has been lost in the public forms of donation. In this most oblique citation of context is the distrust Wordsworth himself had expressed, in poems like 'The Last of the Flock' and 'The Old Cumberland Beggar', for the coercively 'improving' or punishing ambitions of parish and state-sponsored care. In the man's state of second nature, a redemptive providence lives only in the individual. This broken exchange, this failure of communication between Wordsworth and the man, a talking at cross-purposes, is tense with an aporia that the poem is helpless to overcome: the 'diremption of law and ethics'.

It is against this dark background of the public space of law, of the village at night, of a state reaching even to the tropics in colonial war, that Wordsworth's act of insufficient charity must be set. His fussing and patronizing care has shown itself little better. Not only has there been no genuine exchange, there has not even been any real giving. Wordsworth's responses, unreflective and automatic, have disclosed layer upon layer of a *habitus*. But in what this has elicited, the sudden turns and careful markings of a scanning and prosody of experience, the poem has traced a new form of *habitus*. The prescriptive law by which it is governed is only latent within the bleak historical description that is its fountain. Any attempt to extrapolate that form risks being just another emptily abstract 'moral proposition'. If that effort is nevertheless worthwhile, it is precisely because it cannot be translated into a moral code.

The soldier-beggar's 'trust' is not in the passer-by himself, but in his 'eye'. What Wordsworth called his poetry's 'steady look at the subject'[82] was, at its most unsteady, an ethos of close reading. Against the general and external principles imposed by both natural law and positive convention, it tries to decipher an immanent law in the material language of an individuation. But at no point in 'The Discharged Soldier' is Wordsworth's effort characterized by will: he is led by the signs and cues of the object itself, as he follows its unwinding contours. 'We have to try to cure our faults by attention and not by will'[83] – but Wordsworth does not try to do anything at all. Right from the poem's outset, he has been 'step by step led on'. It is in this absence or frustration of purposeful intention, this non-imposition or bafflement of a conscious norm, that we might half-glimpse a potential meaning within Benjamin's cryptic assertion: 'The law which is studied but no longer practiced is the gate to justice.'[84]

The inner law of 'The Discharged Soldier' is that of an 'involute': not a hierarchy of part and whole, but a 'perplexed combination' or 'compound' that is 'incapable of being disentangled'. Bewell's argument that the poem follows the stations of an Enlightenment line of progress, from the 'natural man' to a civilized and cultural humanity, is only partly true – that teleology has been set in motion only to be retroactively dismantled.[85] The poem is not a ladder of stages, as in Payne Knight's *Progress of Civil Society*, with each point an advance on what was left behind, but a configuration of equally valid moments. All are attributes of the man, and each one fails to define him. Each successive interpretation is overturned by what follows, only for that to be revoked in turn. The reader cannot know, and the man cannot be known. This, the poem seems to tell us, and not the project of a sympathetic identity, is the true basis of care.

'The Discharged Soldier' progresses not, *à la* Vico or Rousseau, from the figure of a 'Giant' to the universal 'Man', but in the direction of a proper name. Through its hovering between the literal and the figurative, it does justice to the autonomy of an individual so strange that we do not even know what to call him. It is the poem's map of the inaccessible, its 'configurative discontinuity', rather than any real appellation, which is the true figure of a name. As a pure name, it can have no expression. But to see the unique as truly unique is to see how it points beyond itself: the distance that permits a reading of the marks, or scars, of the 'Nature, Man, and Society' that have shaped it. Mimetic sympathy is a speculative mimesis that, by getting right up close to its minutest letters, tries to combine a picture. Even in exchange there is asymmetry, as we lose ourselves in the object, and are brought up short at its boundaries. Such a rule of comportment might seem impossible, even inhuman – but the poem shows how it might once have come to pass.

And what such a hospitality of the figural eye might mean in terms of real material action, as a law of the community rather than a solitary ethic, can be glimpsed in Wordsworth's defence of his poem 'The Idiot Boy', in the 1802 letter to John Wilson. In sight of another figure of anthropological inscrutability, once more the Swiss mediate between the exotic and the English poor:

> I have often applied to Idiots, in my own mind, that sublime expression of scripture that, '*their life is hidden with God*'. They are worshipped, probably from a feeling of this sort, in several parts of the East. Among the Alps where they are numerous, they are considered, as I believe, as a blessing to the family to which they belong. I have indeed often looked upon the conduct of fathers and mothers of the lower classes of society towards Idiots as the great triumph of the human heart.[86]

In 'The Discharged Soldier', the possible idolatry of such a worship,[87] and the sublimity of what remains only an 'expression' – or moral proposition – have been taken down to the fountain of an uncouth figuring and renewal.

In *The Prelude* version, a final coda was added to the narrative. As the man goes into the cottage, Wordsworth does not follow, but remains standing outside the door. A class distance remains – the Cambridge student has a very different kind of home. He does not yet inhabit an 'Indian bower'. The reader is not introduced to the cottager, or allowed to see or enter into the sympathetic dwelling. Instead, we follow Wordsworth as he walks away, chastened and, for a moment, pacified:

> Back I cast a look,
> And linger'd near the door a little space;
> Then sought with quiet heart my distant home.
> (502–4)

If we cannot see into the interior, we are allowed to linger a little at the threshold. We start to imagine our way in.

CHAPTER 4

The Commonwealth of Song

In his 1798 'Advertisement' to the first edition of *Lyrical Ballads*, Wordsworth hoped that the poems' 'experiment' in language would gratify the reader 'in spite of that most dreadful enemy to our pleasures, our own pre-established codes of decision'.[1] The ballads, mostly written in the spring of that year, immediately following the announcement of *The Recluse*, and shortly after the first composition of 'The Discharged Soldier', were as much as the latter poem an attempt at the disestablishment of what Edward Said would famously call a 'textual attitude'. Such quixotic interpretations through 'hegemonic' discourses, for Said a key feature of European colonialism, will come into play 'when a human being confronts at close quarters something relatively unknown and threatening and previously distant'.[2] The confrontation with an alien culture, that latter-day 'primitive encounter', was for Said an epitome of the 'human tendency to fall back on a text when the uncertainties of travel in strange parts seem to threaten one's equanimity'.[3] This clinging to the familiar text might be operative even in the more homely experience of reading literature. So ingrained were such responses that merely to 'adapt' the 'language of conversation in the middle and lower classes' to metrical verse,[4] hitherto largely associated with elevated and ornate diction, might be enough to trigger the pre-established resistances which codify an 'uncouth shape'. Ironically, this 'strangeness and aukwardness [*sic*]'[5] for the gentle reader would be an effect of the language's sheer ordinariness. The language is strange in its very familiarity, it is homely in an *unheimlich* context – as, in this least occult yet all the more disconcerting of experiences, the uncouth turns into the *uncanny*.

The 'pre-established code of decision' is a state of second nature. As the 1800 Preface to the second edition recognized, it is a form of social contract and commodity exchange: 'It is supposed, that by the act of writing in verse an Author makes a formal engagement that he will gratify certain known habits of association.'[6] Wordsworth breaks the social contract, reneges on his 'promise' and tears up the textual attitude: 'it will appear to many persons that I have not fulfilled the terms of an engagement thus voluntarily contracted'.[7] He has flouted the reader's terms and conditions, as the 'Appendix on Poetic Diction' of the 1802 edition suggests, because the artificiality of poetic language has become so habituated that it appears to be a natural law: 'the taste of men was gradually perverted and this language was received as a natural language: and at length, by the influence of books upon men, did to a degree really become so'.[8] But there is a hidden asymmetry in the contractual exchange of author and reader: the meretricious writer is 'ambitious of the fame of Poets' and seeks 'the character of a man to be looked up to, a man of genius and authority'.[9] In 1818, Hazlitt would accuse Wordsworth, Coleridge and Southey themselves of such a vanity: their efforts at 'bringing poetry back to its primitive simplicity and state of nature' were a levelling attempt to ensure that 'the only thing left remarkable in the world by this change would be the persons who had produced it'.[10] How, then, in *Lyrical Ballads* and the wealth of short lyrics that followed in its wake, might such a desired 'original' or 'natural language' – filtered through the specific and latter-day medium of a 'picture of nature, man, and society' – be in any sense more than unremarkable and ordinary? How might an author speak for anyone or anything other than themselves? What is song in a contemporary state of nature?

'The Nature of Poetry – Its Origin and Progress'

The 1802 'Appendix' sketched the conjectural history of poetry as it arose from a state of nature and underwent its subsequent degeneration into 'poetic diction'. 'The earliest Poets of all nations', Wordsworth affirmed, 'generally wrote from passion excited by real events; they wrote naturally, and as men: feeling powerfully as they did, their language was daring, and figurative.'[11] Wordsworth could write so confidently of the inaccessible past – though no doubt he alludes to figures like Homer too – because characterizations of archaic poetry on these lines had become an Enlightenment commonplace. Rousseau and Vico went even further: the very earliest language as such was entirely poetic and figurative, and for the latter this first language was *sung*, just as 'stutterers' break free of impeded speech by singing.[12] Charles Burney's famous *General History of Music* (1776–89) – which, Duncan Wu claims, albeit speculatively, 'helped establish the thinking behind the *Lyrical Ballads*'[13] – had argued that the language and song 'of every country' were 'nearly coeval' in their origin. Even for the most chauvinistic of armchair ethnographers,[14] a tradition of song could appear as *the* anthropological marker of the human as distinct from the animal: the 'natives of New Zealand, who seem to live as nearly in a state of nature as any animals that are merely gregarious, have their Songs'.[15] For Burney, to burst into song is to break out of the state of nature and enter into culture, however close their proximity.

Wordsworth's account of poetry's origin and decay in tandem with 'the progress of refinement'[16] is close to Hugh Blair's lecture on the 'Nature of Poetry – Its Origin and Progress – Versification', and at times follows it almost word for word.[17] The burgeoning eighteenth-century genre of optimistic universal history had spawned an ironic double in pessimistic narratives of poetry's decline, an immediate effect of the progress of knowledge. Such accounts registered a historical fading of affect and meaning, as passion gave way to elegance and wit, and *mythopoeia* was converted by rational scepticism into arbitrary fancy (the tropes of poetic diction). Francis Jeffrey's stadial history of poetry, in his 1814 *Edinburgh Review* essay on Byron's *Corsair*,[18] and Thomas Love Peacock's *Four Ages of Poetry* (1819) would both (the latter with an ironic, yet not wholly insincere, utilitarian overstatement) dismiss the poetry of Wordsworth's age as the emulation of an archaic vigour that merely fell into anachronism: 'A poet in our times is a semi-barbarian in a civilized community.'[19] In Germany, Carl Jochmann would argue in this period that poetry was a 'regression' in the face of the prosaic rationality necessary for social revolution, even as he invoked the 'triumphal songs' that would inaugurate the new society.[20] The decadence of poetry, and the emphatic intensity of life and language for which it stood, was the great stumbling block for celebratory narratives of European progress and its colonial export. Far from a simple 'evasion' of history, then, as has so often been charged, Wordsworth's poetics must be viewed as a testing of poetry's near-exhausted resources within this widest historical compass – one that led Hegel to proclaim the 'Romantic' as 'the end of art' itself.[21]

The related context of the decline of Christianity and the 'flight' of the pagan Gods would lead Friedrich Hölderlin, in what Heidegger called 'the world's night', famously to ask: 'and why poets in a destitute time?' (*und wozu Dichter in dürftiger Zeit?*).[22] Hazlitt, in the same series of lectures that attacked the Lake School, would judge the keynote of James Macpherson's fabricated *Ossian* poems, which presented its bard as the last dying remnant of a song tradition and culture, to be 'the decay of life, and the lag end of the world'.[23] *Ossian* was 'the old age of poetry', conveying 'the sense of privation . . . the loss of the sap and pith of existence . . . the annihilation of the substance'; its language was a 'sigh and rustle like the dry reeds in the winter winds'.[24] In *Lyrical Ballads*, however, such melancholy pastiche was for the most part avoided; with only a handful of exceptions, the archaic and the exotic appear only obliquely. In the *Biographia Literaria*, Coleridge claimed that its original plan was a division of labour between his own supernatural ballads – antiquarian and exotic in the case of the 'Rime of the Ancyent Marinere' – and Wordsworth's endeavour, as if to rekindle nature's spark in *Ossian*, 'to give the charm of novelty to things of every day, and to excite a feeling analogous to the supernatural, by awakening the mind's attention from the lethargy of custom'.[25] It is an *analogia entis* whose supernatural referent has been left suspended. For Hazlitt, the *Ossian* poems were 'even without God in the world'.[26] Wordsworth's attempt to excite and awaken was, as Mary Jacobus aptly terms *Lyrical Ballads*, an interplay of 'tradition and experiment'.[27] It was an experiment in probing how far – in withered circumstances that Wordsworth does not pretend he can wish away – tradition might still be able to speak.

All that has been left – in the strange familiarity of analogies and correspondences, an awakening of the new and *unheimlich* within the customary and ordinary – is the uncanny. It is this focus on the 'everyday' that distinguishes Wordsworth's task, *contra* Hazlitt, from the restoration of poetry in a state of nature. For Wordsworth in the 'Appendix', what is wrong with the effete verse of eighteenth-century 'refinement' is that it is *too close* to that of the 'earliest poets': its 'mechanical adoption' of archaic 'figures of speech' has lost the 'animating passion' that gave them credence.[28] The 'original figurative language of passion'[29] has been lost because the 'passion excited by real events' has faded. The world has aged. Yet by separating poetry from archaic language per se – unlike Rousseau and Vico – Wordsworth goes on to acknowledge a splitting or rift even at the time of origin: 'It is indeed true that the language of the earliest Poets was felt to differ materially from ordinary language, because it was the language of extraordinary occasions.' Nevertheless, 'it was really spoken by men'.[30] The difference seems to be one of degree rather than kind – only poetic diction has since become *wholly* artificial, a purely textual language that has lost all connection to orality.

A similar ambivalence or oscillation between the extraordinary and an everyday plainness had already threatened to undermine the arguments of the 1800 Preface. The aim of *Lyrical Ballads* is not simply the common, but 'to make the incidents of common life interesting'.[31] What earlier in 1800 in *Home at Grasmere* had been aggrandized into the millennial unveiling of 'paradise' as 'the growth of common day' (*HG* 1001) was in

Lyrical Ballads to be reduced to its barest lineaments, a minimal interest. Yet it is the 'common' that represents humanity in a contemporary state of nature: it exhibits the 'primary laws of our nature' – albeit only as they appear 'in a state of excitement'.[32] The state of nature is a state of excitement. For this reason, 'Low and rustic life' has been chosen for it is less marked by a civilizing process of repression, 'less under restraint'.[33] Not only is their 'language' deemed 'plainer', more ordinary, but it is also more extraordinary: a 'more emphatic language'.[34] And what had been simply the 'language of conversation' in the 1798 Advertisement, the common coin of social exchange, is now 'a selection of the real language of men in a state of vivid sensation'.[35] It is a language of the heightening and intensification of bodily experience. Yet it also speaks for 'the sameness and narrow circle of their intercourse', is not daring and figurative but composed of 'simple and unelaborated expressions', and arises from 'repeated experience and regular feelings'.[36] What is repeatedly experienced and communicated, however, is not the *sensus communis* of a flatly ordinary empiricism, or a convention-bound second nature, but nothing less than the very best that language has to offer: 'such men hourly communicate with the best objects from which the best part of language is derived'.[37] As in 'Yew Trees', in *Lyrical Ballads* the 'essential passions of the heart' are 'incorporated'[38] with nature as an encompassing backdrop, a *theatrum mundi*. In an 1802 revision to the Preface, however, Wordsworth acknowledged that he had seen fit 'to throw over' the poems a 'certain colouring of imagination, whereby ordinary things should be presented to the mind in an unusual way; and further, and above all, to make these incidents and situations interesting'.[39] Rustic life, it seems, is not quite interesting enough. A superadded imagination nevertheless has its own cognitive value: it does not fabricate illusions, but draws out something 'unusual', though genuinely present, within 'ordinary things'. Amid the banalization of the world, it is the instrument of the uncanny.

The Task of the Translator

A tension between the ordinary and the exceptional was also at work in Wordsworth's choice of diction in *Lyrical Ballads*. If rustic diction not only has the widest commonality for Wordsworth, but is also the very 'best part' of language, it has nevertheless undergone a 'selection' process in *Lyrical Ballads*: it has been 'purified . . . from all lasting and rational causes of dislike and disgust'.[40] Yet how might this differ from the 'textual attitude' of the partly domesticated and cleaned up ballads of Thomas Percy's

Reliques of Ancient English Poetry (1775) – a congealing of the fluidly oral and anonymous ballad into its commodified or nationalist 'artifactualization'[41] – as denounced in the unexpurgated anthologies of the antiquarian radical Joseph Ritson?

Wordsworth's effort of mediation nevertheless aimed more to instil sympathy for the foreign than the domestication it equally risked. Helen Maria Williams' 'An Address to Poetry' (1790) – possibly an unacknowledged influence on the Preface – had identified the 'wand'ring bard' of the Pacific islands (9–16), Homer at the banquet of his warring patron (17–24), the impoverished English balladeer (25–32), and the Ossianic 'lonely bard of "other years"' in Scotland (41–8),[42] as a combined voice of nature in opposition to the contemporary 'sphere of art', with its 'various tropes' of false 'splendour' (51) – in other words, poetic diction.[43] For Williams, a Girondin in revolutionary Paris like the young Wordsworth, the vox populi of so-called 'primitive song' was a transhistorical and international Third Estate. As Wordsworth wrote to Sara Hutchinson on 14 June 1802, the issues involved in overcoming her struggle to appreciate the lowborn protagonists of poems such as 'The Leech-Gatherer' and 'Beggars' were 'an affair of whole continents of moral sympathy'.[44] The hyperbole hints at a global ambition.

David Simpson has emphasized Wordsworth's appreciation of difference in 'the anthropological encounter with the "primitive other"'[45] – though, as the voice of a contemporary state of nature, this language is never wholly 'primitive' or indeed purely 'other' for Wordsworth. It is the great crux of Wordsworth's anthropological poetry: the struggle to articulate an individual singularity, even while 'singing a song in which all human beings join with him'.[46] Yet while Wordsworth's project has its historical background in a radical populism, these roots in sentimental humanism have left it vulnerable to critique as a reactionary complacence. Jon P. Klancher has argued that Wordsworth in *Lyrical Ballads* 'seeks out an alien culture, the language of a remote social class . . . only to rescue it from its otherness . . . to make it familiar and unthreatening'. Even as the poems bring together 'two social languages in what Mikhail Bakhtin called a "heteroglot" encounter', they also make a 'gesture that effaces their differences, rendering them "human" rather than social'.[47]

But as Nigel Leask observes, Wordsworth was motivated by a 'generalized concept of the vernacular' rather than 'the Scottish Enlightenment's obsession with defining a non-regional standard English'.[48] Wordsworth 'needed to devise an alternative language for poetry which was (impossibly) based on a rustic lower-class vernacular that was not a regional dialect'.[49]

Nevertheless, the diffused vernacular was to be brought into the homes of a cultivated readership. In this context, Geoffrey Hartman has preferred the term 'conversational' to 'dialogics', for it 'suggests that whenever we deal with style we also deal with social decorum and with a historically specific situation'.[50] Yet the main historical precedent here – Shaftesbury's ideal of polite conversation as a polishing away of social edges[51] – is clearly also at risk from Klancher's asseverations. As Leask implies, there is nevertheless a fundamental asymmetry at work: it is not a privileged urbanity but the generalized vernacular which takes priority.

Another term, introduced in the 1802 Preface, might be more helpful in understanding the contradictions of *Lyrical Ballads*. All conversation is now subordinated to *translation*:

> as it is impossible for the Poet to produce upon all occasions language as exquisitely fitted for the passion as that which the real passion itself suggests, it is proper that he should consider himself as in the situation of a translator, who does not scruple to substitute excellencies of another kind for those which are unattainable by him; and endeavours occasionally to surpass his original, in order to make some amends for the general inferiority to which he feels that he must submit.[52]

What applies even to the educated poet's own 'emotion recollected in tranquillity' is necessary a fortiori in representing the 'elementary feelings' of rustic life. As Wordsworth acknowledges, to translate is necessarily to pass through the second nature of a 'textual attitude' or *habitus*: 'a certain quantity of immediate knowledge, with certain convictions, intuitions, and deductions which by habit become of the nature of intuitions'.[53]

So Wordsworth's embryonic theory of translation must itself be approached through the proliferation of theories that have marked our own time. In Hans-Georg Gadamer's philosophy of cross-cultural dialogue, translation was deemed paradigmatic of all hermeneutic struggles with 'alienness and its conquest',[54] even if the aim was not to convert the foreign into the familiar, but to create a new whole, a 'fusion of horizons'. The danger is made clear in George Steiner's influential account of translation in its 'hermeneutic motion': 'The translator invades, extracts, and brings home.'[55] Just as Wordsworth acknowledges the translator's need 'to make some amends', even 'occasionally to surpass his original', so for Steiner an appropriation must be offset by restitution: 'Where it falls short it emphasizes strengths of the original . . . where it surpasses the original, the real translation infers that the source-text possesses potentialities, elemental reserves as yet unrealized by itself.'[56] But this breaking apart of extremes, an inevitable falling short and surpassing excess, a combination of inadequate testimony and a realization of the unfulfilled, is brought under control by a contractual model of equivalent exchange: 'A translation is, more than figuratively, an act of double-entry; both formally and morally, the books must balance.'[57] Wordsworth, by contrast, lays greatest emphasis on an asymmetric 'general inferiority' and submission to the original. An exchange takes place, but the original has primacy.

The main goal of the translator, for Wordsworth, is an 'exquisitely' mimetic and scrupulous 'fitting' of language to an object of passion – in contrast to John Dryden's famous argument that 'literal' translation had often to be balanced by a 'paraphrase' better adapted to a foreign comprehension.[58] The most celebrated of all appeals to literal translation in the last few decades, of course, has been Walter Benjamin's 1922 essay 'The Task of the Translator'. Benjamin rejects dialogue and hermeneutics almost entirely: translation 'must in large measure refrain from wanting to communicate something, from rendering the sense'.[59] Instead the translator must make their own language resemble the foreign, and 'lovingly and in detail incorporate the original's *way* of meaning [*Art des Meinens*]'.[60] What matters – when the goal is translation rather than description – is less the content of an alien culture than its specific *forms* of thinking, its *poiesis*. In De Quincey's 'literature of power' as opposed to 'knowledge', 'the manner or form of its communication' was 'paramount' over 'the matter to be communicated'. However, as a *poiesis* within thinking, according to the Preface, this might be a form of knowledge as well as power. *Lyrical Ballads* aimed at 'tracing . . . the *manner* in which we associate ideas in a state of excitement'.[61] To unlock a 'form of communication' – an *art* of meaning – as a mode of knowledge as well as power would be the task of criticism itself as a translation.

Any translation of the manner or form of poetry must engage with issues of prosody. An overriding critical emphasis on Wordsworth's handling of diction in *Lyrical Ballads* and the Preface has missed the crucial role of metre as an equally, if not more important social and linguistic medium. In the 1802 'Appendix', metre was very nearly coeval with the 'original figurative language' of poetry: 'To this language it is probable that metre of some sort or other was early superadded.'[62] In a recent 'ethics' of translation, however, the late Henri Meschonnic vehemently rejected not only meaning and the semiotic as the goal of translation, but also metre, and its conventional regularity, in favour of a text's unique rhythm. The rhythmic expresses an individual and embodied subjectivity that rebels against the determining constraints of social discourse.[63] Certainly, in the Preface, metre has a 'tempering and restraining' effect; in the 'danger that the excitement' of powerful emotion 'may be carried beyond its proper bounds', metre offers 'the co-presence of something regular' as 'an intertexture of ordinary feeling'.[64] Metre mediates. It domesticates by bridging the divide between the gentle reader and the 'uncouth shape'. Yet metre too evinces that characteristic tension in the Preface between the ordinary and the extraordinary. Brennan O'Donnell has argued that for Wordsworth versification provides 'a normative "set" against which expressive impulses play'.[65] Metre is regular also in its irregularities, through 'small, but continual and regular impulses of pleasurable surprise from the metrical arrangement'.[66] A singular rhythm not only is interwoven with metre, but emerges from the metrical standard itself as it deviates.

In the twinned lyrical ballads 'The Tables Turned' and 'Expostulation and Reply', written as a gentle rebuke to 'a friend [the young Hazlitt] who was somewhat unreasonably attached to modern books of moral philosophy', the material language that for Wordsworth takes the place of natural law and moral philosophy includes not only birdsong ('The Tables Turned', *LB* 10–16) and the 'mighty sum / Of things for ever speaking' ('Expostulation and Reply', *LB* 25–6). Nature's voice paradoxically extends to mute 'impulses' much like those of 'metrical arrangement':

> One impulse from a vernal wood
> May teach you more of man;
> Of moral evil and of good,
> Than all the sages can.
> ('The Tables Turned', 21–4)

There *is* something outside the text or 'textual attitude' – or only imperfectly caught up in its web. But the purely immediate travels also across a linguistic distance; what it has to teach is left to the one who feels it. That impulse and the 'speaking' of things is the closest we get to a universal language in Wordsworth. Its meaning is humanly accessible only through translation. Yet poetry's 'substitution' of its own 'excellencies' through lack, an inability to translate, also has the potential for Wordsworth to pass into a new affective immediacy. Through the direct impulses of poetry itself, as Wordsworth goes on to state in the 1802 Preface, the verse achieves a truth 'not standing upon external testimony, but carried alive into the heart by passion'.[67]

This language of nature and poetry is both near and yet far from the 'pure language' of the 'creative Word' of God to which translation pointed for the young Benjamin.[68] Benjamin acknowledged that this *reine Sprache* was out of reach amid the plurality of languages. It was to be represented, or aimed at, not immediately but obliquely, as 'the languages themselves, supplemented and reconciled in their way of meaning, draw together'.[69] Benjamin's vision is a *plural* one, at least in the fallen world. To give voice to the universal is not to present it directly, but to participate in multiple acts of translation, a hybrid series of new forms. But as with Wordsworth, the aim is not cultural exchange or 'heteroglossic dialogue', nor a 'fusion' of domestic and foreign 'horizons'. A translation belongs to the original in its 'continued life', its survival even after mortification by historical change.[70] Again, in this asymmetry, it is the original that has priority; a translation should seek in a new cultural context 'that single spot where the echo [of the original] is able to give, in its own language, the reverberation of the work in the alien one'.[71] Such an echo reverberates perhaps most plangently not in *Lyrical Ballads*, but in the way of meaning that Wordsworth's later short lyric 'The Solitary Reaper' would struggle to translate.

'The Solitary Reaper'

Said's constructivist model of a hegemonic discourse in collusion with an expanding European imperialism has been qualified in historical accounts of eighteenth-century travel literature. As Nigel Leask observes, for a traveller to obtain 'credit' with a sceptical readership, the 'textual attitude' had to be played down in favour of exact descriptive protocols.[72] Colonial exploration was characterized by 'vulnerability' and contingency,[73] linguistic incomprehension, and indigenous resistance.[74] Jonathan Lamb has likewise questioned the 'grand narrative' of post-colonial studies by emphasizing the accidents and disasters of the travel narrative, the intractable data and failed experiments that baffled attempts at classification. Explorers became 'periodically distracted' in 'the confusing and sometimes inexpressible experience of extreme conditions'.[75]

Disorientation and hazard might attend even efforts to translate indigenous song. Such a moment was recorded in George Keate's popular travelogue *An Account of the Pelew Islands* (1788), a text drawn upon by Wordsworth for a detail in an attempt to exoticize 'The Blind Highland Boy', which had indeed been criticized (as he anticipated with *Lyrical Ballads*) for its homely and un-poetic ordinariness. The English ships, docked at a bay, face an assembly of three hundred islanders on the beach: 'on a sudden the natives began a song, the shrillness and manner of which made them think it was their war hoop . . . the English instantly took to their arms'.[76] The Captain urges restraint 'until they should find out what the meaning of this should be'.[77] Such were the potential stakes of a hermeneutics of song. Yet bloodshed is averted, with a touch of bathos, 'by finding that they were only tuning their voices, in order to begin a song'.[78] The singing joins together through relay – each verse moving from figure to figure and tent to tent, with periodic choruses – to form an acoustic image of social commonwealth.[79] True to the conventions of sentimental literature, the 'textual attitude' imported into Keate's revision of Captain Wilson's journal, the episode concludes with a sympathetic exchange that conceals an asymmetry. The islanders request some English songs with which 'they were exceeding pleased' – 'Our songs were sea songs, and of battles.'[80]

Michel de Certeau declared a Renaissance frisson of ethno-musicological bewilderment and its resolution – a struggle with what Lamb calls the *je ne sais quoi* of foreign travel – to be the primal scene of modern ethnography itself. For de Certeau, 'the Savage is invented'[81] in an incident from Jean de Léry's *Histoire d'un voyage faict en la terre du Brésil* (1578). On hearing 'the beautifully measured rhythms' of a Tupi assembly, 'especially the cadence and refrain of the ballad, all of them together raising their voices to each couplet', de Léry writes: '"Such a joy it was that I remained completely ravished . . . every time the memory comes back to me, my heart throbs, and it seems as if their music still rings in my ears."'[82] De Certeau observes that this 'absence of meaning opens a rift in time'.[83] But de Léry then turns to his interpreter, and on being told that the Tupis are singing of the primal Flood, 'this passing to meaning . . . transforms the ballad into a product that can be put to good use' – to rework self-loss and the oral into history and the written corpus as '"what most resembles Scripture among them"' – the Biblical Flood.[84] De Certeau goes on to propose that the 'savage becomes a senseless speech ravishing Western discourse, but one which, because of that very fact, generates a productive science of meaning and objects that endlessly writes'.[85]

In an interlacing of the written and the oral, 'The Solitary Reaper' both partakes of this model and resists its dualism – between a non-cognitive pleasure of sheer consumption and a meaning that is arbitrarily produced. Jeremy Prynne has raised the question 'could "The Solitary Reaper" have been a lyrical ballad?' and answered in the negative. Though written (*c.*1805) after the completion of the *Lyrical Ballads* project and set within a different topography, the poem nevertheless foregrounds the problem of translation, and an afterlife of tradition, in an especially acute form. 'The Solitary Reaper' casts a strong retrospective light on *Lyrical Ballads*. For here, as in *terra incognita*, the difficulty of translation has been carried to an extreme:

Wordsworth must translate a song whose language (Scots Gaelic or 'Erse') he cannot understand at all.

'The Solitary Reaper' is the critical revision (disguised as homage) of a moment of senseless ravishment commemorated in a travel journal. The poem was inspired by a 'very beautiful sentence'[86] taken from the 'MS. Tour of Scotland' of Wordsworth's friend Thomas Wilkinson:

> Pass'd by a Female who was reaping alone, she sung in Erse as she bended over her sickle, the sweetest human voice I ever heard. Her strains were tenderly melancholy & felt delicious long after they were heard no more.[87]

Wilkinson's touristic rapture is culinary in its pleasure: the sounds are 'sweet' and 'felt delicious'. This was to set the challenge to which 'The Solitary Reaper' rises. The poem was situated within a widening context of global song and trade, a time in which Herder had collected 'The Songs of the World' as well as local ballads, and in which the 'translation' into verse of world music was becoming as much of an exotic fetish as Chinese porcelain or Indian spices.[88] It belonged to that thirst for stimulation among the reading public, converted by sentimental literature into glossed-over types of 'fusion', that *Lyrical Ballads* was intended (according to the Preface) to counteract.[89] Was it possible to listen without guilt to an alien song tradition, in an ignorance of 'meaning' and local context as profound as that of the most blithe tourist? In the pleasurable shape of its sound alone, its grain and timbre, a song's *way* of meaning, might a form of knowledge lie hidden that is necessarily missed by the antiquarian or ethnographer, bent on transcribing its cultural sense?

It is this effort to translate an art of meaning that distinguishes 'The Solitary Reaper' from the Bakhtinian 'dialogism' which Don H. Bialostosky has employed in a challenging critique of the poem. The 'dialogical' interpretation, despite its potential for a formalistic indifference to the content of the plural meanings that it relativizes, is still bound to the semiotic or hermeneutic through its focus on thematic meaning. In keeping with this emphasis on purposive communication, Bialostosky observes that the poem co-ordinates a triad of 'speaker' (Wordsworth), 'hero' (the reaper) and 'listener' (the reader).[90] The poem's addresses to the reader, Bialostosky observes,[91] are linked to Wordsworth's hope that *Lyrical Ballads* might reform the public taste. From the outset, the reader's attention is cajoled through deictics and imperatives:[92]

> Behold her, single in the field,
> Yon solitary Highland Lass!
> Reaping and singing by herself;
> Stop here, or gently pass!

Alone she cuts, and binds the grain,
And sings a melancholy strain
O listen! for the Vale profound
Is overflowing with the sound.
(*P2V* 1–8)

Yet once the tourist passer-by has been brought to a standstill by this singular vision, all dialogue falls away – to become a listening into, as well as seeing, that is transfixed by its object.

It is also, inevitably, a listening through the 'textual attitudes' and 'pre-established codes of decision' that mediate understanding. The figure is marginal and low in status across several criteria of the age: a young woman, low-born and rustic, a 'barbarian' Highlander singing in a language that the English were trying to stamp out, and engaged in menial hard labour upon another's land. Only through a subtle filtering can Wordsworth and his reader pass through the text and its evaluative norms to reach the singular individual – 'single in the field'. And an inhibiting 'textual attitude' reaches even to the metrical and rhythmic decision. Crucial here is the poem's alternation of a 'gently' approaching prosodic movement with a series of exclamatory jolts. Wordsworth largely uses the four-stress pattern of a regularized 'ballad metre', as occasionally deployed in Percy's *Reliques*; in the 1802 Preface, he had himself judged the 'metre of the old Ballads' to be 'very artless'.[93] Wordsworth, however, departs from ballad convention in the poem's intricate and elongated 'octave stanza', better suited to meditative development, or sustained monody, than to narrative movement. This 'very deliberate hybrid' of ballad and 'art-song'[94] embodies both the reflexive awareness of the translator and a quality of the singing itself. Its sound is already that of a *lyrical* ballad, and its translation through Wordsworth's own rhythms acknowledges distance even as he tries to draw closer.

The fourth line of each stanza is regular in its irregularity, forming a three-stress line, a song-like modulation that alludes to the repeated alternation of tetrameter and trimeter common in ballad metre. The contracted line telescopes an image of recess or distance – 'Stop here, or gently pass!' (4), 'Among Arabian Sands' (12), 'And battles long ago' (20). The reader, pulled up short with the line itself, stands before the withdrawn or self-enclosed, the geographically and historically remote suddenly brought near, even while it remains as enigmatically distant as the girl herself. In the fourth line of the last stanza – 'And o'er the sickle bending' – the girl is doubled up, a contraction that also leans forward, just by a syllable, beyond her immediate activity and environment, as a hypermetrical 'feminine' ending gently exceeds the three-beat line. The end of the third line of the first stanza underscores her singularity as she is introduced 'singing by *herself*', flouting a rhyme scheme that should echo with 'single in the *field*' – as we notice, having gently passed, only in retrospect when the stanzaic pattern has established itself. These small marks or punctures are the minute registrations of a half-conscious moment: when dialogue ceases of itself.

Such infinitesimal differences, felt upon the pulse like tiny electrical charges, if they reach awareness at all, find a more enlarged articulation in the *Prelude* episode 'There was a Boy', first published as a short poem in the 1800 edition of *Lyrical Ballads*. A child's mimicry of hooting owls – less the translation of a non-human language than its simple copying – and the ensuing call-and-response, is suddenly 'mock'd' in a different sense:

> And, when it chanced
> That pauses of deep silence mock'd his skill,
> Then, sometimes, in that silence, while he hung
> Listening, a gentle shock of mild surprize
> Has carried far into his heart the voice
> Of mountain torrents, or the visible scene
> Would enter unawares into his mind
> (*LB* 16–23)

In a sudden dislocation of activity, the caesurae of 'pauses of deep silence' – a momentary estrangement that hangs expectantly listening into a void – a space is cleared for an unexpected language to emerge: a 'voice' of mountain waters. As a 'visible scene' enters 'unawares', this is not merely unconscious but the tangible opening to a new receptiveness; before, it had been unable to 'enter' at all. As with the vernal 'impulse' of 'The Tables Turned', this 'gentle shock of mild suprize' is allied to those 'small, but continual and regular impulses of pleasurable surprise from the metrical arrangement'. Minuscule infractions of prosody form as regular an impulse as its steady though wavering beat. For the pulsations depend upon that formal constraint. It is not a repetition of the same, but a regular enjoyment of the new. Such detail is the timbre and texture of a song.

It is in part through this understated, inconspicuous, indeed barely perceptible way of meaning that Wordsworth's lyrics seek to undermine the 'craving for extraordinary incident' and 'outrageous stimulation' of the commodity culture attacked in the Preface. And its nuances rescue the portrait of 'elementary feelings' from that other side of the commodity, a kitsch banality. For the half-conscious impulse to rise to greater awareness would be a pleasure oriented not to consumption but to the subtle qualities of the object itself. Gently passing through the textual mesh of relations, it is 'carried far into [the] heart' – as the 1802 Preface hoped to leap beyond translation into something 'carried alive into the heart'. What Heather Glen characterizes as 'the shock with which the otherness of even the least articulate can assert itself' in *Lyrical Ballads*[95] is nevertheless qualified by a community of feeling instilled by metre. Shaking 'pre-established codes of decision' by the forceful shock or command alone, interpreted as danger or coercion, might prompt recoil rather than rapture, a withdrawal through avoidance or resistance. The oxymoron of a '*gentle* shock' offered perhaps the nearest possible approach to a non-interpretive intuition that could receive with sympathy, far into the heart – and not simply bury or absorb – a quality of difference.

As with the 'pause of deep silence', a suspension of time and movement, so the poem begins to generate the sense of a continuous suspended present. Timeless seems the rhythm of the girl's work song as it co-ordinates the movements of her limbs, a continuously buoyant rise and fall as 'she cuts, and binds the grain / And sings' (5–6). Along with the regularity that binds the chain of monosyllabic discrete actions, however, is also the gentle shock of a brief cut or incision within the body of the text and its rhythmic cycle – 'Alone she *cuts*,' – accentuated by the placement of a comma. Wordsworth hangs listening to a singular voice that is not homogenous, but gently fluctuates. Yet that voice can be heard only within a lament of conflict and contradiction. There is a suffering that graceful movement cannot master, the 'melancholy strain' (6) of 'plaintive numbers' (17). Nonetheless, 'No sweeter voice was ever heard' (13). Prior to discursive understanding, her song is not heard merely as the 'senseless speech' of ravishment, but as a prosody of affect ('plaintive numbers'). It is already meaningful as a rhythmic inflection of mourning, even as its sweetness baffles an identifiable register.[96] What Bakhtin claimed of discursive signification in art is true here even at the level of sound: 'in every voice . . . two contending voices, in every expression a crack, and the readiness to go over immediately to another contradictory expression'.[97] An inseparably sad and joyous metric, an indeterminate emotional tonality, begin to communicate something beyond the subjective intention of any singer or partner in 'dialogue'.

Flooding over any recognizable content, her song expands into a depth of expressionless sound:

> O listen! for the vale profound
> Is overflowing with the sound
> (7–8)

The heroic or mythic event of the 'earliest poets', the indigenous or biblical Flood, or the 'outrageous stimulation' craved by a jaded culture, have given way to an 'extraordinary incident' in the midst of the ordinary and everyday: the momentary creation of a new language. The natural environment itself translates as it literally provides volume, amplifying the human voice; each becomes more than itself alone. Music is now less a second nature than a new nature. Only this moment, perhaps, truly approaches James H. Donelan's characterization of the poem: 'a moment of pure experience, the experience of pure sound, absolute music'.[98] The expressionless is made articulate through song as an unfathomable expression of the objective.

In the second stanza, the intimation that there must be some meaning to an experience that has so overflowed its boundaries, flooding its singular locus, now drives Wordsworth to situate the event within a 'natural history of man'. As the valley in flood co-ordinated extremes of height and depth, so now the spot becomes a global pivot or axis between polar contrasts. Like a migrating bird, the poem first descends south into the blazing heat, only to swing up far north into an arctic winter. In a state of excited association, the song is first compared to the 'welcome notes' of the nightingale (9–10) heard by 'weary bands' of 'travellers' on arriving at an oasis in the 'Arabian Sands' (11–12). It also recalls a cuckoo's voice heralding the end of a nature reduced to muteness, of winter in the northern Hebrides – 'Breaking the silence of the seas' (15). The bird-like girl has been dehumanized – or rather, something non-human is speaking through her.

She also figures something global – for Bialostosky, the poem sets up its dialogic relays only for the sake of finally collapsing them: to 'abstract' and 'universalize' the girl[99] as the 'trophy' of an 'imperial imagination'.[100] Yet what might be human rather than social emerges only in tiny and singular moments, at a border territory where extremes (the Hebrides and the Sahara) are able to meet. It is the counter-imperial moment in which, as Lamb observes, the traveller is 'distracted' from his mission in the 'inexpressible experience of extreme conditions'. The girl's song hails an end to travel and a rest from labour: a 'Breaking' of the spell cast by an antagonistic domain of sheer survival – of nature as desert, winter silence, or even Highlands croft-farming. What defines the human is ironically its very suspension: an ability to relax and forget oneself in an expression of the non-human – even in the singing of birds.

That such might be the import of a song which accompanies the most monotonous and back-bending labour is either Wordsworth's moral blindness, typical of the tourist or consumer, or the ironic detection of a promise concealed in the heart of its opposite. As if to acknowledge that the subaltern may be able to sing like a bird, but certainly cannot speak, the following stanza by contrast exhibits a pained recognition of historical and cultural distance. Wordsworth becomes exasperated, almost desperate – a tone softened by a whimsically impotent address that includes even the reader – at his inability to translate the specific content of her song. Breaking the enchantment of its sound, the third stanza begins with an abruptly staccato rhythm: 'Will no one tell me what she sings?' (17). The difference between this rhythm and the buoyant monosyllables of lines 5–6 marks the oppositional tension between the two stanzas. As an interrogative in discourse, albeit a 'dialogue' without reply, the line according to its sense is to be read as flatly a-rhythmic, while its metrical undersong might lead us unawares into a softer rise and fall. The potential for gentle shock in such an undecidability of appropriate rhythm is the animating conflict of the poem – the inevitable return of prose sense and history within a blissful escape into song:

> Perhaps the plaintive numbers flow
> For old, unhappy, far-off things,
> And battles long ago
>
> (18–20)

Wordsworth challenges the touristic insouciance of Wilkinson – who had made no such effort to inquire – and in the same breath its very opposite, the whole canon of ethnographic and antiquarian treatises or anthologies, useless at this moment in the field. Wordsworth can rely only on his foreknowledge as an enthusiast for antiquarian verse as he translates an affective materiality of sound ('plaintive numbers') into a recollection of the themes of ballad tradition. Such would be the crushing victory of the English over the Scottish in the medieval battle of 'Chevy Chase'. But in keeping with the poem's inner structure, Wordsworth once more sets up both a conjunction of opposites and an undecidable choice:

> Or is it some more humble lay,
> Familiar matter of to-day?
> Some natural sorrow, loss, or pain,
> That has been, and may be again?
>
> (21–4)

The traditions of heroic lament and domestic complaint are gathered together and dissolved into a repeated flow of mournful sound.

Such a distancing, Bialostosky claims, works to elide (yet perhaps also allude to) the immediate historical context of the Highlands as a 'third-world colonial territory'.[101] The previous half-century had been the era of post-Culloden reprisals, the break-up of the clan system, schemes to replace Gaelic with English, and a mass emigration and depopulation. But Bakhtin himself urged that a 'historical poetics' should view the artwork not only within the immediate history that facilitates a new form, but also 'in *great time*': back across the centuries that build up a tradition of genre, and forwards to 'liberate' the 'immense treasures of potential meaning' as they become apparent in later ages.[102] For Maureen McLane, the minstrel tradition of balladry, as evoked in Walter Scott's hugely popular *Lay of the Last Minstrel* (1805) and the 'ballad genres' of 'The Solitary Reaper', exemplifies Bakhtin's notion of genre as 'chronotope': 'The ballad chronotope – the space–time configuration of oral *poiesis* – here emerges as . . . the image, perhaps nostalgic, of a rooted human community in its full temporal extension.'[103] The Highland chronotope of 'unhappy, far-off things' works also to connect the recent past with a wider tradition of lament: extending from the sufferings of Scotland to all who have been oppressed, domestically and culturally, across 'the great time' of long-term history. The song recalls the linear transmission of oral history through generations, but also, through the solitariness of the girl, the status of tradition as it recedes, the lay of a last minstrel: a line at the point of being finally broken, in a depopulated region as desolate as the winter Hebrides. A historical state of nature or 'chronotope' intertwines the martial and 'natural sorrow'. Natural history is no longer the emergence of the human at an oasis, as in the preceding stanza, but history in the image of the pitiless nature that surrounds it. The human is the voice that complains against it.

Wordsworth is not simply an heir to the great tradition of genre as chronotope, an irrupting of the new from the past as well as the present. He stands before the girl's song as an agent of its own destruction, as the instrument of an English and literate modernity. Restitution cannot now be restoration, but only the liberating of a 'potential meaning' from the historical destruction of the song's content itself: the echo of a way of meaning as it sounds within another language. As the final stanza begins, it is this hermeneutic breakdown, or inability to translate, an oscillation between alternatives that has run through the whole poem, which once more gives voice to the expressionless. Returning to the pure sound of the first stanza, like a refrain or chorus, the poem again opens out into a continuous suspended present:

Whate'er the theme, the Maiden sang
As if her song could have no ending;
I saw her singing at her work,
And o'er the sickle bending;
I listen'd, till I had my fill

(25–9)

The image of a swollen-bellied Wordsworth filling himself up with song, alert to the overflowing dangers of excessive consumption, is 'indeed clumsy' as Prynne acknowledges – even as it admits to 'a hunger or thirst' and a surplus that can be taken 'without stealing'.[104] An 1820 revision of the line would purge this last vestige of the culinary in Wilkinson's 'beautiful sentence'. To listen to tradition now is to lose oneself in its acoustic medium: 'I listened motionless and still' (29). It is an *ek-stasis* that is 'made to stand' or 'stands out' of the inner body. Tradition is now wholly outside. But the poem has allowed us to internalize a gentle shock. In its closing couplet, to 'drink the visionary power' (*Pr.* II.330) of a language that communicates, like birdsong, without signifying, is not to consume but to be haunted:

The music in my heart I bore,
Long after it was heard no more.

(31–2)

This is not the touristic brandishing of a souvenir or trophy, a self-aggrandizing fetish to take home,[105] but the indirect confession of an aching transience. The music will be 'heard no more', and its reverberations, however 'Long', will eventually die down and be forgotten. The poem ends with a suspended pause for something 'more' to emerge in translation – or perhaps just the negation of its fading afterlife.

Aura

In Peter J. Manning's acclaimed historical-political critique of 'The Solitary Reaper' – which for him is not about poetry but about property, an ideological mask for Wordsworth's transition from a republican ideal of small-scale ownership to landed interest Toryism – he argues that 'If Wordsworth eliminated the particularity of the reaper, it was to invest her with the aura of mythic timelessness; and aura, as Walter Benjamin insisted, is a property dependent on the maintenance of distance.'[106] But aura for Benjamin is indeed a 'particularity'. It is the '*unique* appearance... of distance, no matter how close it may be' – *single* in the field – and of a chronotope or spot of time made enigmatic and uncanny: a 'strange weave of space and time'.[107] It is this uniqueness and strangeness that makes the artwork 'transmissable', that is, translatable, and embeds it 'in the context of tradition' in a manner that is changing rather than timeless.[108]

Benjamin's reflections on aura have been linked by Robert Kaufman[109] to his conversations with Bertolt Brecht. They shared a fascination with Shelley's 'anti-Wordsworthian' vision of London in *Peter Bell the Third*, and were largely in solidarity in their rejection of lyric aura as untenable amid the political needs of modernity, with its blinding metropolitan immediacy, abolishing distance, and for Benjamin the mass potential to bring near, or restore to free use, that lay within the media of technological reproduction that counteracted the fetish or taboo of the unique. But as Kaufman notes, from the late 1930s Brecht's short lyrics came increasingly under the influence of Shelley's enlistment of a 'critical-progressive potential of auratic lyric form' that can be drawn even from 'apolitical . . . or . . . downright conservative authors' – 'The precise term for this problem is, in Shelley's vocabulary, *Wordsworth*.'[110] Indeed, Shelley was surely thinking primarily of Wordsworth when, in *A Defence of Poetry* (1821), his famous rejoinder to Peacock's argument for poetry's historical decay in *The Four Ages of Poetry*, he wrote of innovations in poetry and thought as the 'unfailing herald' of 'beneficial change in opinion or institution' – even if the 'persons in whom this power resides, may often . . . have little apparent correspondence with that spirit of good of which they are ministers'.[111] Shelley argues that it is the poet's redefinition of an apparent 'mythic timelessness' (in Manning's phrase), the supposed fixities of the anthropological and natural, which is the source of this historical power: 'At such periods there is an accumulation of the power of communicating and receiving intense and impassioned conceptions respecting man and nature.'[112] The poem alters the way we inseparably consume and produce, translate and invent, or communicate and receive – with an intense passion that transforms our very conception of the human and the natural. This primitive accumulation of power for Shelley must seek discharge or reinvestment; it is prophetic of an entwined change in *doxa* and political constitution. And a potential for social turbulence resides even in the work's impulses of pure language, its way of meaning: 'It is impossible to read the compositions of the most celebrated writers of the present day without being startled with the electric life which burns within their words.'[113]

It is Shelley's ambivalent relation to Wordsworth that brings Kaufman to one of the most unexpected of twentieth-century literary appreciations: that of Brecht's favourable encounter, in August 1940 and during the Battle of Britain, with Matthew Arnold's selected edition of Wordsworth's poems. For Kaufman, while Benjamin had linked aura to a fascist aestheticization of politics, the ensuing journal entry 'explicitly links Brecht's defence of the formal and experimental value of lyric aura to *anti-fascist* sentiment and activity'.[114] As no one could possibly doubt Brecht's credentials (unlike Wordsworth) as a radical and politically engaged artist, it is worth exploring this startling connection a little further than Kaufman does here, as well as its mediation through Arnold. It is all the more relevant since Brecht's journal entry focuses on a poem, 'She was a Phantom of Delight', that is similar in auratic distance to 'The Solitary Reaper', with which it first appeared in *Poems, in Two Volumes*, while also being a short lyric that resembles the 'lyrical ballad'.

Matthew Arnold famously preferred Wordsworth's lyrics to *The Excursion* and even *The Prelude*. If when Brecht 'skimmed', as he put it, *The Poems of Wordsworth*, this included a glance at its great Preface of 1879, his turnabout may even have been influenced by its High Victorian perspective at a moment in history which it shared with Karl Marx: a time of 'great empire' in which 'our upper class is materialized, our middle class vulgarized, and our lower class brutalized'.[115] While Arnold is commonly understood to have rejected Wordsworth's philosophy in favour of his pure poetry, hence the turn to lyric, his position is close to Wordsworth's own in the 'Essay on Morals'. He opposes Wordsworth's negligible philosophy as 'doctrine', its abstract propositions, to its 'moral ideas' as embedded in representations of 'life'. Poetry is 'a criticism of life'[116] – a *literary* criticism, the word implies in this context, of a life whose language-character it seeks. Arnold distinguishes poetic insight from matters of style, which might include prosody, as the non-philosophical dimension of poetry. What is philosophical in Wordsworth, as Shelley also claimed while including the electric life of language, resides in its ideas '"On man, on nature, and on human life"' – or in Wordsworth's earliest formulation, its 'pictures of Nature, Man, and Society'. Poetry is moral not in its maxims or precepts but in its opposition to bare life: 'a poetry of indifference to moral ideas is a poetry of indifference towards *life*'.[117] And 'the best cure for this delusion is to let our minds rest upon that great and inexhaustible word *life*, until we learn to enter its meaning'.[118] But at the end of Arnold's essay, it seems that this does have something to do with style after all. Wordsworth's 'plain manner' is identified with a 'Nature' which seems 'to write for him with her own bare, sheer, penetrating power'.[119] This apparent lack of style, of form-of-life, this denudation of aura, uncovers a language of power in bare life itself.[120] Clothed in an irreducible aura of its own, it is 'accessible universally', the 'source' of '"joy in widest commonalty spread"'.[121] Culture, as Arnold had written in the previous decade – uneasily to be propagated by the state elite –'seeks to do away with classes, to make all live in an atmosphere of sweetness and light'.[122]

Arnold had known Wordsworth personally. For Brecht, who subscribed to a Leninist politics with a more immediate paradox of state-elitist communism, the subsequent history of 'She Was a Phantom of Delight' had imbued it with a much darker aura. The poem is a 'now remote work',[123] to be read across a distance and remove similar to that which separated Wordsworth from the solitary reaper's song and tradition. Even though Brecht's Marxism gives him a convenient enough classification with which to abolish the poem's aura – it is merely a '"petty bourgeois idyll"' – he admits that such 'labels' are 'hazardous': 'how dangerous it is to lay down the law' for poetry even here.[124] Something all-important might go missing. The petty bourgeoisie as a class itself, Brecht observes, harbours 'other kinds of tendencies that conflict' with its narrow-minded conservatism (its 'Philistinism' as Arnold would put it). While the Home Guardsman with a 'shotgun' has 'legitimate enough grounds for blaming his wordsworths',[125] there seems to be a tacit admiration from Brecht for such a pathetically heroic individualism – an afterlife of the 'Commonwealthman' in a militia and Wordsworth's republican affirmations of independence – as it stands helplessly alone against Hitler.[126]

Yet it is 'just in dehumanized situations like these', Brecht insists, that the poem's '"lovely apparition"' and '"moment's ornament"' help 'to conjure up other situations less worthy of the human race'.[127] The sweetness and light of that unique spot of time or chronotope, the 'moment's ornament', has a negative power of evocation when translated into Brecht's moment in time – far more unsettlingly than its direct representation. For it will also speak for situations less unworthy. Without singular 'apparitions' like the Solitary Reaper, in part mere ghostly fictions, the prospect of something different might not be imaginable at all. Nevertheless, it is presumably Brecht's personal sense of contemporary art's didactic mission, of the urgency in extreme conditions of a blunt and direct force, which leads him to conclude: 'certainly ours is a time when the poem no longer serves to "*haunt, to startle, to waylay*"'.[128]

Yet Brecht goes on in part to contradict this assertion, in a remarkable turnaround from the didactic or means–end relation to art with which he is often associated. He begins to develop the implications of an art that occupies both a historical and 'an autonomous sphere'.[129] In a well-known epistolary debate in the 1930s between Adorno and Benjamin, the former had argued vigorously in defence of the social-critical value of (non-auratic) aesthetic autonomy, its procedures heralding a liberated and consciously directed technology, and attributed Benjamin's affirmation of the political value of mass art like film – albeit also in its techniques, its 'way of meaning' – to the damaging influence of Brecht.[130] It is indeed remarkable, then, that the latter should not only (as Kaufman puts it, tongue-in-cheek) have 'gone to sleep one night as Bert, only to awaken and write the next morning as Teddie [i.e., Theodor Adorno]',[131] but that it should be Wordsworth of all poets, so scourged in recent decades by historicist ideology-critique or discourse analysis, who seems to have brought about this conversion and epiphany.

In his unfinished *Aesthetic Theory*, written towards the end of his life, Adorno would revisit the debate one last time. A critical power to go beyond the status quo is now discernible within aura itself: 'Aura is not only – as Benjamin claimed – the here and now of the artwork, it is what goes beyond its factual givenness, its content; one cannot abolish it and still want art.'[132] Aura is an object's capacity to speak for something greater than its thematic meaning. It is the artwork in its material, and thereby necessarily historical, language. This is bound, then, to its way of meaning, its aptness for translation. And Brecht's journal goes on to consider the social value of lyric aura as a way of meaning that is far more critical in its opposition to bare life than its manifest (or ideologically latent) political content. He suggests a 'possible criterion for a work of art' that has emerged from his reading of Wordsworth: 'does it enrich the individual's capacity for experience?'[133] In the case of Wordsworth's lyrics, such enrichment would include not only the ecstatic moment of overflow, but also its scaled down, minute correlation: an ability to feel those subtle, tiny inflections of rhythm, verse form and sense, that undercut a commodified and stereotyped experience.

The 'individual' artist, as Wordsworth argued in remarkably similar terms to John Wilson,[134] for Brecht is an avant-garde explorer 'who goes ahead and is then overtaken by the masses moving in a predictable direction'.[135] The artist as a one-man Leninist vanguard of sensibility, speaking on behalf of a 'mass' progressing uniformly and predictably in the same direction, might seem a notion as remote today as Wordsworth's lyric in the 'world's night' of 1940. Nevertheless, Brecht goes on to argue that poetry 'may enrich the capacity for expression, which is not the same as the capacity for experience'.[136] Not the same, but perhaps not altogether different. Just two days earlier, on 22 August, Brecht had censured Heine, whose attacks on 'Philistinism' so influenced Arnold, for his 'dissipation of the language, because naturalness can be achieved only by small infringements of the formal rules'.[137] Within the flatness of nature as an intentional object, the nature of linguistic convention and the 'textual attitude', expression is marked by the oblique, the half-conscious, the 'gentle shock of mild surprize' at its caesura.

As Brecht writes, prompted by Wordsworth, poetry undermines any rigid distinction between consumption and production, for its 'reception is an operation of the same order as, say, seeing and hearing, i.e., something much more active'.[138] It is not merely an 'expression' of history, but is 'conditioned by history and in turn conditioning it'.[139] Brecht had cited an instance earlier: the individualism of Wordsworth among other writers had silently entered into British tradition. Implicit here too is the potential for a more turbulent influence that Shelley perceived. All true art for Brecht, as he concludes his journal entry, influences by a *Verfremdung* of its historical moment, an 'alienation effect' or state of estrangement that opens up a reflective distance: 'it is the difference between "mirroring" and "holding up a mirror"'.[140] Brecht is surely alluding here to another Englishman and fellow dramatist, namely Shakespeare, for whose Hamlet 'to hold as 'twere the mirror up to nature' in art is inseparable from its entanglement with history – not in its factual givenness, but in its manner or form, its physiognomy in the context of Bakhtin's 'great time': 'to show . . . the very age and body of the time, his form and pressure' (*Hamlet* III.ii.21–4). For Shakespeare as much as Wordsworth, it seems, art holds up the mirror to a contemporary and historical state of nature. For Brecht, this 'pressure' of an ageing 'time out of joint', exerted upon the reader, calls out for something new.

But as the moment of shock which prompts such a reflection, what is carried alive into the heart has the uncanny effect of actualizing the past as the present. If tradition has lost its meaning, a way of meaning might yet persist. The uncanny, for Freud, is that which remains unassimilated from the past, that which will come back, like an irregular refrain, in the form of a *revenant* or apparition.[141] At a time which has lost its faith in either an inspired vanguard or a teleologically driven mass movement, a condition less unworthy of the human race might still enter, almost unawares, in tiny dislocations of the mass commodity in its progress – haunting, startling, waylaying – as a return of the historically repressed. 'A failure of translation – this is what is known clinically as "repression".'[142]

CHAPTER 5

Mimesis

For a 'way of meaning' to translate into the radically contemporary, to speak for the predicament of modernity, old forms are not simply to be copied, transplanted, quoted or interpolated. They are warped and distended on contact with a new medium. It is a looking backwards in order to go forward.[1] Only such a transposition holds out hope for a genuine afterlife, something more than the curating of a tradition, preserved in museum-like stasis, or a 'salvage anthropology' that obsessively records all extant data, as though the archive might compensate for a once-living context. But while such a persisting life of tradition in 'The Solitary Reaper' was largely reduced to a translation of its acoustic medium, the question remains as to how a way of meaning might in the actual *content* of now-distanced beliefs and instinctual responses still be capable of transmission.

Looking back on *Lyrical Ballads* in 1815, Wordsworth declared that his poetic task was the anticipation of a 'sublimated humanity' that combined the 'instinctive wisdom of antiquity' with the 'meditative wisdom of later ages'.[2] His poetry was 'at once a history of the remote past and a prophetic enunciation of the remotest future'.[3] A reference to the 'heroic passions' of antiquity in this passage also reminds that what might be called the 'savage republicanism' of Rousseau *et al.* would lead to the irrationalist myths of fascist primitivism as well as the 'primitive communism' of Marx. But this is counterposed with 'meditative wisdom'. Wordsworth insists here that this should not be an atavistic flight into the irrational. The poet is 'passionate for the instruction of reason'.[4] Reason can learn only through an encounter with its other, the return to a buried mimetic layer in cognition. Such an emphasis on the mimetically particular was famously to provoke Coleridge's objection that rustic discourse, that 'best part of language' for the Preface, was merely that of '*insulated facts*' with no sense of the '*connections* of things' under a 'general law'.[5] Coleridge's denigration of the 'savage' took a similar line:

> The talent for mimicry seems strongest where the human race are most degraded. The poor, naked, half human savages of New Holland were found excellent mimics[6]

Representation as a making oneself similar to an object, as an attempt to mirror back the uniquely particular, was further opposed to conceptual language by Coleridge insofar as the latter extended a bridge towards religious transcendence: 'The extreme difficulty, and often the impossibility, of finding words for the simplest moral and intellectual processes in the language of uncivilized tribes has proved perhaps the weightiest obstacle to the progress of our most zealous and adroit missionaries.'[7] The extreme prejudice of Coleridge's misrepresentations of the 'uncivilized', the rustic, and even Wordsworth himself, nevertheless points to a historical rupture between concept and intuition, an evaluative subordination of mimetic experience, that is not so easily mended. It has been integral to the progressively rationalized forms of scientific, administrative, technological and economic culture. For Adorno and Horkheimer, however, writing during World War II, this rationality of 'processes', 'connections' and 'general law' was itself a form of mimetic adaptation to nature – to nature's 'rigidity', its repeatable and calculable regularities or probabilities, for the sake of power over the natural world and the nature within humanity itself: 'The reason that represses mimesis is not merely its opposite. It is itself mimesis: of death.'[8]

Animate mimesis is relegated to the contingent spheres of art or play. Michael Taussig has recounted the games of mutual mimicry played by the sailors and inhabitants when the *Beagle*, carrying Charles Darwin, arrived at Tierra del Fuego on 18 December 1832. In his journal, Darwin expressed astonishment at the islanders' exact ability to reproduce European speech, without understanding a word that was said: 'They could repeat with perfect correctness each word in any sentence we addressed them, and they remembered such words for some time.'[9] He goes on to ask: 'How can this faculty be explained? Is it a consequence of the more practised habits of perception and keener senses, common to all men in a savage state, as compared with those long civilized?'[10]

The pantomime, on both sides, was mimesis as an instinctual response to the strange and unanticipated, something not yet placed securely under a conceptual or classificatory identity. Taussig observes that mimesis is 'so dependent on alterity that it lies neither with the primitive nor with the civilized, but in the windswept and all too close, all too distant, mysterious sounding space of First Contact'.[11] As Taussig states, the mimetic doubling of sensuous particularity also has the potential to spin off into 'fantastic formations' and a 'chain of images'.[12] As a principle of knowledge, the similar extends into a cosmological perception of analogies and correspondences, or 'sympathetic magic', an action on what is similar to the object one hopes to alter (as with an effigy). In their *Dialectic of Enlightenment*, in an ironic troubling of the Enlightenment genre of progressive historiography, Adorno and Horkheimer drew up a speculative world history of the development of rationality from mimesis, as magical correspondences or animate objects became gods, then metaphysical substances or powers, then Platonic ideas or concepts, and ultimately the formal logic of technical method. For Taussig, the lingering presence of mimesis is a challenge to the arbitrary creation *ex nihilo* that has characterized late twentieth-century theories of 'social constructionism'. Mimesis, for Taussig, is the hinge or articulation between nature and culture – without the two being identified – and what holds social constructions in place through the lived enactment of 'custom' (the *habitus*). For mimesis, as an embodied response, is not simply a copying or detection of resemblance. It is an expression of the other through oneself – Adorno's 'mimetic shudder' – a surge of affect, the register of otherness through feeling, including even, as Taussig writes of one aspect of Walter Benjamin's definition of the 'mimetic faculty', 'the compulsion to become the Other'.[13]

The common eighteenth-century association of the 'primitive' with an astonishingly exact mimesis, an acuity of minute perception to which the generalizing consciousness of the European has become blind, was registered by Wordsworth's wonderment at the uncanny practical wisdom of a Highlander guide on his 1802 tour of Scotland. Dorothy remarked in her journal: 'We were astonished at the sagacity with which our Highlander discovered the track, where often no track was visible to us, and scarcely even when he pointed it out. It reminded us of what we read of the Hottentots and other savages.'[14] Resembling the 'second sight' for which the Highlanders were famous, this 'sagacity' rather than savagery might serve as a model for Wordsworth's own imaginative mimesis, its search for a particularity that points to a track or extends beyond itself. Wordsworth's aim was to restore mimesis to speculative truth. Such moments nestled less in the grandiose claims to unity of an 'intellectual intuition' than in those more fragile instants in his verse that uncover a whole new middle ground of concept and intuition – the unexplored hinterland between naming and abstraction. It was as much a social as an epistemological search for new modes of thinking and engagement.

Affect and Language

The Preface's definition of poetry as the 'spontaneous overflow of powerful feelings'[15] might seem, however, to position Wordsworth within a trend in late eighteenth-century aesthetics that, as M. H. Abrams famously argued, moved away from a mimetic or imitative notion of poetry – Horace's *ut pictura poesis* – to a new 'expressivism'.[16] An emphasis on self-expression, passionate utterance and poetic originality among writers like Herder and Rousseau found its political extension in affirmations of the *Volksgeist*, the 'native genius' of a region or nation. Edward Young's *Conjectures on Original Composition* (1759) rejected the standard imitation of classical models by the 'original' writer, and even 'the richest import from abroad', in favour of an 'Intellectual light' that must 'rise' and 'collect' into a 'body' – ironically as a 'Stranger within'.[17] There is a stranger in our midst to which we must give hospitable welcome; a cultural or self-protectionism harbours an uncanny foreignness, something unfamiliar within the most intimate recesses of the familiar self. And the intellectual light of originality is shaped in terms that suggest the opposite to a pure disembodied cognition: a rising and collecting that forms itself into a body.

Such a corporeal rising is evoked in Wordsworth's short lyric 'The Power of Music', as an old man listens to a street performer: 'Not an inch of his body is free from delight' as 'The music stirs in him like wind through a tree' (*P2V* 34–6). The stirring delight that collects every inch of the body is not an auto-affection but indeed an 'import from abroad': it is the *music itself* that flows through feeling. In 'Lines Written in Early Spring', it is the 'thousand blended notes' (*LB* 1) of birdsong that arouse and attach a native genius to the foreign: 'To her fair works did nature link / The human soul that through me ran' (5–6). The angelic soul of theology, or the 'intellectual light' of a post-Cartesian ghost in the machine, have been translated into something bodily, a stranger within that we have no power to collect into a manageable shape – it 'ran' through Wordsworth, eluding his grasp – yet which is so close as to seem integral to humanity itself: a 'human soul'. Yet its arousal depends on something non-human – a mimetic shudder so intimately familiar to the experience of music, yet so rarely mentioned in the discourses surrounding it: a tingle or trembling, a rush through the body, the hairs standing on end. Something remarkable and singular has occurred. The strangeness within is not only that of an affect which ruptures the ego's self-presence; it is also a 'link' to an outside, a foreign import, a tie to mimesis from which expression is never fully unbound.

At such moments, André Green argued, '*affect is the epiphany of the Other for the subject*'.[18] Green's psychoanalytic study of affect was an attempt to wrest back its centrality to Freud from Jacques Lacan's argument for the linguistic structures of the unconscious. Likewise, the recent development of 'affect theory' has often followed Gilles Deleuze in contrasting affect with representation.[19] But if affect cannot wholly jettison its link to an outside, then as an isthmus between self and world it is necessarily cognitive and representational: it tells us something qualitative about its object. Affect is a language of the foreign. Wordsworth asserted in the Preface that 'our thoughts . . . are indeed the representatives of all our past feelings' – conceptual representation is bound to mimetic affect.[20] André Green noted that 'the general feeling is that the affect sometimes emerges in a state of nature, as it were, without any representation being associated with it'.[21] Yet for Wordsworth, there can be no return to an affective state of nature, for our 'continued influxes of feeling are modified and directed by our thoughts'.[22] What we feel is inseparable from our representations, our language, the values and norms of a *habitus*. But feeling modifies thought for Wordsworth, just as thought modifies feeling. A new affect arising from the foreign can change the nature of our representations.

To trace the link between affect and representation was indeed the goal of Wordsworth's one and only attempt directly to represent an original state of nature in the poetry of his major period – in Book II of *The Prelude*. Yet this too was allied to his more widespread depictions of a contemporary state of nature – it is a reorientation of the phylogenetic state of nature in prehistory to the ontogenetic or individual state of nature in earliest infancy: the relation between the neonate and its mother. Nevertheless, however contemporary a phenomenon, this dyad's inaccessibility to memory would necessitate a conjectural reconstruction as much as the pictures of prehistory:

> Bless'd the infant babe,
> (For with my best conjectures I would trace
> The progress of our being)
>
> (237–9)

In 1793, Dugald Stewart, a late figure of the Scottish Enlightenment, had coined the phrase '*Theoretical* or *Conjectural History*' as an alternative to the 'natural history of Man'. When ignorant of 'how men have actually conducted themselves upon particular occasions' – as in the earliest societies – it is by ascertaining 'the principles of their nature, and the external circumstances of their situation' that the philosopher can fulfil the 'necessity of supplying the place of fact by conjecture'.[23] This was the anthropological motive, for example, behind John Brown's attempt in 1764 to depict *The History of the Rise and Progress of Poetry*: 'Passions and Principles of action, as are common to the whole Race of Man, will be most effectually investigated, as to its Origin and Progress, by viewing Man in his savage, or uncultivated State . . . before Education and Art have cast their Veil over the human Mind.'[24] Wordsworth also seeks the founding principles of poetry before their 'progress' through an advancing socialization. His aim, he states, is to capture

> the first
> Poetic spirit of our human life;
> By uniform controul of after years
> In most abated and suppress'd
> (275–8)

This is not yet poetry as an art form, but a mode of perception and cognition: a buried stratum of mimetic expression.

Returning to consciousness is a poetics now socially *repressed* – 'In most abated and suppressed'. More than just analogous to Freudian psychoanalysis, this is a difficult enterprise that Wordsworth explicitly announces as a poetic psychoanalysis: 'Hard task to analyse a soul' (232). Its historical model, and antagonist, is Enlightenment faculty psychology, challenged by Wordsworth for its arbitrary topography of mind – 'Split, like a province, into round and square' (210) – through a taxonomy of separate entities (reason, will, judgement, etc.) that were fetishized like pseudo-persons:

> to class the cabinet
> Of their sensations, and, in voluble phrase,
> Run through the history and birth of each,
> As of a single independent thing
> (228–31)

Psychoanalysis would discover its own topography of provinces and cabinet of curiosities. Nevertheless, *The Prelude* does attempt a stadial account of what Wordsworth called the 'growth of a poet's mind', above all in Books I–III. The link to Freud is not fortuitous – with its primal scenes and plotted stages of infant development, psychoanalysis was itself an ontogenetic reworking of the state of nature and its progress into social maturity, influenced by the Victorian legacy of the Enlightenment.[25] Like Freud, Wordsworth recounts an emergence from 'primary narcissism' or infantile feelings of omnipotence, and emphasizes the subsequently repressed *eros* of the child's libidinal as well as affective investment in the world. But in Wordsworth these early forms of 'primitive' consciousness are poetic modes of representation with their own claim to cognitive truth.

Book II's conjectural history of the mother–infant dyad, however, is closer to post-Freudian theories of a 'pre-Oedipal' stage, most notably those of Melanie Klein and D. W. Winnicott. And Green, influenced by such 'object relations' theory as well as Freud, went so far as to call Wordsworth's 'infant babe' passage, despite its conjectured and experimental aspect, his 'favourite model of transcription of mother–infant observation'.[26] Yet for Paul de Man, the 'infant babe' passage is not about psychological formation but constitutes 'Wordsworth's essay on the origins of language as poetic language'.[27] This would make it an ontogenetic reworking of the Enlightenment genre of Vico, Condillac, Rousseau and Herder. Nevertheless, as Frances Ferguson observes: 'if Wordsworth portrays the child as an infant – without speech – a related speechlessness, or inability to speak, extends throughout the passage'.[28] What de Man's account overlooks – affect – is what links the passage to psychology, while what a psychoanalytic account risks neglecting – language – is what makes this an inquiry into cognition. The passage retraces the origins of a language of affect. Ferguson, in a sceptical reading, has viewed this affective communication as a deluded unity of subject–object, which she relates to Rousseau's account of the figurative distortions of the first language of passion, and which she contrasts with the 'epitaphic' status of language, in which the word stands for distance and separation, a loss of the object. Language is a mimesis of death. But for Wordsworth, this first language, now mostly repressed, is not simply superseded or an object of mourning: it is uncannily complicit with its 'dead' and 'inorganic' descendant. That is why it is worth going back – and why its repressed content has a tendency to return. Green proposed that 'Eros can triumph over the death drives only if Eros becomes the Eros of Logos and if Logos becomes the Logos of Eros.'[29] Eros, of course, cannot triumph over physical death and loss itself – but as Book II shows, or awakens from death-driven repression, this might not be all that the Logos can represent.

In the 'infant babe' passage, affect is the precondition of language's ability to represent any kind of object at all:

> blest the Babe,
> Nurs'd in his Mother's arms, the Babe who sleeps
> Upon his Mother's breast, who, when his soul
> Claims manifest kindred with an earthly soul,
> Doth gather passion from his Mother's eye!
> Such feelings pass into his torpid life

Like an awakening breeze, and hence his mind
Even in the first trial of its powers,
Is prompt and watchful, eager to combine
In one appearance, all the elements
And parts of the same object, else detach'd
And loth to coalesce.

(239–50)

It is by 'awakening' us from 'torpid life', by responding to a 'passion' that passes into us, that affect drives us to hold a figure together in its integrity. The supposedly 'primitive' delusion of an animistic projection – or rather, combination – is at the root of any coherent perception of shape or identity. All our acts of perceptual synthesis, and by extension all representation and abstraction, begin with an impassioned effort to keep our mother alive. At this stage, affect is not the source of fetishism, but its counter, what stops us from mistaking a part for the whole. What is perceived is a *face*, an individuation. If affect is the basis of language, it is not the general noun, adjective or verb that has priority, but the *name*. The passage sets up a contrast between our habitual identifications and those of a poetic 'making' – a shaping that is animated by love.

Yet there is also an anamorphic perspective here: a collapse of the figure into its component 'parts', a flitting and disoriented movement of the eye from one unrelated detail to another. The face's detached particulars, harbingers of the arbitrary sign, do indeed put up a genuine resistance: they are 'loth to coalesce'. But in that minuscule anthropomorphism – 'loth' – they too have a quasi-animistic power, a 'face' even, of their own. So hard is the task of analysing what is, or is not, a soul. A sense of life is constantly overflowing into what seems non-living, just as what seems most indubitably alive – a resistance, for example, to another's attempt to force an identity upon us – might correspond to an active power of the inanimate.

For de Man, the 'face' in Wordsworth signifies the 'dependence of any perception on the totalizing power of language', an arbitrary 'power to surface from the sea of infinite distinctions in which we risk to drown'.[30] Yet even the most infinitesimal distinction is a kind of face and hence language – the ultimate realization of de Man's vision would be a blindness unable to perceive distinctions at all. What de Man invokes resembles the dizzying spectacle of commodity fetishes in Wordsworth's London:

the same perpetual flow
Of trivial objects, melted and reduced
To one identity, by differences
That have no law, no meaning, and no end

(*Pr.* VII.702–5)

Without a shape with and against which to measure difference, wrestling with and against totalizations, it is distinctions themselves that would drown – into the sea of identity. A rationality of affect would be loath to sacrifice either part or whole, the living or the non-living properties of objects, in the very face of their falling apart.

Melanie Klein claimed that the child's exploration of the mother's body was the origin of 'epistemophilia', the love of knowledge – her analogy was a later Romantic-period poem of the traveller's excitement before *terra incognita*, Keats' 'On First Looking into Chapman's Homer'.[31] No doubt for Klein, the particularities of the face that are loath to coalesce would be displacements of the child's equal urge to destroy the ambivalent mother, alongside its guilt-stricken urge to reparate by reconstruction – though Wordsworth at least acknowledges the conjectural status of his ontogenetic state of nature. The 'infant babe' passage goes on to describe a transition from what Winnicott called the 'environment-mother',[32] the primal landscape of the mother as responsively 'holding' the child, to the natural environment as a field of objects:

> Thus, day by day,
> Subjected to the discipline of love,
> His organs and recipient faculties
> Are quicken'd, are more vigorous, his mind spreads,
> Tenacious of the forms which it receives.
> In one beloved presence
>
> (250–5)

This is the world of our primary fetishism – forms are tenaciously gripped not only insofar as they resemble the maternal face as an independent entity, but also as the mother's presence spreads, with the infant's mind, to undergird or cradle the whole landscape. It is the individual body, as a whole in excess of its parts, which by extension opens up and discloses the whole world to the child. The mythic perception of the universe as a giant cosmic body, with the human as its microcosm, has here been translated into the common experience of mimetic infancy – and as the source of a mature ability to perceive both part and whole in their interrelation, it again speaks for the very opposite of fetishism.

In Wordsworth's 'Essay, Supplementary to the Preface' of 1815, a fetishized landscape and language without 'presence' is that of James Macpherson's contrived Highland poetry: 'everything . . . [is] defined, insulated, dislocated, deadened, – yet nothing distinct'.[33] In this terrain of infinite definitions, nothing is distinct at all. It is like a whirl or procession of commodities from which the libido has been withdrawn. By implication, then, as with the mother's body, for something to be truly distinct, it must have the capacity to spread beyond itself, to communicate something that extends further than itself – to have a kind of language. In the 'Essay', Wordsworth goes on to counterpose what he has actually experienced of landscape to the literary nature of Macpherson's arbitrary signs: 'In nature everything is distinct, yet nothing defined into absolute independent singleness.'[34] In another essay written in 1815, the introduction to his collected *Poems*, an 'absolute independent singleness' is identified as the principle of anthropomorphic fetishism itself. The 'idolatry' of the 'anthropomorphitism of the Pagan religion' is held to have 'subjected the minds' of classical poets to the 'bondage of definite form'.[35] It is a kind of perceptual slavery, for the mind is unable to 'spread' through such a field of objects. Strikingly, then, for Wordsworth here any kind of 'definite form' – a noun, a tool, a flower, a commodity, or any self-contained object – is a piece of idolatry and anthropomorphitism. And the process begins with the mother's body – once the role of affect has been 'suppressed' by 'uniform controul'. Adorno and Horkheimer would famously observe that 'The disenchantment of the world means the extirpation of animism.'[36] But such an extirpation might be harder to execute than it seems. The key distinction for Wordsworth, it appears, is not between animism and an utterly disenchanted or 'deadened' perspective – the 'definite form' of an anthropomorphized corpse – but between the isolated fetish and the physiognomy that illumines a world beyond it.

To get room to move and breathe, the poet must break open the shell of phenomena. It is to travel through the abandoned middle ground between naming and abstraction. The startling power of the 'infant babe' passage is its discovery of this hinterland – and of the suppressed role of affect and physiognomy in the supposedly neutral sphere of objectified language and rationality that emerges from it. As with Wordsworth's characterization of his youthful, Godwin-inspired, cult of pure reason, it is a domain in which 'passions had the privilege to work, / And never hear the sound of their own names' (*Pr.* x.812–13). And it further uncovers just how *social* that pseudo-neutrality really is. It is quite literally, and not sentimentally, an index of lost love.

'The progress of our being'

As Book II progresses beyond infancy into later childhood, Wordsworth goes on proudly to declare his own infantilism, his escape from the uniform repression: 'the infant sensibility, / Great birth-right of our Being, was in me / Augmented and sustain'd' (285–7). Progress is an increase, an augmentation, of infant perception, not its suppression. But at this point the narrative suddenly darkens, and the clear line of progress is diffracted into the 'broken windings' of a 'path . . . / More difficult' (287–9). Something cryptic is said to occur – a 'trouble' of the 'mind' with 'unknown causes' (291–2) – reminiscent of Winnicott's 'trauma of separation' from the mother at the weaning stage,[37] though apparently at a later age and more abrupt in its removal:

> I was left alone,
> Seeking the visible world, nor knowing why.
> The props of my affections were remov'd
> And yet the building stood
>
> (292–5)

The child's state of nature has become a state of estrangement in the most ordinary and everyday sense – it is the very origin of 'common day'. Yet this is not quite that libidinal withdrawal which leaves only the neutral domain of objects standing:

> All that I beheld
> Was dear to me, and from this cause it came,
> That now to Nature's finer influxes
> My mind lay open, to that more exact
> And intimate communion which our hearts
> Maintain with the minuter properties
> Of objects which already are belov'd
> And of those only.
>
> (296–303)

There has been a cooling of ardour, but not a total decathexis – the objects remain 'beloved'. There has been loss, but also gain. The emphasis is no longer on projection, combination, or forms that spread across an extended presence, but on an openness of mind, a new passiveness able to receive that which has no graspable form: 'finer influxes'. The syntax, though slightly ambiguous, seems to suggest that it is through such influxes that the heart is able to commune with objects in their 'minuter properties' – and not, as one might expect, through the searching gaze of an intentional focus. This is not an expression of 'primary narcissism' or of subject–object identity, but its breakthrough.

To ascribe this to 'progress' went against the whole current of Enlightenment historiographies of language. For Lord Monboddo, a 'savage' and 'imbruted'[38] miring in particulars must give way to the 'perfect ideas' of a 'general' and 'arbitrary' language.[39] James Harris' *Hermes* (1751) had earlier asserted that the glory of 'civilized' language was its establishment of syntactical logic, corresponding to the universal grammar of the Logos.[40] With a Humean blend of scepticism and pragmatism, the young Adam Smith, in his 'History of Astronomy' (*c.*1758), had argued that the transition from poetry to scientific order, suppressing the destabilizing effects of 'wonder and surprise', was a necessary effect of world-historical progress, even if it remained at the level of 'mere inventions of the imagination, to connect together the otherwise disjointed and discordant phenomena of nature'.[41] By contrast, progress for Wordsworth is a mimetic exactitude of communion with those 'minuter' particulars that the infant was so anxious to 'coalesce'.

So fine are these inflowing properties that they slip through the mesh of nominal language. Wordsworth can convey them only through their opposite, the language of abstraction. And that language connects them to the larger shape: they are the 'minuter properties / Of objects'. But it is the persisting strength of love that releases them to perception from the forms to which they belong; it is 'only' beloved objects that facilitate such an influx, a sea of infinite distinctions that would otherwise be lost. The reader's own projective imagination has to fill in for what Wordsworth cannot directly represent: the true finesse of detail that inhabits an object when perceived with love. A minute subtlety and delicacy of perception is given here to what has become – though remarkably original in Wordsworth's time – the familiar theme of 'love's knowledge'.

Having partly detached the particular from its object, Wordsworth begins to weave together a counter-Logos of relationships:

> And every season to my notice brought
> A store of transitory qualities
> Which, but for this most watchful power of love
> Had been neglected, left a register
> Of permanent relationships, else unknown
>
> (308–12)

Not only 'neglected' but 'unknown' to the scientific Logos of permanent causal or grammatical or classificatory relations, the lazy ignorance of a negligent logic based on quantity and identity, here the rich store of a 'permanent' knowledge of nature's relationships arises from what is most fleeting, from the 'transitory qualities' of the changing seasons. But again, this language revealed by affect, in mimetic absorption, a 'most watchful power of love', can only be brought to the awareness of the learned community by abstraction. The next line is yet more abstract, paratactic to the point of absurdity: 'Hence life, and change, and beauty' (313). The logical conjunction, 'Hence', prepares us for a rational consequence or result, and what we are given is almost throwaway in its sequence of non sequiturs. Grammatical language seems to have broken down in a 'spontaneous overflow' of affect, an excited or baffled stammering. Maybe what is permanent in these relationships is precisely that sensation of perpetual life and change and beauty – a transitory and qualitative Logos.

With the next paratactic twist of the verse, as the end of line 313 pauses at its turn, Wordsworth does now draw out a greater meaning to these relationships, albeit the surprising one of claiming that this is *social*:

> solitude
> More active, even, than 'best society,'
> Society made sweet as solitude
> By silent in obtrusive sympathies
> And gentle agitations of the mind
> (313–17)

On the one hand, this is solitude as contrasted with society; on the other, this is a radically new sense of society as revealed only in the solitary experience of nature. It is a social language of affect, of 'sympathies', and yet is 'silent'. It had indeed become commonplace since the mid eighteenth century to argue for sympathy as the first principle of the social bond. Later in Book II, recounting his adolescence, Wordsworth will worry that his tendency to animate the natural world has emerged from 'the great social principle of life, / Coercing all things into sympathy' (408–9). An apparently benevolent sympathy, as in sentimental literature, hides a will to dominate and coerce into an identity with the self. Yet in the lines above, sympathy is not coercively projected by the mind, but passively or mimetically received in a gentle shock of otherness: 'gentle agitations of the mind'. A free yet sympathetic association largely suppressed in human social life is granted in loneliness to the finer influxes of a *material* assembly or commonwealth.

What provokes the gentle shock is an array of

> manifold distinctions, difference
> Perceived in things where to the common eye
> No difference is
> (318–20)

This 'manifold' and possibly infinite sea of 'distinctions', invisible to the 'common eye', does not seem to be that set up by linguistic denomination or definition, nor that of a classificatory reason – Wordsworth must again have recourse to abstraction. From the vantage of this minuteness of perceptual mimesis, what is imposed by the coercive identities of common language, determining the way we look and perceive, is nothing more than an *indifference*.

Wordsworth would return to this theme in the following Book III of *The Prelude*. It occurs at a point where he is worrying that his figuratively vital ways of seeing might lead others to believe that he is simply insane. His first line of defence is to claim – in the tradition of Vico, Rousseau and Hugh Blair – that this is the original type of human perception: that of the 'Poets of old time, and higher up / By the first men, earth's first inhabitants' (152–3). In what is a slightly mad claim in itself, Wordsworth declares that he is still in the primordial state of nature. But 'difference' is the therapeutic reality principle in Wordsworth's poetic psychoanalysis. For Wordsworth, it is a searching out of the alien that is his mainstay against derangement:

> It was no madness: for I had an eye
> Which in my strongest workings, evermore
> Was looking for the shades of difference
> As they lie hid in all exterior forms,
> Near or remote, minute or vast, an eye
> Which from a stone, a tree, a wither'd leaf
> To the broad ocean and the azure heavens
> Spangled with kindred multitudes of stars,
> Could find no surface where its power might sleep,
> Which spake perpetual logic to my soul,
> And by an unrelenting agency
> Did bind my feelings, even as in a chain.
>
> (156–67)

These differences are not punctual marks or hard details or definite forms, as with the 'exterior forms' which hide them, but 'shades' analogous to chromatic nuance. It is this degree of mimetic particularity, surprisingly, not rationality itself as might be thought conventionally, that is directly opposed to madness. Again, this is not difference as the common eye, or logic, perceives it. It appears to be as paratactic in sequence as the listing of 'exterior forms' and concatenation of feelings by which the observer forms an attachment to it. Or rather, it is an alternative kind of logic – a language without propositions that 'spake' with its own unique Logos. It is a 'logic', rather than a contingency, because this speaking is 'perpetual'. There is a logos of speech released even from a thing as it decays, as it loses its self-identity – it is to impart a gentle agitation that a 'wither'd leaf' emerges from the catalogue. Within the language of 'exterior forms' – on which the human language that identifies them as general nouns with subordinate adjectives is based – there is another, hidden language of qualities. It is a language that speaks only when freed from identity.

As if troubled, however, by the 'savage' or pagan sensuality of what still remains a visual, if synaesthetic, access to the Logos, Wordsworth's next turn in Book II is to a language 'by form / Or image unprofaned' (325–6). It is an Abrahamic shift from the potential idolatry of the Book of Nature to the linguistic medium of transcendence, the Holy Book of Revelation. Yet this remains a mimetic or sensory experience, still immanent within a book of nature that is no longer read but simply heard:

> For I would walk alone
> . . . and, at that time,
> Have felt whate'er there is of power in sound
> To breathe an elevated mood, by form
> Or image unprofaned: and I would stand,
> Beneath some rock, listening to sounds that are
> The ghostly language of the ancient earth,
> Or make their dim abode in distant winds.
> Thence did I drink the visionary power.
> (321–30)

This is a language that is registered by subjective affect: its 'power' is 'felt'. Yet the 'elevated mood' is not a projection, but an objective affect breathed out by the sound itself – an objectivity marked by an elevation that is no longer the domain of conceptual transcendence but a physical mood or expression. Unable mimetically or conceptually to translate that sound-mood into human language and meaning, Wordsworth profanes it by an image after all: we are led to imagine the sound and listen to it with him as he stands beneath a rock. Yet that rock has something to do with the sound itself. This may be the 'ghostly language of the ancient earth' but it is not that of nature as a totality, for it is distinguished from another language that he was also apt to hear, one that lived in 'distant winds'. If that first language be not the wind as it whistles through a fissure or crevice, and we are not told that it is the noise of a waterfall or brook, then it seems to be the rock and earth themselves that are speaking, a chthonic expressivism or 'native genius' of the earth itself. The 'ancient' is uncannily contemporary; it is still possible to hear language in its state of nature. But its voice is not fully present, it is 'ghostly' and partly disembodied – we cannot be sure that any author or origin is being expressed at all. If, in this language's alternative form, its obscure 'abode' might sometimes lie in 'distant winds', it has nevertheless wandered far hence, somehow projected across a distance. The wind is not actually present. This too, then, is a language that baffles any ascription of identity.

But it is emphatically not a meaningless noise: it is able to communicate a 'visionary power'. Impossible fully to ground contextually, it speaks for something beyond itself. Through a perceptual confusion, or simply illusion, it has acquired an allegorical sign-character. Yet the traditional interpretation of this speaking of earth and wind – the divine language of creation – has been cut away. Unable to gloss its meaning, Wordsworth can only 'drink' it in. Once again we have stepped into the middle ground between intuition and concept, between an appetitive and embodied sensuousness without meaning – an infantile orality of drinking – and a mature cognition of rational or religious import. At a historical hour in which Wordsworth was one of the first to perceive what was close to a nihilistic crisis of tradition, the hope embodied by the highest and for that reason emptiest seeming abstractions – God, spirit, soul, or liberty, equality and fraternity – has become a thirst that can be slaked only through an immersion in sensuous experience. If this is not to drown but to drink hope from a sea of infinite distinctions, it is because mimetic affect breaks through to a meaning on the other side of 'anthropomorphitism'.

In a draft for a passage later transferred to Book II, Wordsworth had written of 'A secret and mysterious soul, / A fragrance and a spirit of strange meaning' in natural appearances.[42] How can a 'meaning' be 'strange'? Is not language the vehicle of meaning, including the hermeneutics of nature, in its lucid presentation of identities, functions and interpretations? A 'strange meaning' would be oxymoronic in the extreme. Nature must somehow hold a form of meaningful language – not just a sonority or visual logic – that is irreducible to human language, perhaps even the opaquely mimetic source from which human meaning is constructively simplified, abstracted, and coerced into sympathy or identity. But even that extra-discursive meaning depends upon a prior sense of human language to be recognized, and indeed a centuries-old tradition of the 'book of nature'. Is it not this very ambiguity, that of a meaning that seems modelled on human discourse and its hopes, while uncannily objective in its affect and resistance to interpretation, that makes it seem so remarkably *strange*? The oxymoronic shape of this 'strange meaning' is made yet stranger by the parallelism of the clauses that contain and mirror it. As so often with the trope of *hendiadys* ('one through two'), the synonymous or complementary terms that qualify the noun do not quite add up[43] – secret/mysterious, fragrance/spirit – just as the parallel clauses do not quite fit together. It is a 'spirit', hence distinct from the body, but this spirituality is as physical as the scent of flowers or perfume. It is emitted by a 'fragrance', as though its spirit were the wholly material distillation of a quintessence. What it signifies is mysterious; there is still a 'secret' that science cannot unlock, but no guarantee that this 'soul' or excess is commensurate with the human.

Yet as though Book II had been progressively building to such a conclusive humanization of nature, an 'expressivist' affirmation of its unified consciousness, Wordsworth's account of childhood and adolescence culminates in a vision of the 'one life' and 'One song' (430–1) of a univocal world. Beyond 'human knowledge', it is nevertheless a cognition of affect: it is 'to the human eye / Invisible, yet liveth to the heart' (423–4). It is mimetically perceptible in the free movements and 'shouts' and songs of animal nature, as also in the motions of the waves (425–6). But this inner life is as fluid and mobile as the human soul that runs through the body when listening to music, as though the whole earth might be felt as a human physiognomy: 'I felt the sentiment of Being spread / O'er all that moves, and all that seemeth still' (420–1). It is easy to object that this is merely an expression of what Wordsworth, just before this passage, had deemed a coercive sympathy. Yet Wordsworth insists that the 'one song' is mimetically 'audible', and then in the next line declares that it is most audible when inaudible, unprofaned by the sensory, when its 'grosser prelude' dies away, and the physical ear 'Forgot its functions, and slept undisturb'd' (433–4). Transcendence is reduced to a sensory blankness or blackout. And immediately in the next verse paragraph, Wordsworth acknowledges that this 'faith' may well be an 'error' (435). The progressive finale pauses for breath, and undoes itself. It is the uncertainty, or potential for delusion, in any cognition of affect. But in the long series of steps that have led up to Book II's leap into faith or identity, closer to paratactic turns than a teleological development, we have been shown the mimetic complexity, the many voices, through which the univocal must inevitably speak.

Just prior to this passage, another material and *plural* basis for sociality had been uncovered. Wordsworth remembers a time in adolescence when he pieced together his own version of a cosmos:

> that interminable building rear'd
> By observation of affinities
> In objects where no brotherhood exists
> To common minds.
>
> (402–5)

It is a Logos in the process of construction. This is not a fixed system or chain of being; it is a play of similarities or 'affinities' without *telos* or end, for it is 'interminable'. Mimesis uncovers a ceaseless building from which the mythological cosmology or scientific machine has been abstracted. Its 'character' is close to, or 'resembling', Wordsworth tells us, the 'poetic' or 'Creative agency' (399–401) – it is a poetics, or music, of nature.

In his *Lectures on the Sacred Poetry of the Hebrews* (translated from Latin in 1787), an influence upon Wordsworth's 1800 note to 'The Thorn',[44] Robert Lowth had posited 'resemblance' as the 'ground-work of the figurative . . . style'. Wordsworth, who wanted at least partly to reincarnate the 'Poets of old time', would have found encouragement for some of his 'primitive' violations of 'civilized' grammar and syntax in Lowth's appreciation for the 'parallelism', pleonasm, and similitudes of Old Testament poetry.[45] For Lowth, such figurative resemblance was not an aesthetic ornament, but the earliest knowledge: 'The whole course of nature, this immense universe of things . . . affords an infinite variety, a confused assemblage, a wilderness, as it were, of images . . . collected as the materials of poetry.'[46] Characteristically, Wordsworth translates the medium, the way of meaning, not the mythical or magical content, of this primitive cosmos of resemblance. But such affinities are not simply poetically created or constructed – Wordsworth insists that they are discerned through a mimetic 'observation of affinities', albeit as hidden to the 'common mind' as their apparent opposite, a manifold 'difference', had been earlier. Here, however, is a new form of commonality: what he calls a 'brotherhood' of sibling resemblances. Objects are related not through a hierarchy of spheres, or causes and effects, as with the vertical model of parent–child, but on the lateral basis of sibling relations. In Book III, the speaking logic of shades of difference had included a sky that is 'Spangled with kindred multitudes of stars' – not an ordering of constellations, but a dazzling and multitudinous kinship of affinities. In the 'infant babe' passage, what the child drew from its mother was not a sense of dependence, but the face-to-face parity of its 'claims' to a 'manifest kindred' (242). The affinities of the material assembly form a remarkably non-human extension of what Marc Shell has called an underground historical tradition that has occasionally risen to the surface, as in forms of Christianity, above all the monastic fraternity and sorority, and in the brotherhood proclaimed by the French Revolution: the idea of a 'universal siblinghood'.[47]

It might, then, be too simple to label as mere ideology Wordsworth's claim, at the end of Book II, that despite the 'melancholy waste of hopes o'erthrown' (449) by political repression in France and Britain, his return to nature is not a 'domestic' (454) retreat – as with John Thelwall's withdrawal from political activism to the Welsh countryside, it has also been termed a form of political travel or 'inner emigration'[48] – but what renews his 'confidence' in humanity (449–59). Such an assurance is based not on the French Revolution's 'levelling' abstraction of rational equality, as Hazlitt would accuse Wordsworth of imitating, but on what Walter Benjamin perceived as a 'homesickness' for the mimetic faculty: for 'the world distorted in the state of similarity, a world in which the true surrealist face of existence breaks through'.[49]

'Similitude in dissimilitude'

How the 'brotherhood of affinities' might relate to the manifold 'shades of difference' – and ward off the threat of madness or a 'demon of analogy', an endless spinning out into delusion of the 'fantastic formations' of mimesis for Taussig – was left unaddressed in Book II. Yet a thinking together of affinity and difference, as a chiasmic intertwining, was announced as the lynchpin of Wordsworth's self-proclaimed 'theory' of his verse in the Preface to *Lyrical Ballads*: as the 'principle' of 'similitude in dissimilitude, and dissimilitude in similitude'.[50] Wordsworth makes the most modest and partial, and the grandest and most sweeping claims for the importance of this principle. It would have been a vital component, 'If I had undertaken a systematic defence of the theory upon which these poems are written.'[51] But it is not the whole of that theory, if it ever existed, and pertains only to one aspect of it, an account of the 'causes' of 'the pleasure received from metrical language' – and even here, it is not the only cause, but 'Among the chief of these causes'.[52] Yet this mere element of something as apparently minor as poetic metre is subsequently affirmed to be no less than the fundamental structure of all cognition: 'This principle is the great spring of the activity of our minds, and their chief feeder.'[53]

Maureen McLane has compared Wordsworth's investigations into the 'savage mind' to similar attempts in twentieth-century anthropology: to Lévy-Bruhl's claim for a 'mystic participation' of so-called primitive consciousness with its objects, and Lévi-Strauss' argument that an equally so-called 'savage thought' builds up a world on the structuralist principles of a classificatory system of binary oppositions, of identities established through difference. Wordsworth's 'similitude in dissimilitude' works between and undermines such polarized conceptions of *pensée sauvage*. As what remains the 'great spring' of 'our minds', this is a highly contemporary state of cognitive nature. Similitude and dissimilitude do indeed 'participate' in each other in Wordsworth's formulation; they are not in binary opposition, but the dissimilar obstructs any subject–object identity. It may represent a mental structure and potential system, but similarities are not identities, and differences are not made absolute but defined negatively: as 'dissimilitude'. As a 'spring', a fountain, of cognitive 'activity', Wordsworth's principle is something like a mimetic under-layer of conceptual thinking – an entwining of what is similar and dissimilar in appearances that is then processed and separated out into rigid identity and difference. Neither similitude nor dissimilitude is granted priority – they are reversible and mutually regulative. This is not a sea of infinite distinctions; without similitude as its measure, dissimilitude could not be perceived at all – and vice versa.

Wordsworth is careful not to make ontological claims for this principle – it is a ground of mental activity, not Being – and yet as a 'feeder' of the mind it emerges from a scrupulous closeness of perceptual mimesis: the 'accuracy with which . . . [something is] perceived'.[54] The description of the mind's basis harbours a prescriptive call for a greater effort of mimetic accuracy – for this faculty to rise from the implicit to a fully owned awareness. This raises the question of how a 'similitude in dissimilitude' might be related to the mimetic replication of a singularity. With reference to the thought of Gilles Deleuze, such a link has been explored by Corinna Russell. Associating Wordsworth's principle with his defence of 'repetition' in the note to 'The Thorn', she collates both with Deleuzean repetition as the reinstatement of a unique singularity, each time involving difference as it enters a new context.[55] The thorn, pond and mossy hill in 'The Thorn' have their own singular 'quiddity' and yet also 'resemble' the human actors and actions of the poem; they 'hint at sameness but deny identity . . . preserving a sense of dissimilitude in similitude'.[56] Russell's thinking is in fact broader here than Deleuze's, whose concept of repetition is specifically targeted against 'resemblance' (without acknowledging its corollary in a singular 'dissimilitude') as much as 'law'.[57] Deleuze's reiterated singularities are locked into isolation and non-communication; similitude in dissimilitude hints at how the singular might enter into relationships. The 'absolute independent singleness' of Deleuzean repetition, despite its ever-new contextualization, is what Wordsworth would call a 'bondage of definite form'. Nothing material is entirely without its 'brotherhood of affinities'. For Wordsworth does not defend tautology in the note to 'The Thorn', but argues that this is only 'apparent tautology'.[58] Repetition is an abstraction, a construction, an identity – mimetically it is only a 'similitude in dissimilitude' that links the present to the past.

Wordsworth's brief yet pregnant exposition of similitude in dissimilitude is not only normative in its appeal to a mimetic 'accuracy'. Its ambition extends to viewing the three separate provinces of philosophy – the true, the good and the beautiful – through their own similitude in dissimilitude.

If mimesis holds a claim to epistemological accuracy, the principle is also linked to the aesthetic pleasure of art, above all of poetic metre, in a manner no longer (as in Kant) upheld as purely 'disinterested'. Indeed for Wordsworth the principle of metrical pleasure is nothing less than the source of the sex drive: 'From this principle the direction of the sexual appetite, and all the passions connected with it, take their origin.'[59] It is an Eros of Logos and the Logos of Eros. And as 'the life of our ordinary conversation',[60] it is the model of a non-identical exchange. It conjoins the aesthetic with the ethical: 'upon the accuracy with which similitude in dissimilitude, and dissimilitude in similitude are perceived, depend our taste and our moral feelings'.[61] Moral behaviour depends not only on sympathy (for 'similitude'), but also on the recognition of, and pleasure in, what is dissimilar and unique. 'Similitude in dissimilitude' might be that utopian moment in which the reality and pleasure principles are at peace.

As a moral principle of lateral rather than hierarchical relations, it is not without its social extension. In a psychoanalytic theory of sibling relations as the model for later peer relations, Juliet Mitchell has supplemented psychoanalysis' stress on vertical relationships of authority with a path-breaking account of the horizontal. The traumas and jealousies of sibling relations stem from a mode of perception that is remarkably close to Deleuzean repetition: siblinghood is structured by 'sameness and difference, uniqueness and replication'.[62] The infant's narcissistic sense of uniqueness is traumatized by the mother's diverted attention to a new baby – alternately perceived as both more of itself, and so loved, and also as a challenge to its uniqueness as a serial replacement, and different as a usurping interloper. This oscillation is in later social life split into the friend–foe distinction.[63] An accurate perception of 'similitude in dissimilitude' would offer a quite different way of viewing peer relations. It is a key dimension within Wordsworth's sense of his poetry as 'an affair of whole continents of moral sympathy'. But this might be not without its own destabilizing effects. Marc Shell points out that the possibility of a 'universal siblinghood' also raises the fear of an incestuous contagion.[64] As Tim Fulford observes of the 'Romantic Indian' in the poetry of the Americas: 'Strangely disturbing and breathtakingly desirable, they were uncanny figures because they suggested that at the heart of the British self was a kinship with the foreign.'[65] As the foreign and domestic, the strange and the familiar, are interwoven with a similitude *in* dissimilitude – not an external conjunction but an internal co-implication – Wordsworth's principle might even stand as an epistemological definition of the uncanny. Insofar as a reversible similitude in dissimilitude is a mimetic chiasmus prior to identity and difference, the uncanny is at the basis of all knowledge.

'The Complaint of a Forsaken Indian Woman'

Similitude in dissimilitude might be called the logic of translation itself. It is at the heart of Wordsworth's one-and-only attempt in *Lyrical Ballads* to represent the *pensée sauvage* of an unambiguously foreign individual: 'The Complaint of a Forsaken Indian Woman'. Such a 'primitive' characterization, from a position of near-total ignorance of such a woman's cultural life, was inevitably patronizing and fantastical for all its sympathy. As if troubled by its dubiousness, Wordsworth never repeated such an experiment again. But the poem is important as a bridge to Wordsworth's more culturally ambiguous figures like 'The Mad Mother'. And the poem has a striking reflexivity, an in-built awareness of its own epistemological blind-spots as an act of translation from travel literature. If it attempts to move from the culturally specific to the 'human', this is because its protagonist has been thrown into a situation in which a social *habitus* has broken down – a contemporary state of nature.

As Alan Bewell points out, the poem has been unfairly denigrated as 'an exercise in primitivist sentimentalism'.[66] But it has not been noted that clear textual parallels show the poem to have been precisely the revision of such an exercise: Coleridge's 'Lewti, Or The Circassian Love Chant', which was withdrawn from the first edition of *Lyrical Ballads* while it was in the press[67] (itself a reworking of Wordsworth's adolescent 'Beauty and Moonlight'). Coleridge's original setting was American ('The Wild Indian's Love Chaunt'), only to be changed in the final draft to the more unusual Circassian habitation. Though 'The Complaint' strongly resembles 'Lewti' in both imagery and versification,[68] it subtly resists the latter's culturally interchangeable sentiment, as well as an ornamental exotic clothing that could be swapped with little fuss from the American to Circassian. By contrast, 'The Complaint' foregrounds the problem of translation even as it searches for 'similitude'.

'The Complaint' eschews not only the simple pathos of unrequited love in 'Lewti', but also the stoic heroism of its other forebear in sentimental exoticism, the immensely popular eighteenth-century tradition of 'dying Indian' songs.[69] Reports of the American Indian 'death song' – the heroic defiance of a captive being tortured to death – had troubled European observers with its violence and cruelty, even as this poetry's stoic devotion to the tribe appealed to a strand of martial republicanism in Adam

Ferguson and Smith, among others, that vied with their economic and cultural progressivism.[70] Its exotic dissimilitude and heroic pathos compelled widespread imitation both in America and across Europe.[71] The two final stanzas of the 'Death-Song of a Cherokee Indian' demonstrate the key features of the genre:

> Remember the wood where in ambush we lay,
> And the scalps which we bore from your nation away.
> Now the flame rises fast, – you exult in my pain;
> But the son of Alknomook can never complain.
>
> I go to the land where my father is gone;
> His ghost shall rejoice in the fame of his son.
> Death comes like a friend, he relieves me from pain:
> And thy son, o Alknomook, has scorn'd to complain.[72]

The dying warrior affirmed his self-identity through a line of heroic deeds tied to his patrilineal name and descent. Writing of Montaigne's account of the Amerindian 'death song' in his famous essay 'On Cannibals', Michel de Certeau has argued that this 'savage ethic of speech', an expression of the whole social group as it survives the perishable body, corresponded to the absence of referent, the 'impossible Word' of the other, in the Western literate discourse that attempted to transcribe it. It is a 'lost-body writing'.[73]

'The Complaint', as its very title indicates, was to present a strikingly different kind of death song. The heroic affirmation of the patriarchal tribe has faded into the lament of a solitary woman. Yet the Preface's gloss on the poem did not identify the woman by culture or gender at all. 'The Complaint' was an effort at 'accompanying the last struggles of a human being at the approach of death, cleaving in solitude to life and society'.[74] As with the masculine death song, here too the dying body clings to the social group – but the independent life of the body is not so easily surrendered. The poem demonstrates how 'life and society' both separate and fall into conjunction. But in the epigraph Wordsworth attached to the poem, this death was located in a sharply particular ethnographic context, drawing on another forbidding American custom. Its source was a travel narrative, Samuel Hearne's *Journey from Hudson Bay*,[75] which had condemned the nomadic 'Northern Indian' (Canadian) practice of abandoning those too ill to keep travelling in the very strongest terms: 'A custom apparently so unnatural is perhaps not to be found among any other of the human race.'[76] Yet this practice was a particularly striking instance of what made the social in general so troubling for Wordsworth: a sacrifice of the individual on behalf of the collective. And having been cast out of the tribe into a contemporary state of nature, Wordsworth's 'forsaken Indian woman' has been exposed to the very limits of the social: the isolation of a mortal body confronted by material nature and death. Hearne's description had made no attempt to enter into the abandoned woman's interior state – here was the gap in knowledge, the lost body, that both licensed and problematized Wordsworth's poetic translation.

Along with the 'death song', this was a custom that appeared to support a widespread European argument that – on the contrary to expressivist primitivism – the 'savage' was distinguished from the 'civilized' by a distinct lack of sensibility. John Millar argued that the survival imperatives of the hunting existence subdued the domestic affections, hence explaining the Indian male's supposedly low regard for women.[77] Millar's *Origin of Ranks* (1771) – alongside historiographies like William Alexander's *History of Women* (1779) and John Adams' *Woman* (1790) – would even consider the estimation of women to be a main teleological force behind the 'progress of refinement'. As luxury, property and entertainment gain in importance, so the status of women rises accordingly. Their influence softens male aggression, and the desire for female approval is a motive to industry, as the warrior male becomes feminized into the man of commerce.[78] Hearne's travel narrative was punctuated with outrage at the Indian male's treatment of women. Jonathan Carver, however, while declaring that the Indian male felt only 'Stoic indifference' on returning to his wife and family after a long absence, nevertheless affirmed that this did 'not proceed from an entire suppression of the natural affections for, notwithstanding that they are esteemed savages, I never saw among any other people greater proofs of parental or filial tenderness'.[79] To emphasize such 'natural affections', Wordsworth would add a detail missing in Hearne's description: the woman is a mother, separated by the custom from her child as well as tribe. Adam Smith's *Theory of Moral Sentiments* had argued for a new balance of 'civilized' sensibility *and* republican stoicism, with the death song forming an extreme type of the latter.[80] Wordsworth's Indian woman would conjoin these antinomies in a strikingly different way.

The poem does, however, begin with a longing for, if not the achievement of, a lost-body writing: 'Before I see another day, / Oh let my body die away!' (1–2). The sentiment is reinforced by its verbatim repetition at the end of the stanza (9–10) in a song-like refrain. The poem is connected to the forms of oral poetry not only through refrains, but through parallelism, short and long lines like modulations of breath, the piling up of appositions, and the rhyming of end-stopped lines. But this 'similitude' between poem and song is then undercut by the dissimilar counterpoint of another kind of music or noise: the strange natural phenomenon that is the sound of the northern lights (the epigraph claims Hearne as its authority here). In her dreams, the woman recalls that, synaesthetically, she 'saw' the 'crackling flashes drive' (6). In the epigraph, the lights make 'a rustling and a crackling noise', while in the 1820 edition the 'crackling flashes' have become a 'rustling conflict'. The lights entered 'among my dreams' (4), just as their crackling or rustling will imperceptibly murmur through the rest of the poem. This sets up the initial reference point for a train of similitude in dissimilitude: a rustling that both evokes and makes newly strange the stock poetic cliché of fluttering leaves in the wind, with a crackling that anticipates and contrasts with the extinct fire of the following stanza. The poem is driven by an anguished and baffled effort to translate this enigmatic language.

The rustling conflict is in echo and counterpoint with the fluctuating pulse of the woman's own thoughts and feelings. The Preface to *Lyrical Ballads* would claim for the poem only the status of faithfully representing an oscillating stillness that was unable to progress: 'the fluxes and refluxes of the mind when agitated by the great and simple affections of our nature'.[81] As with 'similitude in dissimilitude', this is not a formalizable dialectic or logic, but an unpredictable relationship in flux. Generated by shock or agitation, it is mimetically closer than dialectic to the ebb and flow, or buffeting counter-forces of matter in its motion, as at the Simplon Pass: 'Winds thwarting winds, bewilder'd and forlorn' (*Pr.* VI.560). In the Preface, 'language and the human mind' are not one and the same, but 'act and re-act on each other'.[82] What Hazlitt called poetry's lost-body 'music of language, answering to the music of the mind',[83] is shown to depend in its movements upon the friction and resistance of a material and bodily nature.

The conflict is only hinted at in the first stanza. Despite being framed by the expression of a longing for death, the stanza also includes a shock of awakening, literally a waking up from sleep, that is perhaps more than simply gentle: 'And yet I am alive' (8). The shock is measured by a caesura through an ambiguous pause at the end of the line: the regular four-beat pattern has been abruptly truncated into a three-beat measure.[84] That interruption of metre, the shock by which a social contract is broken, reinforces the woman's solitude. It is the suffering as well as jubilation of feeling 'alive', a cry within a contracted space. The woman's 'detachment'[85] is not Smith's equilibrium of stoicism and sympathy, but a 'steady look at the subject': the flux and reflux of a sense of life, and the expressionless complaint of staring at its loss.

The poem's second stanza presents that fluctuation more starkly:

> My fire is dead: it knew no pain;
> Yet is it dead, and I remain.
> All stiff with ice the ashes lie;
> And they are dead, and I will die.
> (*LB* 11–14)

In what is anything but a confidently pantheistic vitalism, an affinity between the material and the living is weighed in the balance of a reversible 'similitude in dissimilitude'. The fire as much as the woman is marked by transience and mortality; in its dissimilitude, it can die without feeling pain – but through an uncanny similarity, its flickering warmth was once undeniably living. With a monosyllabic stiffening of rhythm, the shock of ashes 'stiff with ice' anticipates the lost body in its frozen rigor mortis. The parallel clauses are in opposition more than apposition. 'I remain' and 'I will die' stand as undecidable alternatives on the other side of a caesura marked by the 'dead'. Wordsworth was no doubt recollecting what Hearne, a highly prejudiced and unreliable narrator, had written of the 'Northern Indians': 'I never found any of them that had the least notion of futurity.'[86]

The following stanzas set up a new arena of conflicting impulses: the woman's longing to be restored to the social, a sense of her total solitude as a living death, and a muted protest against the group for its abandonment of her. The woman partly remonstrates against her tribe – 'Alas! you might have dragged me on / Another day, a single one!' (21–2) – while acknowledging that it was at her request, in agony, that she was left in the forest. Wordsworth, unlike Hearne, is careful not to demonize the Indians. But the woman claims a bitter irony – she is now 'strong and without pain' (29). Yet this is also to draw her closer in 'similitude' to the fire's death with 'no pain'.

In the fourth stanza, she remembers being severed not only from the tribe, but also from her own infant child, now passed to another mother for fostering:

> When from my arms my babe they took
> On me how strangely did he look!
> Through his whole body something ran,
> A most strange something did I see;
> As if he strove to be a man
> (33–7)

The child's struggle to emulate the father – an impossible effort that ironically recalls the identification with the father's name in the warrior death song – is an example of mimetic behaviour at its most social: the copying of a public role. The 'Immortality Ode' would invoke the child's 'endless imitation' (*P2V* 107) of adult behaviour – 'the little Actor cons another part' (102). In that poem, it is a joyous and playful reorientation of the child's mimetic responses to its environment, ominously unaware that this marks the beginning of a deadly conformism, the 'prison-house' (67) of social immanence that will enclose the adult. In 'The Complaint', the infant has been pushed into that stage prematurely. But through its very failure, the mimetic strain of translating the foreign is what releases a 'most strange something'. It 'ran' through the child's body, like the rising of affective energy through music. The mother and her child, as much as Wordsworth, are engaged in the difficulty of translating another's subjectivity – even that of one's own son or father.

In the next stanza, the woman's reproaches to her tribe indirectly attest to its denial of her voice as an individual – and also, it is perhaps implied, as a woman:

> Oh wind that o'er my head art flying,
> The way my friends their course did bend,
> I should not feel the pain of dying,
> Could I with thee a message send.
> Too soon, my friends, you went away;
> For I had many things to say.
>
> (45–50)

Unlike the warrior male, she has no audience for a 'message' or death song on dying. If the wind bears a 'similitude' to the Indian caravan in its flight, it is also shown in its dissimilitude as a medium – for all its ghostly language, it can carry no human message. And that message is also withheld from us. The poem now acknowledges that the woman's subjectivity, the lacuna that Hearne had left open for projection, has only been partially covered over. What Bewell calls the woman's social 'epitaph'[87] is indirectly acknowledged in its cultural 'dissimilitude' to be inaccessibly remote to the European reader. As with the 'timely utterance' that gives 'relief' (23) to Wordsworth in the 'Intimations Ode', the consoling word of a lost-body writing has not been granted to us. We know only that the woman 'had many things to say'. While the warrior yoked a set of heroic exploits to the single patronymic, here what might represent a life is evoked only as a plural configuration of 'many things'. The poem's 'message' remains an enigma. A silence conditions its rustling and agitated music.

The first person narration means that in the final stanza the woman's end is also left suspended – we do not see her die. But while earlier she had affirmed her revived strength, now she acknowledges what seems like her impending demise:

> My journey will be shortly run,
> I shall not see another sun,
> I cannot lift my limbs to know
> If they have any life or no.
>
> (61–4)

Even here, there is an acknowledgement of not knowing, of not being able confidently to translate even the feeling, or its absence, of what is most intimate of all – one's own body. The numbness of her limbs may yet conceal a revival of immanent life. The encroaching loss of feeling, withdrawing from the extremities and rising upwards – reminiscent of the poisoned Socrates' spreading numbness in the *Phaedo* – is close to a negative image of that 'most strange something' as it runs through the excited body. For Adam Ferguson, the warrior death song was the achievement of a 'rising above' the body through its concentration upon a single idea.[88] Here, a withdrawal of conscious attention from the body is only an accident of somatic estrangement. It is a part of the poem's discretion that this is not claimed as an intimation of transcended embodiment.

The poem ends with the woman claiming that she might die happily were she to have her son 'close' to her again (65–8). If the social cannot avert death, the intimacy of its presence, if only through kinship, might nevertheless make all the difference to its terrible solitude. But in the isolation that the social has conditioned here – not the heroic appropriation of an individuating 'being-towards-death' but the woman's forced reduction to a monadic loneliness – another form of assembly has been adumbrated by the poem: a commonwealth of song that speaks through, not against, an individual voice.

'Of these was neither, and was both at once'

Brennan O'Donnell has observed some of the structural and thematic correspondences that link 'The Complaint' with 'The Mad Mother' and 'The Last of the Flock', to suggest that they form a kind of set. All three are composed of ten-line stanzas, with similar rhyme schemes; all treat of parental love and emotional distress 'in direct speech'; all involve protagonists who are culturally distanced from the reader.[89] But 'The Complaint' is also different, mediating Wordsworth's transition towards an entirely new genre: the song of an exotic figure transplanted into England, hybridized with the rustic (and archaic) ballad, in a state of suffering that gives rise to a new self-consciousness. Such a mutual transformation of the primitive and the modern, the local and the foreign, was a focus for the aspirations of *Lyrical Ballads* as a whole.

Poems like 'The Female Vagrant' had shown the corrosive effects at a local level of economic crisis, the centralization of land ownership, imperial war and colonial settlement. Individuals were uprooted from communities and Europeans were taken to, and non-Europeans taken from, the colonies in increasing numbers. Such individuals, as they fell out of, or in between, familiar cultural moorings, the victims of an incipient globalization, presented the contemporary state of nature in a markedly colonial light. Alone among his contemporaries, Wordsworth set out to write the songs of these hybridized individuals. The nearest precedent was perhaps Robert Southey's 1797 *Botany Bay Eclogues*, political satires that took the viewpoint of the transported English in Australia. What captured Wordsworth's imagination, however, was the reverse: the exotic figure translated into rural England. This might take the form even of a purely figurative 'similitude in dissimilitude', as in 'The Last of the Flock', in which a West Country shepherd, forced to sell his property, the basis of his self-identity, appears uncannily outlandish. A supposedly 'primitive' extroversion of grief emerges in apparently the least likely of places, pastoral England:

> In distant countries have I been,
> And yet I have not often seen
> A healthy man, a man full grown,
> Weep in the public roads, alone.
> (*LB* 1–4)

That figure becomes considerably ironic when placed alongside Wordsworth's later suspicion in the poem 'Beggars', in which a gypsy, herself a hybridized 'Egyptian brown', speaks of misery that 'on our English land . . . could never be' (*P2V* 15–16) – a complacency that perhaps itself cannot be taken at face value.

Just as the 'Forsaken Indian Woman' – like the Solitary Reaper and Discharged Soldier – remained nameless, so almost none of Wordsworth's hybrid and uncanny figures is granted the secure individuation, and cultural locus, of a proper name. In the poem 'Ruth', in striking contrast to the eponymous English heroine, the 'Youth from Georgia's Shore' (*LB* 13), who has lived among the Indians, is said to have 'spake the English tongue' and to have 'a soldier's name' (20–1) – but we are not told what it is. The unnamed 'Mad Mother' is said to have come to England 'far from over the main' (*LB* 4), and yet her speech 'is in the English tongue' (10). As O'Donnell indicates,[90] the poem alludes at several points to a minstrel ballad, 'Lady Bothwell's Lament', while employing a non-ballad metre and stanzaic form. The poem is located somewhere between genres, as well as places and languages. As its very term suggests, the 'lyrical ballad' was an inherently hybridized form. The woman's knowledge of forest lore, including how to build 'an Indian bower', would seem to identify her as an American Indian woman that an Englishman has seduced and brought back from the colonies. But if so, she has grown estranged from her culture to the extent even of losing her own language; she has been not only abandoned by her husband, but also rejected by the local community, whose 'taunts' (71) hold her child to be illegitimate – and whose prejudice is presumably behind her exclamation, 'And what if my poor cheek be brown?' (68). The collapse of all her social relationships, above all the desertion of love, has induced a mental breakdown, and it is only that barest social unit, the mother–infant dyad, that is able to sustain her. As if it were incredible that there should be an English-speaking American Indian woman living as a vagrant in the West Country, Wordsworth would later emphasize that he had first-hand evidence of her through 'a lady of Bristol who had seen the poor creature'.[91]

Within the poem itself, however, the narrator's introduction had worked to distance the figure from any empirical prototype:

> The sun has burnt her coal-black hair;
> Her eyebrows have a rusty stain
>
> (2–3)

Her physical identity as an American has become blurred through her exposure as a vagrant in the English countryside – as if, fantastically, it is by catching fire from the sun's rays that the woman has gained a 'Red Indian' pigmentation, albeit a colour scorched through only her eyebrows and possibly hair. It is an irruption of the *lyrical* within the ballad. The distance of a social context that has now been irrevocably lost can be recalled only through this most oblique citation. As Wordsworth wrote of the poem in an 1836 letter to John Kenyon:

> [she is] either of these Islands, or a North American. On the latter supposition, while the distance removes her from us, the fact of her speaking our language brings us at once into close sympathy with her.[92]

Cultural distance and linguistic proximity make her a figure of 'similitude in dissimilitude'. Even Wordsworth was unsure of her origin. She is both American Indian *and* English, yet also *neither* – as in the dream-logic of Book v of *The Prelude*, whose errant figure (also nameless) appears to be both an Arab and Don Quixote: 'Of these was neither, and was both at once' (126). Similarly, the 'leech-gatherer' of 'Resolution and Independence' speaks only '*Like* grave Livers' (*P2V* 104) in Scotland (my emphasis) – this may or may not be his cultural background. Without a rooted identity, he is also uncannily 'Like a man from some far region sent' to admonish Wordsworth (118) – a figure of the exotic as it recedes into the transcendent.

For all his later attempts to reconcile the individual, community and empire, it was Wordsworth's exploration of this border territory – on the model of the Lakes as a 'primitive' boundary between England and Scotland – that was haunted by the oblique signs of a new world. In *Lyrical Ballads*, the inhabitants of Wordsworth's empire are the homeless, the solitary, the insane, the bereaved, the abandoned and the dispossessed, all those without identity, citizenship or nation-state. Theirs was the vox populi of social suffering, a fragmentation of cultures, and loss of tradition. To the extent that they can communicate, can translate the foreign into 'the English tongue', they represent that fragile commensurability between cultures that is necessary for any kind of hybrid interchange to occur at all. And as with the 'Mad Mother', their lyricism is a defiance of fate:

> And I am happy when I sing
> Full many a sad and doleful thing
> (13–14)

It is a fugitive happiness in what remains only the partial eclipse of a binding context or theme. Yet insofar as a similitude in dissimilitude draws us closer to that 'most strange something', the breakdown of secure cultural identity might yet offer genuine commonwealth instead of madness.

CHAPTER 6

'Man working for himself'

In Book II of *The Prelude*, the developing 'infant babe' becomes a 'creator and receiver both' (273). Its work is to translate and invent the world in a state of attuned mimesis: 'Working but in alliance with the works / Which it beholds' (274–5). There is no escape from work, it might seem, even in infant perception. Its building of affinities or physiognomies is not merely 'writing' or construction – nor is it simply received, flatly 'out there'. Creation and reception place the cognitive or working subject *in medias res*, caught up in an entanglement to be made conscious, worked through, not 'abated and suppress'd'. Production and consumption have yet to be split, for the infant, into the poles of labour and leisure. What is perceived is 'works' – with their own history of creation. They have activity embedded within them. The child works not *upon* the world, but in alliance *with* it. A potential activity within the created 'works' is drawn out and made actual: the child becomes 'An inmate of this *active* universe' (266). As the child works effortlessly in alliance with the material, such work is not unilateral, but a relationship of flux and reflux. It becomes, without any kind of pseudo-animation, an *intersubjective* partnership. And like any relationship, it also has the potential to break down.

Yet the child does not *try* to do anything in what is a form of play as much as a 'tenacious' labour of love. Its work is as much inactive as efficacious, a driven though unconscious shaping of intuition. The child, in a sense, is completely idle. This is both the harbinger of adult labour, perceptual and physical, and something that has been 'suppress'd' – hence, ever liable to return, even in the most ordinary behaviour. It is not simply utopian, then, but a comportment that, in uncanny, varying and unstable, dejected, lifeless and vitally transported ways, is in actuality always still with us – at the same time as it has been lost. It is against this ontogenetic state of working nature that Wordsworth's efforts poetically to translate an adult labour must be measured.

In the second half of the eighteenth century, the schism between production and consumption, or creation and reception, was played out between rival pioneers of social science. While theories of the state of nature had posited a uniform human nature, attention began to shift to determining bases of human activity that could account for widespread cultural differences. In 1748, Montesquieu's *Spirit of the Laws* had placed the emphasis squarely on reception: the effects of differing climates and geographies, passively absorbed, led to corresponding manners, which in turn created differing institutions and laws.[1] From the 1760s, however, the political economies of Turgot and Adam Smith upheld a new paradigm of cultural difference: now the explanatory principle was firmly that of labour and production. Their 'four-stage' or 'stadial' theory, systematized by numerous thinkers of the Scottish Enlightenment, was to map the unilinear progress of global history as it developed from a hunting stage to pasturage and then to agriculture, peaking with the industrial commerce of contemporary Europe. The theory received its most thoroughgoing exposition in John Millar's *Origin of Ranks* (1771), whose overriding stress upon the economic base as the foundation of culture was hailed by the Marxian economist Ronald L. Meek as a discovery of the 'great master-principle', giving birth to the first fully 'materialist conception of history'.[2] The 'base–superstructure' theorem, the notion that history is driven 'in the last instance' by material rather than cultural factors, that work is the anthropological definition of the tool-using human 'species-being' – all these *doxa* of economism and productivist ontology, Marxian or otherwise, were anticipated by four-stage theory. For Adam Ferguson, 'improvement' was an anthropological 'force, [that] like the power of a spring, silently presses on every resistance'.[3] Humanity is defined by labour and invention: 'art itself is natural to man'.[4] The state of nature is a state of work.[5]

Certainly, by the mid-1810s, Wordsworth had partly internalized this schema; the River Duddon sonnets do indeed plot history according to the four stages of the Scottish Enlightenment. Already in the Preface to *Lyrical Ballads*, Jon P. Klancher has perceived the sketch of a 'historical materialist' understanding of taste in its account of the cultural transformation wrought by urban industrialism:[6]

> the great national events which are daily taking place, and the increasing accumulation of men in cities, where the uniformity of their occupations produces a craving for extraordinary incident which the rapid communication of intelligence hourly gratifies.[7]

This is undoubtedly a historical account, but it is not exclusively materialist; Wordsworth attributes the change in public taste to 'a multitude of causes, unknown to former times'.[8] The welter of influences includes the environmental (the city), the demographic (an urbanizing population), the political event, the media of public communication, *and* a 'stadial' emphasis on 'occupation' (of which the factory work drawing rural labourers to the towns was perhaps the most 'uniform' of all). Yet it is a plurality, for Wordsworth, that is monistic in effect: 'acting with a combined force to blunt the discriminating powers of the mind'.[9] Wordsworth's hope is to counterpose this with something 'indestructible': 'certain inherent and indestructible qualities of the human mind, and likewise of certain powers in the great and permanent objects that act upon it'.[10] In an indiscriminate world that task is a historical and critical one – an ignition of 'qualities' and 'powers'.

The urban culture of uniform production and narcotic consumption, with its incessant flow of information, has become a 'tendency of life and manners'.[11] Mark Salber Phillips has observed that there is hardly a more eighteenth-century phrase than 'manners and customs'.[12] He argues that Enlightenment historiography was characterized by a new focus upon the 'social' or 'civil society' rather than politics – the domain of everyday manners, as well as trade, sociability and art. This sphere was now considered to be the real motor of long-term change. Phillips points out that 'manners' were also important to the Scottish Enlightenment, and not just labour conditions and property relations.[13] Even Meek admits that John Millar noted the occasional survival of manners despite economic change, and conceded an important, though subordinate, role to climate in influencing the constitution of peoples.[14] Phillips suggests that Millar could pay an equal attention to manners and the economy because he 'wrote . . . at a time when there was no pressure to choose between materialist and cultural explanations'.[15]

In the wake of the French Revolution, Wordsworth's hopes for change underwent a similar reorientation from the political to the social. It remained a governing contradiction: an increasingly conservative political stance was coupled with a radical view of society's inner potential. A hope of 'good to come' became something that must be 'sought' or read within a physiognomy of everyday life:

> The promise of the present time retired
> Into its true proportion; sanguine schemes,
> Ambitious virtues, pleased me less, I sought
> For good in the familiar face of life
> And built thereon my hopes of good to come.
> (*Pr.* XII. 64–8)

Wordsworth had become less pleased, if not wholly displeased, by the 'sanguine' over-optimism of ambitiously scheming programmes. The problem with such a politics is that it must be enforced from the top-down, not rise from the base upwards:

> in the men
> Who thrust themselves upon this passive world
> As Rulers of the world, to see in these,
> Even when the public welfare is their aim,
> Plans without thought, or bottom'd on false thought
> And false philosophy
>
> (71–6)

The falsity of such 'Rulers', or committees of public safety, is not a consequence of being too theoretical, as Burke and other conservatives had argued. It is that their plans are not philosophical at all – 'without thought' – or grounded ('bottom'd') in a *false* philosophy. The political superstructure has misunderstood the base itself. The Jacobin revolution had been false because the 'world' was wrongly conceived as 'passive' from the start. A true politics demands a true philosophy.

A thrusting of the political scheme upon a passive base corresponded to a social division into 'cultural' and 'material' levels: what Wordsworth, in the serious whimsy of 'To the Spade of a Friend' (*c.*1806), would call 'The labouring many and the resting few' (*P2V* 8). Wordsworth's friend, Thomas Wilkinson, is singled out as a bridge across that divide, one 'Whose life combines the best of high and low' (7). He is both a gentleman agriculturalist and a subsistence farmer, working alone with the spade rather than the plough. This man of 'elegant enjoyments' (11) also hears 'the Poet sing / In concord with his river murmuring by' (13–14). It is, of course, only a wish-image of reconciliation: it was Wilkinson who first took culinary enjoyment, clearly bordering on touristic exploitation, from the mellifluous hard labour of 'The Solitary Reaper'. But while the privileged Wilkinson can only hear the poet singing from a distance, and the reaper's song is only an accompaniment to her labour's repetitive rhythm, Wordsworth's project was at once deeper, more radical and more quixotically extravagant. His poetics aims not only to locate the forms of labour within poetry, but the poetry that might be 'indestructible' within labour itself. That effort, of course, was fraught with idealization and denial – but it is also what makes such images so uncanny and disturbing, the hallmark of something suppressed, struggling to achieve full consciousness. And the project had its own tradition. Earlier eighteenth-century Georgic verse had reworked

Virgil's pun on the *versus* as both the poetic line and the ploughman's furrow.[16] Wordsworth wanted to be, as he wrote of Robert Burns, a poet who 'walked . . . Behind his plough' ('Resolution and Independence', 45–6), if only in his ambulatory mode of composition. Hazlitt recalled that 'Wordsworth always wrote (if he could) walking up and down a straight gravel-walk, or in some spot where the continuity of his verse met with no collateral interruption.'[17] Moments of 'collateral interruption', however, are just what distinguish Wordsworth's poetics of the line from the flattening effects of a productivist labour. Wordsworth's search is for those forms of immanent experience that must inevitably leap into a speculative claim on behalf of transcendence. At such moments for Wordsworth, the cultural becomes a cognitive attempt to know and express the *life* of the material.

Industry

Book XII of *The Prelude*, as Phillip Connell is perhaps the only critic to acknowledge,[18] has been quite remarkably neglected. For in Book XII Wordsworth explicitly claims that the major social goal of his verse is nothing less than a critique of political economy. Book XII takes its point of departure, through an allusion to *The Wealth of Nations*, from the 'classical' economic theory of Adam Smith, probably the first proponent of stadial theory.[19] Smith is here singled out as the arch-embodiment of 'false philosophy'. More than just manners, it was 'solid life' that negated Smith's anthropology:

> having brought to the test
> Of solid life and true result the Books
> Of modern Statists, and thereby perceiv'd
> The utter hollowness of what we name
> The wealth of Nations, where alone that wealth
> Is lodged, and how encreased, and having gain'd
> A more judicious knowledge of what makes
> The dignity of individual Man,
> Of Man no composition of the thought,
> Abstraction, shadow, image, but the man
> Of whom we read, the man whom we behold
> With our own eyes
>
> (76–87)

It is hard to conceive of a more shocking and radical statement. It is close to Rousseau in its social iconoclasm. The dramatic increase in social wealth that Smith's painstaking structural analysis had related to the state and market economy, with its division of labour, new industries and international trade, is utterly worthless and hollow. The whole planet of globalization, in the face of a single man, falls into crisis and crashes down. Wordsworth appeals to the bearer of rights – without mentioning their 'Abstraction', for he would be more concretely 'judicious' than the Statists – the 'dignity of individual man'. It is Wordsworth's physiognomic reading of familiar life, so he claims, beheld with his own eyes, that has performed the critique of political economy. Its abstract indices of growth mean nothing face-to-face with the living and working individual. What is required is a form of philosophical travel, a comparative fieldwork of the workplace itself, in contradistinction to the armchair synthesis (the 'composition of the thought' and its *Homo œconomicus*) that is the work of the moral philosopher. Wordsworth goes so far as to boast that his meetings with vagabonds and the labouring poor on 'the public road' have been invested with the 'grandeur' of the tropical explorer, the 'Mariner' and 'Wanderers of the Earth' (145–60). What this experience has brought about is no less than a critique of value itself – 'where alone that wealth / Is lodged, and how encreased'. Long before the Ricardian socialists, let alone Marx, Wordsworth had undertaken his own *Wertkritik*. Value is not just somewhere other than where the political economists think it is, but it can actually, as much as accumulated and reinvested capital, be 'encreased'.[20]

If Smith had allowed space for 'manners', nevertheless in his 1762–3 Glasgow lectures the notion that modes of subsistence were all-determining was certainly presented as an angle of perspective: 'in a certain view of things all the arts, the sciences, law and government, wisdom and even virtue itself tend all to this one thing, the providing meat, drink, rayment and lodging for men'.[21] Yet a 'certain view' risks eclipsing all others. The problem remains in *The Wealth of Nations*, where economics becomes the royal road to fulfilling Smith's definition of moral philosophy as an inquiry as to 'wherein consisted the happiness and perfection of a man, considered not only as an individual, but as the member of a family, of a state, and of the great society of mankind'.[22] Society here is constituted not by politics, religion, civil society or even 'moral sentiments', but solely by an exchange of the products of labour. Far from an independent 'dignity of individual man', Smith describes a society of producers wholly reliant on the social exchange of divided labour, a national and global network of interdependence: 'Every man thus lives by exchanging', for the 'far greater part' of 'a man's wants' are supplied 'by exchanging that surplus part of the produce of his own labour, which is over and above his own consumption, for such parts of the produce of other men's labour as he has occasion for'.[23] In terms that Marx took over from Smith, 'value in use' is manufactured for the sake of its 'value in exchange'.

What for Mandeville was the 'private vice' of self-interest, indirect in its 'public benefits', now becomes both private and public virtue: 'capital has been silently and gradually accumulated by the private frugality and good conduct of individuals . . . to better their condition. It is this effort . . . which has maintained the progress of England towards opulence and improvement.'[24] It is the market's 'invisible hand' that redistributes the primitive accumulation of the frugal individual. It is this new anthropomorphism, this new Leviathan, not the miserly capitalist, that holds 'virtue' in its hands. Even Smith's earlier *Theory of Moral Sentiments*, while arguing for 'sympathy' as the social nexus, had affirmed the new state of estrangement: 'Society may subsist among different men, as among different merchants, from a sense of its utility, without any mutual love or affection; and though no man in it should owe any obligation, or be bound in gratitude to any other, it may still be upheld by a mercenary exchange of good offices according to an agreed valuation.'[25]

The wage-labourer's 'good office' was no more than an individual *sacrifice*: 'he must always lay down the same portion of his ease, his liberty, and his happiness' – a regularly quantified and ever-same alienation of the free time of leisure.[26] Ill at ease, in chains and unhappy, labour has no value in itself, but only in exchange. In his 'Letter to the Authors of the Edinburgh Review' (1755), Smith attacked Rousseau by claiming that the *Discourse on Inequality*, 'intending to paint the savage life as the happiest of any, presents only the indolent side of it to view'.[27] Smith's unhappy view of labour – an unvoiced longing for happy indolence – went back to the state of nature. He had no qualms in projecting the measurement of value by sacrificed time – bringing portions of time as well as objects into abstract equivalence – all the way back to the earliest hunting stage: 'If among a nation of hunters, for example, it usually costs twice the labour to kill a beaver which it does to kill a deer, one beaver should naturally exchange for or be worth two deer.'[28] It is an evacuation of space as well as time: place is reduced to an exchange of hunting domains.

But Smith was not unaware of the division of labour's challenge to the 'dignity of individual man':

> The man whose whole life is spent in performing a few simple operations . . . has no occasion to exert his understanding, or to exercise his invention in finding out expedients for removing difficulties which never

> occur . . . and generally becomes as stupid or ignorant as it is possible for a human creature to become . . . this is the state into which the labouring poor, that is, the great body of the people, must necessarily fall, unless government takes some pains to prevent it.[29]

The 'invisible hand' demands state intervention. In *The Excursion*, Wordsworth would also call for a scheme of national education. Smith's 'great body of the people' had by 1814 become perceptible as 'A savage Horde among the civilised', a 'servile Band among the lordly free!' (IX.308–9). At the level of consumption rather than production, the Preface to *Lyrical Ballads* had already condemned the 'almost savage torpor' induced by a sensationalist culture, including the higher-class as well as servant consumers of 'frantic novels', 'sickly and stupid German tragedies' and 'extravagant' verse, as a cultural decline that had arisen, in part, from 'uniform occupations'.[30] What is '*almost* savage' here – Wordsworth is prejudiced enough to make the distinction – was a craving for relief from sheer boredom.

The burgeoning proletariat – and the commodification of taste – was a secret double of the 'savage' as a conceptual persona. Rousseau's *bon sauvage* was the reverse image of what Meek has called the 'ignoble savage' of the Enlightenment.[31] What Smith assigned to industrial production was ascribed by Montesquieuan environmental determinism to the 'savage'. Buffon's *Natural History* (1749) judged the American Indian to be 'no more than an animal of the first order', weakened by a harsh climate: 'the activity of his body is less an exercise or voluntary movement than an automatic reaction to his needs; take from him hunger and thirst, and you will destroy at the same time the active cause of his movements; he will remain either standing there stupidly or recumbent for days on end'.[32] The 'savage' automaton was a projection from the machine: La Mettrie's *L'homme machine* (1748). The fiction of savage life as a 'bare minimum' corresponded to the *stricte nécessaire* of wage subsistence, the minimum wage to sustain life and the reproduction of labour while maximizing profit.[33] Agamben's 'bare life' must be tied to the figure of the 'mere worker'.

On their Scottish tour of 1803, Dorothy recorded how she, William and Coleridge had stumbled upon 'a large machine or lever' for lifting water from a mine: 'it seemed to have made the first step from brute matter to life and purpose . . . William made a remark to this effect, and Coleridge observed that it was like a giant with one idea'.[34] Industrialization and its mechanical world-view was the real savagery. But this isolated

Watt steam engine, in its own unique idiom, speaks the language of a contemporary state of suffering nature, with even a caesura to catch its breath: 'It heaved upwards once in half a minute with a slow motion, and seemed to rest to take breath, its motion being accompanied with a sound between a groan and a *jike*.'[35] Not just the labourer and the American Indian as savagely desiring machines, but even the Cyclopean and robotic engine itself, belonged to that 'Abstraction, shadow, image' of sheer passivity, 'bottom'd on false thought', for which Wordsworth had attacked the 'Statists'.

In Book VIII of *The Excursion*, it is the factory and the state that practise a savage idolatry of human sacrifice:

> Within this temple – where is offered up
> To Gain – the Master Idol of the Realm,
> Perpetual sacrifice.
>
> (185–7)

There are no savage workers here, or any individuals at all – they have all been sacrificed. In this temple there is only 'never-resting Labour's eyes', the 'unnatural light' of the factory lamp, as it keeps shift-work going on around the clock (169–70). Progress has reverted to an archaic horror. The tone rises to a pitch of bitter irony: 'Economists will tell you that the State / Thrives by the forfeiture' (285–6). Political economy is a poetics of allegory: as with poetic diction, its Leviathan or Moloch relies on a 'personification of abstract ideas'.[36] The base is already contaminated by the superstructure of a state religion in disguise.

The Excursion does not reject industrial production altogether; it is a good thing in 'due proportion' to the 'Country's need' (215).[37] An inquiry into such 'proportion', 'need' and 'real worth', as opposed to idolatrous 'Gain' – now indifferent to the claims of the nation-state – had been announced in Book XII of *The Prelude*. Wordsworth asks of the Adamite 'dignity of individual man':

> Why is this glorious Creature to be found
> One only in ten thousand? What one is
> Why may not many be? What bars are thrown
> By nature in the way of such a hope?
> Our animal wants and the necessities
> Which they impose, are these the obstacle?
> If not; then others vanish into air.
> Such meditations bred an anxious wish
> To ascertain how much of real worth
> And genuine knowledge, and true power of mind

Did at this day exist in those who liv'd
By bodily labour, labour far exceeding
Their due proportion, under all the weight
Of that injustice which upon ourselves
By composition of society
Ourselves entail.

(90–105)

The logic of this passage is not quite easy to follow, and its gravity must be weighed carefully. It seems after all that only 'one in ten thousand' has the glorious 'dignity of individual man' – forcing us to wonder if Wordsworth has ever seen such a creature at all. We must take the claim on trust, for Wordsworth is quite adamant that at least 'one is', and so why not the 'many', the labouring multitude? There is some kind of 'bar' or 'obstacle' of 'nature', a stumbling-block, an original sin or natural state that stands in the way of progress. This may be an effect of the 'animal' urges in their necessity, an imposed and ineluctable automatism – though the question is left open. It may not be this at all – 'if not', then 'others', whatever these may be, though the plural suggests the 'bars', will 'vanish into air'. The obstacles do not exist, truly, if they are not an effect of natural necessity. They will be merely contingent and hence changeable. These 'meditations' without issue, and questions without answer, make Wordsworth 'anxious'; the dilemma seems insoluble.

This is the prompt for a more systematic inquiry into labour. Yet the question of natural necessity is now left abruptly hanging, and the focus becomes less to do with individual character and more internal to labour itself: the extent to which it is capable of 'real worth', 'genuine knowledge' and 'true power of mind'. The implication is that these are dignities that might remove or transform the natural 'bars' or 'obstacle' – a problem undecidably singular or plural – as counter-necessities or freedoms. Again it is an open question as to just how much virtue, if any at all, labour might contain. Wordsworth representations of 'bodily labour', it is announced, have the open-ended character of an experiment. But its working hypotheses are remarkable. Bodily labour, associated with the machine-animal and its 'necessities', might not only be creative of a 'real worth' beyond value-in-exchange. It might also have a cognitive import, a 'genuine knowledge' – not the 'false thought' of the 'Statists' – and show a 'true power' of mind as well as body. Manual labour, it seems, might be the most 'glorious' of all activities.

But it seems not, for here the passage turns again. What before was possibly or probably a natural 'obstacle' now seems in apposition to a social 'weight'. As with the factory, this is an excessive labour that is 'far' out of 'due proportion'. If labour has its own dignity, this has nothing to do with working all hours of the day. It needs to be drastically reduced, as much as possible – made proportionate only to what is duly required, a quantity that is left indeterminate.[38] The 'weight' bearing down upon the worker is a new obstacle or stumbling-block, a *scandalon*. It is the scandal of an outright social 'injustice'. Wordsworth does not just acknowledge his own complicity, but drags in his whole readership as well, all who live off such bodily labour without having to practise it themselves – 'we entail' it. It is an effect of the 'composition of society', the stratified division of labour, a weight that bears down also 'upon ourselves' – the weight of guilt. And one that determines the pressure of our own activities. Might this social weight, rather, be the 'bar' or 'obstacle' to Wordsworth's hopes for an individual dignity? Again, there is no answer. The solution might involve both nature *and* society – the problem of a contemporary state of nature.

In Book VII, Wordsworth had explicitly acknowledged the base–superstructure model of Enlightenment determinisms *and* the relative autonomy of the creative mind. He admitted of his famously transfigured vision of a 'blind beggar' in London that 'Though rear'd upon the base of outward things, / These, chiefly, are such structures as the mind / Builds for itself' (624–5). No statement better exposes the possibly scandalous discrepancy between an independent invention and the impoverished base upon which it builds. The project announced in Book XII, however, in potential all the more scandalously, seeks to locate such a 'true power of mind' within an indigent labour itself. While many critics have pointed to the supposedly 'mystified' labour and social relations in Wordsworth's aesthetics,[39] extraordinarily little attention has been paid to its obverse: a search for the forms of poetry within labour itself. At least in Book XII, that project is dedicated not to a glorification of manual labour, which must be reduced to its 'due proportion', but to the hope for a new kind of human being, and, by extension, a new form of labour, already present in embryo 'at this day'. If our work and understanding of the 'base' were to change, the whole superstructure might change with it – and yet the latter belongs to the very weight that blocks such a change. Both must change at once. This is the aporia that keeps Wordsworth's questions so open and unanswerable and yet salutary: what gives his project such a capacity to haunt.

The project inevitably conjures the troubling 'spectres of Marx': his now ghostly call to abolish 'the enslaving subordination of individuals to the division of labour, and thereby also the antithesis between mental and physical labour... [to bring about a condition in which] labour has become not only a means of life but life's prime want'.[40] Indeed, two recent accounts of Wordsworth's political economy have engaged with differing attempts at a radical rereading of Marx. Simon Jarvis has drawn on Michel Henry's phenomenology of affect as the true immediacy and basis of the self, and his argument that this is the source of what Marx called 'living labour'.[41] Henry's Marx is emphatically a philosopher of the 'dignity of individual man' as agent of praxis.[42] Far from being a 'petty bourgeois idyll' that must be supplanted by collectivist labour, individual praxis must be reclaimed from its alienation by the imposed social abstractions of class and productive forces. The exchange of the individual with nature, the basis of history prior to the secondary class struggle, must be won back from its estrangement by an interposing market exchange. Henry's Marx seeks a new society of material abundance and emancipated labour that will facilitate an 'opening up to nature, to the totality of beings... such that in this relationship beings are given to feeling, *become sensuous*'.[43]

Jarvis has drawn attention to an image of the living labour of affect in Wordsworth within social production itself. In an illuminating analysis of a passage from MS. B of *Home at Grasmere*, he shows how Wordsworth's 'materialism of the beautiful' links his aesthetic 'gifts / Of feeling' (*HG* 652–3) to the Grasmere peasantry's 'little boons of animating thought / That sweeten labour, make it seem and feel / To be no arbitrary weight imposed / But a glad function natural to man' (689–90). They are free gifts of love that nevertheless 'spring' from an intensity of pragmatic involvement, an apparent necessity of 'self-respecting interests' and an 'individual sense / Of anxiousness' (670–7). As such feelings 'refine the selfishness from which they spring' (675), this is 'to allow the gift to animate social exchange'.[44] Jarvis suggests that the passage works to question political economy's split between the absolutely self-interested donation of commerce – the offices of Smith's famous baker – and the absolute disinterest of private charity. The bars and obstacles of 'animal' necessity and self-interest are not necessarily in opposition to generosity. The gift of concrete labour already haunts the abstract labour of quantified time – it is from a labour in excess of what is strictly required, from the worker's ability to produce more than the capitalist has to pay to ensure the reproduction of that labour, that 'surplus value' is extracted.

The 'gifts of feeling' or 'boons of animating thought' in labour seem allied to its potentially 'true power of mind' in Book XII. But it is not clear how this links to their 'real worth' and 'genuine knowledge'. To assess the importance of 'value' for Wordsworth, David Simpson has drawn on Moishe Postone's reinterpretation of Marx.[45] For Postone, Marx is the great critic of proletarian labour – seeking to abolish rather than affirm it, and not just end or mitigate its exploitation (*contra* 'traditional Marxism'). Only capitalism, not earlier social formations, in its historical specificity operates a 'labour theory of value' that constitutes social relations. Capitalist value is determined by the expenditure of human labour as measured by time – by the 'socially average' amount of time it takes to produce a commodity as the fundamental basis for measuring its value against other commodities. This is 'abstract labour' or 'social labour'. The only way to measure this productivity on a commensurate scale is through hours of the working day, regulated and standardized by clock-time. Human life becomes devastated by the domination of abstract time. Individual producers, products and acts of production are all rendered abstract and interchangeable in the web of interdependent labour that in capitalism constitutes society.

Simpson argues that Wordsworth's 'spots of time' are constituted *in toto* by this industrial paradigm – they are a ghost of the value-form itself. The dance of the daffodils in Wordsworth's most famous poem is a spectral double of the 'assembly line form . . . which only seem to move together while each is always rooted to the spot'.[46] Memory for Wordsworth is a capitalization of time, a 'deposit' or investment reduced to its value in exchange, whose surplus is later withdrawn to affirm his self-identity and mastery: as he remembers the daffodils on his couch, he is 'cashing in his accumulated "wealth"'.[47] Simpson is certainly right to emphasize, for the first time, the importance of 'value' in Wordsworth's treatment of political economy – and above all, its crucial role in the 'spots of time'. For Book XII, however, this is a search for 'real worth', explicitly set against Smith's 'wealth of nations'. Does a ghostly analogue between types of value automatically mean their identity or complicity?

For Simpson, Wordsworth's figures of the real display a 'profound poetic understanding' of England's 'evolution into a culture governed by industrial time, machine-driven labour and commodity form' around 1800.[48] There are 'historical affiliations' between the 'death-in-life aura' of Wordsworth's 'encounters' and how Marx understood 'the figurative imagination' to work within 'commodity capitalism'.[49] Simpson links a tendency in Wordsworth to animate the material and reify the human to Marx's account of commodity fetishism: capital's translation of rigidified social relations of production into the pseudo-social relation of commodities in lively though abstract exchange. Drawing on Derrida's well-known 'deconstruction' of Marx in

Specters of Marx (1993), Simpson argues that such figures are characterized by their 'spectrality'.

For Derrida, that spectrality is more original than industrial capitalism; it is irreducible, 'non-deconstructible'. This leads him to 'deconstruct' Marx's 'metaphysical' appeals to a 'pure and simple' concrete individuality of living labour and use-value. Living labour is haunted by the 'work of mourning' that is repetition, while use-value, even in its most minimal state of potential, as the 'form' of a basic material, is 'promised to iterability, to substitution, to exchange, to value' as 'an idealization that permits one to identify it as the same throughout possible repetitions'.[50] And in its excess beyond 'pure use', it also harbours the '*out-of-use*': 'A culture began before culture – and humanity.'[51] It is a not un-Wordsworthian insight. But Derrida accepts the 'analytic power' of Marx's distinctions.[52] He argues for the 'co-implication' of Marx's oppositions but not their identity; to think that complicity together calls for 'a more refined and more rigorous restructuration' in the interest of the 'progress of the critique'.[53] In a mere aside, Derrida confesses that his 'deconstruction' is not enough but must itself be supplemented by a new, more subtle *critical theory*: and precisely that of political economy. That critique might work to avert the coming on of a 'night in which all cows are black' – or mistily grey on grey – risked by an unqualified dissolution of all phenomena into 'spectrality': a universally blurry and undifferentiated world of phantasmagoria. This would not be to claim that we can just throw ourselves into an iridescent particularity. Not only are use-value and living labour pervasively invaded by abstract exchange in capitalism, so they in turn become increasingly abstract and standardized in character, but, as Derrida reminds us, use-value imposes its own abstraction, along with language, perception and even form itself. But it would mean an opening up of *differences*, of historically varying degrees and kinds of spectrality. And here Wordsworth's passionate and minute efforts of mimesis, his attention to experiences that are not just held within, but seep through the meshes of language, cultural norms and systematically 'false philosophy' – to the *critical* purchase of experience within the social text, not just an immanent reading and destructuring of the linguistic text – might open up a process of revaluation.

It would mean the difference between the dance and a conveyor belt. Or a 'similitude in dissimilitude' more finely discriminated than the repetitive 'iterability' of a singular form. It is a turn within the double movement of the commodity that Wordsworth seems to replicate: the reification of persons, and a personification of things.[54] At work within that dualism is a 'life-in-death' as well as 'death-in-life' aura. Weaving through the 'textual attitude' is a language of phenomena in affect. As it travels through *terra incognita* in the interval between concept and intuition, it might stop to listen to a 'ghostly language' of the material as it haunts the evaluative discourse of comparative quantities and equivalence: 'value . . . is the sphere in which the linen relates to the coat in a language we cannot speak, "a language with which it alone is familiar"'.[55]

Wordsworth's wager was that labour might hide a 'real worth' within its creation of an abstract language of value-equivalence. This spectre was not necessarily that of use-value. The distinction between intrinsic 'worth' and commercial value was nothing new: it went back at least as far as Locke. But the young Marx had tried to open up an intriguing distinction within use-value itself. It might emerge within a society beyond property in which 'nature has lost its mere *utility* in the sense that it has become *human* use'.[56] This humanization of 'animal wants', however, metabolically absorbing the useful in its cultivation, remains a form of property in its seizure of nature. It is a contradiction in the young Marx, who also argued – as is sometimes forgotten in criticisms of his 'Prometheanism' – that the 'wage slavery' imposed by private property 'estranges from nature'.[57] Does the unalienated liberty finally to get down to one's own work upon nature inevitably entail its domination? The imposition of a subjective or human valuation upon 'Being' was of course Heidegger's objection to Nietzsche's 'revaluation of all values': its indifference to the non-anthropological proclaimed a severe nihilism and 'will to power'.[58] But Marx compares a sense of 'human use' to the development of a musical ear; he writes that 'the dealer in minerals sees only the commercial value, and not the beauty and peculiar nature of the minerals'.[59] A human use breaks through into an uncanniness of the non-human – a 'peculiar nature'. Interest and disinterest might enter into a new relationship, but in which the latter has priority. Human use becomes a mode of translation. Its attention to the peculiar is to raise the ghost of an *objective* value: a 'real worth'.

This is the germ of a 'labour theory of value' with a difference. No longer is labour the source of all value; it is of value precisely insofar as its utility is able to surpass itself. It is a glimmer of 'genuine knowledge'. That is to say, it is a labour on behalf of *transcendence*: not as a secure metaphysics, but as something evermore about to be, beyond the labouring subject. In a state of second nature, access to the non-human is not necessarily an immediate given. It might require an intense work of subjectivity, a 'true power of mind' – and not just a labour of the concept or work of the negative – to reach a point where the subject can relinquish itself.

This is the trajectory of Wordsworth's peculiar theory of an *objective* 'genius'. It occurs at the very beginning of Book xii, as if announcing the ideal template, or at least the high-cultural analogue, for the revaluation of labour that will follow. What Wordsworth calls 'Genius' follows the 'twofold influence' of nature's 'moods', an 'interchange / Of peace and excitation' (1–9). The moodiness of creative genius receives inspiration from the changing atmosphere of a *genius loci* itself. That 'interchange' evokes Book viii's earlier account of the shepherd's rhythm: a life of 'hard labour interchanged / With that majestic indolence so dear / To native Man' (388–90).[60] Both work and leisure are somehow intrinsic to being 'native', the feeling of being at home in a place. In his *Discourse on Inequality* – as though anticipating Smith's later critique of the state of nature's idleness – Rousseau had praised the earliest 'savage' state of culture as the very greatest human achievement, holding a balanced 'mean between the indolence of the primitive state and the petulant activity of our own pride'.[61] In Book xii's account of genius, however, labour and leisure are a fluctuating 'interchange' within creative activity itself. And it is characterized by an interchange with nature in which the latter has priority:

from her receives
That energy by which he seeks the truth,
Is rouzed, aspires, grasps, struggles, [wishes, craves]
From her that happy stillness of the mind
Which fits him to receive it, when unsought.
(10–14)[62]

Even the most productive of forces must depend upon a supply of 'energy'. The animating gift of labour, its struggle to grasp, is of value only insofar as it fails. It must collapse into a grace of the unintentional, a quality of attention fit to receive the 'unsought'.

Book xii goes on to characterize a genuine work with nature as a mode of *intersubjectivity*. But again, it is the object that has priority. The rural worker, Wordsworth insists, not only experiences 'love' – apparently that most blindly subjective of valuations – but does so in a way not 'falsely deem'd / A gift . . . / Of vulgar Nature' (185–8). In a striking reversal, love is not a 'gift of feeling' from the worker to his material; it is given *to* him. Yet this is not, apparently, the gift of a metaphysical subject of nature, easily 'deconstructible' into spectrality. It is as 'vulgar' in material origin as the common worker was held to be. Yet it is subsequently called 'Nature's self' (199). This wholly material, that is, *vulgar* subjectivity appears to present a different kind of spectrality to use and exchange value.

But as if aware of a possible idealization of the vulgar here, Wordsworth remains troubled by its potential opposition to the mere worker:

> where grace
> Of culture hath been utterly unknown
> And labour in excess and poverty
> From day to day preoccupy the ground
> Of the affections, and to Nature's self
> Oppose a deeper nature, there indeed
> Love cannot be
>
> (195–201)

The gift of nature is not enough on its own, nor that of pure labour; they require at least *some* 'grace of culture' to fall in love. The selfishness of labour cannot be refined on its own, and a superstructure cannot arise purely from the base – there must be some degree of leap into cultural grace. The labouring life will remain loveless, a deadening of affect, without another life of cultured leisure to infuse it. A social poverty and excessive labour block access to an objective (a truly 'vulgar') love. The 'affections' are preoccupied at their 'ground' by a baser self-interest, or at least an insistent drive to self-preservation. It is a 'deeper nature' than the vulgar surface of nature's physiognomy – a primal egoism of natural law, an interiority so deep that it goes back to the state of nature, profound enough to be the *natura naturans* itself. For Phillip Connell, the passage acknowledges a Malthusian nature of need and scarcity against an idealized natural benevolence – a contradiction that Wordsworth's authorship was unable to resolve.[63] But this deeper nature, apparently a priori, has in fact emerged a posteriori. It has been brought to the surface by a socially conditioned 'poverty' and its 'labour in excess'. The passage cries out for a grace of culture: a reduction of socially necessary labour-time.

The contemporary state of nature is what freezes 'natural history' to a standstill. If Derrida's punning *hantologie* of the spectral is only *quasi*-transcendental, as he repeatedly states – conditioned by the empirical as much as conditioning it – it is because it is also a species of natural history. Its supposed transcendence is itself an apparition: the ghost of a state of estrangement. The life and death that it works between are also its outer limits. Wordsworth sought a labour that pushed towards those boundaries in the heart of spectrality itself. It was a hope accessible only in *language*. But this was not just a 'grace of culture', or inventive fiction, vouchsafed by words. Labour for Wordsworth might also be grasped by a cognitive language of affect:

> Theirs is the language of the heavens, the power,
> The thought, the image, and the silent joy;
> Words are but under-agents in their souls;
> When they are grasping with their greatest strength
> They do not breathe among them
>
> (270–4)

So mystical is this passage in its grandeur that it comes as a shock to realize that this is rural labour. The worker seems to break through into a paradisal state of nature – but language marks a spectral distance even here. There is a cultural grace of 'words', quasi-transcendental as 'under-agents', added to an experience they interpret. Such words might include a phrase like 'the heavens', a promise of joyful transparency.

Yet the passage is anything but clear. Just what is being grasped here? Do its power, thought and image belong to a nature that is pointing to transcendence? But nature is not even mentioned here. The referent is that of 'the heavens'. Only it is not the heavens themselves, but their language. It is an experience of *pure language*. For that very reason, it is non-verbal: at its 'greatest strength' words fall away, the hermeneutic circle is breached. *There is no referent.* We have broken through the rank of ghosts, even words, to reach a pure experience of meaning. But that is also why it is haunted by language, a heavenly signification. It is only in retrospect that the experience becomes spectral, breaking apart into thought, image, word and feeling, the *analogia entis* or 'similitude in dissimilitude' of a labouring distance from paradise. Indeed, just how on earth, rather than in the heavens, might this be an experience of hard labour? There has been some kind of 'image', presumably one of nature. And its combination of 'thought' and affect, its 'silent joy', seems to have something to do with the physical body – its attempts to 'grasp' also involve an effort to 'breathe'. That struggle is accompanied by a jettisoning of words. To articulate or interpret here is a grasping or intake of breath.

The fragile power of that metaphysical experience – in defiance of a spectral ubiquity – may not be a rare or mystical privilege, but common and everyday. It might be as common as a change in our breathing as we grasp something that surprises us:

> Points have we all of us within our souls,
> Where all stand single; this I feel, and make
> Breathings for incommunicable powers;
> Yet each man is a memory to himself
>
> (186–9)

What constitutes our singleness is a variety of unrepeatable experiences – or a plurality of such punctual moments even in a single day. The universal has been compressed into a singularity of point. There is another paradox. Wordsworth says that he cannot express such 'powers', they are singularly 'incommunicable', and is able at the same time to 'make / Breathings for' them. They can be channelled by a making, a poiesis, a shaping of individual breath. But the experience must also turn back into spectrality: 'Yet each man is a memory to himself.'

The singular nature of the breath mechanism might even subtend the factory-like machine. There is a spectral persistence of life-in-death in the very rhythm of mechanical labour. In 'She was a Phantom of delight', Wordsworth makes breathings for a 'thoughtfulness' that keeps on respiring as his wife becomes estranged by the machine:

> And now I see with eye serene
> The very pulse of the machine;
> A Being breathing thoughtful breath;
> A traveller between life and death
> (*P2V* 21–4)

This is not La Mettrie's *L'homme machine* or Baron d'Holbach's *Système de la nature* (1770). Its pulse is a ghost not *in* the machine, but *of* it – a systole and diastole that is both uniformly regular *and* organically quavering as it travels between life and death. The repetition of 'breathing' and 'breath' is not a redundancy. Not only is 'Being', when conceived as living and individual, intimately related to the 'breathing' into which it expands as a near-homonym. A 'thoughtful' quality of perception converts a mechanical process ('breathing') into a substantive duration ('breath') – at the point of receiving a name.[64] And the line itself is the making of a breath: a pulse of the metrical machine, a syllabic regularity suffused and distended by drawn-out aspirates, culminating in the 'thoughtful' weight placed upon its final emission of 'breath'. A passage from William Bartram's *Travels* through south-eastern America (1773–6), proposed as a source here,[65] indicates how that breathing might correspond to a singular 'vibration' that subtly inflects even a natural causality: 'At the return of morning, by the powerful influence of light, the pulse of nature becomes more active, and the universal vibration of life insensibly and irresistibly moves the wondrous machine.'[66] It is a tiny margin of plasticity that is a promise of happiness not death: a 'phantom of delight'.

The poem was perhaps less the 'petit-bourgeois idyll' and closer to the critique of political economy – in its capacity to enrich our experience – than Brecht realized. We begin to glimpse what Wordsworth might have meant, in his 1802 sonnet addressed in support of the Haitian slave leader imprisoned by Napoleon, 'To Toussaint L'Ouverture', when he wrote that every 'breathing of the common wind' was among 'Powers that will work for thee' (10–11) in opposition to slave labour. But what right had Wordsworth so sublimely to transfigure the worker's struggle and effort? Rather embarrassingly, he appears clumsily to disclose such a guilt when Book XII announces: 'In Nature's presence: thence may I select / Sorrow that is not sorrow, but delight' (244–5). An unkind gloss might read: 'the rural worker's sorrow can hardly be called sorrow when the beauty of its natural backdrop allows a poet-onlooker like me to project such delightful transports into his groaning and sighing breath'. There is also the more modest possibility, in what Wordsworth points out is only a selection, that even the labouring life of sorrow might yet contain a promise of happiness. The very conditions of sorrow, an exposed and affective vulnerability, might also be the condition of delight.

For Book XII, that promise is held out by a moment of 'interchange'. Nature's vulgar self issues a 'summons' as it 'intermingles' with labour:

> the forms
> Of nature have a passion in themselves
> That intermingles with those works of man
> To which she summons him, although the works
> Be mean, have nothing lofty of their own;
> And that the genius of the Poet hence
> May boldly take his way among mankind
> Wherever Nature leads, that he hath stood
> By Nature's side among the men of old,
> And so shall stand for ever.
>
> (289–98)

What is proposed here would be the most crucial link between a poetic and manual labour, for it is what validates the sheer effrontery of the poet as anthropological traveller's claim to participate in the whole of human experience, 'boldly' to enter into any form of life and labour – however trivial an occupation may be in itself, there is something in it that is ineliminably poetic. Intermingling with use- and exchange-value is an even stranger spectrality: the forms of a passion-in-itself.

A clue to what such a paradoxically inanimate passion might possibly mean is offered by an analogous expression in a letter Wordsworth wrote to John Thelwall, in mid-January 1804, on poetic metre. Wordsworth argues that while he agrees with Thelwall that prose sense should predominate in reading a poem (i.e., the prosodic rhythm should not awkwardly interrupt the syntactic units of the poem's 'meaning'), nevertheless at the end of a line the syntactic sequence is inevitably broken by a metrical pause. This caesura is 'not called out for by the passion of the subject, but by the passion of metre merely'.[67] 'Nature's self' did not necessarily imply an 'anthropomorphitism'. An 'inanimate' passion can be genuinely registered by the senses insofar as something intractably resistant to the 'passion of the subject' – the resistance lacking in assembly-line work for Smith – is at intervals able to break through production. That material 'passion' – the *passio* of a helpless suffering as well as delight – is the shock or grace of an unanticipated gift. An arbitrary linguistic convention, a visual end-stopping that necessitates a pause in breathing, stands for what intermingles with the flux and reflux of labour: a matter that breaks through with the vitality of its own rebounding force.

Almost 180 years later, Giorgio Agamben would also argue that it is enjambement alone, 'the opposition of a metrical limit to a syntactic limit, of a prosodic pause to a semantic pause', that is uniquely specific to poetry.[68] It is due to this, he suggests, that 'the word *versure*, from the Latin term indicating the point at which the plow turns around at the end of the furrow, be given to this essential trait of the verse'[69] – for 'poetry lives in the unsatisfied tension between the semiotic and the semantic series alone'.[70] Human sense or use must intermingle with semiotic matter, as we work with a language of nature – this is what a living labour means for Wordsworth.

If a poetic thinking, let alone the conventions of metre, seems now at the opposite remove from social and political science, there was a time when they were deemed essential to an understanding of the social. Plato had argued for the intimate connection between a moral-political order and its *mousike*, 'a term that includes but is not confined to music: it encompasses euphony in poetry, and rhythm in gymnastics'.[71] Coleridge would complain that the decadence of English prose as well as manners showed that 'Fact bears Plato out even in Music, in its stricter or narrower sense as Metre and Tune.'[72] While poetry as an artistic genre has grown ever more marginal, in disguised forms it has never lost its centrality – if only in the body's rhythms at work and play in its syncopation with machinery. If *mousike* for Plato was a fortifying discipline of order,[73] it might also be the vehicle of a shaping of breath that intermingles with the passion of language.

Hunting

Book XII's revaluation of labour is not just an island or interlude within the development of *The Prelude*. It brings to a head what had been an ongoing, though partially hidden, concern with the relation of work to nature throughout the poem. What was to become, in the Duddon sonnets, an explicit use of 'four-stage theory' as a structural device for the long poetic sequence was already present in *The Prelude* in a ghostly and incomplete form. In early 1798, just before his announcement of *The Recluse*, Wordsworth had read Richard Payne Knight's *The Progress of Civil Society*, which was divided into Books corresponding to the stages of Scottish Enlightenment historiography. Its first book was entitled 'On Hunting' – and it is surely no accident, then, that this is also the main theme of Book I of *The Prelude*. The passions of nature are intermingled with, not indifferent to, the historically varying forms of attention bestowed upon them.

Wordsworth's pictures of an infantile hunting are a part of his reorientation of anthropological inquiry from the phylogenetic to the ontogenetic. Alan Bewell is both right and wrong when he argues for 'the complementarity of the history of the individual and of the species that was of such importance to Wordsworthian autobiography'.[74] Wordsworth's 'spots of time' stand out from, more than represent, a model of linear development. For Wordsworth the spots of time hold a 'distinct pre-eminence' and their resurgence inspires with a 'renovating virtue' (XI.259–60). Going back has a capacity to illuminate the present, to make everything new again. Not only do the 'spots of time' invoke elementary forms of labour, they also present a contrast to them – they are said to lift the 'deadly weight / In trivial occupations' (262–3). They are not interchangeable in their value, but as patterns of behavioural response that inter-knit, with a long-term influence on unconscious comportment and disposition, they are linked together by a 'similitude in dissimilitude'. Far from the abstract determination of time that characterizes wage labour, a homogenous continuum divided into fixed hours, they represent moments in which time flows and is qualitatively charged with an unusual pressure and intensity. And as *spots* of time, they work against not just an evacuation of time, but also a flattening of space.

In Book I, a rupture or frustration of the childhood hunt is the seed of a genuine awareness of place. It corresponds to what Geoffrey Hartman identified as the 'halted traveller' motif central to Wordsworth's authorship[75] – in the form of the halted hunter. The structure of these episodes can be traced back as far as *Descriptive Sketches*, in which a man hunting chamois, oblivious to the Alpine scenery, is punished by sinking into an avalanche as he is captivated by an anthropomorphic raven (*DS* 366–407). It is clear, then, that the childhood forays of *The Prelude*, though less crudely vindictive, and far more ambivalent, originated in a questioning of the hunt as an actual labour – as a stance and attitude towards nature.[76] Following

The Prelude, two works related to *The Recluse – The Tuft of Primroses* (1808), and the River Duddon sonnets – would both image a hunter stumbling upon a paradisal bower after losing track of his prey.[77] Hunting, it seems, is somehow what keeps us from entering into paradise.[78] Yet it is also a primitive form of what Book XII would present as the productive force of 'genius': a struggle to grasp that succeeds only as it fails. What leaps out – beyond subjective intention – is a claim on behalf of truth itself: the ghost of an objective value.

As childhood episodes within the 'growth of a poet's mind' or Wordsworth's poetic psychoanalysis – his 'hard task to analyse a soul' – they represent what is closer to an Oedipal stage than the 'pre-Oedipal' account of the 'infant babe' with its mother in Book II. While it would be reductive to say with the young William Empson that mountains in Book I are a mere 'totem or father-substitute',[79] and that what foils the boyhood hunt is a kind of 'castration' or prohibition of (quasi-incestuous) intimacy with nature, an institution of the adult law, nevertheless they force an acknowledgement of self-limitation and transcendence.[80] The child Wordsworth still resembles what Freud famously called 'His Majesty the Baby'. Infantile feelings of omnipotence are here expressed through attempts to annihilate or conquer the external world. As Wordsworth writes of his sweetly innocent childhood self: 'I was a fell destroyer' (35).[81] But this infantile death-drive or demonism is also bound up with a form of Eros, with 'expectation' and 'strong desire' (42).

The first hunting episode of Book I opens with an apostrophe to 'Gentle powers', as if in anticipation of a pacifying *telos* or educative result. What occurs, however, leads to a shock that is anything but gentle:

> Gentle powers!
> Who give us happiness and call it peace!
> When scudding on from snare to snare I plied
> My anxious visitation, hurrying on,
> Still hurrying hurrying onward, how my heart
> Panted; among the scattered yew-trees, and the crags
> That looked upon me, how my bosom beat
> With expectation. Sometimes strong desire,
> Resistless, overpowered me, and the bird
> Which was the captive of another's toils
> Became my prey;
>
> (35–45)

The child is 'scudding on', gliding swiftly and easily, as if skimming across a frictionless surface. Wordsworth moves effortlessly from snare to snare, just as in a related lyric, 'To a Butterfly' (1802), he writes of his childhood butterfly-catching: 'A very hunter did I rush / Upon the prey: – with leaps and springs / I follow'd on from brake to bush' (*P2V* 14–16). As desire overpowers the 'resistless' ego, such is the propulsive force that it effortlessly leaps over the snares and brakes of a material resistance. Key to what makes the hunting episodes so ambivalent is this wonderful moment of *grace* and transcendence.

Yet these movements are not truly gracious, but quite the contrary: they are 'anxious'. The boy hurries and hurries and hurries on, as if repeatedly exhorting himself to push forward. The child imposes an accelerated time upon a deserted space to repress an obstacle that has not been truly vaulted, for it returns uncannily as his own double – the yew-trees and crags that in turn look upon him. The pounding insistence of the bodily shudder, a bosom that beats with expectation, is more an impatient fear than an eager anticipation of what it will seize. If desire, as Wordsworth states, was only 'Sometimes' able to overpower him, then the child already has an internal resistance or sense of guilt. It is not quite a primal scene – the child is to some degree already socialized.

And the world of adult labour has quite physically marked the landscape in Wordsworth's spot of time. The woodcocks stolen by the child are the 'captive of another's toils' – snares ('toils') laid out by the labour of another (that other sense of 'toils'). And so when the child seizes its prey, that implicit guilt assumes an objectified form as a more persecutory and uncanny doubling. The hunter is hunted in turn:

> and when the deed was done
> I heard among the solitary hills
> Low breathings coming after me, and sounds
> Of undistinguishable motion, steps
> Almost as silent as the turf they trod.
>
> (45–9)

With the 'indistinguishable motion' of a frictionless prosody – and a sinister 'low breathing' that resembles the child's panting anxiousness more than a careful shaping of breath – the hunter too is 'scudding on'. Yet as the personification of this 'spot of time', this ghostly counter-attacker's indeterminacy is also the negative image of a *genius loci* that the child has evacuated and stolen from. As such it might resemble a guilt of the traveller as much as the labourer. In November 1797, Wordsworth suggested to Coleridge that 'The Ancient Mariner' should include an event inspired by descriptions of the albatross in George Shelvocke's *Voyage Round the*

World by the Way of the Great South Sea (1726): '"Suppose," I said, "you represent him as having killed one of these birds on entering the South Sea, and that the tutelary spirits of these regions take upon them to avenge the crime."'[82] As an elementary structure, the theft of the woodcocks has obvious colonial resonances. Two forms of property have here been brought together: the product of an individual's toils and what belongs to a sense of independent place. What had seemed a dead object there for the taking is instead to be represented by what is living and individual – the form of a passion in itself.

The experience of guilt becomes yet more powerful in Book 1's famous episode on Ullswater. Here the boy, having stolen a boat – again appropriating the property of another's labour – sets off in a self-propelling 'cadence' that 'struck the oars and struck again' (87–8). That phrase would become an image of violence in an 1820 revision to another poem of 1799, *Peter Bell*, whose 'savage' protagonist 'struck – and struck again' (*PB* 200) a fallen donkey. But the boy's rowing is not quite a prosody of violence. It is 'like a man who walks with stately step' in a grace of 'stealth' (89–90). No longer 'scudding on', that elegance of movement is too measured to be an 'undistinguishable motion', even if its stealth might hide a furtive anxiety. For it too, 'bent on speed', harbours the guilt of a 'troubled pleasure' (90–1). It is even quasi-sexual as it 'dipped' then 'rose upon the stroke' (104–5) – 'lustily' in the 1805 text (*Pr.* 402). The Preface, of course, was to associate the 'similitude in dissimilitude' of metre with 'sexual appetite'. Yet there is only a 'similitude' without 'dissimilitude' in these enthusiastically regular iambics of the oar. They align the child with a fixed point of orientation, a crag it has seen ahead in the distance, a visual object that it has claimed in a sublimated mode of capture. If the hunt for an object of pleasure is not here the erotic violence of 'Nutting' – where it is figured as a form of rape – it remains an oblivious drive. It is not yet an Eros of *knowledge*.

But the child is dramatically awakened from his self-absorption: suddenly emergent from behind the horizon is an unexpected cliff which 'like a living thing, / Strode after me' – 'With measured motion' (113–14). As the boy later reflects on this representative of 'unknown modes of being', a 'blank desertion' descends on his 'thoughts' (120–4). In a reading of this passage from a book that takes its point of departure from Karatani's notion of the 'parallax view', a theorist who has likewise argued for a return to the critique of political economy, Slavoj Žižek, has claimed that the cliff is not a 'Kantian Thing-itself', but 'its inherent opposite': 'what appears as the excess of some transcendent force over the "normal" external reality, is the very place of the direct inscription of my subjectivity into this reality . . .

the objectivization . . . of my own gaze'.[83] Wordsworth himself would claim, worryingly, that in 'spots of time' the mind is 'lord and master' (XI.272). The passage, however, is precisely the account of a dizzying parallax view, an intersection of mutually transformative viewpoints upon an object. If such an 'anthropomorphitism' is the projection of a primitive or even 'imperial' imagination – as Alison Hickey characterizes Wordsworth's 'figuring of the blank'[84] – its involuntary propulsion is not under the ego's conscious control. More crucial is the element of guilt, the double as a return of the repressed. It is the figure of a 'dissimilitude'. What creates the blackout here is that images like the cliff 'do *not* live / Like living men' (127–8; my italics).

Leaping out at the caesura, the break in rhythm, such imaginative forms now 'moved slowly through my mind' and dreams (128–9) – slowly not lustily – with a passion of metre that is inhuman. The child is now haunted, rather than hunted, by what is more than a spectral equivalence akin to the commodity. These 'huge and mighty forms' are contrasted with the interchangeable 'familiar shapes / Of hourly objects' (422–3) – the products of measured clock-time. If there has been progress here, it is not in the direction of an affect-less object relation. The child has already reached that stage of 'mature' recognition. It is precisely through subjective affect, a spectrally distorting animation, that a deeper sense of objectivity has been gained. Developing a feeling for what is truly alien in its object, it is a knowledge inseparable from a sense of the 'unknown'. There is life here, but not as we know it.

The thing-in-itself can only be glimpsed in the form of a passion-in-itself. The child has reached the ultimate limits of representation: the figurative truth of an alien life.[85] In another childhood episode of Book I, as Wordsworth hangs from a cliff-edge, hunting for eggs in ravens' nests – pausing at the end of a poetic line – his attention is suddenly diverted by a peculiarly non-representational language: 'With what strange utterance did the loud dry wind / Blow through my ears!' (64–5). If 'utterance' has been projected onto this 'loud' noise, it is not as an effort of intentional consciousness: the ears are not listening; it blows through them. What makes it resemble language is not just its sonority, but its physicality, the dry breath, blowing through the ears as an aperture. Language here is not a working up into identification, but what happens when hourly objects lose their familiar identity: 'the sky seemed not a sky / Of earth, and with what motion moved the clouds!' (65–6). The apparent tautology of 'motion' and 'moved', the shift from a verb to a noun, is what makes this 'spot of time' a substantive duration – a noun as it turns towards a name. There is a quality of unknowing to this strange experience, a question mark hidden in its exclamation: what is it that bears such an emphasis, what is that motion moving the clouds?

The 'spots of time' are an education in a qualitative time and space, not the abstracted base upon which one works – 'hurrying hurrying onward' in a race against the clock. And as part of the 'growth of a *poet's* mind', they are the dawn of a prosodic sensibility. That process is announced in Book I's very first 'spot of time' as the primal scene of poetic metre: Wordsworth evokes a River Derwent that 'loved / To blend his murmurs with my Nurse's song' (2–3). Its 'ceaseless music' is also a 'steady cadence, tempering our human waywardness'; it 'composed my thoughts / To more than infant softness' (9–12). Even in the cradle, Wordsworth would like to believe, he was getting a training in metrical thinking. This is not the quasi-martial discipline of Plato's *mousike*; it instils a 'softness', a tempering, of the extravagant urge to grasp. It is 'a dim earnest of the calm / Which Nature breathes' (14–15) – a shaping of that breath. For Paul Fry, Wordsworth's prosody is that of Book II's now communal image of the childhood hunt, of horse-hooves thudding on the level sand in unison, 'a hypnotic sense of the same' in 'mechanical regularity' that echoes the repetition of Being itself: 'the Foucauldian disappearance of man is heralded'.[86] But the steady cadence, the measured motion, is in interchange with a murmur of music, and blended with the human warmth of a Nurse's song. The cadence is contrapuntal. Repetition – a prosody of the hunt or factory – has unfolded into a 'similitude in dissimilitude', a crossing-over of nature's rhythms with the human. This is the ghostly metric of a passionate or softly tender, not anonymous Being; it has the regular irregularity of 'continual impulses of pleasurable surprise', not a univocal and monotonous iterability. It is constantly liable to interruption – and always at the end of a line. The disappearance of abstract labour is heralded.

Just how that might be anticipated in existing labour practices is peculiarly made visible in another episode of 'apt admonishment', a poem about a mode of subsistence related to the hunter – the *gatherer*.[87] 'Resolution and Independence' was, of course, originally entitled 'The Leech-Gatherer'. Working between production and consumption, labour and leisure, or action and contemplation, to gather here is introduced as a 'steady look at the subject':

> he the Pond
> Stirred with his Staff, and fixedly did look
> Upon the muddy water, which he conn'd,
> As if he had been reading in a book
>
> (*P2V* 85–8)

The man's steady attention evokes a magical reading in the book of nature. The eponymous protagonist of the 1798 *Peter Bell* also stares into a pond: 'He looks, he cannot chuse but look, / Like one that's reading in a book, / A book that is enchanted' (*PB*, MSS. 2 and 3, 558–60). But what Peter Bell sees is only a dead body with no hope of magical revival. As the leech-gatherer stirs the pond with what resembles a wizard's staff, the image seems a labour as much of play as of earnestness. Lewis Carroll's well-known parody of 'The Leech-Gatherer' would indeed present the man's labour as a whimsically fantastical and magical activity.[88] But the enchanted close reading of a ritual or magical labour has here been translated into a form of meditative attentiveness, a fixed search within the muddy blank for the appearance of something meaningful, of something that has a language. The man stares at the pond in the hope that something will leap out at him.

A magically or lyrically productive mode of subsistence would indeed be providential here. For in the opening stanzas Wordsworth had been troubled by the possibility that his feckless vocation, neither toiling nor spinning, had merely exploited the labour of others: 'But can He expect that others should / Build for him' who 'for himself will take no heed at all?' (40–2). It is what drives Wordsworth's almost desperately repeated question, 'What kind of work is that which you pursue?' (95). He becomes distracted at the thought of the 'Cold, pain, and labour' that the man appears to represent, and the fatal 'misery' of impoverished and neglected poets (123–4) that seems to correspond to it. 'My question eagerly did I renew' (125), he claims; in the 1815 edition, he is furthermore 'Perplexed' with a 'longing to be comforted'. It is as though he does not want to hear that this is, after all, the most prosaic, painful and meagre subsistence imaginable: a gathering of leeches.

But the hoped-for response had already been given:

> His words came feebly, from a feeble chest,
> But each in solemn order follow'd each,
> With something of a lofty utterance drest;
> Choice word, and measured phrase
>
> (99–102)

The minute discrimination in the 'conning' or attentive reading of the man's labour has inflected even the contours of his speech patterns, a shaping even of 'feeble' breath. In the 'solemn order' of a prosody, and with the 'choice' diction of a thoughtful care for language, its cadences are those of the independent worker, 'the dignity of individual man'. As such, it has the capacity also to dissolve into that substantive duration, that 'strange utterance', which breathes or flows through the natural:

> But now to me his voice was like a stream
> Scarce heard; nor word from word could I divide;
> (114–15)

The man's speech is the intermingling of a 'measured' and 'indistinguishable' motion. Embedded in his work and way of life is an interchange of metre and murmur. But it can only split apart from a semantic discourse of 'Cold, pain, and labour' which it cannot fully accompany or reconcile. It remains only an image, viewed across a divide; Wordsworth's 'longing to be comforted' has been only partially appeased. Standing face-to-face, the poet and leech-gatherer remain poised, or rather suspended, at the juncture of manual and poetic labour.

Shepherding

After Book I, *The Prelude* immediately deviates from the trajectory of stadial theory, though not of course from its ontogenetic inquiry. Nevertheless, in Book VIII's recollections of the 'rambling School-boy' Wordsworth's awed perception of Lakeland shepherds, at this subsequent stage in his childhood development following the hunting escapades, there is something of a transition to the subsequent pastoral stage. He sees them immediately as stalking giants, much as he did the cliff at Ullswater, only now as if the preparatory and interrupted chase were no longer required.

But there is nothing in *The Prelude* that evokes the agricultural stage, with its complex division of labour and hierarchical social structure – the great historical catastrophe in Rousseau's Second Discourse. *The Prelude*, for all its organic metaphors of the 'seed-time' and ripening cultivation, leaps over agriculture to the final stage of industrial commerce. This is represented not by the factory, but by the dazzling yet finally unsatisfying consumer spectacle of London in Book VII, the 'great Emporium' (VIII.749) at the centre of international trade; its traditions of festive leisure, as at Bartholomew Fair, have become superimposed with the image of 'one vast Mill' (VII.693), 'a type not false' of the 'mighty City' at large (696–7). On the rare occasions when crop farming is valued by Wordsworth – who grew vegetables in his garden – it is in the form (as in 'To the Spade of a Friend') of that ideal of agrarian republicanism, an individual rather than divided labour, in hardy independence on a small-scale plot of land. For the most part, Wordsworth was to take this agrarian discourse and transfer it to shepherding.

It was not the alienated work of social labour, even in co-operative form[89] – aside from the family 'cottage industry' (as in 'The Brothers') – that was attractive to Wordsworth, but the individual labour of self-subsistence that most resembled the contemporary poet's social isolation. His ideal was that of the shepherd in Book VIII:

> Man free, man working for himself, with choice
> Of time, and place, and object; by his wants,
> His comforts, native occupations, cares,
> Conducted on to individual ends
> Or social, and still followed by a train,
> Unwooed, unthought-of even: simplicity,
> And beauty, and inevitable grace.
>
> (*Pr.* VIII.152–8)

Here an individual labour might also have social 'ends' – but the point is that this work has a freedom of choice quite different to a selling of labour on the market. It includes even a liberty to choose which spots of time – 'time, and place' – the individual wishes to cultivate. The idealization of the passage seems to propel it beyond necessary labour into the dream of Marx, emphasized by both Henry and Postone: the reduction of social labour-time to its very minimum, freeing up an unalienated and individual labour – with potentially social as well as individual ends. Far from rejecting the aesthetic, Marx held the composition of music to be the very paradigm of an emancipated labour.[90] Such a work, then, would unfold from the 'deeper nature' of Mandevillian vice or self-interest – or a Spinozan *conatus* – not a pure selflessness, even as it loses itself in the object it has chosen. Wordsworth's desperately idealized vision of the shepherd nevertheless speaks for that deeper nature, an inner voice or impulse of suffering – prior to abstract right – which cries out for the freedom to work for oneself.

Such a labour of 'wants' and 'comforts' remains haunted, for the shepherd, by the persistence of 'cares'. The shepherd's work is a mode of subsistence and a labour of necessity, whatever its potential freedom. Wordsworth's hope was that even a condition of necessary labour, a contemporary state of nature, might nevertheless be capable of a grace of culture. The very care and anxiousness that make such a work a genuine engagement are also a characteristic of the love relationship. A mechanical necessity might even become the vehicle of grace itself: the shepherd's work has an 'inevitable grace'. A patient care might invoke a lavish help. That secular theology is unorthodox to say the least, even blasphemous, with a grace no longer freely bestowed – or the arbitrary gift of a capricious deity – but compelled. It troubles easy distinctions between grace (or culture) and nature, humanity and animality, freedom and necessity, even contingency and teleology. Uncanny and undecidable, it is a 'pulse of the machine'. What gives it the character of grace rather than works is that it surpasses an intentional (and selfish) consciousness: 'unwooed, unthought-of even'. It is an invisible hand or law of unintended consequences with a difference.

While Book VIII, in contrast to Book I's hunting episodes, observes the pastoral only at a distance, it is in the poem 'Michael' that Wordsworth most intensely seeks to portray the shepherd's life from within. The poem is shot through with ambivalence. At first sight, as much as Defoe's original Robinsonade,[91] it seems a perfect illustration of Max Weber's thesis that the Puritan vocation was translated in the eighteenth century into the 'inner-worldly asceticism' of the entrepreneur (the frugal good conduct of Smith's hoarding then reinvesting capitalist).[92] Only here, a confusion of the religious and mercantile ethos has been further complicated by an aesthetics of nature. The poem is undoubtedly replete with unconscious ironies, false idealizations and outright mystification. But it might be possible to read it differently. On the one hand, the poem takes us deep within the ideological dream-work and imaginary of a speculating proprietor; we feel its genuine enchantment at work in experience. But in its pathos and loneliness we feel it speak for something else. Another language is speaking through it, crying out to be heard. There is a longing in the poem that makes its whole framework tilt on its axis. It has entered into a mode of deluded life and turned it in the direction of something new – subtended by a pulse of the machine. Through that subtle shift, a minute dislocation of perspective, the poem's irony speaks for a complex awareness of distance. But the new language that cries and sings and blasts through the poem has the capacity wholly to redefine it. Or at least continue to haunt it. It might even rewrite the lexicon of political economy itself – as though, after this poem, words like 'frugality', 'business', 'industry' and 'gain' will never be the same again.

Wordsworth introduces the shepherd by telling us that 'his mind was keen, / Intense, and frugal, apt for all affairs' (*LB* 44–5). It is a sharp and frosty, northern and Presbyterian intensity – like the Leech-Gatherer, he resembles a 'grave liver' in Scotland. Michael's passionately work-focused and Puritan 'frugal' thriftiness, for all its practical or business aptitude, seems oblivious in its self-interest to anything outside his own 'affairs'. But as we move on to his employment history and work experience, to what gives him a competitive advantage over 'others', we are told that it is the very intensity of his vocation, this austere removal of distractions, that invokes a music and language that those less preoccupied, those who apparently confirm the aesthetic as a luxury, 'heeded not':

> And in his Shepherd's calling he was prompt
> And watchful more than ordinary men.
> Hence had he learn'd the meaning of all winds,
> Of blasts of every tone, and often-times
> When others heeded not, He heard the South
> Make subterraneous music, like the noise
> Of Bagpipers on distant Highland Hills.
>
> (46–52)

What this 'frugal' perception opens up is precisely a moment of excess. The man stands like the *genius loci* or spirit of a place that extends into, and is traversed by, something that transcends its boundaries. Through a sentence of seven lines, the literate reader is brought to an awareness of their own ignorance, and the shepherd's unlettered erudition, as an inscrutable 'meaning' is tantalizingly withheld from us. It resembles an aesthetic labour at the borders of music and sheer cacophony; it is 'like the noise / Of Bagpipers' in the Highlands. The meaning of these 'blasts of every tone' – clarion calls that trumpet across the full range or spectrum of qualities – appears to have something in common with the high-flying pitches and steady drones of the bagpipe. But the comparison makes this language even stranger: the wind is heard impossibly sounding underground, and what is low down and far south resembles an echo from what is high up and far north, and so also impossible to hear, even at the Lakeland borders. There is an ineliminable magic – or at least a speculative mimesis – in such a perception. An enigmatic pattern has been formed, a correspondence to be read like a constellation of stars. And so the chiasmus of 'subterraneous music' and 'distant Highland hills' – a chiasmus that also cuts across visually in the positioning of the words at the beginning and end of the lines – is not simply the flattening of space to a uniform equivalence. There is some kind of 'similitude in dissimilitude' at work. Perfectly oriented, the shepherd stands on his ground as if one at home everywhere, like a sacred figure at the *axis mundi* of a ritual space, or the bagpipe's droning root-note. But he is more a figure of the prophet than the priest: what has 'summon'd him' (57) is a 'warning' (53) that others 'heeded not' (50), as if the *mene tekel* of an imminent, even apocalyptic, threat to culture by a repressed and avenging nature – a warning that is legible only to him, for only he listens carefully enough. But when the interpretation is finally given, the writing on the winds is that of an all-too-literal and commonplace 'storm' (56) from which he must protect his sheep, not the destiny of mankind. It is hard not to feel a sense of deflation.

For critics like Francis Jeffrey, this was Wordsworth's characteristic bathos – a transport of sublime sentiments to the low or commonplace. But to redefine the manual and material 'base' was to question the critical principle, or prejudice, that an art of sinking to the depths to rise up in lofty utterance was inevitably in bad taste. Wordsworth's wager is that the perfect poise of a correctly oriented reading might also articulate a *disorientation* of storm and music. A genuine poetic intentionality might be implicit in such an exact scrutiny, a conviction that whatever of semantic value might be withdrawn from such a reading, its language will inevitably spill over, or bleed through, into the strange meaning of a semiotic noise or music. The conflation – or rather *translation* – of poetic and manual labour is to speak for an outlandish hope: that the historical splitting it hopelessly tries to cover over might be an affair more of contingency than necessity. If so, this would not only give Wordsworth's poetics a real ground in the most basic praxis, hidden though 'heeded not' in the material base itself, a hope of 'good to come' with the widest anthropological foundation. It would provide the substantive basis – alongside his self-identification as a poet with their isolation, neglect and suffering – of an unflinching solidarity with the poor. Or at least the potential to transform that base; for it is they whose 'grace of culture' is most immersed in, and daily forced to confront, the spectacle of the 'vulgar'.

In a draft passage for the poem (MS. 2),[93] Wordsworth insists that such a poetics is not merely one of his own invention or self-projection. He admits that the shepherd would not even understand the question as to whether he loved the mountains; he would simply reply that they were 'frightful to behold' (5). Yet what the man lacks is not a sense of natural beauty, but an awareness that it can be detached from the labour he performs upon it:

> but had you then
> Discours'd with him in some particular sort
> Of his own business, and the goings-on
> Of earth and sky, then truly had you seen
> That in his thoughts there were obscurities
> Wonders and admirations – things that wrought
> Not less than a religion in his heart.
>
> (5–11)

Such 'obscurities' resemble *The Prelude*'s effort to translate a reading of the winds into a poet's making of breath: 'Visionary Power / Attends upon the motions of the winds / Embodied in the mystery of words' (*Pr.* v.619–21). And to the extent that this obscure language of the heart, of earth and sky and heaven, is prior to words, it is a 'religion' without doctrine. A frugal keenness, that most spiritless and practical of visions, might in its very alertness perceive something other than its own self-interest – even in the discourse of 'business'.

This is why the shepherd's labour of interpretation, in another draft passage from MS. 2,[94] is not only the 'propelling power' of a mind that calculates how to foster and increase its livestock capital. It is a speculative 'gain in special sort':

> in his mind
> There was an active and propelling power
> Which finding objects in his daily gains
> And in the love of gains, in special sort
> Attach'd him to his calling.
>
> (8–12)

Wordsworth is almost shameless in his intermingling of poetic and material speculation, of imaginative projection and forecast value, in this Puritan and profiteering vocation. Or so it seems – it is not quite clear just what is being propelled by this loving power of mind as it goes forward. It may or may not be the potential gain in the future, a commercial expansion, implied by Michael's 'daily gains', in what is close to a co-implication of use and exchange-value. It resembles the ambivalence of the commodity itself: the co-presence of two different values. Greed is good. A *cupiditas* not only binds him to his work, but makes him love every object that he finds. But within, not outside, the daily gain and its projective worth is a 'special sort' of new language – the gain of a love object, a physiognomy, and the promise of happiness that reaches beyond it. It is a gain of something not yet ambivalent.

And in the published text, we get a more specific sense of what these objects and gains might be. His tract of land or 'spot of time'

> like a book, preserv'd the memory
> Of the dumb animals, whom he had sav'd,
> Had fed or shelter'd, linking to such acts
> So grateful in themselves, the certainty
> Of honorable gains;
>
> (70–4)

To read the book of nature is to allow the dumbly animal to speak. This is not gain as the master-idol of production, but gain as preservation, sheltering something that would otherwise be lost. It is to preserve each creature's image in a book of emblems, like an allegorical labour of redemption or salvation – and a quite literal saving and protecting of animal life. So attached is the man to the nameless animals he exploits, albeit 'honourably' – we are not told whether he leads them to slaughter – that his land reminds him of them even when they have died. And this is inseparably linked to his practical investment in them. But his acts of protection are 'grateful in themselves' – they both are, and are not, linked to material 'gains'. Yet they too forge a link between disinterest and self-interestedness – they are gratifying. To weigh the degrees of interest or disinterest here, for the sake of praise or blame, is to miss the whole point. 'We do not need to reason on behalf of our good actions, we feel internally their beneficent effect.'[95]

Such a feeling may, however, stem from a moral-rational blindness. This is the ambivalence of Wordsworth's wish-images: a conservative and paternalistic concern, a patronizing version of pastoral secretly driven more by 'gain' than by necessity, a valorization, as Simpson suggests, of 'spots of time' – and an almost desperate insistence that our material action must break through into the fostering of an alien life and language. It is the only perceptible fore-image of a truly free labour of care for our environment.

The shepherd, however, seems incapable of dissociating the environment, as landed property, from his own ego:

these fields, these hills
Which were his living Being even more
Than his own Blood – what could they less? had lay'd
Strong hold on his Affections, were to him
A pleasurable feeling of blind love,
The pleasure which there is in life itself.

(74–9)

Yet the animating sense of property, the spot of time upon which one works, has been translated into something quite different. The source of his 'forward looking-thoughts' (155), his far-reaching commercial speculations, has become something he is unable to look at: 'A pleasurable feeling of *blind* love'. The land is not just more than an extension of himself – it is bizarrely more himself than he is. He has not taken possession of it – it has laid a 'Strong hold' upon him. The invisible hand that has clasped him is closer to his own 'living Being' than the mortmain of a seizure of title deed.

As so often in Wordsworth's verse, the spectre of 'Being' is not an impersonal and repetitive givenness that envelops the human subject. It is living and individual. The apparently given is haunted by a norm or value. As Wordsworth writes of the 'infant babe': 'Emphatically such a Being lives' (*Pr.* II.265). Yet this most spectral of emphases, this animation or 'sentiment of Being' – a word almost always capitalized by Wordsworth when it bears such a force, one that can apply equally to the ontic individual (e.g., 'She Was a Phantom of Delight') and the ontological moment alike – is also the most intense experience of immediacy. Michael's own 'living Being' has been turned inside out – his life is directly out there in front of him. It is not bare life, but 'life at every turn'.[96] Only such a life, Wordsworth seems to be saying, is worthy of the appellation of Being. It is 'the pleasure which there is in life itself' – a pleasure of blind love. Life itself is more than itself.

Yet such a living Being remains questionable insofar as it depends upon a sense of property or belonging. It is always liable to be alienated. And having reached such a pitch, 'Michael' then charts the process by which the sense of Being falls into estrangement. The poem now descends from lyric to its main narrative of sacrifice. Yet while critics have tended to focus on the latter, and to leap over the lyrical introduction, it is only from the perspective of the former that we can gauge just how much has been lost. As often noted, the story alludes to Abraham's (averted) sacrifice of his son, Isaac. At the heart of the poem, then, is that most central of social fears for Wordsworth: human sacrifice. And it is a sacrifice exacted by political economy. Heavily in debt, Michael packs off his son, Luke, to the city in the hope that he will get rich enough to bail his parents out. Luke falls into dissolute ways, and in disgrace flees from England to the tropics – like so many other figures in Wordsworth, he seeks to escape from social shame in the oblivion of a (colonial) state of nature. For Marjorie Levinson, the poem's ideology is thereby a form of 'spiritual economics' in which Michael's new-found detachment after the loss of his son and consequently much of his land, corresponding to the 'aesthetic sublimation' by which Wordsworth rises above the labourer,[97] is 'realized *through* material loss'.[98] Yet this is to forget that the whole tenor of the poem's introduction – its delight in every sense of material *gain* – had worked to co-implicate such a base–superstructure distinction. If a poetic sublimation does step in to recount a narrative of material loss, it is as a work of mourning a way of life in which a poiesis was able to work in the world.

To understand the poem's ambivalence we must see that Michael's working practices are both pregnant with a transfigured and unalienated labour and precisely that which blocks it. For Michael's individual work is in fact a social labour: it is entangled in the quid pro quo of a sacrificial economy.

He gives away his son in the full expectation that he will get everything back. His son will come back as a return of profit on what was freely alienated as an investment. It is this moment of present sacrifice that makes the tragic difference. Michael's earlier love of anticipated gain had been at one with the immediate gratification of the 'daily'.

His mistake arises from an inability to separate the love of his child from a love of property. In a 9 April 1801 letter to Thomas Poole, Wordsworth described Michael as a man 'agitated by two of the most powerful affections of the human heart; the parental affection, and the love of property, *landed* property, including the feelings of inheritance, home, and personal and family independence'.[99] On one level then, the poem follows a process of recognition, as the love of property and the love of family come apart. But love of property for Wordsworth also involves a love of 'family independence' – Michael's affections are interdependent, and it is this agitation which breaks him. Flux and reflux, a similitude in dissimilitude, is the source of the living relationship, the very medium of reconciliation in Wordsworth – and also the source of catastrophe as its forces break out into conflict.

A blind feeling of belonging prior to self-conscious property has now hardened into contradicting types of ownership. But these remain, Wordsworth tells us, forms of love. To pay off a debt incurred by his nephew, Michael is faced with the obligation to sell half the 'patrimonial fields' (234) of his ancestors. His 'endless industry' (97) – a Puritan zeal lauded by Wordsworth and Michael's neighbours, and allegorized by a constantly burning lamp that makes them call the farmhouse 'The Evening Star' (ironically anticipating the round-the-clock light of manufacturing industry in *The Excursion*) – is embedded within the new credit economy. But he is driven by an archaic 'second nature' of social custom, a patriarchal need to maintain the family inheritance and pass it on to a male heir. There is no trace here of that 'majestic indolence so dear' to the 'native' shepherd in *The Prelude*.

But if Michael works more than is strictly necessary, indeed all hours of the day, and then at home repairing tools and carding wool in the evening, it is because his work is so hugely enjoyable. He extracts a lyrical surplus as well as profit in the objects he finds. For it is a kind of artistic game with nature: 'The winds are now devising work for me!' (55), he says, as if rubbing his hands with glee, or at least an affectionate smile. There is an almost whimsical cheerfulness, a nearly sentimental and nostalgic glow, to much of the poem before its turn into sacrifice. It is a serious matter that there should be a silliness, a light-hearted play as well as grave rigour, in the man's intent reading of the winds. What could be more ridiculous, as well as sublime, than hearing a blast as a bagpipe, and the south wind blowing up from underground?

The bathos with which Jeffrey *et al.* charged Wordsworth was an important part of the point. To read and write a 'meaning' in nature's noise might indeed be quite patently absurd. There is an intimation or atmosphere of childhood in this Puritanism at play.[100] With a haunting lightness, uncannily ordinary yet animate phenomena weave in and out of the poem: the 'many thousand mists / That came to him and left him on the heights' (59–60). It is with a light and gentle stroke that Michael plays with nature's meaning, as he speaks of his life in 'the open sunshine of God's love' (239), something 'free as is the wind / That passes over' their land (256–7). Nature is transformed by the touch of language, on the basis of its real 'emanations' (211). But this is not an effort of will. Such 'Feelings and emanations' are said to come to Michael from his child, giving a 'Light to the sun and music to the wind' – a language or music of nature that is no mere projection, for it is no different from really seeing the light – so 'that the Old Man's Heart seemed born again' (211–13). With a shock we realize that Michael's aged and mortgaged heart had not quite been so open before. There has been a hint of mechanical compulsion in his workaholic relentlessness. He is incapable of doing anything else. What has changed in aura is so gentle in nuance, so nearly imperceptible in its love – a tiny difference, somehow, in the apparent tautology of daylight and a 'Light to the sun' – that it is recognized only under the threat of material sacrifice. Faced with selling half his land, the atmosphere has hardened again. In the light of loss, Michael becomes desperate. Within the utopian breeze that blows freely through this poem, such is the spectrality – or counterpoint – of its articulation 'of every tone'.

And in an MS. 1 draft passage,[101] we get another sense of what Michael has been forced to sacrifice. As interrupting spots of time intermingle with his business time – as when his child unsettles a tuft of snow that, as it falls, gathers further snow drifts with it 'till the mountain seem'd / Raced over by a thousand living things' (18–19) – we are told:

> at such a busy time
> The dear beloved Boy would sometimes send
> Forgetfulnesses through the father's thoughts,
> And he would stand beside him like a man
> Robb'd of all purpose
>
> (3–7)

It is as if Michael has been stopped in his tracks by the ghost of his own childhood. His sense of the aesthetic does *not* depend upon a correlative 'purpose'. The forgetting of his personal teleology, his 'forward-looking thoughts' of gain, rescues another sense of life from oblivion. To be a shepherd of living Being is to attend to a 'thousand living things' – beyond a sense of livestock capital.

And the 'cottage industry' of this hard-working family is further marked by ambivalence. The incessant domestic labour of his wife, Isobel, is bound to the *oikos*; we never glimpse her out in the fields of Michael's 'blind love'. At one point she is referred to simply as 'the Housewife' (116). Social relations have necessitated sacrifice from her too – and the provision of children seems solely dictated by Michael's need for an heir; she seems to have no say in the matter. At one point the house-keeping division of labour is transgressed, but only by Michael tending to his son:

> Old Michael, while he was a Babe in arms,
> Had done him female service, not alone
> For dalliance and delight, as is the use
> Of Fathers, but with patient mind enforc'd
> To acts of tenderness
>
> (163–7)

There is something almost sinister in this pulse of the machine, the inevitable grace of a mechanical drive that enforces its opposite in 'tenderness'. The father, incapable of playful 'dalliance' alone, rocks a child in his arms who has been spectrally overdetermined by a patrilineal self-identification. Michael is not only unlike other fathers; this arch-patriarch even emasculates himself in 'female service' or nursing. The drive is close to an obsessive compulsion, even mania. Yet through this uncanny image, a reconciliation of grace and necessity, displacing gender norms, is nevertheless still speaking.

The poem does not have the didactic aim of showing that Michael should have placed his love of family before love of property. In 'The Last of the Flock', the impoverished shepherd's need to sacrifice his livestock is what erodes his affection for his family. What makes the sacrificial relationship binding, with no way out, is that whatever Michael does, he is in the wrong, for something must be given up. After the disappearance of Michael's son, 'As before', we are told, he still 'Perform'd all kinds of labour' and 'listen'd to the wind' (466–7). Nothing has changed, and everything has changed. The concrete and living labour of music has become an abstract work of repetition. Even a solitary labour of love is bound to its relations of production.

And so Michael's work of mourning – his continued work on the sheepfold that had been an allegorical labour of Abrahamic covenant with his son – is more often unable to carry on: 'many and many a day he thither went / And never lifted up a single stone' (474–5). Despite seven years' effort, he 'left the work unfinished when he died' (481). In a devastating final image of ambivalence, the poem reaches its broken climax in an ultimate robbing of purpose – an abandonment of labour in loss, and the end to work at death. The poem culminates in its own negation. It ends with the vanity of all labour in the face of bereavement and extinction – the blackout for which no work of mourning can compensate. There were days when Michael could only sit down and stare into space. But it is the negative image of a future state of 'majestic indolence'. What had emanated from his child as it worked and played with a 'thousand living things' was an effortless action in which nullity is at the heart of labour itself. It has no point or 'purpose' beyond 'the pleasure that there is in life itself'. Such a life, and such a death, has left the state of spectrality. In the poem's grief remains a longing for that possibility half-glimpsed in its opening: a life of gain without sacrifice.

In a coda to the poem, the progress of world history has now triumphed as if with a silent inevitability: 'the ploughshare has been through the ground' (486). But in a draft version from MS. 1,[102] the traveller is halted by something that remains behind. It is not only the condition of all labour and 'progress', but also the possibility of its interruption. The inalienable rights of a nature both living and individual – the *genius loci* of a spot of time or state of nature – make their very own declaration of independence:

> [when] I have waked at length
> From dream of motion in some spot like this
> Shut out from man, some region – one of those
> That hold by an inalienable right
> An independent life, and seem the abode
> Of nature and of unrecorded time
>
> (3–8)

But in this isolation, the traces of labour, 'Some vestiges of human hands', perhaps even Michael's ruined sheepfold, are like 'the sudden sound / Of music to a blind man's ear' (12–13). In this splitting apart, this differentiation of two forms of independent life, is the possibility of their reconciliation in music. Such traces inspire Wordsworth to 'look into past times as prophets look / Into futurity' (17–18). To preserve 'like a book' the memory of now superseded, and what were always in part broken forms of life, to translate their dumbness into eloquence, was not merely a 'salvage anthropology' or nostalgia. The almost negative synaesthesia that tries to redeem the blank – a seeing without eyes, a music that cannot be heard except in allegorical fragments – is an effort to discern what both is, and is not yet visible. It is the blind image of what can have no image: the longed-for transformation of labour in 'futurity'.

CHAPTER 7

Progress

Wordsworth's poetry can have no conclusion, or cannot be concluded yet. As he showed in the drafts for 'Michael', a backward glance at history was a prophetic reading into the future. It is a constitutive ambiguity, an endemic problem of reference. Even a steady look at the present was aimed at the invisible and yet to come. In lines first written for *Home at Grasmere* in 1799–1800, and in 1814 made a 'Prospectus' for the whole *Recluse*, to stand at the head of the entire authorship, that future was no less than the blinding *eschaton* itself: the 'great consummation' (*HG* 1004). Wordsworth asks us to evaluate his work in the light of utopia. But that light has yet to fall upon us. And there seems to be no guarantee, even likelihood, that it will – though Wordsworth, for one, was in no doubt.

It is astonishing how few critics have read this poetry on its own terms as an avowedly utopian project.[1] Wordsworth's strange confidence, and the avoidance or good sense of his readers, become more explicable when we see that this utopia has been timed to coincide with *right now*: the 'blessed hour' is a 'growth of common day' (1001–2). And so, after all, this is a poetry of the here-and-now. But before we can read it properly, we might be in for a long wait. For 'long before the blessed hour arrives', Wordsworth is condemned to 'sing in solitude' (1002–3). Paradise is spread all across the earth, and only he can see it.

Yet Wordsworth insists that he is 'Speaking of nothing more than what we are' (1005). The 'growth' has sprung up fully – or is in need of cultivation, a seed planted but yet to germinate. The millennium might be more a potential than an inevitability. What does invoke 'Paradise' (996) is an art of philosophical travel. The 'Elysian' (997), Wordsworth declares, 'waits upon my steps, / Pitches her tents before me when I move' (994–5). Always a step ahead, it might be something 'evermore about to be'. The Promised Land is more the pastoral nomad, or a servant-beggar at Wordsworth's feet. Even as the messianic arrives, it might be ignored or pass unnoticed.

A marriage needs to be arranged. This is a 'spousal verse' (1003), an epithalamium. It would proclaim the bans of no more, but also no less, than the wedding of subject and object, of mind and matter. This was only to take up a cry already raised by the empiricism of Francis Bacon, the 'happy match between the mind of man and the nature of things'.[2] For Wordsworth too, they are already 'fitted' together, 'exquisitely' so (1009) – just cause enough to make Blake speak out that he knew of no such fixture and fitting.[3] But the honeymoon booked for these nuptials is to travel far beyond – or within – the empirical. This tour within 'the mind of Man / My haunt, and the main region of my song' (989–90), however, though it evokes the Romance tonality of a Renaissance travel, a search for the 'marvellous',[4] in reality seems closer to a Quixotic model so frequent in eighteenth-century travel, a landscape of progressive disenchantment.[5] For it will raise an apocalyptic bridal 'veil' (979) that is only the Emperor's New Clothes – none other than those of 'Jehovah' himself (982). This philosophical travel will progress beyond not only his entourage of angels, but all 'personal forms' (981) of the supernatural, and even the 'Heaven of heavens' itself (979). In a shocking spirit of romance and carefree levity, with even a tone of the ideal world – a blasphemy that made Blake sick to his stomach[6] – Wordsworth says that he will 'pass' by these spectral and harmless enchantments 'unalarmed' (984). He will reach the *eschaton* of the Enlightenment: a whole history of 'superstition' has been simply travelled past.

But we are not in holiday sunshine. Wordsworth trembles in 'fear and awe' (987). There seems to be a deeper Godhead. Our travels have followed a *via negativa* to the impersonal and formless. But with a shock we are told that *this itself* is 'the mind of Man' (989). As the most extreme form of a sceptical debunking has stripped literally everything but the mind away, in the blithe spirit of what is supposed to be a wedding song, it is only at this point of ultimate disenchantment that a real enchantment breaks through. We are awestruck. For we remain tourists: it is something we can only 'look / Into' (988–9). Within the deepest region of mind, at the heart of our self-identity, there is some kind of contradiction or non-identity. The mind has split apart within itself. In apocalyptic 'fear and awe', it eludes our cognitive grasp. We are deep into *terra incognita*. Immediately we move on – a non sequitur with no transition – to 'Beauty, whose living home is the green earth' (991). The 'great consummation', it seems, is to take that fearful 'mind' and bring it down to beautiful earth.

This is Wordsworth's maximal vision. Only a beauty of matter that has consummated its union with a sublimity at the heart of mind can satisfy the intention of utopia. But at least one of its poles has been totally obscured from us. What we see when 'the light of sense / Goes out in flashes that have shewn to us / The invisible world' (*Pr.* VI.534–6), a mind that is 'A thousand times more beautiful than the earth' (*Pr.* XIII.447) – all this is left in total blackout. As Donald Davie wrote of our 'fiduciary' stake in Wordsworth, we are called upon to trust an abstraction.[7] Blake wrote in the margin of the 'Prospectus': 'Jehovah dropped a tear & follow'd him by his Spirit into the Abstract Void.'[8] Yet this void is then identified by Blake with 'the Divine Mercy'.[9] It might be a merciful release from the rigours of judgement and determinate form. There seems to be a concealed tension in Blake himself, let alone Wordsworth, between the formless or 'Spirit' and its 'personal forms'. Yet the seemingly 'Abstract Void', Wordsworth has told us, is 'the main region of my song'. But there is another region: our 'common day'. As a poetry of their marriage, somehow the two regions are superimposed or fitted together. Our everyday life is an eschatology. If the 'great consummation' would announce the end of history, then the 'fear and awe' of mind in its daily presence on earth is the work of history itself. This would seem to be Coleridge's 'esemplastic' power of imagination, the demiurgic struggle of its 'shaping spirit' with a recalcitrant matter. But Wordsworth's travels in the 'Prospectus' anticipate a revelatory moment in excess of intention, a leaping out of mind and earth together. The 'great consummation' cannot be brought about by will. Wordsworth can only show us where to look, and how to work, what value we should be cultivating. But as De Quincey was to write of spousal verse: 'The epithalamia of Edmund Spenser are the most impassioned that exist; but nobody reads them.'[10]

Lamb has written of the voyager's wild transports and ecstatic mania, a vain 'gloriation of mind' that Hobbes compared with Don Quixote, and their infatuated visions of terrestrial paradise in the maritime age of island discovery – the Prospectus announces 'Paradise and groves / Elysian' like 'those of old / Sought in the Atlantic Main' – in terms that irresistibly recall the Prospectus' two poles:

> The utopia in the brain and the paradisal possibilities of the *terra incognita* provide political philosophers as well as mariners opportunities for finding more than nothing in a blank space. The metaphor of the psyche as a map of uncharted territory overlaps the metaphor of the voyage as a probe of the secrets of the mind, giving a global space to the difficulties of the je ne sais quoi.[11]

Lamb's account of the traveller's fall from civil society into anti-social, vainglorious and delusional efforts at self-preservation in *terra incognita* might seem abruptly to puncture the ecstatic hopes of the Prospectus. But even here, there is 'more than nothing': there are 'possibilities', 'opportunities', 'secrets' and 'difficulties'. There is plenty of scope for colonial, or philosophical, self-aggrandizement and exploitation. But there are also 'secrets' and 'difficulties' of expression. It is such moments of resistance, even in Wordsworth's most extravagantly utopian verse, which remain a stumbling-block 'that is not to be put by'.

As a 'growth' of the common, Wordsworth had faith in a *telos* that was not identical to historical 'progress'. This was to mark him out from other 'millenarians' in the 1790s – one of those rare and always brief periods in history, like the 1650s, the 1920s and the 1960s, in which it was not altogether uncommon to be utopian.[12] For rational Dissenters as varied as Joseph Priestley and William Godwin, the collapse of belief in a revolutionary instant after the Reign of Terror – which claimed the life of the most famous 'perfectibilist', Condorcet – was offset by the rational progress towards perfection that it had helped to set in train.[13] The messianism of the Commonwealth-period sects was grafted onto an Enlightenment teleology. Arguing that we must chart the progress of world history and abandon the impossible effort to picture the state of nature, Adam Ferguson had stated that humanity's 'emblem is a passing stream, not a stagnating pool'.[14]

Wordsworth never quite shook off the progressivism of his youth. As late as his 'Reply to Mathetes' in 1809, he was able confidently to affirm 'a belief in the progress of human Nature towards perfection'[15] as imaged by the passing stream or river – but this was now precisely a matter of 'belief', not a rational inevitability. Wordsworth struggled to fit *The Recluse* into a historiography, a drawing of the line of history:

> The progress of the Species neither is nor can be like that of a Roman road in a right line. It may be more justly compared to that of a River, which both in its smaller reaches and larger turnings, is frequently forced back towards its fountains, by objects which cannot otherwise be eluded or overcome, yet with an accompanying impulse that will ensure its advancement hereafter, it is either gaining strength every hour, or conquering in secret some difficulty, by a labour that contributes as effectually to further it in its course, as when it moves forward uninterrupted in a line, direct as that of the Roman road with which we began the comparison.[16]

The passage's elaborately winding syntax exemplifies its own principle: pushing back then forwards, repeatedly turning, before finally doubling back on itself, only to spring directly ahead once more. The novelty of this historiography – he is unique among writers of the period in this turning of the 'Roman Road'[17] – may well be indebted to the convoluted line of development in *The Prelude*. Progress is not only driven back by the stumbling-block of obstacles or resistances that it brings to light; it depends on going back to 'fountains', states of nature, for replenishment. But in the interspace, 'A whole generation may appear even to sleep.'[18] In such periods, 'truth and virtue' are served 'by scattered and solitary minds'.[19] This seems to be a labour of preparation. For the dormant 'multitude' is gathering 'energy' for a later 'fury': a surge that breaks 'the chains of the people'.[20] Possibly thinking of figures like Rousseau and Tom Paine in the decades leading up to 1789, or republicans like Milton and Harrington after the Restoration, an essay on the river of progress has suddenly turned into a theory of *revolution*.

Such was the eschatological or utopian longing – even if revolution here is a progressive leap rather than end of history – that so often hid in teleological postponements. Coleridge's idea of *The Recluse*, however, was emphatically chiliastic and anti-progressive – albeit itself a millennial progress or 'scheme' with a difference, for though its lineaments were fully visible, it had yet even to begin. When Coleridge finally, after entreaties from Wordsworth going back to the early 1800s, sketched his plan for *The Recluse* in a letter of 30 May 1815, it was to follow a stadial progress that was no more than a comparative history of the postlapsarian: 'Fallen men contemplated in the different ages of the World, and in the different states – Savage – Barbarous – Civilized . . . and not disguising the sore evils, under which the whole Creation groans, to point out however a manifest Scheme of Redemption from this Slavery, of Reconciliation from this Enmity with Nature.'[21] Wordsworth's task was nothing less than the reversal of Original Sin. It is little wonder, then, that he was later reported to confess, while comparing *The Recluse* in 1838 to another unfinished moral-philosophical long poem, Thomas Gray's *The Alliance of Education and Government*, that 'he had undertaken something beyond his powers to accomplish'.[22]

When Wordsworth did try to present an image of history as straight-ahead progress, in the Duddon sonnets – a tacit response to Coleridge's letter, and an acknowledged effort (in its preface) to fulfil the stadial and riverine scheme of what was probably the original impetus for *The Recluse*, Coleridge's unwritten 'The Brook' – it was only as a picture of 'Fallen' nature. In sonnet XIII, as Wordsworth reaches the physical clearing that will lead to the triumph of progress, the 'Open Prospect' of agriculture, the stage of history omitted by *The Prelude*, he leaps into an exuberant apostrophe: 'Hail to the fields' (1–3). Nature's enmity, however, has not been overcome. It reappears in a distorted reflection of the violence now imposed upon it: 'the stiff lance-like shoots of pollard ash' (6). Clearing the prospect exposes it to the 'roar' of 'bleak winds' (5) – ironically compared to the winds that 'lash' the perimeter of the sheltering forests at Ontario, 'By wasteful steel unsmitten' (9). To treat anything as an object rather than a subject – even material nature – will create effects of resistance. The progress of history has gradually escalated into an all-out two-way war.

The 'Prospectus' gave evidence of a younger and more imaginative Wordsworth's refusal to defer historical gratification. He simply wanted to live and write as if utopia were already with us. His poetry was an experiment in pressing that aspiration right up against the most severely concrete. Keats observed how, in his famous allegory of Wordsworth's progress, an 'intoxicated . . . Maiden-Thought' of wondrous sense-experience

> becomes gradually darken'd and at the same time on all sides of it many doors are set open, but all dark, all leading to dark passages. We see not the balance of good and evil. We are in a Mist. *We* are now in that state. We feel the 'burden of the Mystery.' To this point was Wordsworth come, as far as I can conceive, when he wrote 'Tintern Abbey, and it seems to me that his Genius is explorative of those dark Passages. Now if we live, and go on thinking, we too shall explore them.[23]

The progressive in Wordsworth is simply an opening of doors that might be ways out of the state of estrangement. There is no guarantee of light at the end of their 'dark Passages'. To see into the life of things would recede for Wordsworth into a negative capability that was not sheer night, but 'recognitions dim and faint' and 'gleams of half-extinguish'd thought' ('Tintern Abbey', 59–60). It is 'a dim and undetermin'd sense / Of unknown modes of being' (*Pr.* 1.420–1). What was crucial for Keats is that this is a verse that opens things up rather than closes them down. It is this inconclusiveness, this tentative open-endedness, which gives it an afterlife – Keats himself will become a 'thinking' explorer through its *terra incognita*.

At its subtlest moments, a 'Reconciliation from . . . Enmity with Nature' in this verse was a latent quality more than a 'manifest scheme'. The problem with natural law, or a progressive 'natural history of man', was that they were not quite natural enough. The schematized nature of philosophical anthropology – in which actual physical nature was all but forgotten in rational sketches of the socio-historical or human totality – had to be confronted with the social expression of nature as legible in physiognomies or 'pictures of Nature, Man, and Society'. Society was to be challenged with the question of which state of nature it wished to represent. Wordsworth's 'humanization of nature and naturalization of man' was to show how our moral-political life is bound up with our stance towards nature. Our comportment towards objects is inseparable from persons, for there is matter in our bodies and a strange life in the material. To give voice to that life in an industrializing age was to search for what might leap out in the way of progress. The conservative and transformative forces in Wordsworth's verse cannot be neatly separated out. But there is genuine hope in this verse's prophecy of the future through an image of the past: the revaluation of a newly poetic work, building and technology that seek to articulate the nuance and delicacy, as well as affective power, the rich differentiation and embodied particulars, which give nature its alien language. Wordsworth reminds us that in our state of second nature, a *habitus* masquerading as immediacy built up through millennia of tradition and domination, we have simply no idea of what the natural state might actually mean.

Wordsworth's insistent desire for an inner 'life of things', qualified as a possibly 'vain belief' ('Tintern Abbey', 49–51), drew back into felt moments of inanimate passion in which the mythic heritage disqualified by an Enlightenment with its own version of myth, the 'Block / Or waxen Image' of abstract forms, might be retrieved as the source of a genuine engagement, an intersubjectivity, not an ineluctable power of natural forces. Progress had to go backwards in order to spring forwards: to the rescue or redemption of animism. What spoke through the face of a physiognomy was a real individuation – and the historical scars of its shaping. It was to revive the archaic tradition of hospitality to the 'stranger as such': a strangeness that might conceal a visitation of the divine. To approach the alien body required a new mode of *habitus*, and it is in such poetic structures that a 'spousal verse' of humanity and nature begins to grow faintly visible – a criss-crossing similitude in dissimilitude, a processual openness to revision, a prosody that makes breathings for its interruption. Or a rhetoric that does not arrogate or subsume within the identity principle but in the same gesture opens up differences and hitherto unsuspected relationships: litotes, hendiadys, parataxis, oxymoron, even an 'apparent tautology'. As this verse goes back in the direction of material nature and rural modes of life, that archaism or traditionalism is haunted by a potential leap ahead that cannot be imaged in any other way. Memory, poetry and history are enjoined with the task of translation. Only this might prevent an acting out by which the past or the archaic reiterates itself blindly. Wordsworth's scattered and isolated acts of translation can only point to it – or in Novalis' words: 'I show that I have understood a writer only when I can act in his spirit, when, without constricting his individuality, I can translate him and change him in diverse ways.'[24]

There was no straight road back to the paradisal state of nature. The ageing individual cannot return to childhood and youth:

> The days gone by
> Come back upon me from the dawn almost
> Of life; the hiding-places of my power
> Seem open, I approach, and then they close;
> I see by glimpses now, when age comes on
> May scarcely see at all
>
> (*Pr.* VI.333–8)

This is not only what undermines 'progress'. It is also the source of the blind drive that pushes it forward:

> the soul,
> Remembering how she felt, but what she felt
> Remembering not, retains an obscure sense
> Of possible sublimity, to which,
> With growing faculties she doth aspire,
> With faculties still growing, feeling still
> That whatsoever point they gain, they still
> Have something to pursue.
>
> (*Pr.* II.331–41)

The pursuit is driven by the ontological question of childhood. Just what did the child experience? But Wordsworth can only move in the opposite direction: towards death. We can only try to 'find / Strength in what remains behind' ('Ode', 182–3), a minimal remainder, he enjoins, in a joyous cry of despair: 'Oh joy! that in our embers / Is something that doth live' (132–4).[25] Wordsworth's poetry was soon to enter its own terminal phase of dessicated ageing. The 'death-in-life' of his figures of withered maturation – such as 'Old Man Travelling', 'The Leech-Gatherer' or 'The Discharged Soldier', regressing like Freud's death-drive, but not wholly, to the condition of inanimate matter – might also be the image of a life-in-death sobriety. The ambivalence is explicit: 'the young behold / With envy, what the old man hardly feels' (*LB* 13–14, 'Old Man Travelling').

The age and body of Wordsworth's own historical time seemed to be growing old with him. His belief in the future squared up against the fear of an oncoming 'age of iron'. In his 1833 poem, 'To the Utilitarians', this is his phrase for what their 'economic rage' (*LP* 1–2) held in store. As late as the year after his opposition to the Reform Bill, Wordsworth was still identifying the millenarian *telos* of labour, a reconciliation of 'effort with the end of Being', with the 'true agreeing / Of objects with internal seeing': the utopia of the 'Prospectus'. He even lays claim to abstract right: it is here we find the 'ideal rights / Of Human-kind' (10–13). But this is counterposed to the utilitarian goal of relieving social poverty. It is the major contradiction in what had become Wordsworth's anti-politics of a sensuously material, hence bodily, as well as spiritual happiness – the 'blissful hour'. Yet an economic rationality blindly exclusive of other concerns is itself irrational, a form of 'rage'. The aporia points to the 'spousal verse' of Wordsworth and the Utilitarians – a 'consummation', however, to which they do not add up.[26]

In Book v of *The Prelude*, Wordsworth was quite capable of envisioning not only the annihilation of humanity, but the entire destruction of the planet's surface. In that Book, the utopian tradition of poetry has come to nothing. Yet even at that prospect, he clings to a hope that the 'living Presence' will 'still subsist' in a 'sing'd and bare' matter, with 'kindlings like the morning', a pre-dawn in darkness that anticipates 'a returning day' (32–6). In a state of estrangement – perhaps more truly Wordsworth's 'main region' – that apocalypse has already taken place. Wordsworth's maximal vision – his unappeasable drive for happiness, his desire to have it all – has now receded into a bare utopian *minimum*: a fixed and steady look at 'what remains behind'.

Scraps and Fragments

Wordsworth's haunted gaze at the minimal remainder, latent with hope in the very embers of common day, led him to search for the germinal seeds of poetic life within the most inconspicuous and ordinary modes of behaviour. An anthropological basis for poetry had to be found in 'nothing more than what we are' – not only in the passions of labour, but also in the intervals of vacancy. A man whose life seemed nothing else was 'The Old Cumberland Beggar', one of the 1798 'pictures' of *The Recluse*. So extreme is this man's state of estrangement that he seems to present a test or limit case in Wordsworth's search for the indestructible, for 'what remains behind'. But the pathological is only the normal *in extremis*. We read this poem wrongly if we evade our own complicity. The abstract sentimentality of the poem's egalitarian axiom or proposition – 'we have all of us one human heart' (146) – is to be put to the test of 'solid life'. For the man seems to be singularly heartless. The beggar offers no thanks for the charity he receives on his habitual round, and does not even perceive, let alone acknowledge, anyone else. The instinct of self-preservation, the ground of individual rights, is exposed at its point of greatest reduction as an undead and machinic drive. Yet Harold Bloom has been able to call its mendicant 'Wordsworth's finest vision of the irreducible natural man, the human stripped to the nakedness of primordial condition and exposed as still powerful in dignity, still infinite in value'.[27] While he resembles one of Rousseau's solitaries, however, this is emphatically a *contemporary* state of nature: a social condition of vagrancy. What has distanced him from human beings is inextricable from a withdrawal so severe he is unable even to look up at the sky. An automatism of survival keeps him moving on, while rotating in a circle of villages, his eyes fixed on the ground.

Yet Wordsworth insists that even this man will remain half-conscious of something other than his own self-interest:

> Thus, from day to day,
> Bowbent, his eyes for ever on the ground,
> He plies his weary journey, seeing still,
> And never knowing that he sees, some straw,
> Some scatter'd leaf, or marks which, in one track,
> The nails of cart or chariot wheel have left
> Impress'd on the white road, in the same line,
> At distance still the same.
>
> (51–8)

Estrangement has reduced the three-dimensional world to a one-dimensional surface, as flat as a blank sheet of paper – 'Impress'd', nonetheless, by a form of *writing*. The living particulars that make up a face, or the minute grading of 'shades of difference', have now shrunk back into sheer graphemes without meaning, arbitrary scratchings that merely space out a line. As with printed words, the spaces between them are even identically distanced, 'still the same' – impressed with the automated prosody of a turning wheel, as inexorable a repetition as that of the man's own life. Here then – if anything in experience might be – is undeniably a 'pre-text', a world of sheer writing, with nothing outside its textual relations. Even a steady look, rather than half-conscious glance, might be hard-pressed to see how, as Bloom writes of the poem as a whole, the 'matter of fact . . . is itself a transfiguration'.[28] Yet Wordsworth insists that these bare marks have the power to break through into the man's distracted consciousness, even unawares – he remains haunted, without even knowing it, by what Book v would call a 'living Presence'. A hint is given by an ironic counterpoint: in his 1804 letter to Thelwall on metre, Wordsworth singled out the very line that underscores the linear uniformity of these impressions – 'Impress'd on the white road, in the same line' – as, in terms of regular metre, the 'most dislocated line I know of in my writing'.[29] As with the shape of the verse line, the marks deposited by the wagon are not points in mathematical space – they have been inscribed with a *punctum*. There is a sharpness of point to this hard-edged syllabary, 'nails of cart' that dig into the line, and decorate it – even in its regular and abstract locomotion. The only 'transfiguration' here is the minuscule difference by which the straws, ruts and loose detritus have been marked out from bare matter: a singularity of impression that dislocates, like an individual word, even while concatenated in a line or series. What remains behind is a language of materiality, and the materiality of language itself.

To find something more in an apparent waste matter might even be in the man's own self-interest. As he stares at the food he has been given:

> He drew his scraps and fragments, one by one,
> And scann'd them with a fix'd and serious look
> Of idle computation.
>
> (*LB* 10–12)

As James Chandler observes, the beggar is 'made to seem very like an animal in this description, drawing out his scraps and scanning them dumbly', below the villagers in the 'great chain of being', but above the birds which collect the crumbs that fall from him (18–21).[30] His absorbed interest in the merest scraps of food, like that of the birds, seems to confirm that he is able 'To breathe and live but for himself alone' (158). Yet the poem appears to reorient this evaluative *habitus* towards a *telos* that is not hierarchical but horizontal: there is 'a spirit and pulse of good, / A life and soul to every mode of being / Inseparably link'd' (77–9). Wordsworth does not explicitly defend the chain, only its links. There is somehow an end of 'good', a 'pulse' of the machine, even in the scraps themselves. There is a vital spark of generosity even within an 'animal' self-interest.

Searching for that 'pulse' as a differential, it suddenly seems important that the man's gaze is that of an '*idle* computation'. The noun indicates a self-interested calculation, a 'computation'. Yet its adjective is 'idle', without purpose. The oxymoronic look is not motivated by appetite or even an anticipated satisfaction. It is a counting that adds up to nothing. Indeed, he seems already to have counted his fragments a moment before, as he drew them out 'one by one' – the mere line of a monosyllabic series. What was already a superfluous measuring without numbering is now exacerbated by an even more useless secondary computation. And it is hard to gauge just how this computing might receive its coded inputs: for the scraps are not tallied up, but merely 'scanned'. The scan might be a negligent glance over, a close examination, a panoramic survey, or even the qualitative counting of a prosody, a metrical scansion. The man's behaviour seems pregnant with all these forms of a not wholly self-interested behaviour. It recalls the leech-gatherer's 'Choice word, and measur'd phrase' (*P2V* 102) in 'Resolution and Independence' – a drawing out, one by one, of syllables whose accompanying rhythm at the same time dissolves these phonemes into a 'stream' of discourse: 'nor word from word could I divide' (114–15). Like the double movement of a prosodic comportment, working between the chariot wheel of a measured motion and an inchoate flow, the beggar's partly distracted attention is at once a painstaking calibration and a stream or pulsing through. Moreover, line 11 is itself not quite precise in its counting. With no elision indicated to the word 'serious', the line terminates in a hypermetrical eleventh syllable, momentarily held in suspense by a fixated and excessive 'look'.

When Wordsworth tells us that the 'vital anxiousness' of the beggar's material 'hope' as he struggles against the elements is what 'Gives the last human interest to his heart' (170–1), it is in this sense that the apparently 'animal' is also a '*human* interest'. He is capable of hoping for something better. What might be genuinely 'human' is a resurrection of the animal. It is defined against the 'House, misnamed of industry' (172), the workhouse system that would outlaw any form of idleness, yet would set him to an idle and useless, incessant labour for its own sake – without anxiousness, and also without hope. What makes the poem so disquieting, no less than an affirmation of anxiety and pain, is also the potential for its torpid life to awaken. It offers a very different model of counting to that of any utilitarian calculation of the 'greatest happiness of the greatest number' – the Benthamite workhouse project to which those who did not make the count were to be sacrificed.[31] The poem's conservatism is inseparable from its resistance to the progress of anaesthesia.

Its teleological intuition or 'transfiguration' settles precisely on that which has no *telos* – or has been diverted from its identity and function, like the accidentally fallen crumbs that the birds consume, disturbingly imparting a pulse of good even to the man's 'palsied hands', or the wall that the beggar sits upon to eat, intended only as a base for remounting horses at the foot of a hill (2–6). The pulse of good or the machine is a gift of excess in all things. As in 'Resolution and Independence', it is a 'peculiar grace' (*P2V* 50) – as enigmatic as the 'strange utterance' of nature, a language of things, actions and events as they disrupt the normal purposes or course of the everyday in minute infractions. Seemingly arbitrary, the afterlife of this miracle of the apparently ordinary and non-supernatural intervention is able to haunt with the supernatural power of the uncanny. What makes something idle, or beyond computation, is what gives it a capacity to turn. The teleological intuition is a perception of things as unidentifiably open-ended.

The man's sweeping gaze is the absolute barest, most extreme reduction of Wordsworth's faith in a river of progress as an invisible force of nature: 'the mighty stream of tendency'. Wordsworth sought a stream or flow that might uphold the figures of individuation. In *The Spirit of the Age* (1825), Hazlitt would identify that progressive hope with the ideology of the age: '"the mighty stream of tendency" as Mr. Wordsworth in the cant of the day calls it'.[32] But Wordsworth did not identify that natural teleology with history. In its material resistance was a counter-progress, a discipline of natural necessity. It was a vulnerable position: on 15 January 1804, Coleridge wrote to Thomas Poole to boast that he had recently cured Wordsworth from being 'even to Extravagance a Necessitarian'.[33] But 'the mighty stream of tendency' would later resurface in *The Excursion* (IX.86). It is an oral language, a 'clear sonorous voice' (90) which is paradoxically – by this point in Wordsworth's progress towards spiritualized doctrine and alienated experience, the dwindling away of a hauntingly concrete experience with an unidentifiably allegoric resonance into the arbitrary sign – an *almost* fully allegorical writing. For it is indeterminately of nature, 'the voice / Of waters, with invigorated peal / From the full River' (67–9), albeit now 'All unsubstantialized', as well as of the 'invisible world' (87). The direction of its *telos* and its relation to history is left undisclosed – it is 'inaudible' to the 'fret and labour' of the 'vast multitude' (90–4) – but occurs in a poem in which a now fully conservative Wordsworth affirms the progress of British imperialism, helping to explain Hazlitt's reaction.

The mighty stream was first announced in a draft for 'The Pedlar' from the late 1790s as a stance of 'wise passiveness' – the sages

> rest upon their oars
> Float down the mighty stream of tendency
> In a calm mood of holy indolence
> A most wise passiveness in which the heart
> Lies open and is well content to feel
> As nature feels and to receive her shapes
> As she has made them.

John Rieder quotes these lines as part of his study of Wordsworth's 'counterrevolutionary turn'.[34] Yet this too is a revolutionary turn: a renunciation of the will to power and control, maybe even Coleridge's reconciliation from 'Enmity with Nature'. It leads to what is perhaps the most strange of all Wordsworth's invocations of an objective affect: the drifter feels 'As nature feels'. This is how nature feels when it has not been prefigured in advance. It is what remains behind when even the will to change the world has fallen into estrangement. And it is precisely the feeling of a new world. Except that this is to stream through the shapes of nature, not history. It is an opportunity to surrender to the currents of nature, a heart lying open to the foreign, but whose oars will be taken up again. Just how its flow might enter into action in the world has been left open-ended: the enigma of an 'idle computation'.

In another draft of this period – the turn of the century was the high-water mark of Wordsworth's millenarian enthusiasm – the feeling has now become mutual:

Thus disciplined
All things shall live in us and we shall live
In all things that surround us. This I deem
Our tendency

(*RC*, MS. B, 78–81)

This is Wordsworth's maximal vision of 'tendency'. Yet an incorporation, as well as projection, would also imply the resistance, the indigestible strangeness, of what remains behind in the observer. For this vital immediacy is haunted by a sense of distance: it is to 'multiply / The spiritual presences of absent things' (*RC*, MS. B, 27–8). No phrase better exemplifies the problem of reference in Wordsworth. But what is absent can also hold a strongly material presence. In 'Tintern Abbey', this is the hendiadys of a 'motion' as well as a 'spirit' (*not* a 'spiritual motion') – as with the 'pulse' accompanying a 'spirit of good' – in a stream of tendency that is merely the line of a paratactic series

Whose dwelling is the light of setting suns,
And the round ocean, and the living air,
And the blue sky, and in the mind of man,
A motion and a spirit, that impels
All thinking things, all objects of all thought,
And rolls through all things.

(98–103)

In his lecture 'On Liberty and Necessity', Hazlitt would interpret this passage in teleological as much as pantheist terms: 'Perhaps the doctrine of philosophical necessity was never more finely expressed than in these lines.'[35] Yet Wordsworth's repetition of the word 'all', no less than three times, a teleological hammering into unity, deflects from what had been a catalogue of qualitatively distinct moments. This motion dwells only in the light of setting suns – not in the poem's earlier 'many shapes / Of joyless day-light' (52–3), the horror of common day, of atoms in empty space writ large. Its sky is blue, its air tangibly 'living' in atmosphere. But Wordsworth immediately follows this list with another whose nouns are flatly neutral and without aura: 'Therefore am I still / A lover of the meadows and the woods, / And mountains' (103–5). Such lists, so numerous in Wordsworth, seem to confess a decay of affect in the very act of affirming its ubiquity.

There is just this, and this, and that, in an endless and deadening line. The list is the most primitive form of writing, held by scholars to have characterized the first appearance of written signs in Mesopotamia, the inventory or 'accountant's script' as a mnemonic technique.[36] Its oral precedents might include the genealogical recitation or the catalogue of names in epic. But in a key passage of *The Prelude*, there is a minimal remainder of spiritual presence even in the barest series – and precisely in the matter of its language:

> Visionary Power
> Attends upon the motion of the winds
> Embodied in the mystery of words.
> There darkness makes abode, and the all the host
> Of shadowy things do work their changes there,
> As in a mansion like their proper home:-
> Even forms and substances are circumfus'd
> By that transparent veil with light divine;
> And through the turnings intricate of Verse
> Present themselves as objects recognis'd,
> In flashes, and with a glory scarce their own.
> (v.619–29)

Visionary power only *attends upon* the motion of the winds; as with 'a motion and a spirit', they might as readily come apart. And so nature's language is not only translated into human words: this is their 'proper', or at least more secure, 'home'. But nature's meaning remains insecure: it belongs to the 'mystery of words'. The lines seem to embody that obscurity in their own resistance to interpretation – just what is this legion of 'shadowy things' and their darkly magical agency, an ability to 'work changes' or metamorphoses? This is not language as the 'light divine' of Platonic ideal forms – the language of identity. It seems closer to a restless materiality of language in a flux and reflux that resembles the winds. But that movement in turn transforms the identifying noun. The recognition of a genus or species appears only in 'flashes', an instant of release from the stream of language. And this is a special effect of verse. Unlike ordinary language, it is distinguished by its 'turnings intricate': its caesurae or pauses, enjambement, transitions and subtle modulations, its minute deviations from metre or rhythmic emphases.

If a *poiesis* is a making, the *versus* is a turn. In excess of a recognizable identity, it delivers up the object in a flash of singular 'glory'. Closer to the name than the general noun, the isolated word communicates a force that is greater than itself – the power of language itself. And a trace of that glory might find a refuge, if not a 'mansion', in even the most minuscule *punctum* of the serial list. But this is also a rhythm of transience, like the destructive processes of nature; the object disappears at the very moment it leaps out, the condition of another turning up. That is all that remains here of a natural teleology. Yet it resembles not only nature as a bending or turning river; it is a form of prosodic comportment, even a mode of travel. What remains behind, when experience has lost its glory, is sealed up within language. When the key has gone missing, when we can no longer interpret the winds – 'the heavy and the weary weight / Of all this unintelligible world' ('Tintern Abbey', 40–1) – what verse can still do, as it articulates language itself in flashes, is to let things speak for themselves.

As the stream of an egalitarian metaphysics withdraws, this is all that can now co-ordinate the strange particulars, as well as general nouns, that haunt rather than inhabit Wordsworth's verse: the noise of splitting gorse seeds, the 'burr' of an 'idiot boy', a wet and slimy stone, a mouldering staff on a rock. No previous writer had granted such phenomena this kind of claim to dignity. At times they might even offset the whole world. To Coleridge's chagrin, Wordsworth spent much of the spring and early summer of 1802 – shortly after writing the despairing opening stanzas of the 'Ode' and another 'crisis-poem', 'Resolution and Independence' – avoiding *The Recluse* and writing short lyrics about flowers and birds: the epoch of 'The Small Celandine'. Such commonplace singularities were tangible with the presence of something absent:

> But there's a Tree, of many one,
> A single Field which I have look'd upon
> Both of them speak of something that is gone.
>
> ('Ode', 51–3)

The tree is not just the bare remnant of a lost whole: it stands out from the 'many'. It is a dejected afterimage of the turn of a flashing word in verse, an eclipse of context by which it loses its ground. A singularity of point seems to have leaped out of the void. A faded image of life at its most intense is held together with a blackout.

In the 'Ode', Wordsworth would imagine a child's view of the grave as 'A place of thought where we in waiting lie' (123). Shortly after the first draft for the 'Ode', in the spring of Wordsworth's flower poems, Dorothy Wordsworth recorded an eccentric moment when she lay motionless in a ditch alongside William, who imagined that he was lying in the grave – listening to 'the *peaceful* sounds of the earth'.[37] With 'his eyes shut', he also hears what can be called a waterfall only in the language of identity: 'There was no one waterfall above another – it was the sound of waters in the air – the voice of the air.'[38] Having lost its ground – suspended in mid air – the waterfall gives voice to a living vacancy. Wordsworth hung listening into the dark, the hiatus or caesura of the poetic line, Coleridge's 'trances of the blast'. The true contrary to a state of estrangement in this verse is not a driven engagement. It is to stare deep into estrangement itself – until something opens up or leaps out at us. In the 'Ode' this became the vigil of a personal ageing, 'an eye / That hath kept watch o'er man's mortality' (200–1). But what remains at the end of the 'Ode' is an expressionless thought, the gift of an inscrutably singular, yet common life:

> To me the meanest flower that blows can give
> Thoughts that do often lie too deep for tears.
> (205–6)

The North-West Passage

What has remained behind of Wordsworth's poetry most conspicuously in recent years has been its unrecognized afterlife within the largely journalistic trend of 'psychogeography'. This fashion in turn is only a bare remnant of the more vitally charged and politically radical 'driftings' of Situationism in the 1950s and 60s. A vogue for drawing out the scraps and fragments of the aimless stroll, in self-conscious rejection of a utilitarian or consumerist *telos*, most often in the cityscape, is also at risk of the serial list: the warehouse, the littered verge, the graffitied underpass, and docklands canal. What such a geography appears to lack is precisely the *psyche*. The missing body of a physiognomy is often compensated in this literature by a factual and historical reading of a station's hidden or former life. But such a 'psychogeography' is in danger of becoming what it would least like to be: a new search for the picturesque or antiquarian.

For Guy Debord, writing in 1955, Situationist psychogeography meant a study of the 'specific effects of the geographical environment, whether consciously organized or not, on the emotions and behaviour of individuals'.[39] As with Wordsworth's travels in search of the *genius loci*, it recorded the 'moods' of a place, its objective affect. A critical reading of a milieu oppressed and disfigured by capitalism was also to undertake its lived or imagined reconstruction and *détournement*, a new turn given to the alienation and manipulation of what Debord famously called the 'society of the spectacle': 'detourned to serve in constructions of more interesting ambiences'.[40] The psychogeographical drift or *dérive* was a political reconnaissance, acting out in advance a scene's post-revolutionary conversion into a theatre of 'situations', of poetic encounters made actual. The privatization of this festive programme might now seem as inevitable as Wordsworth's turn in *The Prelude*, as outlined by Jacques Rancière, from a drift through the signs of a democratic reason in nature in revolutionary France to the lonely wanderings of the autonomous lyric subject.[41]

What remains of Debord's project is perhaps best located in a passage from De Quincey's *Confessions of an English Opium-Eater* that became its major touchstone. That precedent draws a line back from Debord not just to the Surrealist wanderings through Paris in search of the peculiar grace of an 'objective chance', but also, via his erstwhile disciple De Quincey, directly back to Wordsworth himself. First quoted in compressed form in Debord's 1957 account of a *dérive* in 'Psychogeographical Venice', De Quincey in 1821 characterized his own drifts through night-time London as the physical analogue of a moral and philosophical travel:

> Some of these rambles led me to great distances, for an opium-eater is too happy to observe the motion of time; and sometimes in my attempts to steer homewards, upon nautical principles, by fixing my eye on the pole-star, and seeking ambitiously for a north-west passage, instead of circumnavigating all the capes and head-lands I had doubled in my outward voyage, I came suddenly upon such knotty problems of alleys, such enigmatical entries, and such sphynx's riddles of streets without thoroughfares, as must, I conceive, baffle the audacity of porters and confound the intellects of hackney coachmen. I could almost have believed at times that I must be the first discoverer of some of these *terræ incognitæ*, and doubted whether they had yet been laid down in the modern charts of London. For all this, however, I paid a heavy price in distant years, when the human face tyrannised over my dreams, and the perplexities of my steps in London came back and haunted my

> sleep, with the feeling of perplexities, moral and intellectual, that brought confusion to the reason, or anguish and remorse to the conscience.[42]

For Debord, these private and nocturnal ambles shed a world-historical light: 'The hopeless condition of very large numbers of people – experienced at the same time that the power of human society over nature had increased immensely – appeared from then on in the culture of the innovators as an even-more acute contradiction between the affirmation of superior passionate possibilities and the reign of a certain kind of nihilism.'[43] De Quincey's passionate sense of a possible breakthrough from estrangement, 'seeking ambitiously for a north-west passage' homewards, was only to get lost in 'enigmatical entries' and 'riddles of streets without thoroughfares' – '*terræ incognitæ*' that returned to haunt him 'with the feeling of perplexities moral or intellectual'. The *terra incognita* is an involute, the 'perplexed combination', 'incapable of being disentangled', of a spot of time. It is a dark reflection of Wordsworth's own perplexities as he travelled in a rural daylight. The philosophical mind is brought down to earth through travel at the sheer physical knot of an aporia, a tangle of streets, through which there can be no passage.

De Quincey suggests, nonetheless, that if there is a way forward it can lie only in the direction of such enigmas and riddles, not along the cleared highways and major thoroughfares of progress. In his unfinished poetic meditation on homecoming – *Home at Grasmere* – Wordsworth would compare the 'passing traveller' in the Lakes to an explorer in *terræ incognitæ* whose 'way / Lies through some region then first trod by him' (*HG*, MS. B, 698–9). Here the tangled aporia is an effect of progress itself:

> which way e'er he goes,
> Something on every side concealed from view,
> In every quarter some thing visible,
> Half seen or wholly, lost and found again –
> Alternate progress and impediment,
> And yet a growing prospect in the main.
> (704–9)

In a flow of revelation and concealment, like a child's *fort-da* game, Wordsworth plays with the loss and gain of a more than mother nature. An inability to reach a final transparency, a north-west passage, seems written into experience itself. Progress throws up its own counter-movement or 'impediment' of resistance. To lay claim to something will make something else withdraw. Yet the obstacle is a necessary rule of the game's pleasure, a hide-and-seek of the visible and invisible that would be ruined if its nature were just out there, exposed, ready for data collection – the nature of the Enlightenment and 'curious' traveller – if it were not inexhaustible to this insatiable adult-child. Somehow, by accretion, all this has a cumulative effect of larger progress, of gathering vision in a sense of 'growing prospect'. But it seems to look forwards into nothing more than its own incessant march onwards. And this aimlessly philosophical travel, a utopian drift, must also 'cast a painful look / Upon unwelcome things' (712–13). Wordsworth is forced to reject a pure correspondence theory of truth: 'Truth justifies herself' only insofar as she 'dwells / With hope' (500–1). Truth is as internally split between the visible and inaccessible as the Lakeland territory itself.

Travel becomes an endless meandering in the isthmus between an irrecoverable origin, the state of nature, and the goal of future progress – or death. It is to these prospects, Wordsworth claims in his first 'Essay on Epitaphs' (1810), that the child's fresh sense of *terræ incognitæ* is directed. The innocent question of childhood is an ontological question: when children ask what the source of a river might be, the question '*whither*' is implied in the '*whence*' for 'Origin and tendency are notions inseparably co-relative'.[44] The child is also asking '"Towards what abyss is it in progress? what receptacle can contain the mighty influx?"' – a question that contains its own implicit answer: for the child a river is heading towards 'nothing less than infinity'.[45] The child's instinctive sense of progress is directed towards a point or goal, a north-west passage, which swallows up all points – to the infinitely open and unbounded.

In the 'Ode', however, it is striking that Wordsworth offers 'thanks and praise' (143) not for the child's 'simple creed' of 'Delight and liberty' (139) or feeling of immortality, but for its sense of radical doubt:

> those obstinate questionings
> Of sense and outward things,
> Fallings from us, vanishings;
> Blank misgivings of a Creature
> Moving about in worlds not realiz'd
> (144–8)

The child's worlds are 'not realiz'd' for they have not yet been objectified as totally other to the self. The question of substance in such a psychogeography will return for the adult in the travel experience. The traveller's effort to realize his world is what Anthony Pagden has called the 'principle of attachment'. The explorer grows accustomed to an alien terrain by visualizing it within the framework of a domestic familiarity.[46] As David

Bunn has shown in relation to Wordsworth's friend, Thomas Pringle's 1820s 'picturesque' poems of South Africa, the exotic environment was aesthetically valorized only insofar as it evoked the landscape of home, a 'transitional object' in Winnicott's terms, which cushioned a feeling of 'ontological shock' at the foreign.[47] It could also be the mnemonic of a less homely, more imperial sense of origin – as in Mungo Park's exclamation on his first visit to West Africa to discover the teleological direction of its main river: 'I saw with infinite pleasure the great object of my mission; the long sought for, majestic Niger, glittering to the morning sun, as broad as the Thames at Westminster, and flowing slowly *to the eastward*.'[48] Wordsworth's 'The Idiot Boy', a tale of travel in *terra incognita* in which the boy leaves home to journey out at night for the first time in his life, is on one level a hermeneutic parable of misrecognition, a satire on the transitional object. On return home, he provides a digest of the experience, 'like a traveller bold', in just one mimetic and repeated statement: '"The cocks did crow to-whoo, to-whoo, / And the sun did shine so cold"' – 'And that was all his travel's story' (*LB* 458–63). The traveller's story is a tale told by an idiot, signifying nothing new.

Yet the boy's reverie is also a peculiar 'similitude in dissimilitude', a salutary estrangement of new and old in unsettling juxtaposition. In Wordsworth the home terrain as transitional object is more frequently set into reverse. When, in Book I of *The Prelude*, he compares himself to a 'naked Savage' child sporting in the 'thunder shower', the hills become 'bronz'd with a deep radiance' (301–5) as though acquiring a 'Red Indian' complexion themselves. Dorothy's journal of their Highlands tour insistently compares its landscapes to an America they were never to visit. In 'The Solitary Reaper' the Highlands suddenly leap towards the Sahara and the Hebrides; a shepherd in Book VIII of *The Prelude* can emerge from the mist like a polar bear in Greenland (402). For the 'Prospectus' to *The Recluse*, utopia was the reorientation of foreign travel to the here-and-now: 'Paradise and groves / Elysian', like 'those of old / Sought in the Atlantic Main', were not a 'history only of departed things', or a 'mere fiction', but remained a 'living presence of the earth' in its 'beauty' (47–51). Wordsworth attempted to revive the utopian tradition of travel at the very moment in history when it had at last been abandoned as a large-scale hope. The final heir to a *Terra Australis*, Mount Purgatory, Eldorado and Fountain of Eternal Youth that had all conspicuously failed to show up – Louis Antoine de Bougainville's raptures on discovering Tahiti in 1768, hailed as the 'Elysian Fields' and a 'garden of Eden' – had been quickly debunked the following year by Cook's longer stay on an island now marked by the painful sight of inequality, prostitution and infanticide.[49] As in the Quixotic model that dominated eighteenth-century literary travel, most notably in Samuel Johnson's *Rasselas*, an enchanted travel gave way to a progressive disenchantment. For Michael Wiley, the utopia of Wordsworth's landscapes is a blank negativity, like the largely unmapped interior of Africa in the period, a displacement of existing structures to create space for an indeterminate possibility.[50] Yet Wordsworth insists that paradise is a 'living' presence of the earth. But it was also a spiritual presence of absent things, an interference of spaces, unfolding the familiar into the strange. Paradise is to feel at home within the sensation of foreignness.

As the failure of the French Revolution was compensated by a faith in progress, so utopian travel became supplanted by the teleological drive. With the mapping of islands completed by Cook, late eighteenth-century travel shifted to the exploration of continental interiors. The traveller was the advanced guard of progress, discovering new territory and gathering scientific, ethnographic and commercial intelligence in preparation for colonization, or at least the opening up of new markets. Now the charting of continental rivers, as the main arteries of trade, goods and rapid mobility, became the central task. The river became the vector of a world-historical progress. With the failure of the coastal navigations of Cook and Vancouver to find the legendary 'North-West Passage', the river or ocean that would link the Atlantic to the Pacific through the Americas, the emphasis was now placed on finding the river or river-system that might extend from one coast to the other. Even Chateaubriand, in flight from the French Revolution, went off in search of such an inland north-west passage, as did Samuel Hearne in Canada and the famous Lewis and Clark expedition across America in 1804. As Bernard DeVoto stated of the latter: 'There had to be such a river; the logic of geography, of teleology, and of desire required one.'[51] In *The Excursion*, that Passage to the future was deemed as inaccessible by the Solitary – who, like Chateaubriand, is driven from revolutionary France to America, albeit due to disappointed radicalism rather than conservative reaction – as his fantasy of the state of nature, the 'Primeval Nature's Child' (III.928) of the American Indian (a now disavowed corollary to the Swiss shepherd in *Descriptive Sketches*), whom he had once imagined walking along the banks of 'that Northern Stream / Which spreads into successive seas' (940–1).

The Solitary had spoken for the perplexing enigma of origin and tendency through a comparative mythography of the river. An 'American' myth is adduced in which 'the first Parents of Mankind' had 'Leapt out together from a rocky cave' (*Exc.* III.245–7) – that moment of chthonic magic, or leaping out, in even a material account of origins. By contrast, he appeals to an Indian myth of the Ganges as emerging 'from a skiey fount', allowing the Hindu to 'deduce the Stream of human Life / From seats of Power divine' (260–2). This psychogeography of myth then turns to the River Niger, whose terminus (like that of the Nile) had baffled classical and modern geography alike, and that must 'be engulfed' within 'impenetrable sands / And utter darkness', an image of the 'comfortless' thought of death as annihilation (266–9). Wordsworth was perhaps alluding here to Mungo Park's fatal second journey to West Africa in 1805, an attempt, as he wrote in November that year to Lord Camden, Secretary of State for War and the Colonies, 'to discover the termination of the Niger or perish in the attempt'[52] – in the (mistaken) hope that it would link up with the river Congo. Park had disappeared upriver, and Wordsworth wrote two concerned letters to Park's friend, Walter Scott, regarding his uncertain fate.[53] For the Solitary, it seems, the teleological drive was shot through with an eschatological tension.

While Park was driven by 'tendency', an earlier Scottish traveller James Bruce's self-consciously archaic quest for the source of the River Nile, with a sublimated rather than territorial desire to take personal and colonial possession, was inspired by a passion for the origin. Alan Liu has plausibly suggested that the famous episode at the Simplon Pass in *The Prelude*, Book VI, is indebted to Bruce's account in 1790 of arriving at what he claimed to be the unique Ethiopian source of the river in 1772.[54] Bruce drew upon the symbolism of Book X of Lucan's *The Civil War*: '"Nature has disclosed to no one his secret spring, and men have not been allowed to see thee, Nile . . . she has withdrawn thy hiding-places."'[55] It was the psychogeographical correlate of the unreachable 'hiding-places' of Wordsworth's 'power' in childhood. Bruce's quasi-imperial triumph over the conquerors of antiquity (Julius Caesar and Alexander the Great had sent failed expeditions to the source) gives way to a progress of disenchantment, as he is left 'considering the Nile indeed as no more than rising from springs, as all other rivers do'.[56] The Nile is then belittled in favour of Bruce's native rivers of Scotland, and he calls on the Providence that has made his journey triumphant to escort him back to the motherland. In an 1801 notebook entry, Coleridge would register the nominalistic damage: 'N.B. to make a detailed comparison in the manner of Jeremy Taylor between the searching for the first Cause of a Thing & the seeking the fountains of the Nile – so many streams each with their junction &c–&c– at last, it all comes to a name.'[57] In his Fenwick note to the Duddon sonnets, Wordsworth would admit: 'It is with the little Duddon as it is with most other rivers, Ganges and Nile not excepted, – many springs might claim the honour of being its head.'[58] Wordsworth is stubbornly driven to invent one: 'In my own fancy I have fixed its rise.'[59] For Liu, it is the arbitrary and subjective assertion of an 'imperial imagination' that links Wordsworth to Bruce and a larger colonialism.[60]

Wordsworth's 'dull and heavy slackening' (549) in Book VI, on learning that he has prematurely reached his sublime *telos* and already crossed the Alps, does indeed recall Bruce's dejection. Yet the experience is a loss of 'imperial' control:

> Imagination! lifting up itself
> Before the eye and progress of my Song
> Like an unfather'd vapour; here that Power,
> In all the might of its endowments, came
> Athwart me; I was lost as in a cloud,
> Halted without a struggle to break through,
> And now recovering to my Soul I say
> I recognise thy glory
>
> (525–7)

The passage does seem modelled on that favourite 'spot of time' in travel literature, like Bruce at the Nile, the providential rescue of the despairing traveller – in the 1850 text, imagination is like a 'vapour that enwraps / At once some lonely Traveller' (*14BkPr.* 596–7) – but with a Copernican turn. Its *habitus* is turned in a new direction that is the abandonment of direction, the Providential guide to a goal or back home. Imagination does not rescue the traveller, but is the source of danger itself. In a sudden irruption, it seems 'unfathered' like a first cause or innate idea. But as David Ferris observes, a metrical emphasis underscores that imagination is only *like* something unfathered.[61] It is also like a 'vapour' or 'cloud'. It is not quite true, as Hartman famously claimed of the passage, that it fully signals 'the independence of imagination from nature' or that the two phenomena are '*intrinsically* opposed'.[62] There is a 'similitude in dis-similitude' between them. This is not in any simple sense the 'egotistical sublime' or triumphant ego of self-preservation, for it has thwarted the lost traveller's progress, created a resistance, an overthrow of self-consciousness by what resembles a nature in the subject. Recovering, the 'I' is carefully distinguished from the 'soul' to which it is inferior, addressed in the second person. Despite that positive identification, the nebulous sensation belongs with 'visitings / Of awful promise' (533–4) and 'harbours' with 'hope that can never die' (537–40). Again, whatever truth harbours in such a resistance is indeterminately split between present and future. Yet it seems related, if not perhaps identical, to what Wordsworth called the 'human soul', a surcharge of bodily feeling. The passage both draws on a romance or rhetoric of imperialistic crusade – 'the mind' is 'beneath' (not above) 'banners militant' – and explicitly redirects and opposes that *habitus*, for it 'Thinks not of spoils, trophies' (543–4). The ego has not been denied, but its appetent or imperial cravings have been turned towards fulfilment by what it cannot claim or seize, but within which it dissolves. Once the ego has recovered from the shock to its self-image, it can relax enough to recognize the real content of its overthrow: it is an 'access of joy' (547).[63] As a point expands and floods the ego, it 'hides' the mind in a foreignness of sensation 'like the overflowing Nile' (548). Only later might it fertilize an uncertain or symbolic interpretation – as in the 1850 text, in which Wordsworth has his own claim to have discovered a source of the Nile: the 'fount' of its flood at least in 'Abyssinian clouds' (*14BkPr.* 615–17).

For Liu, the passage's truth is an alternative first cause: 'the grounded or demystified Nile that is history'[64] – to Liu, no more than Bruce's or Napoleon's imperialism. Imagination, however, which Wordsworth both lifts above and associates with 'progress', might be closer to the inventions or passions of a 'natural history of man'. As Book VI moves on, and Wordsworth moves backwards as so often to go forwards, back from the Gondo Ravine along the Simplon Pass that took him to the end of the Alps – a north-west passage that has led to nowhere – an image appears of a nature and history now peacefully and adjacently parallel in tendency: 'The brook and road / Were fellow-travellers' (553–4). In the 1793 *Descriptive Sketches*, the millennial river of a revolutionary Reason of 'Heroes of Truth' against mystification had 'swept in anger' all who resist 'its progress' to 'Sink' and 'rise no more!' But what would emerge from this vindictive apocalypse had been left as blank as the 'long-parched lands' of world history it was meant to sweep over with 'Nile-like wings!' (*DS* 655–64). Such 'banners militant' led to Napoleon's expeditions to both Switzerland and Egypt. Back at the Simplon Pass, what is seen now is not an imperial or utopian blank. The veil lifted by the flood of joy is the revelation of a language of the particular and individual: '*Characters* of the great apocalypse' (570, my emphasis). The hope that dwells with truth in this private apocalypse, its public hope for the 'great consummation', is a sudden passage into what is 'first, and last, and midst, and without end' (572) – not a merely linear sequence, for the whole, the first and last, is attained in the 'midst' of an endlessness that has no goal to aim at, for it is reached at every point.

This natural temple, however, contains both 'the darkness and the light' (567) – a nature that is pregnant with historical suffering. The tradition of lament, the 'still, sad music' of a humanity unable to progress, has been accelerated to fever pitch. It is the psychogeography of an unredeemed nature in mourning, of 'Winds thwarting winds, bewilder'd and forlorn' (560). The progress of this 'gloomy Pass' (554) is a 'giddy prospect', a 'sick sight', with a 'stream' now 'raving' (564–5). As so often in the field of colonial travel, the explorer's prospect through this allegory of natural history is one of disorientation, disease and madness. Apocalyptic 'characters' write only of the destruction of meaning. They can speak, but have no voice: 'Black drizzling crags that spake by the way-side / As if a voice were in them' (564–5). Almost sinisterly close, alien enough to drizzle through the accents of a raving and forlorn history, the crags dislocate the line and its prosody. The scene has the dual valence of the apocalyptic, both catastrophic and revelatory: an allegorical nature of the 'types and symbols of eternity' (571) as well as history, a duration voiced only through what brings history instantly back, a permanent transience and decadence: 'woods decaying never to be decayed' (577). Recalling De Quincey's humbler perplexities at the involute, the enigmatic riddle of London, we are halted before 'the darkness and the light' of a final aporia.

The Simplon Pass had been crossed, however, not at *The Prelude*'s estuarine conclusion, but only half way through its progress. It has to be offset by that last great set-piece of the poem, Book XIII's narrative of a climb up Mount Snowdon. At one point, in his 1804 drafts (MS. W),[65] Wordsworth had intended to draw a direct comparison between Snowdon as a 'spot of time' and key moments from the literature of travel. What is striking about these dramatic episodes in world exploration is that they are moments in which an imperial progress is not affirmed but dislocated. Once more an exotic space is mapped onto a familiar (Welsh) scenery. As with the child's questionings, they record the 'fallings' and 'vanishings' of a world yet to be fully realized.

They begin with the Elizabethan traveller Sir Humphrey Gilbert, on a global circumnavigation, who braves a storm by sitting on deck reading the Bible, only to be swept away by a wave. It is an image of death as entirely arbitrary in its blasphemous providence. After another storm, the seventeenth-century pirate and state-sponsored explorer William Dampier, he who could see the Native Australians only through the lens of litotes, now renounces world travel in 'Bitter repentance for his roving life' (99). The passage then turns to Christopher Columbus, as for the first time in history a compass needle is seen 'faltering in its office', taking 'another course' away from 'the Pole' (63) – as a journey to the Indies is suddenly turned in the direction of *terra incognita*. When lastly, Wordsworth turns to a 'Land Traveller, living yet' (80), he recounts a key moment from Mungo Park's first expedition to West Africa:

> when, from the Moors escap'd,
> Alone & in the heart of Africa,
> And having sunk to earth worn out with pain
> And weariness that took at length away
> The sense of Life, he found when he awaked
> His horse in quiet standing at his side
> His arm within the bridle & the Sun
> Setting upon the desart.[66]

It was a point in Park's narrative that had seemed altogether to negate world travel: 'and whilst I reflected on the awful change that was about to take place, this world, with its enjoyments, seemed to vanish from my recollection'.[67] Like Wordsworth's traveller on Salisbury Plain, in an extreme condition of hunger and thirst, 'sickness and giddiness', an estranged Africa had just been reduced to the bare matter of a colonial state of nature: 'I cast a melancholy look over the barren Wilderness, but without discovering the most distant trace of a human dwelling. The same dismal uniformity of shrubs and sand every where presented itself, and the horizon was as level and uninterrupted as that of the sea.'[68] Yet though Park has 'sunk to earth' in blackout, unlike the Solitary's Niger, he does not 'sink engulfed' but reawakens. The heart of Africa is of light, not darkness. What has flashed out from all these episodes is not an overarching providence, but an inscrutable 'sense of Life'.

The colonial explorer is an adult relative of the child as 'halted hunter' in Book I. At the beginning of the Snowdon episode, Wordsworth climbs at the head of his band 'With forehead bent / Earthward, as if in opposition set / Against an enemy' (XIII.29–31). The image conjures not only the traveller or imperial foot-soldier at the vanguard or frontline of progress, genocidally implacable. Setting out to conquer the mountain, it invokes an entire world history of progressive 'Enmity with Nature'.

What wakes him to awareness is at first a gentle shock: 'at my feet the ground appear'd to brighten' (36). A flash of recognition leaps and falls out:

> instantly a Light upon the turf
> Fell like a flash: I look'd about, and lo!
> The Moon stood naked in the Heavens, at height

Immense above my head, and on the shore
I found myself of a huge sea of mist,
Which meek and silent, rested at my feet:
A hundred hills their dusky backs upheaved
All over this still Ocean, and beyond,
Far, far beyond, the vapours shot themselves,
In headlands, tongues, and promontory shapes
Into the Sea, the real Sea, that seem'd
To dwindle and give up its majesty,
Usurp'd upon as far as sight could reach.
Meanwhile the Moon look'd down upon this shew
In single glory

(39–53)

Wordsworth is careful to point out that on one level this 'sea of mist' is just a 'shew', a *spectacle* – a vaporous, even vapid illusion. Its headlands, tongues and promontory shapes are as imaginary as De Quincey's 'capes and headlands' in London.[69] So striking is the phantasmagoria that Wordsworth has to remind himself or the reader that 'the Sea' is not that of the mist, but the genuine article, 'the real Sea'. The two kinds of sea have become hard to distinguish – so much has the spectacle 'Usurped upon' the real that the latter seems almost to have vanished. Indeed, the latter 'seemed' – but only seemed – to diminish in comparison and surrender its claim to given authority, its 'majesty'. There is no resistance to that invasion save for one shady glimmer of the active universe: the dusky hills that appear to have 'upheaved' their 'backs' in an ineffectual uprising against it. Indeed, the conquering mist seems preferable even to the 'real' setting in its spectacular enchantment. In this 'spot of time', this sustained duration, only by small clues does Wordsworth snap us out of our contemplative reverie to alert us to the possibility that this 'shew', a semblance or performance, for all its captivation, is only an evanescent haze of intangible and wispy shapes.

But there is a stronger resistance to the usurpation:

and from the shore
At distance not the third part of a mile
Was a blue chasm, a fracture in the vapour,
A deep and gloomy breathing-place thro' which
Mounted the roar of waters, torrents, streams
Innumerable, roaring with one voice.
The universal spectacle throughout
Was shaped for admiration and delight,
Grand in itself alone, but in that breach
Through which the homeless voice of waters rose,

> That dark deep thorough-fare had Nature lodg'd
> The Soul, the Imagination of the whole.
>
> (54–65)

It is this 'dark deep thorough-fare' – not the misty promontory that laps at the 'real Sea' – that is the north-west passage that leads to the ocean. It seems to gather up all rivers, all 'waters, torrents, streams'. The 'blue chasm' is a 'fracture' that is also a breakthrough, a way beyond the 'universal spectacle'. The latter is not disparaged; it fills Wordsworth with 'admiration and delight'. It is, after all, the spectacle that has created its own 'breach'. A difference opens up between the beguiling spectacle that usurps and covers over 'the real' and one that makes spaces in which another language – a 'roar' and 'voice' non-human and not normally heard – has finally been given a 'breathing-place'. It is not the 'real Sea' in all its positivity that truly has the capacity to affect us – it is no more real than the mist, deceptive only as its semblance – but the *punctum* of this 'blue chasm' and its shaping of breath. Its language is 'homeless' – its resonance, if not its physicality, does not belong to the spectacle. It is 'dark' and 'gloomy'. It speaks of something absent and invisible, out of place and in exile. Yet it is this which redeems the 'whole'. The paradox is that the 'universal' is only truly a whole, rather than a usurpation, when it offers us a way out, an exit, beyond its apparent totality. What the spectacle had lacked is precisely the psyche, the 'Soul', of a genuine psychogeography. 'Soul' and 'Imagination' are lodged in the image itself. The physiognomy of nature's face or mood, the *genius loci* in its objective affect, has now become so charged with language that even something that might seem so impassably subjective as 'Imagination' is out there in the object itself. This too is part of the spectacle, an effect of the illusion. But something has genuinely leaped out and 'Mounted' a resistance. To make a 'breach' through the spectacle is not simply its unveiling towards 'the real', but the caesura by which a voice pierces, tears a hole in the cover of the real. It is the sound of a living vacancy. In their dissonant homelessness, its voices are crying out for translation, for 'a mansion like their proper home'.

The universal only gives us a breathing-place when it gives voice to what appears to break through it. While this remains as material as a rush or crash of waters, its language is not at home in the world and its ontology. Yet this is as much a semblance as the sea of mist – the voices only seem 'homeless' because their source is out of sight. Is the invisible surge really that of 'innumerable' currents? Language has touched language. It is an image of that 'consummation' of imagination and earth announced by the 'Prospectus'. It is perhaps in this sense, as Blake would claim, that what Wordsworth 'Writes Valuable is Not to be found in Nature'.[70] As in the child's or traveller's experience of radical doubt, a world not realized, the psyche cannot be separated from its geography. But at the same time, this deracinated language is not a pure illusion or poeticization. What the object emits, its properties – a sound of waters in mid air – are not fully reducible or identical to the object itself. The object might even be the most spectacular illusion of all. Spread across the earth as though refracted through a prism is a language of qualities, an excess of things in their pure surface that begins to pull us into an infinite depth.

Unusually, Wordsworth goes on in the next verse paragraph to give the experience an allegorical interpretation. The 'fear and awe' of the 'Prospectus' is at last given an image, and it remains just as unidentifiable:

> it appear'd to me
> The perfect image of a mighty Mind,
> Of one that feeds upon infinity,
> That is exalted by an underpresence,
> The sense of God, or whatso'er is dim
> Or vast in its own being
>
> (68–73)

It is also an image of Wordsworth's own brooding upon vacancy. There is something almost disturbing in this mind that 'feeds' – munches, sucks, nibbles or swallows up the infinite – like a ravenous animal. Have we really broken through the spectacle of consumption? But for Wordsworth, just as the 'superstructure' inhabits the 'base', so a baser instinct or appetite might drive our spiritual cravings – and it is the former that makes the latter not merely a sublimation, but just as real a need.

Yet is this not, after all, the 'imperial imagination' of a devouring ego? It is reminiscent of a draft passage from MS. Y, in which a child tries to propel its mind through the infinite depth of a night sky: 'Resolving into one great faculty / Of being bodily eye and spiritual mind' (*Pr2* 155–6). Line 156 was transcribed by the passage's first editor as 'Of being bodily eye and spiritual *need*' (my italics).[71] There is a similar feeding frenzy: 'if the one / Be insatiate the other is inexhaustible' (176–7). Yet the mind-body and space retain their non-identity in a 'converse' (157) of similitude in dissimilitude: 'With difference that makes the likeness clear' (182). The mind is not satiated; its resemblance, but also its other, eludes it. It is not a mode of consumption, for it has nothing substantial to feed upon. Nothing has been harmed or appropriated in this experience, an image of fulfilment precisely because it can never reach its fill of what is inexhaustible. Far from being 'lord and master', the mind is humbled through being 'exalted' by an 'underpresence' that exceeds it – an experience that is not necessarily divine, for it might include whatever is 'dim / Or vast in its own being'. What had seemed a void is an individuation. The mind 'feeds', depends upon, something that is greater than itself. A hunger for what is near identical to an imperial exploitation has been turned into its very contrary.

It is a strikingly different way of drawing nourishment from the world to its mere consumption alone – one that might enter even into our *habitus* of material consumption itself. Wordsworth goes on to argue that the radically objective Imagination of Snowdon belongs to moments in which nature appears to shape appearances into physiognomies or pictures with a creative agency: it 'molds them and endues, abstracts, combines' (79). This too stands in a relation of similitude in dissimilitude to human creativity: it is 'the express / Resemblance', the 'genuine Counterpart / And Brother' (86–9) of the 'glorious faculty' of imagination – as its sibling rather than imperial antagonist. Such an interplay or translation, if actualized, would be a revolution not only in everyday life. Its imaginative forms might even rebuild, or at least 'de-turn', the psychogeography of the city itself. 'What are those Golden Builders doing / Near mournful ever-weeping Paddington'?[72]

The creative agency of a poetics, a 'building of affinities', might yet reclaim the mythical given. In 1979, Guy Debord insisted that the 'supersession of art is the "North West Passage" of the geography of real life that had so often been sought for more than a century'.[73] The past tense speaks, against Debord's hopes, for a lost ambition: the construction of a poetically active environment, rather than a passively consumed – or the virtual compensations of a media participant – spectacle. If a now mediatized 'psychogeography' has its own truth, it is because it states baldly what has become (as one of its best-known practitioners has stated of a 'drift' through the Paris suburbs) an 'urban environment . . . so decoupled from any element of the felt or experienced life'.[74] Yet it is precisely through Wordsworth's sheer 'Necessitarian' passivity, because his poetry does not depict the individual on a stroll manipulating and moulding their environment at will, but rather distracted and self-absorbed in private cares – suddenly overcome and arrested by what is completely unanticipated – that the scraps and fragments of its 'felt or experienced life' might even yet remain behind.

We are step by step led on, syllable by syllable, to the caesura. For all our inexorable progress, there is always a 'sudden turning of the road'.

After the Snowdon episode, Wordsworth goes on to compare the whole of *The Prelude* to a river as it turns: its 'stream' has emerged in earliest infancy from 'darkness'; it is 'faintly heard' in childhood, and more consciously perceived by the adolescent in 'Nature'; it is 'bewilder'd and engulph'd' on entrance into society, then rises 'once more' when 'reflecting' the 'works of man', presumably via the shepherd and Book XII's revaluation of labour (172–81). And 'lastly, from its progress', he has 'drawn / The feeling of life endless, the one thought by which we live' (182–4). And it seems that it is an aimless travel, a drift or flow forwards, which gives us that feeling. *The Prelude*'s progress has been aimed not towards a point or goal, but at the 'endless' itself. But the reference is ambiguous – might it not be the Snowdon episode that has provided this feeling? That is, precisely an interruption of travel, a cessation of movement, obliged to stare into the caesura?

Near the conclusion of Book XIII, as Wordsworth turns to the river-image one last time, it is only to acknowledge his deceased patron, Raisley Calvert, whose financial legacy to Wordsworth had given him the much-needed leisure to write. The condition of all *The Prelude*'s progress has been a relief from material care. A poem of the river that has comprehensively redefined the material 'base' will almost end at the bottom-line. It is turned towards a supersession which history remains unable to find:

> He clear'd a passage for me, and the stream
> Flow'd in the bent of nature
>
> (XIII.366–7)

Notes

INTRODUCTION

1 *EY*, p. 212.
2 Alan Bewell, *Wordsworth and the Enlightenment: Nature, Man, and Society in the Experimental Poetry* (New Haven: Yale University Press, 1989).
3 To Joseph Cottle, in *Collected Letters of Samuel Taylor Coleridge, 1785–1834*, ed. Earl Leslie Briggs, 6 vols. (Oxford: Clarendon Press, 1956–71), vol. I, *1785–1800*, pp. 320–1.
4 John Millar, *The Origin of the Distinction of Ranks* (Bristol: Thoemmes Antiquarian Books, 1990; reprint of 1806 edition), pp. 3–13.
5 *The Correspondence of Edmund Burke*, ed. George H. Guttridge (Cambridge: Cambridge University Press, 1961), pp. 350–1.
6 Millar, *The Origin of the Distinction of Ranks*, p. 14.
7 Alexander Pope, *The Major Works* (Oxford: Oxford University Press, 2006), p. 271.
8 For example, an 11 March 1798 letter to James Losh announces '*The Recluse or views of Nature, Man, and Society*'. *EY*, p. 214.
9 'Letters to a Young Man Whose Education Has Been Neglected'; *The Collected Writings of Thomas De Quincey*, ed. David Masson, 14 vols. (Edinburgh: Adam and Charles Black, 1890), vol. X, p. 48n.
10 *Ibid.*, p. 48.
11 *Ibid.*, p. 47.
12 Kojin Karatani, *Transcritique: On Kant and Marx*, trans. Sabu Kohso (Cambridge, MA: MIT Press, 2005).
13 Cited in Jonathan Lamb, *Preserving the Self in the South Seas, 1680–1840* (Chicago: University of Chicago Press, 2001), p. 48.
14 *Ibid.*, p. 6.
15 William Bartram, *Travels through North and South Carolina, Georgia, East and West Florida* (Philadelphia: James and Johnson, 1791), pp. 45–6. This text was a favourite source of allusion for both Wordsworth and Coleridge.
16 *William Bartram on the Southeastern Indians*, ed. Gregory A. Waselkov and Kathryn E. Holland Braund (Lincoln: University of Nebraska Press, 1995), pp. 202–3.

17 Ann Talbot, *'The Great Ocean of Knowledge': The Influence of Travel Literature on the Work of John Locke* (Leiden: Koninklijke Brill NV, 2010), chapter 7.
18 John Locke, *An Essay Concerning Human Understanding*, I.ii.27, ed. Roger Woolhouse (London: Penguin, 2004), p. 73.
19 The statement appears in a manuscript ('General Draft') written between September 1798 and March 1799; Novalis, *Philosophical Writings*, trans. and ed. Margaret Mahony Stoljar (New York: State University of New York Press, 1997), p. 135.
20 Jean-Jacques Rousseau, *The* Discourses *and Other Early Political Writings*, trans. and ed. Victor Gourevitch (Cambridge: Cambridge University Press, 1997), 'Discourse on the Origin and Foundations of Inequality Among Men *or* Second Discourse', p. 209. Cited hereafter as Second Discourse.
21 Stephen Greenblatt, *Marvellous Possessions: The Wonder of the New World* (Oxford: Clarendon Press, 1992), p. 54.
22 *Ibid.*
23 Clifford Siskin, 'The Year of the System', in Richard Cronin (ed.), *1798: The Year of the Lyrical Ballads* (Basingstoke: Macmillan, 1998), p. 27. Siskin does not refer to *The Recluse*, but does include *Lyrical Ballads* here. Malthus' *Essay on Population* is another of his examples from this year.
24 Kenneth K. Johnston, *Wordsworth and The Recluse* (New Haven: Yale University Press, 1984), p. 13.
25 In a review of *Lyrical Ballads* in 1799, Charles Burney, the musicologist and friend of Samuel Johnson, had discerned a Rousseauan state of nature hidden in the contemporary setting of 'Lines composed a few miles above Tintern Abbey', a condition of 'men . . . born to live in woods and wilds, unconnected with each other'; unsigned review of *Lyrical Ballads* in *Monthly Review* 29 (June 1799), pp. 202–10; in Robert Woof (ed.), *William Wordsworth: The Critical Heritage*, vol. I, *1793–1820* (Routledge: London, 2001), p. 78. Francis Jeffrey argued in 1802 that Wordsworth's 'sources' lay first of all in 'The antisocial principles . . . of Rousseau' and 'his discontent with the present constitution of society'; unsigned review of Robert Southey's *Thalaba* in *Edinburgh Review* 1 (October 1802), pp. 63–83; in *ibid.*, p. 153. Two years later, he associated the 'charitable endeavours' of Wordsworth's writings with Paine's addresses to 'the common people'; unsigned review of *Popular Tales* by Maria Edgeworth, *Edinburgh Review* 8 (July 1804), p. 330; in *ibid.*, p. 128. William Hazlitt famously identified this 'Jacobin poetry' – though Wordsworth of course, like Paine, had been a Girondin – with a 'levelling muse' emergent from the French Revolution.
26 Mary Jacobus, *Romantic Things: A Tree, a Rock, a Cloud* (Chicago: University of Chicago Press, 2012), chapter 3, pp. 61–78.
27 The only exception in Wordsworth's 'major period', surprisingly unmentioned by Jacobus, occurs in draft material for the poem 'Michael' – and here indeed this refers to a natural landscape rather than 'human rights' (see chapter 6, p. 179).
28 Maureen N. McLane, *Romanticism and the Human Sciences: Poetry, Population, and the Discourse of the Species* (Cambridge: Cambridge University Press, 2000), p. 69.

29 Bewell, *Wordsworth and the Enlightenment*, p. 90. McLane's emphasis on Wordsworth's replacement of primitive anthropology with history and culture is derived from Bewell, as she acknowledges.
30 David Bromwich, *Disowned by Memory: Wordsworth's Poetry of the 1790s* (Chicago: University of Chicago Press, 1998), pp. 5–7.
31 Quoted in Susan Buck-Morss, *The Dialectics of Seeing: Walter Benjamin and the Arcades Project* (Cambridge, MA: MIT Press, 1989), p. 59.
32 James Chandler, *Wordsworth's Second Nature: A Study of the Poetry and the Politics* (Chicago: University of Chicago Press, 1984), pp. 16, 62–70, 129–39.
33 Edmund Burke, *Reflections on the Revolution in France*, in *The Works of the Right Honourable Edmund Burke*, revised edition, 12 vols. (Boston: Little, Brown & Co., 1865–7), vol. III, p. 312; cited by Chandler, *Wordsworth's Second Nature*, p. 34.
34 Praise for Burke had appeared long before 1832 in his 'Two Addresses to the Freeholders of Westmoreland' of 1818. But from 1798 until at least the 1810s, Wordsworth's overt politics (as *doxa*, rather than verse thinking) are almost impossible to pin down amid the 'winds thwarting winds' of conflicting tendencies – many of which remained operative if subterranean until the end of his life. If he was keen in that decade and after to plead a continuity with his earlier views, this is because certain principles, like an affirmation of 'independence' derived (as with Rousseau) from both republicanism and the rights tradition, were to broad enough to be adaptable to changing political emphases.
35 Duncan Wu suggests that Wordsworth probably read Paine's *Rights of Man, Part 1*, in spring 1791 (it appeared in February that year); *Wordsworth's Reading 1770–1799* (Cambridge: Cambridge University Press, 1993), pp. 109–10.
36 Quoted by Woof in *Critical Heritage*, p. 320.
37 *PW* 1.103.
38 Arthur Young, *Travels During the Years 1787, 1788, and 1789; undertaken more particularly with a View of ascertaining the Cultivation, Wealth, Resources, and National Prosperity of the Kingdom of France*, second edition, 2 vols. (London and Bury St Edmunds, 1794); quoted in David Simpson, *Romanticism, Nationalism, and the Revolt against Theory* (Chicago: University of Chicago Press, 1993), p. 52.
39 Simpson, *Romanticism, Nationalism, and the Revolt against Theory*, p. 52.
40 *Ibid.*, p. 153.
41 *Ibid.*
42 *PW* 1.103.
43 *Ibid.*
44 *Ibid.*
45 Ernesto Grassi, *Rhetoric as Philosophy: The Humanist Tradition* (University Park: Pennysylvania State University Press, 1980), p. 20.
46 Lynn Hunt, *Inventing Human Rights: A History* (New York: W. W. Norton, 2007).
47 *Ibid.*, p. 118.

48 Simon Jarvis, *Wordsworth's Philosophic Song* (Cambridge: Cambridge University Press, 2006), p. 27.
49 *Ibid.*, p. 31.
50 Jarvis, *Wordsworth's Philosophic Song*, p. 29.
51 In his 'Prospectus' to *The Recluse*, Wordsworth speaks of his verse's 'high argument', a phrase derived from Milton's 'great argument' in *Paradise Lost*. Like *theoria*, the word 'argument' had etymological roots (Latin, *arguere*) that wavered between description and prescription: 'showing', 'proof', 'accusation', and also the 'summary of contents' in an epic poem.
52 Pierre Bourdieu, *The Logic of Practice*, trans. Richard Nice (Cambridge: Polity Press, 1990), p. 14.
53 *Ibid.*, pp. 14, 108. In his *Protrepticus*, Aristotle compared theoretical contemplation to watching the Olympic Games.
54 *Ibid.*, p. 15.
55 *Ibid.*, p. 52.
56 *Ibid.*, p. 41.
57 *Ibid.*, p. 54.
58 *Ibid.*, p. 72.
59 *Ibid.*, p. 69.
60 Michel de Certeau, *The Practice of Everyday Life*, trans. Steven Rendall (Berkeley: University of California Press, 1984), p. 58.
61 Letter to John Wilson, 7 June 1802. *EY*, p. 355.
62 Jonathan Lamb, 'Scurvy and the Terra Incognita', *Public Domain Review*, 6 May 2015. Available at http://publicdomainreview.org/2015/05/06/scurvy-and-the-terra-incognita/.
63 *Ibid.*
64 *Ibid.*
65 On Darwin and eighteenth-century medical discourse in relation to Wordsworth and the delusions and nostalgias of travel, see Kevis Goodman, '"Uncertain Disease": Nostalgia, Pathologies of Motion, Practices of Reading', *SiR* 49 (2010), pp. 197–227.
66 David Hume, *A Treatise of Human Nature*, vol. 1, p. vii, ed. Ernest C. Mossner (Harmondsworth: Penguin, 1985), p. 311.
67 *Ibid.*
68 Immanuel Kant, *Critique of Pure Reason*, trans. and ed. Paul Guyer and Allen W. Wood (Cambridge: Cambridge University Press, 1998), p. 339.
69 One of his students in his later professorial years in Berlin, Ludwig Michelet, reported that this was a frequent characterization of his youthful *summa* by Hegel. A biographer has indeed termed this a 'cliché', while acknowledging that it is 'particularly apt' given the work's foundational and 'experimental character'; Terry Pinkard, *Hegel: A Biography* (Cambridge: Cambridge University Press, 2000), p. 203.
70 Edmund Husserl would write of his attempts to suspend the 'natural attitude' (his term for theoretical presuppositions along with prejudgements of the real) in a phenomenology of direct experience: 'he who for decades instead

of speculating concerning a New Atlantis has really wandered in the trackless wilds of a new continent and undertaken bits of virgin cultivation, will not allow himself to be diverted by the refusals of geographers who judge the reports in the light of their own experiences and habits of thought, and on the strength of this exempt themselves from all the trouble of making a journey into the land proclaimed to be new'; 'Introduction' (1931) to *Ideas: General Introduction to Pure Phenomenology*, trans. Boyce Gibson (London: Routledge, 2012), p. xliv.

71 *MY* II.238.

72 Less attention will be paid to Wordsworth's later phase roughly from 1808 in which, as *The Excursion* often typifies when it is not reworking his earlier draft poetry, we see a new turn from the latter-day primeval towards a greater historical traditionalism, not unrelated to an increasing 'Burkeanism', be it the feudal-Christian or antiquarian, or a comparative myth and ritual.

1 *SALISBURY PLAIN*

1 Thomas Hobbes, *Leviathan*, ed. Richard Tuck (Cambridge: Cambridge University Press, 1996), p. 89.

2 Rousseau, Second Discourse, p. 132.

3 Hobbes, *Leviathan*, p. 89.

4 *Ibid.*, pp. 96–7.

5 *Ibid.*, p. 97.

6 Lamb, *Preserving the Self*, p. 112.

7 Quoted in *Ibid.*, p. 111. As Lamb points out (p. 112), Jonathan Swift would turn the tables in his parody of Dampier in *Gulliver's Travels*. In its last book, the two poles of the state of nature, reason and animal instinct, supposedly reconciled in enlightened self-interest, have now split apart. Gulliver remarks in wonder at the Houyhnhnms' purely rational state of nature (as contrasted with the animal state of the Yahoos): 'Here were no Gibers, Censurers, Backbiters, Pick-pockets, Highwaymen, House-breakers, Attorneys, Bawds.' The list runs on for nearly a paragraph until it concludes: 'No Lords, Fidlers, Judges or Dancing-Masters'; *The Writings of Jonathan Swift*, ed. Robert A. Greenberg and William B. Piper (New York: W. W. Norton, 1973), p. 242.

8 Lamb, *Preserving the Self*, p. 112.

9 Agamben, *Homo Sacer*, p. 105.

10 *Ibid.*, p. 106.

11 *Ibid.*, p. 125. Agamben's italics.

12 *Ibid.*, p. 127.

13 Rousseau, Second Discourse, p. 132.

14 Paul Hamilton, *Metaromanticism: Aesthetics, Literature, Theory* (Chicago: University of Chicago Press, 2003), p. 51.

15 Rousseau, Second Discourse, p. 218.

16 *Ibid.*, p. 161.

17 *Ibid.*, p. 134.

18 *Ibid.*, p. 157.
19 Jean Starobinski, *Jean-Jacques Rousseau: Transparency and Obstruction*, trans. Arthur Goldhammer (Chicago: University of Chicago Press, 1988), p. 308.
20 Rousseau, Second Discourse, p. 139.
21 *Ibid.*, p. 82.
22 See Paul Kelley, 'Rousseau's *Discourse on the Origins of Inequality* and Wordsworth's *Salisbury Plain*', *Notes and Queries*, NS 24 (1977), p. 323; cf. Chandler, *Wordsworth's Second Nature*, pp. 130–1.
23 For a brief exception in terms of Wordsworth's differing evaluation of sympathy, see Chris Jones, *Radical Sensibility: Literature and Ideas in the 1790s* (London: Routledge, 1993), p. 200.
24 Samuel Taylor Coleridge, *Biographia Literaria*, ed. Nigel Leask (London: J. M. Dent, 1997), p. 54.
25 Richard Gravil, for example, has argued (not without grounds) that *Guilt and Sorrow* is by far the superior version; *Wordsworth's Bardic Vocation, 1787–1842* (Basingstoke: Palgrave Macmillan, 2003), p. 79.
26 This is also linked to the pastoral genre as William Empson conceived it: 'a pastoral or Robinson-Crusoe situation where one meets only the fundamentals of human life'; *The Structure of Complex Words* (London: Chatto & Windus, 1951), p. 124.
27 See, of course, Starobinski, *Jean-Jacques Rousseau.*
28 This is more than just an implication: in a later passage of *Adventures*, the livelihood of an independent fisherman is ruined when he refuses to sell his 'hereditary nook' to a new 'mansion proud' before which, progressively, 'cottage after cottage owned its sway'; *SP* 300–8, p. 133.
29 Walter Benjamin, 'On Some Motifs in Baudelaire', in *Selected Writings*, vol. IV, *1938–1940*, trans. Edmund Jephcott and others, ed. Howard Eiland and Michael Jennings (Cambridge, MA: Belknap Press, 2003), p. 366.
30 Quoted in *ibid.*, p. 327.
31 Wordsworth seems to have conceived of *Salisbury Plain* as an exact inversion of the latter-day rhapsodic state of nature evoked in the opening two verse paragraphs of *Descriptive Sketches*. The Alpine paradise of the Swiss peasant is also a domain of 'Unfathom'd dells and undiscover'd woods' (10), but 'Dear is the forest frowning o'er his head' (23) to the cottage-dweller on a pensive stroll. Here too, there is a 'far-off spire' for orientation in every sense, the peasant's 'evening bourn!' (22). The protective nature defined only by litotes in *Salisbury Plain* is present here in abundance: 'Kind Nature's charities his steps attend, / In every babbling brook he finds a friend' (27–8). The most striking parallel is the 'Host of his welcome inn, the noon-tide bow'r, / To his spare meal he calls the passing poor' (31–2).
32 At its most extreme, for the traveller in the blankness of *terra incognita* that longing might even produce hallucinations. Such was the famous 'calenture' of sailors in the ferocious heat of dead calm tropical seas, as evoked by Wordsworth in 'The Brothers'. Here, Leonard, a former shepherd, frequently leans across

the rail of his ship on the 'cloudless main', and in 'the bosom of the deep' sees 'mountains', 'the forms of sheep that grazed / On verdant hills', and grey-clad 'Shepherds', along with 'inland sounds / Of caves and trees' in more rapid water – 'Even with the organs of his bodily eye' (45–62). In his reading of Coleridge's tropical and hallucinatory 'Ancient Mariner', Jonathan Lamb has sought to explain the 'calenture' as an effect of scurvy, or what he calls 'scorbutic nostalgia'; *Preserving the Self*, chapter 4, 'Scurvy', pp. 114–31. The calenture, however, more directly presents itself in historical terms: as the most radical manifestation of colonial litotes.

33 *SP*, p. 217. For Hobbes, international politics was a contemporary survival of the 'war of all against all'; *Leviathan*, Part I, chapter 13.

34 William Stukeley, *Stonehenge, a Temple Restor'd to the British Druids* (London, 1740). On Wordsworth's classical and modern sources regarding the Druids, see Gravil, *Wordsworth's Bardic Vocation*, chapter 1.

35 See Jarvis, *Wordsworth's Philosophic Song*, pp. 40–4.

36 While 'savage' and 'barbarian' had become quasi-technical terms for different historical stages in some eighteenth-century social theories (e.g., for Rousseau and Adam Ferguson), their prejudicial connotations nevertheless made them often interchangeable in normal usage; see J. G. A. Pocock, *Barbarism and Religion*, vol. IV, *Barbarians, Savages and Empires* (Cambridge: Cambridge University Press, 2005), pp. 1–2. In a letter to William Mathews on 19 May 1792, Wordsworth would employ both terms while recounting the violence and fear surrounding the revolutionary army's retreat at Lille, disturbingly archaic in the supposedly enlightened context of the Revolution: 'An ignominious flight, the massacre of their general, a dance performed with savage joy round his burning body, the murder of six prisoners, are events which would have arrested the attention, of the reader of the annals of Morocco, or of the most barbarous of savages' (*EY*, p. 77).

37 *Ibid.*, p. 112. Much of the phrasing here is taken from the initial draft's account of Druidic sacrifice (and would be restored to that section in subsequent drafts).

38 Hunt, *Inventing Human Rights*, p. 94.

39 Henri Hubert and Marcel Mauss, *Sacrifice: Its Nature and Function*, trans. W. D. Halls (London: Cohen & West, 1964), p. 100.

40 René Girard, *Violence and the Sacred*, trans. Patrick Gregory (Baltimore: Johns Hopkins University Press, 1977).

41 In *Homo Sacer*, Agamben is at pains to distinguish the 'state of exception' from sacrifice. In the former, the individual is killed or degraded without being hallowed (unlike, say, the ritual victim or the fallen soldier). But the 'state of emergency' also involves the sacrifice of individuals for the supposed benefit of the community.

42 Walter Benjamin, 'Critique of Violence', in *Selected Writings*, vol. 1, *1913–1926*, ed. Marcus Bullock and Michael Jennings (Cambridge, MA: Belknap Press, 2004), pp. 236–52.

43 Rousseau, Second Discourse, pp. 171–2.

44 *Ibid.*, p. 173.
45 William Godwin, *An Enquiry Concerning Political Justice and its Influence on General Virtue and Happiness*, 2 vols. (London: G. G. J. and J. Robinson, 1793), vol. 1, p. 35.
46 Gravil, *Wordsworth's Bardic Vocation*, p. 82.
47 Letter to Francis Wrangham, 20 November 1795; *EY*, p. 159.
48 As Lynn Hunt observes, 'Because punishment was a sacrificial rite, festivity inevitably accompanied and sometimes overshadowed the fear. Public executions brought thousands of people together to celebrate the community's recovery from crime's injury' (*Inventing Human Rights*, p. 94).
49 *Salisbury Plain* seems to conflate, or at least implicitly draw comparison between, the period of the American War and the rural crises during the war with France after 1793.
50 Jean Baudrillard, *America*, trans. Chris Turner (London: Verso, 2010), p. 67.
51 Coleridge, *Biographia*, p. 54.
52 In the last decade of his life, Wordsworth finally resolved his fascinated horror at executions and ritual sacrifice by notoriously celebrating them in his 'Sonnets on Capital Punishment'.
53 'The Two-Part Prelude of 1799', in *The Prelude, 1799, 1805, 1850*, ed. Jonathan Wordsworth, M. H. Abrams and Stephen Gill (New York: Norton, 1979), p. 569.
54 John Locke, *Two Treatises of Government*, ed. Peter Laslett (Cambridge: Cambridge University Press, 1988), second treatise, chapter 2, p. 274; Locke's italics.
55 There has been a marked shift in Wordsworth's attitude to 'superstition' from the final stanza of the 1793–4 *Salisbury Plain*, which had prophesied 'Heroes of Truth' to destroy 'Superstition's reign', leaving 'not a trace' apart from Stonehenge as the monument of something finally overcome (541–9). Yet Wordsworth here has not quite yet reached the Wanderer's view, in the 1814 *Excursion*, that the 'illusions' of rural custom are 'mainly outward ministers / Of inward conscience' (IV.833–6).

2 BUILDING, DWELLING, EMBODYING

1 Thomas Aquinas, following Aristotle, upheld a hierarchical ('relative') natural law on account of the Fall. But calls to reclaim the Edenic state of equality were a feature of anti-clerical Christian sects such as the 'Brethren of the Free Spirit' in the Middle Ages, and would become prominent in radical Protestantism.
2 See Norman Cohn, *The Pursuit of the Millennium: Revolutionary Millenarians and Mystical Anarchists of the Middle Ages* (London: Paladin, 1970), pp. 187–9; Ernst Bloch, *Natural Law and Human Dignity*, trans. Dennis J. Schmidt (Cambridge, MA: MIT Press, 1986); and Leo Strauss, *Natural Right and History* (Chicago: University of Chicago Press, 1953).
3 Bloch, *Natural Law*, p. xxx. Bloch's study is an attempt within Marxism itself to counterbalance Marx's critique of human rights as a legal-formal rather than substantive freedom and equality.

4 *Ibid.*, p. xxiv.

5 Locke, *Two Treatises*, p. 323.

6 This rationality of natural law is what separates Wordsworth's figure from the radical Christian state of nature to which it is nevertheless allied. Norman Cohn cites a medieval 'Free Spirit': '"I belong to the Liberty of Nature, and all that my nature desires I satisfy . . . I am a natural man"'; *The Pursuit of the Millennium*, p. 178. But the obscurity of the law in Wordsworth's passage already points to his later 'pictures', which can be chalked up neither to moral law nor to antinomianism.

7 Quentin Skinner has identified Milton with 'the radical political theory of the Reformation, according to which the state of liberty is the natural condition of mankind' – 'Milton summarises the conventional wisdom with magnificent assurance at the start of *The Tenure of Kings and Magistrates* in 1649 when he announces that no one "can be so stupid to deny that all men were naturally borne free, being the image and resemblance of God himself"'; *Liberty before Liberalism* (Cambridge: Cambridge University Press, 1998), p. 19. It is one of the many ironies of *Paradise Lost* that Satan as much as Adam has the upright towering stature, and the inward freedom of will, that bespeak a divine origin.

8 Elsewhere in *Descriptive Sketches*, the 'pastoral Swiss' (450) becomes an Old Testament figure, a second Abraham, 'Bless'd with his herds, as in the patriarch's age' (456).

9 Knud Haakonssen, *Natural Law and Moral Philosophy: From Grotius to the Scottish Enlightenment* (Cambridge: Cambridge University Press, 1996), p. 331.

10 Michel Foucault, 'Preface' to Gilles Deleuze and Félix Guattari, *Anti-Oedipus: Capitalism and Schizophrenia* [1972], trans. Robert Hurley, Mark Seem and Helen R. Lane (London: Athlone Press, 1984), p. xiv. The later Foucault, of course, became more oriented to the autonomous individual through his interest in Kant and a 'care of the self'.

11 *Ibid.*

12 In *Descriptive Sketches* we find the 'softer prospect' of a 'deep secluded vale' of 'Calm huts, and lawns between, and sylvan slopes'; these too are 'low brown wood-huts' (264–75). The passage that leads up to the invocation of humanity in the state of nature also includes a glance at 'cabins, woods, and lawns' (502).

13 See, for example, Adam Ferguson, *An Essay on the History of Civil Society* (Edinburgh: Millar & Cadell, 1767), 'Of Rude Nations prior to the Establishment of Property', pp. 123–45.

14 Joseph Rykwert, *On Adam's House in Paradise: The Idea of the Primitive Hut in Architectural History* (New York: Museum of Modern Art, 1972).

15 J. H. Prynne, 'Huts', *Textual Practice* 22, 4 (2008), pp. 613–33.

16 *Ibid.*, p. 621.

17 Henri Lefebvre, 'Preface to the Study of the Habitat of the "Pavillon"', in *Key Writings*, ed. Stuart Elden, Elizabeth Lebas and Eleonore Kofman (New York: Continuum, 2003), p. 123.

18 See Adam Sharr, *Heidegger's Hut* (Cambridge, MA: MIT Press, 2006).

19 Martin Heidegger, 'Letter on Humanism', in *Basic Writings*, ed. David Farrell Krell (London and New York: Routledge, 2011), p. 174.
20 Jonathan Bate, *The Song of the Earth* (London: Picador, 2000), p. 205.
21 *Ibid.*, p. 266.
22 *Ibid.*, p. 75.
23 For another interpretation of Wordsworth's 'poetic dwelling' between earth and sky that builds on Heidegger, see John Kerrigan, 'Wordsworth and the Sonnet: Building, Dwelling, Thinking', *Essays in Criticism* 35, 1 (1985), pp. 45–75.
24 Heidegger, 'Building, Dwelling, Thinking', p. 246. Ontological or 'quasi-transcendental' formalisms, so characteristic of post-Heideggerean and 'post-structuralist' thought, can be accused, as Rousseau declared of theories of the state of nature, of transporting concepts gained in society back into the foundational. This is true not only of Heidegger's 'building', but also, for example, of Derrida's 'writing before writing' or, to take an extreme example, his notion of a 'messianicity without messianism' – the Messiah is a historical category par excellence. This effacement of the historical by the foundational through conjuring tricks of language might instead be conceived as pointing to contemporary states of nature – not as a fixed ontological structure, but in their changing configurations.
25 Prynne, 'Huts', p. 631.
26 In 'Building, Dwelling, Thinking', Heidegger, while acknowledging the 'hard and bitter' post-war housing shortage, downgrades its importance relative to the 'proper plight of dwelling', the need to address modernity's 'homelessness' within cosmological 'being'; *Basic Writings*, p. 254. 'The Old Cumberland Beggar' shows how intertwined these aspects might become at a particular moment, rather than at some supposedly quasi-transcendental level.
27 This is the basis for Leonardo's drawing, the 'Vitruvian Man', perhaps the most famous of all ideal representations of the upright body, with a geometry modelled on Vitruvius' 'canon of proportions' between body parts.
28 See Rykwert, *Adam's House*, p. 109. For Vitruvius, although the first humans live 'like the wild beasts, in woods, caves, and groves', it is the first stretching upwards from the ground of the upright body – as human beings become social following the discovery of fire and language – that is the natural origin of human superiority and its expression in architecture: 'finding themselves naturally gifted beyond the other animals in not being obliged to walk with faces to the ground, but upright and gazing upon the splendour of the starry firmament . . . they began in that first assembly to construct shelters'; Vitruvius, *The Ten Books on Architecture*, trans. Morris Hicky Morgan (New York: Dover, 1960), p. 38.
29 Marc-Antoine Laugier, *Essai sur l'architecture* (Paris, 1753), p. 2. Quoted in Rykwert, *Adam's House*, p. 44.
30 *Ibid.*
31 Karsten Harries, *The Ethical Function in Architecture* (Cambridge, MA: MIT Press, 1998), p. 114.
32 Rykwert, *Adam's House*, pp. 46–7.

33 Dalibor Vesely, *Architecture in the Age of Divided Representation: The Question of Creativity in the Shadow of Production* (Cambridge, MA: MIT Press, 2004), p. 384.
34 *Ibid.*, p. 64.
35 *Ibid.*, p. 363.
36 J. F. Blondel, *Cours d'architecture*, 6 vols. (Paris, 1771–7), vol. II, p. xii. Quoted in Vesely, *Architecture*, p. 361.
37 Vesely, *Architecture*, p. 363.
38 David P. Haney, *William Wordsworth and the Hermeneutics of Incarnation* (University Park: Pennsylvania State University Press, 1993), p. 75.
39 Emmanuel Levinas, *Totality and Infinity*, trans. Alphonso Lingis (The Hague: Martinus Nijhoff Publishers, 1979), p. 66.
40 'Uniqueness', in Emmanuel Levinas, *Entre Nous: Thinking-Of-The-Other*, trans. Michael B. Smith and Barbara Harshav (London and New York: Continuum, 2006), p. 168.
41 David P. Haney, 'Wordsworth and Levinas: Making a Habit of the Sublime', in Melvyn New with Robert Bernasconi and Richard A. Cohen (eds.), *In Proximity: Emmanuel Levinas and the Eighteenth Century* (Lubbock: Texas Technological University Press, 2001), p. 367.
42 Levinas, *Totality and Infinity*, p. 79.
43 Harries, *Ethical Function*, p. 4.
44 *Ibid.*, p. 115.
45 " . . . Poetically Man Dwells . . . ", in *Poetry, Language, Thought*, trans. Albert Hofstadter (New York: Harper & Row, 1971), pp. 221–5.
46 Heidegger, 'Building, Dwelling, Thinking', p. 255.
47 Coleridge, *Biographia*, p. 175.
48 William Wordsworth, *Guide to the Lakes, The Fifth Edition (1835)*, ed. Ernest de Selincourt (Oxford: Oxford University Press, 1977), p. 72.
49 *Ibid.*, p. 59.
50 *Ibid.*, p. 74.
51 Michael Wheeler, *The Lamp of Memory: Ruskin, Tradition and Architecture* (Manchester: Manchester University Press, 1992), p. 106.
52 Letter to Wordsworth, 30 May 1815; Coleridge, *Collected Letters*, vol. IV, p. 575.
53 Coleridge, *Biographia*, p. 114.
54 This was pulled down by De Quincey in 1811, but the site is now marked by a wooden summerhouse at Dove Cottage that has been named 'The Indian Bower'. The original's conception may well stem from Dorothy and William's 1803 tour of the Highlands, where at Linn they came upon a 'pleasure-house . . . called the Fog-house, because it was lined with *fog*, namely moss. On the outside it resembled some of the huts in the prints belonging to Captain Cook's Voyages, and within was like a hay-stack scooped out. It was circular, with a dome-like roof, a seat all round fixed to the wall, and a table in the middle, – seat, wall, roof, and table all covered with moss in the neatest manner possible. It was as snug as a bird's nest; I wish we had such a one at the top of our orchard, only a great deal smaller'; *Journals of Dorothy Wordsworth*,

2 vols., ed. Ernest de Selincourt (London: Macmillan, 1952), vol. I, p. 224. It makes sense, then, that Dorothy should make especial note of the fact that her revision of the Tour journal, begun in 1803, had concluded on 'May 31st 1805 in the Moss Hut at the top of the orchard'; DC. MS. 54; cited in J. H. Prynne, *Field Notes: 'The Solitary Reaper' and Others* (Cambridge: privately printed, 2007), p. 4. The whole tour is as much a journey from hut to hut as between lakes, glens and mountains. Repeated appraisals of the Highlands hut often swing between enthusiastic approval and harsh censure – as if Dorothy and William were seeking to test and disprove Samuel Johnson's well-known horror at the poverty and squalor of Highland dwellings on his own famous tour with Boswell, but were unable, at times, to overcome their middle-class domestic instincts.

55 Thomas McFarland, *Romanticism and the Forms of Ruin: Wordsworth, Coleridge, and Modalities of Fragmentation* (Princeton: Princeton University Press, 1981), p. 135.

56 *Ibid., passim.*

57 Such an image might be that of the Highland houses spotted by William and Dorothy on the shore of Loch Lomond at Luss in 1803: 'there were *wild* gardens, as beautiful as any that ever man cultivated, overgrowing the roofs of some of the cottages – flowers and creeping plants. How elegant were the wreaths of the bramble that had "built its own bower" upon the riggings in several parts of the village; therefore we had chiefly to regret the want of gardens, as they are symptoms of leisure and comfort, or at least of no painful industry'; *Journals of Dorothy Wordsworth*, vol. I, p. 248. As with 'The Ruined Cottage', it is also a picture of misery.

58 *The Journals of Dorothy Wordsworth*, vol. I, p. 259.

59 E. P. Thompson characterized the plight of weavers from 1780 as a loss of 'security' and of a 'status' that had been 'debased' to that of a 'proletarian outworker, who worked in his own home, sometimes owned and sometimes rented his loom, and who wove up the yarn to the specifications of the factor or agent of a mill or of some middle-man'; *The Making of the English Working Class* (New York: Vintage Books, 1963), p. 271. Thompson quotes a Belfast MP's statement to the House of Commons on 28 July 1830, which recounts the decline in the linen-weaving district of his constituency in terms strikingly close to Dorothy: 'a quarter once remarkable for its neatness and order . . . their whitewashed houses, and their little flower gardens . . . These houses were now a mass of filth and misery'; *ibid.*, p. 269.

60 Letter to Mrs John Marshall, 30 November 1795. *EY*, p. 162.

61 William Wordworth, *The Major Works*, ed. Stephen Gill (Oxford: Oxford University Press, 2000), p. 686, editor's note to page 33, line 99.

62 Gaston Bachelard, *The Poetics of Space*, trans. Maria Jolas (Boston: Beacon Press, 1994), Introduction, *passim.*

63 *Ibid.*, p. 50.

64 Lord Henry Home Kames, *Elements of Criticism*, third edition, 3 vols. (Edinburgh: printed for A. Millar, 1765), vol. II, p. 441.

65 Anthony Vidler, *The Architectural Uncanny: Essays in the Modern Unhomely* (Cambridge, MA: MIT Press, 1992), pp. xi–xii.
66 Jarvis, *Wordsworth's Philosophic Song*, chapter 6.
67 Michel Henry, 'Dessiner la musique: théorie pour l'art de Briesen', *Le Nouveau Commerce* 61 (1985), p. 81.
68 *Guide*, p. 55. Wordsworth is quoting Richard West's *Antiquities of Furness.*
69 *Ibid.*, pp. 56–7.
70 'Two Addresses to the Freeholders of Westmoreland' (Kendal: printed by Airey and Bellingham, 1818), p. 46.
71 Vesely, *Architecture*, p. 14.
72 *Ibid.*, p. 366.
73 It is characteristic of the 'traditionalism' of the later Wordsworth's verse that it does pay an increasing attention to temples and ritual worship – almost absent (in non-ruined form) in his poetry of the 1790s and 1800s. See, for example, his poem 'Humanity'.
74 Hugh Sykes Davies, *Wordsworth and the Worth of Words*, ed. John Kerrigan and Jonathan Wordsworth (Cambridge: Cambridge University Press, 1986), pp. 132–3.
75 Thomas De Quincey, 'Suspiria De Profundis', in *Confessions of an English Opium-Eater and Other Writings*, ed. Grevel Lindop (Oxford: Oxford University Press, 1996, second edition), p. 104.
76 Geoffrey Hartman, *The Unremarkable Wordsworth* (Minneapolis: University of Minnesota Press, 1987), p. 139.
77 *Journals of Dorothy Wordsworth*, vol. I, p. 254.
78 Prynne, 'Huts', p. 631.
79 'Building, Dwelling, Thinking', p. 254.
80 Theodor W. Adorno, *Lectures on Negative Dialectics: Fragments of a Lecture Course 1965/1966*, ed. Rolf Tiedemann, trans. Rodney Livingstone (Cambridge: Polity Press, 2008), pp. 41–2.
81 Paul H. Fry, *Wordsworth and the Poetry of What We Are* (New Haven: Yale University Press, 2008), p. 22.
82 *Ibid.*, p. xii.

3 'THE DISCHARGED SOLDIER'

1 See Bewell, *Wordsworth and the Enlightenment*, pp. 78–81.
2 Quoted in Walter Benjamin, 'Problems in the Sociology of Language', in *Selected Writings*, vol. III, *1935–1938*, ed. Howard Eiland and Michael W. Jennings (Cambridge, MA: Belknap Press, 2002), p. 69.
3 *The Collected Works of Samuel Taylor Coleridge, Marginalia*, 3 vols., ed. H. J. Jackson and George Whalley (Princeton: Princeton University Press, 1992), vol. III, p. 400.
4 Etienne Bonnot de Condillac, *Essay on the Origin of Human Knowledge*, trans. and ed. Hans Aarsleff (Cambridge: Cambridge University Press, 2001).
5 *Ibid.*, pp. 114–15.

6 *Marginalia*, p. 402.
7 Hans Aarsleff, 'Introduction' to Condillac, *Essay*.
8 *Ibid.*
9 Jacques Derrida, *The Archeology of the Frivolous: Reading Condillac*, trans. John P. Leavey, Jr. (Pittsburgh: Duquesne University Press, 1980), p. 102.
10 Locke, *Two Treatises*, p. 305.
11 *Ibid.*, p. 319.
12 *Ibid.*, p. 295.
13 Adam Smith, *An Inquiry into the Nature and Causes of The Wealth of Nations*, ed. Edwin Cannan (Chicago: University of Chicago Press, 1976), p. 17.
14 As Strauss writes, quoting Locke, 'all knowledge of the law of nature is acquired by study: to know the law of nature, one must be "a studier of that law"'; *Natural Right and History*, p. 225.
15 Locke, *Two Treatises*, p. 298.
16 See David Murrary, *Indian Giving: Economies of Power in Indian–White Exchanges* (Amherst: University of Massachusetts Press, 2000), and David Graeber, *Towards an Anthropological Theory of Value: The False Coin of Our Own Dreams* (Basingstoke: Palgrave Macmillan, 2001), chapter 5.
17 Mary Jacobus, *Tradition and Experiment in Wordsworth's Lyrical Ballads (1798)* (Oxford: Clarendon Press, 1976), p. 163.
18 The poem 'Beggars' is one exception, however, though even here Wordsworth implies that his gift is partly too generous, for the beggar woman, he believes, has tried to mislead him – 'on English Land / Such woes I knew could never be' (15–16). Yet the moral complication is heightened when we recall Wordsworth's frequent comparisons of rural English poverty to a supposedly 'savage' state of destitution. The statement is surely ironic – or is it? The main point, *contra* the literature of sensibility, is that such encounters are impossible to assimilate and overcome – triggering self-justification and repression.
19 Bromwich, *Disowned by Memory*, pp. 39–40.
20 Condillac, *Essay*, p. 114.
21 *Ibid.*, p. 115.
22 *Ibid.*, p. 37.
23 Mungo Park, *Travels in the Interior Districts of Africa: Performed under the Direction and Patronage of the African Association in the Years 1795, 1796, and 1797*, second edition (London: W. Bulmer & Co., 1799), p. 82. It was read by Wordsworth at some point before 1804 – see Duncan Wu, *Wordsworth's Reading 1800–1815* (Cambridge: Cambridge University Press, 1995), p. 162. On Park as a figure of 'sensibility', see Mary Louise Pratt, *Imperial Eyes: Travel Writing and Transculturation* (London and New York: Routledge, 1992), pp. 71–84.
24 See Pratt, *Imperial Eyes*, pp. 32–3. Under 'African', Linnaeus will list physical characteristics (type of hair, nose, etc.) followed by 'moral' characteristics ('negligent', etc.) as though there is an undisclosed correspondence (see *ibid.*, p. 32). This early attempt to systematize prejudice anticipates the biological racism of the nineteenth century.

25 Condillac, *Essay*, p. 118.
26 *Ibid.*
27 Kames, *Elements of Criticism*, vol. II, chapter XVIII, section IV ('Versification'), p. 98.
28 Richard Payne Knight, *The Progress of Civil Society: A Didactic Poem, In Six Books* (London: W. Bulmer & Co, 1796), vol. I, pp. 223–7. Lucretius – whose didactic epic was able to give the Enlightenment long poem, with its rebuilding of history from the first principles of a hypothetical origin, a reassuring feeling of standing on classical ground – may also have supplied a point of departure. In *De rerum natura*, language develops from animal noises as an instinctual response to affective phenomena (5.1028–90).
29 *Ibid.*, p. xi.
30 *Ibid.*
31 Coleridge, *Biographia*, p. 265.
32 *Ibid.*, p. 250.
33 *Ibid.*
34 *Ibid.*
35 Christoph Menke, *The Sovereignty of Art: Aesthetic Negativity in Adorno and Derrida*, trans. Neil Solomon (Cambridge, MA: MIT Press, 1998).
36 *Ibid.*, p. 254.
37 Menke, *The Sovereignty of Art*, p. 31.
38 Paul Valéry, *Rhumbs*; in *The Collected Works of Paul Valéry*, vol. XIV (Princeton: Princeton University Press, 1970), p. 211.
39 Menke, *The Sovereignty of Art*, pp. 46–7.
40 *Ibid.*, p. 105.
41 *Ibid.*, pp. 156–7.
42 *Ibid.*, p. 60.
43 *Ibid.*
44 Theodor W. Adorno, '*Vers une musique informelle*', in *Quasi una fantasia: Essays on Modern Music*, trans. Rodney Livingstone (London: Verso, 1998), p. 272.
45 Robert Kaufman, 'Lyric's Expression: Musicality, Conceptuality, Critical Agency', in David Cunningham and Nigel Mapp (eds.), *Adorno and Literature* (London and New York: Continuum, 2006), p. 105.
46 Bertolt Brecht, *Journals*, ed. John Willett, trans. Hugh Rorrison (New York: Routledge/Theatre Art Books, 1996), p. 91. See chapter 4, pp. 104–8, for a discussion of Brecht's striking response to Wordsworth.
47 Gillian Rose, *The Broken Middle: Out of Our Ancient Society* (Oxford: Blackwell, 1992).
48 George Steiner, *After Babel: Aspects of Language and Translation*, third edition (Oxford: Oxford University Press, 1998), p. 81.
49 Jonathan Bate, *Romantic Ecology: Wordsworth and the Environmental Tradition* (London: Routledge, 1991), p. 91.
50 Jacques Derrida, *Of Grammatology*, trans. Gayatri Chakrovorty Spivak, corrected edition (Baltimore: Johns Hopkins University Press, 1997).

51 Andrew Bennett has undertaken a 'deconstruction' of Wordsworth's undoubted predilection, at times, for the oral and immediate; *Wordsworth Writing* (Cambridge: Cambridge University Press, 2007). It is important, however, not to forget his equal attention to the mark, the sign and nature's 'characters' – and not just those he inscribes himself.

52 Such ideas were still widespread in the 1790s, and Wordsworth did not perhaps need to derive this notion of language from Coleridge, for whom it was an obsession in his poetry of the period. It is central to the seventeenth-century writings of Jacob Boehme – a favourite of the young Coleridge, and a presence in Wordsworth's library at least at the time of his death – in his account of 'divine signatures' in the appearances of nature. In the second half of the eighteenth century, variants of the notion still asserted themselves vigorously through J. G. Hamann, Swedenborg, the young Schelling and innumerable others.

53 On 'autoptic' authority in travel literature, see Anthony Pagden, *European Encounters with the New World: From Renaissance to Romanticism* (New Haven: Yale University Press, 1993), pp. 51–87.

54 See Introduction.

55 Henry Mackenzie, *The Man of Feeling*, ed. Brian Vickers (Oxford: Oxford University Press, 1967), p. 84.

56 Jarvis, *Wordsworth's Philosophic Song*, chapter 3.

57 David Simpson, 'Wordsworth and Empire – Just Joking', in Peter De Bolla, Nigel Leask and David Simpson (eds.), *Land, Nation and Culture: Thinking the Republic of Taste* (Basingstoke: Palgrave Macmillan, 2005), pp. 188–201.

58 Coleridge, *Biographia*, p. 284.

59 *EY*, p. 357.

60 Coleridge, *Biographia*, p. 250.

61 Swift, *Writings*, p. 193.

62 Giambattista Vico, *New Science* (third edition), trans. David Marsh (London: Penguin, 2001), p. 148 and *passim*. This is the ultimate source of Grassi's theory of the *archai*; Vico, for Grassi, was the culmination of Renaissance Humanism's theories of rhetoric.

63 Bewell, *Wordsworth and the Enlightenment*, pp. 78–81. Cf. Celeste Langan, *Romantic Vagrancy: Wordsworth and the Simulation of Freedom* (Cambridge: Cambridge University Press, 1995), pp. 198–9.

64 David Simpson, discussing the 'giant' in 'A Narrow Girdle . . . ', relates it to the notorious exaggerations of travel literature, such as Commodore Byron's report of a giant Patagonian chief in 1764. The rumour of Patagonian giants, cited by several thinkers as fact, was finally debunked on the first Cook voyage; 'Wordsworth and Empire', p. 193.

65 His acknowledged source is Thomas Ashe's 1808 *Travels in America*.

66 *PW* II.9–10.

67 Emphasizing a kinship between the two poems, lines 43–7 were later (*c.*1800) transferred to 'A Narrow Girdle of Rough Stones'. The extended family includes

'Old Man Travelling', 'Resolution and Independence' and 'The Old Cumberland Beggar'.

68 Bewell, *Wordsworth and the Enlightenment*, p. 90.

69 Mary Jacobus, *Romanticism, Writing and Sexual Difference: Essays on The Prelude* (Oxford: Oxford University Press, 1989), p. 74.

70 On the 'The Discharged Soldier' as a reworking of the theme of military history in *Salisbury Plain*, see Alan Bewell, *Romanticism and Colonial Disease* (Baltimore: Johns Hopkins University Press, 1999), pp. 108–20.

71 'Love and Liberty – A Cantata', in *The Songs of Burns*, ed. Donald A. Low (London: Routledge, 1993), pp. 139–43.

72 In keeping with this, in the *Prelude* version – which, though it cuts numerous powerful details, here shows a remarkably exact attention to the poem's latent 'rules' – the first version's sole extended passage of reported speech (128–34), in which the former soldier explained not only the physical reasons why he had stationed himself by the road against a milestone, but how he had been feeling and what was upsetting him, was culled.

73 As Bewell points out (*Romanticism and Colonial Disease*, p. 116), Wordsworth was drafting 'The Discharged Soldier' at roughly the same time (Jan.–Feb. 1798) as Coleridge was completing 'The Ancient Mariner'. The latter, of course, is replete with ghosts, life-in-death and fluent supernatural movement.

74 Jacobus, *Romanticism, Writing and Sexual Difference*, p. 73; cf. Langan, *Romantic Vagrancy*, pp. 194–5.

75 Geoffrey Hartman, 'Toward Literary History', *Daedalus* 99, 2 (1970), p. 355.

76 Bewell, *Romanticism and Colonial Disease*, p. 117. See pp. 108–20 for an exhaustive account of the history alluded to in the poem: the enormous loss of life from yellow fever during the 1790s colonial wars with France in the West Indies. In this reading, Bewell does not even refer back to his earlier 'anthropological' interpretation of the poem, in *Wordsworth and the Enlightenment*, as the critique of a misrecognized primitivism. The contradiction is explained when we view the poem as the exploration of a latter-day, that is, *historical*, state of nature.

77 In the explanatory speech of the first version, cut from *The Prelude*, the man's immediate anguish and complaint when Wordsworth first saw him, he recounts, had stemmed from the barking of the mastiff dog: '"I do not know / What ailed him, but it seemed as if the dog / Were howling to the murmur of the stream"' (134–6). Not only is the man's 'dead complaint' in mimetic sympathy with that stream, but the chained dog's howling, through all its violence, seems to be crying out to it for release. Like Wordsworth, the soldier here too is engaged in a figural close reading.

78 This is given added credence when we recall that Wordsworth and the man 'measure back / The way'; at the beginning of Book II of *The Prelude*, Wordsworth says of his efforts to 'retrace' his childhood in Book I that he has 'measured back / The way I travelled when I first began' (2–4). The itinerary of 'The Discharged Soldier' moves progressively forwards and upwards, in a

straight line, only to be knocked off course at a 'sudden turning', and then moves backwards towards a new starting point.

79 It is perhaps also not a coincidence that it is the very absence of such a dwelling which turns the fields of *Salisbury Plain* into the 'unknown plains' of the state of nature for the traveller.

80 Suspended at this moment of a revived interest within apathy, the man might even prefigure, though almost as negatively, the desideratum of Adorno: 'Spell-bound, the living have a choice between involuntary ataraxy – an esthetic life due to weakness – and the bestiality of the involved. Both are wrong ways of living. But some of both would be required for the right *désinvolture* and sympathy'; *Negative Dialectics*, p. 364.

81 In the *Prelude* version, the cottager is sentimentalized and given a 'ready heart' (458).

82 'I have at all times endeavoured to look steadily at my subject'; *Wordsworth and Coleridge: Lyrical Ballads*, ed. R. L. Brett and A. R. Jones (London and New York: Routledge), p. 296.

83 Simone Weil, *Gravity and Grace*, trans. Emma Crawford and Mario von der Ruhr (London: Routledge, 2002), p. 116.

84 Walter Benjamin, 'Franz Kafka', in *Selected Writings*, vol. II, part 2, *1931–1934*, trans. Rodney Livingstone and others, ed. Michael W. Jennings, Howard Eiland and Gary Smith (Cambridge, MA: Belknap Press, 2005), p. 815. This is at least a more concrete interpretation than Agamben's equally cryptic gloss of Benjamin's statement as a messianically playful study that deactivates the law, at last freed from the bare life of legal violence: 'One day humanity will play with law just as children play with disused objects'; *State of Exception*, trans. Kevin Attell (Chicago: University of Chicago Press, 2005), p. 64. This, however, does resemble the children playing with myth and ritual in 'Rural Architecture'. And an ethos of close reading has its own element of play.

85 A similar process occurs in 'Resolution and Independence', in which the leech-gatherer at first resembles a rock, then a 'sea-beast', before finally appearing as human. Although following a process of evolution, perhaps even recalling the evolutionary theories of Monboddo, Rousseau and Erasmus Darwin, this progress of humanization draws attention in retrospect to material and animal dimensions of the human that persist.

86 *EY*, p. 357.

87 He is presumably referring to the veneration of the *mastana*, the holy madman, in India.

4 THE COMMONWEALTH OF SONG

1 *Wordsworth and Coleridge: Lyrical Ballads*, p. 49.

2 Edward W. Said, *Orientalism: Western Conceptions of the Orient* [1978] (London: Penguin, 1995), p. 93.

3 *Ibid.*

4 *Wordsworth and Coleridge: Lyrical Ballads*, p. 49.

5 *Ibid.*
6 *Ibid.*, p. 288.
7 *Ibid.*, p. 289.
8 *Ibid.*, p. 367.
9 *Ibid.*, p. 366.
10 'On the Living Poets' (1818). In *The Selected Writings of William Hazlitt*, 9 vols., ed. Duncan Wu (London: Pickering & Chatto, 1998), vol. II, p. 316.
11 *Wordsworth and Coleridge: Lyrical Ballads*, p. 365.
12 Vico, *New Science*, p. 96.
13 Wu, *Wordsworth's Reading, 1770–1799*, p. 178.
14 Burney shared this disdain with his friend Samuel Johnson. His review of *Lyrical Ballads* would attack what he perceived as its evocation of the Rousseauan 'savage' (see p. 214n).
15 Charles Burney, *General History of Music: From the Earliest Ages to the Present Period*, 2 vols., ed. Frank Mercer (London: G. T. Foulis, 1935), vol. I, pp. 560–1. Burney may well have taken this argument from Monboddo's similar point concerning the songs of the Maori assembly.
16 *Wordsworth and Coleridge: Lyrical Ballads*, p. 367.
17 Hugh Blair, *Lectures on Rhetoric and Belles Lettres*, ed. Linda Ferreira-Buckley and S. Michael Halloran (Carbondale: Southern Illinois University Press, 2005), lecture XXXVIII. On these borrowings, possibly mediated through William Enfield's 'Is Verse Essential to Poetry?' (*Monthly Magazine*, July 1796), see M. H. Abrams, *The Mirror and the Lamp: Romantic Theory and the Critical Tradition* (Oxford: Oxford University Press, 1953, paperback edition 1971), pp. 95–105.
18 See Mark Salber Phillips, *Society and Sentiment: Genres of Historical Writing in Britain, 1740–1820* (Princeton: Princeton University Press, 2000), pp. 289–93.
19 David Bromwich (ed.), *Romantic Critical Essays* (Cambridge: Cambridge University Press, 1987), p. 209.
20 See '"The Regression of Poetry," by Carl Gustav Jochmann', in Benjamin, *Selected Writings: 1938–1940*, pp. 356–80.
21 For Hegel, art is no longer a central expression of the historical *Geist* and so no longer embedded in the social, practical and 'ethical life' of the community: 'Art, considered in its highest vocation, is and remains for us a thing of the past. Thereby it has lost for us genuine truth and life, and has rather been transferred into our *ideas* instead of maintaining its earlier necessity in reality and occupying its higher place'; *Hegel's Aesthetics: Lectures on Fine Arts*, 2 vols., trans. T. M. Knox (Oxford: Clarendon Press, 1975), vol. I, p. 11.
22 'Bread and Wine'; quoted in Martin Heidegger, 'Why Poets?' (1946), in *Off the Beaten Track*, ed. and trans. Julian Young and Kenneth Haynes (Cambridge: Cambridge University Press, 2002), p. 202.
23 Hazlitt, *Selected Writings*, vol. II, p. 178.
24 *Ibid.*
25 Coleridge, *Biographia*, pp. 179–80.
26 Hazlitt, *Selected Writings*, vol. II, p. 178.

27 Jacobus, *Tradition and Experiment.*
28 *Wordsworth and Coleridge: Lyrical Ballads*, p. 366.
29 *Ibid.*
30 *Ibid.*
31 *Ibid.*, p. 289.
32 *Ibid.*, p. 290.
33 *Ibid.*
34 *Ibid.*
35 *Ibid.*, p. 287.
36 *Ibid.*, p. 290.
37 *Ibid.*
38 *Ibid.*
39 *Ibid.*, p. 289n.
40 *Wordsworth and Coleridge: Lyrical Ballads*, p. 290.
41 Susan Stewart, 'Scandals of the Ballad', *Representations* 32 (1990), pp. 134–56.
42 Helen Maria Williams, *Poems on Various Subjects* (London: G. and W. B. Whittaker, 1823), pp. 3–17.
43 On Wordsworth's early enthusiasm for Williams, who inspired his first adolescent effusion in poetry, see Wu, *Wordsworth's Reading 1770–1799*, pp. 149–50.
44 *EY*, pp. 366–7.
45 Simpson, 'Wordsworth and Empire', p. 190.
46 *Wordsworth and Coleridge: Lyrical Ballads*, p. 302.
47 Jon P. Klancher, *The Making of English Reading Audiences, 1790–1832* (Madison: University of Wisconsin Press, 1987), p. 147.
48 Nigel Leask, 'Burns, Wordsworth and the Politics of Vernacular Poetry', in *Land, Nation and Culture*, p. 203.
49 *Ibid.*, p. 216.
50 Geoffrey H. Hartman, 'Reading: the Wordsworthian Enlightenment', in Helen Regueiro Elam and Frances Ferguson (eds.), *The Wordsworthian Enlightenment: Romantic Poetry and the Ecology of Reading* (Baltimore: John Hopkins University Press, 2005), p. 31.
51 In his *Characteristics of Men, Manners, Opinions, Times* (1714), ed. Lawrence E. Klein (Cambridge: Cambridge University Press, 1999).
52 *Wordsworth and Coleridge: Lyrical Ballads*, p. 300.
53 *Ibid.*, p. 301.
54 Hans-Georg Gadamer, *Truth and Method*, second revised edn, trans. Joel Weinsheimer and Donald G. Marshall (London: Sheed & Ward, 1989), p. 387.
55 Steiner, *After Babel*, p. 314.
56 *Ibid.*, p. 318.
57 *Ibid.*, p. 319.
58 In the Preface to his translation of Ovid's *Epistles* (1680).
59 Benjamin, 'The Task of the Translator', in *Selected Writings*, vol. 1, p. 260.
60 *Ibid.*, my emphasis.
61 *Wordsworth and Coleridge: Lyrical Ballads*, p. 290, my emphasis.
62 *Ibid.*, pp. 366–7.

63 Henri Meschonnic, *Ethics and Politics of Translating*, trans. and ed. Pier-Pascale Boulanger (Amsterdam and Philadelphia: John Benjamins, 2011).
64 *Wordsworth and Coleridge: Lyrical Ballads*, pp. 305–6.
65 Brennan O'Donnell, *The Passion of Meter: A Study of Wordsworth's Metrical Art* (Kent, OH: Kent State University Press, 1995), p. 181.
66 *Wordsworth and Coleridge: Lyrical Ballads*, p. 306.
67 *Ibid.*, p. 301.
68 Benjamin, 'Task', p. 261.
69 *Ibid.*, p. 259.
70 *Ibid.*, p. 258.
71 *Ibid.*
72 Nigel Leask, *Curiosity and the Aesthetics of Travel Writing, 1770–1840: 'From an Antique Land'* (Oxford: Oxford University Press, 2002), p. 15. This too, however, is a 'textual attitude', though (not always) diligently regulated.
73 *Ibid.*, p. 16.
74 *Ibid.*, p. 22.
75 Lamb, *Preserving the Self*, p. 7.
76 George Keate, *An Account of the Pelew Islands*, ed. Karen L. Nero and Nicholas Thomas (London: Leicester University Press, 2002), p. 100.
77 *Ibid.*
78 *Ibid.*, p. 101.
79 *Ibid.*
80 *Ibid.*
81 Michel de Certeau, 'Speech, or the Space of the Other: Jean de Léry', in *The Certeau Reader*, ed. Graham Ward (Oxford: Blackwell, 2000), p. 130.
82 *Ibid.*
83 *Ibid.*
84 *Ibid.*
85 *Ibid.*, p. 147.
86 Fenwick note; *P2V*, p. 415.
87 *Ibid.*
88 *Wordsworth and Coleridge: Lyrical Ballads*, p. 294.
89 *Ibid.*, p. 293.
90 Don H. Bialostosky, *Wordsworth, Dialogics, and the Practice of Criticism* (Cambridge: Cambridge University Press, 1992), p. 138.
91 *Ibid.*, pp. 144–5.
92 *Ibid.*, p. 139.
93 *Wordsworth and Coleridge: Lyrical Ballads*, p. 306n.
94 Prynne, *Field Notes*, pp. 8–10.
95 Heather Glen, *Vision and Disenchantment: Blake's Songs and Wordsworth's Lyrical Ballads* (Cambridge: Cambridge University Press, 1983), p. 6.
96 This sense of a material affect that cannot be reduced to the identity principle, to any familiar and recognizable emotion, might even be deemed a new imperative for non-commodified art. It is a resurrection of the objective affect of nature's moods.

97 Mikhail Bakhtin, *Problems of Dostoevsky's Poetics*, ed. and trans. Caryl Emerson (Minneapolis: University of Minnesota Press, 1984), p. 30.
98 James H. Donelan, *Poetry and the Romantic Musical Aesthetic* (Cambridge: Cambridge University Press, 2008), p. 110.
99 Bialostosky, *Wordsworth*, p. 147.
100 *Ibid.*, p. 143.
101 *Ibid.*, pp. 146–7.
102 Mikhail Bakhtin, 'Response to a Question from the *Novy Mir* Editorial Staff', in *Speech Genres and Other Late Essays*, trans. Vern W. McGee, ed. Caryl Emerson and Michael Holquist (Austin: University of Texas Press, 1986), p. 5.
103 Maureen McLane, *Balladeering, Minstrelsy, and the Making of British Romantic Poetry* (Cambridge: Cambridge University Press, 2008), p. 232. See also McLane, *Romanticism and the Human Sciences*, pp. 79–83.
104 Prynne, *Field Notes*, p. 92.
105 Prynne writes: 'In Wordsworth's terms, it is not wrong to speak here of '*my* heart', because this is not anonymous impersonal feeling or collective memory, but is specifically assigned (by poetic vocation) into his care; but also, the feeling does not belong to him as some kind of character asset, he is rather its ethical custodian. That is what being a poet means for him'; *Field Notes*, p. 94.
106 Peter J. Manning, *Reading Romantics: Texts and Contexts* (Oxford: Oxford University Press, 1990), p. 255.
107 Walter Benjamin, 'A Little History of Photography', in *Selected Writings*, vol. II, part 2, p. 518.
108 Walter Benjamin, 'The Work of Art in the Age of its Technological Reproducibility (Third Version)', in *Selected Writings*, vol. IV, pp. 254–6.
109 Robert Kaufman, 'Aura, Still', in Andrew Benjamin (ed.), *Walter Benjamin and Art* (London and New York: Continuum, 2005), pp. 121–47.
110 Kaufman, 'Aura', p. 140.
111 Percy Bysshe Shelley, *Shelley's Poetry and Prose*, second edition, ed. Donald H. Reiman and Neil Fraistat (New York: W. W. Norton, 2002), p. 535.
112 *Ibid.*
113 *Ibid.*
114 Kaufman, 'Aura', p. 140.
115 Matthew Arnold, 'Wordsworth', in *Selected Poems of Wordsworth*, ed. Harrison Ross Steeves (New York: Harcourt, Brace and Company, 1922), p. 4.
116 *Ibid.*, p. 12.
117 *Ibid.*, p. 13.
118 *Ibid.*, p. 12.
119 *Ibid.*, p. 20.
120 From this perspective, the counter to bare life is not to clothe it in a form of life – for it is the very stripping of such a form that constitutes bare life. Rather, it is a capacity to perceive that bare life itself is never truly bare. Only that might act as a powerful enough barrier to halt the violence or indifference that bare life elicits. As Arnold reminds us, Wordsworth had a unique ability to expose this 'penetrating power'.

121 *Ibid.*, pp. 17–18.
122 Matthew Arnold, *Culture and Anarchy*, ed. Jane Garnett (Oxford: Oxford University Press, 2006), p. 52.
123 Brecht, *Journals*, p. 90.
124 *Ibid.*, p. 91.
125 *Ibid.*
126 On 3 October 1803, with England in panic expectation of a Napoleonic invasion, Wordsworth enlisted (together with almost all the men in his village) in the Grasmere Volunteers; Mary Moorman, *William Wordsworth, a Biography: Early Years, 1770–1803* (Oxford: Clarendon Press, 1957), pp. 602–3.
127 Brecht, *Journals*, p. 91.
128 *Ibid.*
129 *Ibid.* Cf. chapter 4, p. 69.
130 See Ernst Bloch *et al.*, *Aesthetics and Politics*, trans. and ed. Ronald Taylor (London: Verso, 1980).
131 Kaufman, 'Aura', p. 141.
132 Theodor Adorno, *Aesthetic Theory*, ed. Gretel Adorno and Rolf Tiedemann, trans. Robert Hullot-Kentor (London: Continuum, 2002), p. 45. In his late essay 'On Some Motifs in Baudelaire', Benjamin now connects aura with the *hic et nunc* as it binds itself to the redemptive force of the *mémoire involuntaire*, reclaiming the oblivion of the past (and present). But that aura is vulnerable to history – modernity has swept it away in the city as a state of nature (see chapter 1, p. 28).
133 Brecht, *Journals*, p. 91.
134 See Introduction, p. 12.
135 Brecht, *Journals*, p. 91.
136 *Ibid.*
137 *Ibid.*, p. 90.
138 *Ibid.*, p. 91.
139 *Ibid.*
140 *Ibid.*
141 Sigmund Freud, 'The Uncanny' (1919), *The Standard Edition of the Complete Psychological Works of Sigmund Freud*, vol. XVII *(1917–1919)*, ed. and trans. James Strachey (London: Hogarth Press, 1953), pp. 219–52.
142 Sigmund Freud, *The Complete Letters of Sigmund Freud to Wilhelm Fliess, 1887–1904*, ed. and trans. J. M. Masson (Cambridge, MA: Belknap Press, 1985), letter 6 December 1896, p. 208.

5 MIMESIS

1 The late Jack Goody argued that this kind of 'renaissance' or 'renascence' is a feature of all literate societies, insofar as books and other artefacts form a durable record of the past to which a culture may always turn back; *Renaissances: The One or the Many?* (Cambridge: Cambridge University Press, 2010).
2 'Essay, Supplementary to the Preface', *PW* III.84.

3 *Ibid.*
4 *Ibid.*, p. 65.
5 Coleridge, *Biographia*, p. 209.
6 *Ibid.*, p. 50n.
7 *Ibid.*, p. 210.
8 Max Horkheimer and Theodor W. Adorno, *Dialectic of Enlightenment: Philosophical Fragments*, ed. Gunzelin Schmid Noerr, trans. Edmund Jephcott (Stanford: Stanford University Press, 2002), p. 44.
9 Quoted in Michael Taussig, *Mimesis and Alterity: A Particular History of the Senses* (New York: Routledge, 1993), p. 75.
10 Quoted in *ibid.*
11 *Ibid.*, p. 72.
12 *Ibid.*, pp. 43–4.
13 *Ibid.*, p. xviii.
14 *Journals of Dorothy Wordsworth*, vol. 1, p. 372.
15 *Wordsworth and Coleridge: Lyrical Ballads*, p. 307.
16 Abrams, *The Mirror and the Lamp.*
17 Edward Young, *Conjectures on Original Composition. In a letter to the Author of Sir Charles Grandison* (London: A. Millar, and R. and J. Dodsley, 1759), p. 53.
18 André Green, *The Fabric of Affect in the Psychoanalytic Discourse*, trans. Alan Sheridan (London and New York: Routledge, 1999), p. 215. Green's emphasis.
19 See Melissa Gregg and Gregory J. Seigworth (eds.), *The Affect Theory Reader* (Durham, NC: Duke University Press, 2010).
20 *Wordsworth and Coleridge: Lyrical Ballads*, p. 291.
21 Green, *The Fabric of Affect*, p. 3.
22 *Wordsworth and Coleridge: Lyrical Ballads*, p. 291.
23 Dugald Stewart, *An Account of the Life and Writings of Adam Smith, LL.D.* (New York: Kelley Reprint, 1966), pp. 33–4. Stewart's italics.
24 John Brown, *The History of the Rise and Progress of Poetry, Through its Several Species* (Newcastle: J. White, 1764), p. 9.
25 In *Totem and Taboo*, Freud would present his own theory of the 'primal horde' (based on Darwin's speculations) and its emergence from a state of nature into contract law.
26 Green, *The Fabric of Affect*, p. 284.
27 Paul de Man, 'Wordsworth and the Victorians', in *The Rhetoric of Romanticism* (New York: Columbia University Press, 1984), p. 90.
28 Frances Ferguson, *Wordsworth: Language as Counter-Spirit* (New Haven: Yale University Press, 1977), p. 136.
29 Green, *The Fabric of Affect*, p. 215.
30 De Man, *The Rhetoric of Romanticism*, pp. 91–2.
31 Melanie Klein, 'Love, Guilt and Reparation', in *Love, Guilt and Reparation and Other Works 1921–1945* (London: Vintage, 1998), p. 335.
32 Green's enthusiasm for the 'infant babe' passage can probably be traced to Winnicott, who joked of it: 'He seems to have read my books!' See Mary

Jacobus, 'Wordsworth and Winnicott', in *The Poetics of Psychoanalysis: In the Wake of Klein* (Oxford: Oxford University Press, 2005), pp. 148–69.

33 *PW* III.77.

34 *Ibid.*

35 *PW* III.34.

36 *Dialectic of Enlightenment*, p. 2.

37 D. W. Winnicott, *Playing and Reality* (London and New York: Routledge, 2005), p. 107 and *passim*.

38 Lord Monboddo, *The Origins and Progress of Language*, 6 vols. (Edinburgh: A. Kincaid and W. Creech, 1773), vol. I, p. 130.

39 *Ibid.*, vol. II, p. 6.

40 On Monboddo's and Harris' theories, see Olivia Smith, *The Politics of Language, 1791–1819* (Oxford: Clarendon Press, 1986), pp. 20–9.

41 *The Essential Adam Smith*, ed. Robert L. Heilbroner and Lawrence J. Malone (Oxford: Oxford University Press, 1986), pp. 22–36.

42 *RC*, MS B, lines 84–5, p. 46.

43 See George T. Wright, 'Hendiadys and *Hamlet*', *PMLA* 96, 2 (1981), pp. 168–93.

44 See Wu, *Wordsworth's Reading 1770–1799*, p. 89.

45 For a detailed account of Lowth's influence on Wordsworth, see Corinna Russell, 'A Defence of Tautology: Repetition and Difference in Wordsworth's Note to "The Thorn"', *Paragraph* 28, 2 (2005), pp. 106–18.

46 Robert Lowth, *Lectures on the Sacred Poetry of the Hebrews,* facsimile ed., 2 vols. (London: Routledge/Thoemmes Press, 1995), vol. I, pp. 115–17.

47 Marc Shell, *The End of Kinship: 'Measure for Measure,' Incest, and the Ideal of Universal Siblinghood* (Stanford: Stanford University Press, 1988).

48 Nicholas Roe, *Wordsworth and Coleridge: The Radical Years* (Oxford: Clarendon Press, 1988).

49 Benjamin, 'On the Image of Proust', in *Selected Writings*, vol. II, Part I, *1927–1930*, ed. Michael W. Jennings, Howard Eiland and Gary Smith (Cambridge, MA: Belknap Press, 2005), p. 240.

50 *Wordsworth and Coleridge: Lyrical Ballads*, p. 307. Wordsworth's theory is in part a reclamation of 'similitude' for knowledge that harked back to the premodern. Michel Foucault's famous account of resemblance as the Renaissance 'episteme' saw it as tapering off by the end of the sixteenth century; *The Order of Things: An Archaeology of Human Knowledge* (London and New York: Routledge, 2002), chapter I. It had, however, never quite gone away, above all in discourses at the edge of science and mysticism (as in Emmanuel Swedenborg's theory of correspondences). But it is also countermanded by a sense of 'dissimilitude' that brings it close to Aquinas' medieval theory of the *analogia entis*, which insisted on the difference as much as the similarity between, say, human goodness and the absolute Good as an attribute of deity. Wordsworth's largely secularized 'similitude in dissimilitude', however, operates on the lateral rather than vertical plane of relations.

51 *Wordsworth and Coleridge: Lyrical Ballads*, p. 306.

52 *Ibid.*
53 *Ibid.*, p. 307.
54 *Ibid.*
55 Russell, 'A Defence of Tautology'.
56 *Ibid.*, p. 113.
57 Gilles Deleuze, *Difference and Repetition*, trans. Paul Patton (London: Continuum, 2004). It is no coincidence that Deleuze's argument, influenced like just one tendency in Wordsworth by Spinoza's monistic 'expressivism', culminates in the metaphysics of a univocally singular Being; *ibid.*, p. 378. It can say only one thing repeatedly, though each moment differently. Amos Funkenstein has related Foucault's observation of a shift from a Renaissance paradigm of 'similitude' to a seventeenth-century emphasis on 'sameness' and 'difference' to the scientific desire for a univocal language and homogenous world; *Theology and the Scientific Imagination: From the Middle Ages to the Seventeenth Century* (Princeton: Princeton University Press, 1986), p. 28. The divine language of nature becomes mathematical (*ibid.*, p. 29). The object in a state of similitude, however, is equivocal in what it says.
58 *Wordsworth and Coleridge: Lyrical Ballads*, p. 333. For a discussion of 'apparent tautology', see Goodman, '"Uncertain Disease"', pp. 223–7.
59 *Ibid.*, p. 307.
60 *Ibid.*
61 *Ibid.*
62 Juliet Mitchell, *Mad Men and Medusas: Reclaiming Hysteria and the Effects of Sibling Relations on the Human Condition* (London: Penguin, 2000), p. 346.
63 Juliet Mitchell, *Siblings: Sex and Violence* (Cambridge: Polity Press, 2003).
64 Shell, *The End of Kinship*, *passim.*
65 Tim Fulford, *Romantic Indians: Native Americans, British Literature, and Translatlantic Culture 1756–1830* (Oxford: Oxford University Press, 2006), p. 32.
66 Bewell, *Wordsworth and the Enlightenment*, p. 197.
67 *LB*, pp. 767–9.
68 They share the same 10-line stanza, rhyme scheme and four-beat 'ballad metre'. Lewti's lament that a cloud 'floats away, / Away it goes – away so soon! / Alas it has no pow'r to stay' (*LB* 28–30) is clearly transferred to the natural imagery, and tribal context, of 'The Complaint' (see lines 44–50), whose tone it strongly resembles, only here as an image of lost love rather than mortality.
69 For other readings of 'The Complaint' in relation to the 'Indian death song' with differing emphases, see Jacobus, *Tradition and Experiment*, p. 193, and, with an account of pastiche 'Romantic Indian' poetry in general, Fulford, *Romantic Indians*, pp. 141–55.
70 Ferguson, *Essay*, pp. 68–72. On Smith, see below.
71 Goethe and Schiller, among many others, wrote 'Indian death songs'.
72 Cited in Joseph Ritson, 'Historical Essay on the Origin and Progress of National Song', in *A Select Collection of English Songs*, 3 vols. (London: J. Johnson, 1783), vol. 1, p. iin; quoted in Jacobus, *Tradition and Experiment*, pp. 193–4.

73 Michel de Certeau, 'Montaigne's "Of Cannibals": The Savage "I"', in *Heterologies: Discourse on the Other*, trans. Brian Massumi (Minneapolis: University of Minnesota Press, 1986), pp. 67–79.
74 *LB*, p. 745.
75 Samuel Hearne, *A Journey from Prince of Wales Fort in Hudson's Bay to the Northern Ocean, 1769, 1770, 1771, 1772*, ed. Richard Glover (Toronto: Macmillan, 1958), pp. 131–2.
76 Hearne, *Journey*, p. 132.
77 Millar, *The Origin of the Distinction of Ranks*, pp. 14–56.
78 See Phillips, *Society and Sentiment*, pp. 163–4.
79 Jonathan Carver, *Travels through America, 1766–68*, ed. Norman Gelb (New York: John Wiley, 1993), p. 124.
80 Adam Smith, *The Theory of Moral Sentiments*, ed. D. D. Raphael and A. L. Macfie (Oxford: Clarendon Press, 1976), pp. 206–7, 288. Smith goes on to argue that classical Stoicism 'prepared a death-song', the 'most animated and spirited song' of all philosophies in the face of mortality (p. 283).
81 *Wordsworth and Coleridge: Lyrical Ballads*, p. 292.
82 *Ibid.*, p. 288.
83 On Poetry in General', in *Selected Writings*, vol. II, pp. 174–5.
84 Brennan O'Donnell and Simon Jarvis have discussed the expressive significance of 'hypermetricality' in Wordsworth, but this extends also to Wordsworth's contractions of an expected line length.
85 Bewell, *Wordsworth and the Enlightenment*, p. 200.
86 *A Journey*, p. 220. Cf. Bewell, *Wordsworth and the Enlightenment*, p. 198.
87 Bewell, *Wordsworth and the Enlightenment*, p. 201.
88 Ferguson, *Essay*, p. 68.
89 O'Donnell, *The Passion of Meter*, pp. 118–19, 124–9. 'Lewti', too, shares these characteristics, missing only the kinship theme.
90 O'Donnell, *The Passion of Meter*, p. 129.
91 Fenwick note; quoted *LB*, p. 353.
92 *LY* 3.292–3.

6 'MAN WORKING FOR HIMSELF'

1 The theory was still largely dominant at the end of the eighteenth century. Asked what he thought of it by John Wilson in 1801, Wordsworth argued that while the environment might be formative in isolated communities, in nations with varying geographies and social groups, like Britain, that influence was counteracted.
2 Ronald L. Meek, *Social Science and the Ignoble Savage* (Cambridge: Cambridge University Press, 1976), pp. 164, 161.
3 Ferguson, *Essay*, p. 10.
4 *Ibid.*, p. 9.

5 This was to historicize aspects of Locke's account of the state of nature, in which labour was posited as the origin of private property. As Leo Strauss writes: 'Locke identifies the rational life with the life dominated by the pain which relieves pain. Labor takes the place of the art which imitates nature; for labor is, in the words of Hegel, a negative attitude toward nature . . . The way towards happiness is a movement away from the state of nature, a movement away from nature . . . Life is the joyless quest for joy'; *Natural Right and History*, p. 251.
6 Klancher, *The Making of English Reading Audiences*, p. 147.
7 *Wordsworth and Coleridge: Lyrical Ballads*, p. 294.
8 *Ibid.*
9 *Ibid.*
10 *Ibid.*
11 *Ibid.*
12 Phillips, *Society and Sentiment*, p. 147.
13 *Ibid.*, pp. 182–5.
14 Meek, *Social Science*, pp. 164–5.
15 Phillips, *Society and Sentiment*, p. 185.
16 See Kevis Goodman, *Georgic Modernity and British Romanticism: Poetry and the Mediation of History* (Cambridge: Cambridge University Press, 2004), p. 1.
17 'On My First Acquaintance with Poets' (1823). In Hazlitt, *Selected Writings*, vol. IX, p. 106.
18 Philip Connell, *Romanticism, Economics, and the Question of 'Culture'* (Oxford: Oxford University Press, 2001), pp. 43–4.
19 Meek, *Social Science*, pp. 99–130.
20 Connell argues that the reference to Smith is 'misleading' for the real engagement in Book XII is with Malthus' *Essay on Population* (*Romanticism*, p. 45). As Connell's impressive analysis demonstrates, Malthus' political economy is certainly a valid context for some of Book XII's themes. That focus, however, misses Book XII's more central preoccupation with labour and value – which is presumably why Wordsworth alludes to Smith rather than Malthus. The passage, however, is a swipe at all such 'Statists', just as the 'Essay on Morals' had condemned the 'whole tribe' of moral philosophers.
21 Adam Smith, *Lectures on Jurisprudence*, ed. R. L. Meek, D. D. Raphael and P. G. Stein (Oxford: Clarendon Press, 1978), p. 20.
22 Smith, *Wealth of Nations*, p. 293.
23 *Ibid.*, p. 26.
24 *Ibid.*, p. 367.
25 Smith, *The Theory of Moral Sentiments*, p. 86.
26 Smith, *Wealth of Nations*, p. 37.
27 *The Early Writings of Adam Smith*, ed. J. R. Lindgren (New York: Kelley Reprint 1967), p. 25.
28 Smith, *Wealth of Nations*, p. 53.
29 *Ibid.*, pp. 303–4.
30 *Wordsworth and Coleridge: Lyrical Ballads*, p. 294.

31 Meek, *Social Science*, *passim*. Both versions of the 'savage', loftily idealist and cravenly empiricist, as mutually conditioning projections are found in the Solitary's account of his American experience in Book III of *The Excursion*.

32 Quoted in P. J. Marshall and G. Williams, *The Great Map of Mankind: British Perceptions of the World in the Age of Enlightenment* (London: J. M. Dent, 1982), p. 216. Similar representations occur in Cornelius de Pauw and in William Robertson's hugely influential *History of America* (1777).

33 See Jarvis, *Wordsworth's Philosophic Song*, pp. 85–8. As Jarvis observes, in opposition to such an anthropology of need, in Wordsworth 'needs' are always shading into 'wants'.

34 *Journals of Dorothy Wordsworth*, vol. I, p. 208. Six years later, Coleridge would call Thomas Clarkson a 'Giant with one Idea', whose abolitionist crusade was that of a 'moral Steam-Engine'; letter to Daniel Stuart, February 1809, *Collected Letters*, vol. III, p. 179. It is ironically appropriate that Clarkson's single-minded opposition to slavery should here be conflated with industrial production.

35 *Journals of Dorothy Wordsworth*, vol. I, pp. 207–8.

36 *Wordsworth and Coleridge: Lyrical Ballads*, p. 295.

37 See Alison Hickey, *Impure Conceits: Rhetoric and Ideology in Wordsworth's 'Excursion'* (Stanford: Stanford University Press, 1997), p. 100.

38 This helps to qualify Gary Lee Harrison's study of Wordsworth's indebtedness to contemporary discourses that extolled the ceaselessly industrious, and hence 'virtuous' poor, against the villainous 'idle poor'; *Wordsworth's Vagrant Muse: Poetry, Poverty, and Power* (Detroit: Wayne State University Press, 1994).

39 Most notably in Marjorie Levinson, *Wordsworth's Great Period Poems: Four Essays* (Cambridge: Cambridge University Press, 1986), and David Simpson, *Wordsworth's Historical Imagination: The Poetry of Displacement* (New York: Methuen, 1987).

40 Marx, 'Critique of the Gotha Program', in Karl Marx and Friedrich Engels, *Collected Works*, 50 vols. (London: Lawrence and Wishart, 1975–2005), vol. IV, p. 87.

41 Jarvis, *Wordsworth's Philosophic Song*, chapter 3.

42 Michel Henry, *Marx: A Philosophy of Human Reality*, trans. Kathleen McLaughlin (Bloomington: University of Indiana Press, 1983).

43 *Ibid.*, pp. 120–1; Henry's italics.

44 Jarvis, *Wordsworth's Philosophic Song*, p. 107.

45 David Simpson, *Wordsworth, Commodification and Social Concern: The Poetics of Modernity* (Cambridge: Cambridge University Press, 2009); Moishe Postone, *Time, Labor, and Social Domination* (Cambridge: Cambridge University Press, 1993).

46 Simpson, *Wordsworth, Commodification and Social Concern*, p. 169.

47 *Ibid.*

48 *Ibid.*, p. 4.

49 *Ibid.*

50 Jacques Derrida, *Specters of Marx*, trans. Peggy Kamuf (London and New York: Routledge, 2006), p. 200.
51 *Ibid.*, p. 201.
52 *Ibid.*
53 *Ibid.*, p. 204.
54 The non-identity of Wordsworth's figures with the commodity is evoked by a famous phrase of the young Marx himself: his call for a 'naturalization of man' and the 'humanization of nature'.
55 Simpson, *Wordsworth, Commodification and Social Concern*, p. 128, citing Marx, *Capital*.
56 Marx, 'Economic and Philosophical Manuscripts (1844)', in *Marx: Early Writings*, trans. Rodney Livingstone and Gregor Benton (Harmondsworth: Penguin, 1975), p. 352.
57 *Ibid.*, p. 353.
58 Martin Heidegger, *Nietzsche*, trans. David Farrell Krell *et al.* (London: Harper & Row, 1979), 4 vols.
59 *Early Writings*, p. 353.
60 Such an alternation is later evoked in the revised *Descriptive Sketches* of 1836; in his Arcadian state of nature, the Swiss peasant's 'Brisk toil, alternating with ready ease, / Feeds the clear current of his sympathies' (17–18).
61 Rousseau, Second Discourse, p. 115.
62 The verbs in parenthesis were deleted from MS. A, though kept in MS. B (see *Pr.*, editor's note, p. 305).
63 Connell, *Romanticism*, pp. 57–9.
64 As with Wordsworth's other figures of the uncanny, his wife is not mentioned by name in the poem.
65 Charles Norton Coe, *Wordsworth and the Literature of Travel* (New York: Bookman Associates, 1953), p. 68.
66 Bartram, *Travels through North and South Carolina*, pp. 24–5.
67 *EY*, p. 434. Cf. O'Donnell's analysis of this letter's importance to Wordsworth's prosody; *The Passion of Meter*, p. 27.
68 Giorgio Agamben, *The End of the Poem: Studies in Poetics*, trans. Daniel Heller-Roazen (Stanford: Stanford University Press, 1999), p. 109.
69 *Ibid.*, p. 111.
70 *Ibid.*, p. 114.
71 James Vigus, *Platonic Coleridge* (London: Legenda, 2009), p. 65.
72 Quoted in *ibid.*, p. 66.
73 This is its role, on a par with military training, as central to the *paideia* or education of Guardians who will govern in *The Republic*; in the *Laws* it is essential to 'choral' order, should not be led by pleasure and innovation, and should instil harmonious and regulated conduct. *Mousike* is to shape appetite and affect into consonance with the ideal forms of reason.
74 Bewell, *Wordsworth and the Enlightenment*, p. 14. This qualification also applies to the same argument as made by Howard Erskine-Hill, *The Poetry of Opposition and Revolution: Dryden to Wordsworth* (Oxford: Clarendon Press, 1996),

pp. 187–90, and John Barrell, 'The Uses of Dorothy: "The Language of the Sense" in "Tintern Abbey"', in *Poetry, Language and Politics* (Manchester: Manchester University Press, 1988), pp. 137–67.

75 Geoffrey H. Hartman, *Wordsworth's Poetry, 1787–1814* (New Haven: Yale University Press, 1964), pp. 3–30.

76 Uneasily, this mirrors Thomas Jefferson's policy in this period as American president (1801–9), which actively sought to displace the Indians from their lands and resettle them as small-scale farmers. For Jefferson's agrarian republicanism, the Indians could only be 'civilized' through a shift from hunting to the settled virtue of agriculture. Wordsworth would reproduce such prejudices in his account of the wayward bands of Indians in 'Ruth'. Yet the way in which Book I's spots of time both allude to, and distance, an American Indian hunting is made clearer in a draft introduction for the poem 'Nutting'. Here the boy Wordsworth's rapacious hunt for hazelnuts in the forest is mirrored in a 'Half cruel . . . eagerness' of his sister's gaze (10). She resembles 'A houseless being in a human shape', 'An enemy of nature' (13–14). That demon is 'one who comes / From regions far beyond the Indian hills' (14–15); *LB*, pp. 302–3. As supernatural and exotic distance grow confused, the demon is yet further away than the American Indian hunter from the European, as though also a deeper spectre within the universally primitive self. It is not identified with the American, but evokes something that the tribe might try to ward off or propitiate.

77 *TP* 402 ('some straggling Hunter led by chance'); and *SSI*, sonnet VIII.

78 The ghost of utopia explicitly haunts a poem written around the same time as Book I, 'Hart-Leap Well'. It is written about a deserted spot where a hart, being hunted, fell to its death. Hunting corresponds to an evacuation of place. Wordsworth plays with the notion that this is no ordinary wasteland but a site of mourning created by 'The Being, that is in the clouds and air' (161). The spot will return to life at the dawn of the millennium, the 'milder day' (171).

79 William Empson, *Seven Types of Ambiguity* (London: Chatto & Windus, 1949), p. 20.

80 For Wordsworth, this remains salutary for the adult too. In the draft introduction to 'Nutting', that poem's troubled relationship to hunting makes a further connection to *The Prelude*'s revaluation of labour in Book XII. It contains a passage, later transferred to Book XII, which proposes that childhood hunts such as that of 'Nutting' had 'early taught' Wordsworth to reject 'the pompous names / Of power and action' and instead to look with 'fraternal love / Upon those unassuming things which hold / A silent station' (28–33). Against the vertical imposition of 'power and action', as in labour upon the flattened base, Wordsworth proposes a new form of sibling relationship.

81 *The Prelude, 1798–1799*, ed. Stephen Parrish (Ithaca: Cornell University Press, 1977). References to Book I in this section will be to this edition unless otherwise indicated.

82 Fenwick note, quoted in *LB*, p. 347.

83 Slavoj Žižek, *The Parallax View* (Cambridge, MA: MIT Press, 2006), pp. 151–2.

84 Hickey, *Impure Conceits*, pp. 140–1.

85 The episode may even have been influenced by the 'Ulysses' Canto 16 of *The Inferno* – Wordsworth knew Dante well. The story told by Ulysses is familiar: having returned to Ithaca, he is seized with wanderlust again, and persuades a band of men to sail out with him beyond the borders of the charted universe (the Pillars of Hercules). He fires his crew with enthusiasm by stating that they are not born to live like animals but to seek 'virtue and knowledge'. At the edge of the ocean, an unknown mountain leaps out at them: Mount Purgatory. As they sail towards this taboo object for the living, their ship is capsized by a giant wave, 'as pleased Another'.

86 Fry, *Wordsworth*, p. 107.

87 Stadial theory had been largely indifferent to 'gathering' as a mode of subsistence in what was not yet called 'hunter-gathering'. And celebrations of a 'savage republicanism' would likewise overlook its gendered division of labour. Adam Smith was especially dismissive: 'Their women plant a few stalks of Indian corn at the back of their huts. But this can hardly be called agriculture'; *Lectures on Jurisprudence*, p. 29. But the marginality of these women seems to have haunted Wordsworth. In *The Prelude*, their apparition suddenly emerges in Europe itself, in the Alpine recess of Como, with its 'garden plots / Of Indian corn tended by dark-eyed Maids' (VI.592–4). Such a gathering might still offer an image of the commonwealth of song: the American Indian women in 'Ruth', in a passage inspired by William Bartram, with 'dance and shout' leave their settlement to 'gather strawberries all day long / Returning with a choral song' (*LB* 52–3).

88 'Knight's Song' in *Through the Looking Glass*, in *The Penguin Complete Lewis Carroll* (Harmondsworth: Penguin, 1982), pp. 225–7.

89 After Book VIII's long account of shepherd life, Wordsworth asks rhetorically 'Why should I speak of tillers of the soil?' (498). It heads a list of co-operative social labours that Wordsworth will not discuss: 'the Ploughman and his Team', the young and old raking the soil together, the 'Quarry-man', 'Fishermen in pairs', and the 'melancholy' labour of the miner in darkness (499–510). The rhetorical question speaks more for an avoidance than what can safely be taken for granted. Wordsworth's exclusive focus on the 'Robinsonade', his failure to investigate whether there might be value, in his sense, in mutual or group labour, is the greatest weakness of his revaluation of labour. But the 'dignity of individual man' was a critical point of vantage against the social labour of the 'wealth of nations'.

90 'Really free working, e.g., composing, is at the same time precisely the most damned serious, the most intense exertion'; Karl Marx, *Grundrisse: Foundations of the Critique of Political Economy (Rough Draft)*, trans. Martin Nicolaus (London: Penguin, 1993), p. 611. The passage is an example of Marx's problematically one-sided humanism – satisfying work is an overcoming of obstacles, a self-realization through objectification. It is his counter not only to Smith's sacrificial account of labour, but also to Charles Fourier's 'shop-girl' vision of a group labour converted into fun or amusement. But as what is more than just

the metaphor of 'playing' a musical composition indicates, its gliding freedom as well as exertion, the intense reality of a social and historical opposition of work and play need not be ontological.

91 Hazlitt reported that *Robinson Crusoe* and books of voyages and travels were Wordsworth's favourite reading matter.
92 Max Weber, *The Protestant Ethic and the Spirit of Capitalism*, trans. Talcott Parsons (London and New York: Routledge, 2001).
93 *LB*, p. 330.
94 *Ibid.*, p. 331.
95 'Essay on Morals', *PW* I.103.
96 The phrase appears in a draft passage in MS. Y on childhood experience.
97 Levinson, *Wordsworth's Great Period Poems*, p. 75.
98 *Ibid.*, p. 60.
99 *EY*, p. 322.
100 On the importance of games to the Puritan ethos, see Bruce C. Daniels, *Puritans at Play: Leisure and Recreation in Colonial New England* (Basingstoke: Macmillan, 1995).
101 *LB*, p. 327.
102 *LB*, pp. 325–6.

7 PROGRESS

1 Notable exceptions include Jarvis, *Wordsworth's Philosophic Song* (see especially, pp. 26–7), Michael Wiley, *Romantic Geography: Wordsworth and Anglo-European Spaces* (Basingstoke: Macmillan, 1998), Morton D. Paley, *Apocalypse and Millennium in English Romantic Poetry* (Oxford: Clarendon Press, 1999) and M. H. Abrams, *Natural Supernaturalism: Tradition and Revolution in Romantic Literature* (New York: W. W. Norton, 1973).
2 'In Praise of Knowledge' (1592), in *The Letters and Life of Francis Bacon*, ed. J. Spedding, vols. VIII–XIV (London, 1861–74), vol. VIII, p. 123. Bacon, as much as Wordsworth, would also acknowledge the distortions of the *habitus*, the mental 'idols' by which we see through a glass darkly.
3 Blake wrote in the margin next to this statement: 'You shall not bring me down to believe such fitting & fitted'; 'Annotations to *The Excursion*' (1826), *Poetical Writings*, ed. Geoffrey Keynes (Oxford: Clarendon Press, 1972), p. 784.
4 See Greenblatt, *Marvellous Possessions*.
5 See Thomas M. Curley, *Samuel Johnson and the Age of Travel* (Athens: University of Georgia Press, 1976).
6 According to Crabb Robinson, Blake told him that the lines had caused him a 'bowel complaint' that almost killed him.
7 Donald Davie, 'Syntax in the Blank Verse of Wordsworth's *Prelude*', *Purity of Diction in English Verse* and *Articulate Energy* (London: Penguin, 1992), pp. 294–305. In his corrosively sceptical and misanthropic study, *History and Utopia*, the philosopher E. M. Cioran concludes his survey of illusion with a startling about-turn. Utopia is suddenly affirmed after all, only now

as a hidden point within the self: 'However pitiless our denials, we never quite destroy the object of our nostalgia: our dreams survive our waking and analysis. Though we have stopped believing in the geographical reality of paradise, and in its various figurations, it resides within us nonetheless, a supreme *given*, a dimension of our original ego; now the question is to discover it there. When we succeed, we enter into that glory the theologians call *essential*; but it is not God we see face to face, it is the eternal present, wrested from becoming and from eternity itself... a void that affords plenitude, a fulfilling void – does it not contain more reality than all history possesses from beginning to end?'; *History and Utopia*, trans. Richard Howard (London: Quartet Books, 1996), pp. 116–18. In the 'Prospectus', however, such an experience, whatever it might be, is to be confronted again with geography and history.

8 *Poetical Writings*, p. 784.

9 *Ibid.*

10 'On Wordsworth's Poetry', *The Collected Writings of Thomas De Quincey*, vol. XI, *Literary Theory and Criticism*, ed. David Masson (Edinburgh: Adam and Charles Black, 1890), p. 303.

11 Lamb, *Preserving the Self*, p. 37.

12 See W. H. Oliver, *Prophets and Millennialists: The Uses of Biblical Prophecy in England from the 1790s* (Auckland: Auckland University Press, 1978).

13 Blake, of course, also emerged from this Dissenting background – though there is only the negative teleology of a quasi-Gnostic history of the Fall in his Prophetic Books, despite the creative counter-labour that they affirm. The 'Harvest of the Nations' appears at their end as though out of nowhere.

14 Ferguson, *Essay*, p. 10.

15 *PW* II.13.

16 *Ibid.*, 3–4.

17 Vico had argued for the *ricorso*, the cyclical return of history, as on occasion would Shelley (influenced by Machiavelli), but Wordsworth's image of *reculer pour mieux sauter* is quite different.

18 *PW* II.12.

19 *Ibid.*

20 *Ibid.*

21 Coleridge, *Collected Letters*, vol. IV, p. 575.

22 *Life, Letters, and Journals of George Ticknor*, ed. George S. Hillard, 2 vols. (Boston: Osgood, 1876), vol. II, p. 167.

23 Letter to J. H. Reynolds, 3 May 1818; *Selected Letters of John Keats, Revised Edition*, ed. Grant F. Scott (Cambridge, MA: Harvard University Press, 2002), p. 124.

24 Novalis, *Philosophical Writings*, p. iv.

25 For a full and penetrating account of the 'Ode' in its relation to teleology and the eighteenth-century 'progress poem', see James Chandler, 'Wordsworth's Great Ode: Romanticism and the Progress of Poetry', in James Chandler and

Maureen N. McLane (eds.), *The Cambridge Companion to British Romantic Poetry* (Cambridge: Cambridge University Press, 2008), pp. 136–54.

26 A liberal political economist and philosopher influenced by Utilitarianism, John Stuart Mill, wrote of how Wordsworth's poetry helped to pull him out of his personal 'age of iron' and state of estrangement: 'What made Wordsworth's poems a medicine for my state of mind, was . . . [that] they seemed to be the very culture of the feelings, which I was in quest of. In them I seemed to draw from a source of inward joy, of sympathetic and imaginative pleasure, which could be shared in by all human beings; which had no connexion with struggle or imperfection, but would be made richer by every improvement in the physical or social condition of mankind. From them I seemed to learn what would be the perennial sources of happiness, when all the greater evils of life shall have been removed. And I felt myself at once better and happier as I came under their influence'; *Autobiography of John Stuart Mill* (Oxford: Oxford University Press, 1940), pp. 124–5. The 'age of iron' has yet to fulfil Mill's hopes. But Wordsworth's poetry of labour is written in the hope that sensibility might become an enriching value that is inside, not outside, 'physical improvement'.

27 Harold Bloom, 'The Myth of Memory and the Natural Man', in *Wordsworth: A Collection of Critical Essays*, ed. M. H. Abrams (Englewood Cliffs, NJ: Prentice-Hall, 1972), p. 103.

28 *Ibid.*

29 *EY*, p. 434.

30 Chandler, *Wordsworth's Second Nature*, p. 92.

31 As John Reider suggests, although there is no evidence that Wordsworth was familiar with Benthamite proposals in the 1790s, the poem can be read as strongly critical of any over-emphasis on 'rational calculation'. See *Wordsworth's Counterrevolutionary Turn: Community, Virtue, and Vision in the 1790s* (Newark: University of Delaware Press, 1997), p. 69.

32 Hazlitt, *Selected Writings*, vol. VII, p. 172.

33 Letter to Thomas Poole. Coleridge, *Collected Letters*, vol. II, p. 1036.

34 Rieder, *Wordsworth's Counterrevolutionary Turn*, p. 81.

35 *The Complete Works of William Hazlitt*, ed. P. P. Howe, 21 vols. (London: J. M. Dent, 1930–4), vol. II, p. 268.

36 Hans J. Nissen, Peter Damerow and Robert K. Englund, *Archaic Bookkeeping: Writing and Techniques of Economic Administration in the Ancient Near East*, trans. Paul Larsen (Chicago: University of Chicago Press, 1993), p. 30.

37 29 April 1802, *Journal*, vol. I, pp. 139–40; Dorothy's italics.

38 *Ibid.*, p. 139.

39 'Introduction to a Critique of Urban Geography', *Situationist International Anthology*, revised and expanded edition, ed. and trans. Ken Knabb (Berkeley: Bureau of Public Secrets, 2006), p. 8.

40 *Ibid.*, p. 9.

41 Jacques Rancière, *The Flesh of Words: The Politics of Writing*, trans. Charlotte Mandell (Stanford: Stanford University Press, 2004), pp. 9–20.

42 De Quincey, *Confessions*, pp. 47–8.

43 Debord, 'Psychogeographical Venice'. Available at www.notbored.org/psychogeographical-venice.html.
44 *PW* II.51.
45 *Ibid.*
46 Pagden, *European Encounters*, chapter 1 and *passim*.
47 David Bunn, '"Our Wattled Cot": Mercantile and Domestic Space in Thomas Pringle's African Landscapes', in W. J. T. Mitchell (ed.), *Landscape and Power* (Chicago: University of Chicago Press, 1994), pp. 127–73.
48 Park, *Travels in the Interior Districts of Africa*, p. 194. Park's emphasis.
49 Bernard Smith, *European Vision and the South Pacific*, second edition (New Haven and London: Yale University Press, 1982), p. 42.
50 Wiley, *Romantic Geography*, pp. 5–7.
51 Editor's 'Introduction', *The Journals of Lewis and Clark*, ed. Bernard DeVoto (Boston: Houghton Mifflin, 1953, reprinted 1981), p. xxxviii.
52 Quoted in Mark Duffill, *Mungo Park, West African Explorer* (Edinburgh: NMS Publishing, 1999), p. 126.
53 On 18 August and 10 November 1806. *MY* I.73, 97.
54 Alan Liu, *Wordsworth and the Sense of History* (Stanford: Stanford University Press, 1989), pp. 3–4. He had discovered the source of the Blue but not the White Nile, neglecting to mention the forking of the river into two channels at Khartoum.
55 James Bruce, *Travels to Discover the Source of the Nile, in the Years 1768, 1769, 1770, 1771, 1772, & 1773*, 5 vols. (Edinburgh: G. G. G. and J. Robinson, 1790), vol. III, p. 597.
56 *Ibid.*, p. 598.
57 *The Notebooks of Samuel Taylor Coleridge*, 3 vols., ed. Kathleen Coburn (London: Routledge & Kegan Paul, 1957), vol. I, p. 180.
58 *SSI*, p. 99.
59 *Ibid.*
60 Liu, *Wordsworth and the Sense of History*, p. 24.
61 David Ferris, *Theory and the Evasion of History* (Baltimore: Johns Hopkins University Press, 1993), p. 137.
62 Hartman, *Wordsworth's Poetry*, pp. 41, 33.
63 If this resembles the traveller's 'gloriation of mind', it also recalls another tradition to which Jonathan Lamb has briefly drawn attention; he writes of the seventeenth-century Cambridge Platonist Henry More: 'the soul's recognition of itself constitutes a surprise, a kind of inward impression that Descartes calls joy'; *The Evolution of Sympathy in the Long Eighteenth Century* (London: Routledge, 2009), p. 21.
64 Liu, *Wordsworth and the Sense of History*, p. 23.
65 *Pr2*, pp. 289–93.
66 *Pr2*, 401, p. 295.
67 Park, *Travels in the Interior Districts of Africa*, p. 177.
68 *Ibid.*

69 De Quincey was one of only a handful of people to have been granted access to *The Prelude* by 1821, and he retained a good, even verbatim, recall of it. The description of his night-time walks may well have been strongly influenced by the Snowdon episode.

70 Blake, *Poetical Writings*, 'Annotations to Wordsworth's *Poems*', p. 783.

71 *The Prelude, or Growth of a Poet's Mind*, ed. Ernest de Selincourt (Oxford: Clarendon Press, 1926), line 154, p. 557.

72 William Blake, *Jerusalem*, 27:25–6.

73 Debord, Preface to the Fourth Italian Edition of *The Society of the Spectacle*. Available at www.notbored.org/debord-preface.html.

74 Will Self, 'Guy Debord's *The Society of the Spectacle*', *The Guardian*, 14 November 2013. Available at www.theguardian.com/books/2013/nov/14/guy-debord-society-spectacle-will-self.

Bibliography

Aarsleff, Hans. Introduction. In Etienne Bonnot de Condillac. *Essay on the Origin of Human Knowledge*. Trans. and ed. Hans Aarsleff. Cambridge: Cambridge University Press, 2001.

Abrams, M. H. *The Mirror and the Lamp: Romantic Theory and the Critical Tradition*. Oxford: Oxford University Press, 1953, paperback edition 1971.

Natural Supernaturalism: Tradition and Revolution in Romantic Literature. New York: W. W. Norton, 1973.

Adorno, Theodor W. *Negative Dialectics*. Trans. E. B. Ashton. London: Routledge, 1973.

Vers une musique informelle. In *Quasi una fantasia: Essays on Modern Music*. Trans. Rodney Livingstone. London: Verso, 1998.

Aesthetic Theory. Ed. Gretel Adorno and Rolf Tiedemann. Trans. Robert Hullot Kentor. London: Continuum, 2002.

Lectures on Negative Dialectics: Fragments of a Lecture Course 1965/1966. Ed. Rolf Tiedemann. Trans. Rodney Livingstone. Cambridge: Polity Press, 2008.

Agamben, Giorgio. *Homo Sacer: Sovereign Power and Bare Life*. Trans. Daniel Heller-Roazen. Stanford: Stanford University Press, 1998.

The End of the Poem: Studies in Poetics. Trans. Daniel Heller-Roazen. Stanford: Stanford University Press, 1999.

State of Exception. Trans. Kevin Attell. Chicago: University of Chicago Press, 2005.

Arnold, Matthew. Wordsworth. In *Selected Poems of Wordsworth*. Ed. Harrison Ross Steeves. New York: Harcourt, Brace and Company, 1922, pp. 1–22.

Culture and Anarchy. Ed. Jane Garnett. Oxford: Oxford University Press, 2006.

Bachelard, Gaston. *The Poetics of Space*. Trans. Maria Jolas. Boston: Beacon Press, 1994.

Bacon, Francis. *The Letters and Life of Francis Bacon*. Vols. VIII–XIV. Ed. J. Spedding. London, 1861–74.

Bakhtin, Mikhail. *Problems of Dostoevsky's Poetics*. Ed. and trans. Caryl Emerson. Minneapolis: University of Minnesota Press, 1984.

Response to a Question from the *Novy Mir* Editorial Staff. In *Speech Genres and Other Late Essays*. Ed. Caryl Emerson and Michael Holquist. Trans. Vern W. McGee. Austin: University of Texas Press, 1986.

Barrell, John. The Uses of Dorothy: 'The Language of the Sense' in 'Tintern Abbey'. In *Poetry, Language and Politics*. Manchester: Manchester University Press, 1988, pp. 137–67.

Bartram, William. *Travels through North and South Carolina, Georgia, East and West Florida*. Philadelphia: James and Johnson, 1791.

William Bartram on the Southeastern Indians. Ed. Gregory A. Waselkov and Kathryn E. Holland Bround. Lincoln: University of Nebraska Press, 1995.

Bate, Jonathan. *Romantic Ecology: Wordsworth and the Environmental Tradition*. London: Routledge, 1991.

The Song of the Earth. London: Picador, 2000.

Baudrillard, Jean. *America*. Trans. Chris Turner. London: Verso, 2010.

Benjamin, Walter. Problems in the Sociology of Language. In *Selected Writings*, vol. III, *1935–1938*. Ed. Howard Eiland and Michael W. Jennings. Cambridge, MA: Belknap Press, 2002, pp. 68–93.

The Work of Art in the Age of its Technological Reproducibility (Third Version). In *Selected Writings*, vol. IV, *1938–1940*. Ed. Howard Eiland and Michael Jennings. Trans. Edmund Jephcott and others. Cambridge, MA: Belknap Press, 2003, pp. 251–283.

On Some Motifs in Baudelaire. In *Selected Writings*, vol. IV, *1938–1940*. Ed. Howard Eiland and Michael Jennings. Trans. Edmund Jephcott and others. Cambridge, MA: Belknap Press, 2003, pp. 313–55.

'The Regression of Poetry', by Carl Gustav Jochmann. In *Selected Writings*, vol. IV, *1938–1940*. Ed. Howard Eiland and Michael Jennings. Trans. Edmund Jephcott and others. Cambridge, MA: Belknap Press, 2003, pp. 356–80.

Critique of Violence. In *Selected Writings*, vol. I, *1913–1926*. Ed. Marcus Bullock and Michael Jennings. Cambridge, MA: Belknap Press, 2004, pp. 236–52.

The Task of the Translator. In *Selected Writings*, vol. I, *1913–1926*. Ed. Marcus Bullock and Michael Jennings. Cambridge, MA: Belknap Press, 2004, pp. 253–63.

On the Image of Proust. In *Selected Writings*, vol. II, Part, *1927–1930*. Ed. Michael W. Jennings, Howard Eiland and Gary Smith. Trans. Harry Zohn. Cambridge, MA: Belknap Press, 2005, pp. 237–47.

Franz Kafka. In *Selected Writings*, vol. II, part 2, *1931–1934*. Trans. Rodney Livingstone and Others. Ed. Michael W. Jennings, Howard Eiland and Gary Smith. Cambridge, MA: Belknap Press, 2005, pp. 794–818.

A Little History of Photography. In *Selected Writings*, vol. II, part 2, *1931–1934*. Ed. Michael W. Jennings, Howard Eiland and Gary Smith. Trans. Rodney Livingstone and others. Cambridge, MA: Belknap Press, 2005, pp. 507–30.

On The Mimetic Faculty. In *Selected Writings*, vol. II, part 2, *1931–1934*. Ed. Michael W. Jennings, Howard Eiland and Gary Smith. Trans. Rodney Livingstone and others. Cambridge, MA: Belknap Press, 2005, pp. 720–2.

Bennett, Andrew. *Wordsworth Writing*. Cambridge: Cambridge University Press, 2007.

Bewell, Alan. *Wordsworth and the Enlightenment: Nature, Man, and Society in the Experimental Poetry*. New Haven: Yale University Press, 1989.

Romanticism and Colonial Disease. Baltimore: Johns Hopkins University Press, 1999.

Bialostosky, Don H. *Wordsworth, Dialogics, and the Practice of Criticism*. Cambridge: Cambridge University Press, 1992.

Blair, Hugh. *Lectures on Rhetoric and Belles Lettres*. Ed. Linda Ferreira-Buckley and S. Michael Halloran. Carbondale: Southern Illinois University Press, 2005.

Blake, William. *Poetical Writings*. Ed. Geoffrey Keynes. Oxford: Clarendon Press, 1972.

Bloch, Ernst. *Natural Law and Human Dignity*. Trans. Dennis J. Schmidt. Cambridge, MA: MIT Press, 1986.

Bloch, Ernst *et al. Aesthetics and Politics*. Trans. and ed. Ronald Taylor. London: Verso, 1980.

Blondel, Jean-François. *Cours d'architecture*, 6 vols. Paris, 1771–7.

Bloom, Harold. The Myth of Memory and the Natural Man. In *Wordsworth: A Collection of Critical Essays*. Ed. M. H. Abrams. Englewood Cliffs, NJ: Prentice-Hall, 1972, pp. 95–106.

Bourdieu, Pierre. *The Logic of Practice*. Trans. Richard Nice. Cambridge: Polity Press, 1990.

Brecht, Bertolt. *Journals*. Ed. John Willett. Trans. Hugh Rorrison. New York: Routledge/Theatre Art Books, 1996.

Bromwich, David. *Disowned by Memory: Wordsworth's Poetry of the 1790s*. Chicago: University of Chicago Press, 1998.

Bromwich, David (ed.). *Romantic Critical Essays*. Cambridge: Cambridge University Press, 1987.

Brown, John. *The History of the Rise and Progress of Poetry, Through its Several Species*. Newcastle: J. White, 1764.

Bruce, James. *Travels to Discover the Source of the Nile, in the Years 1768, 1769, 1770, 1771, 1772, & 1773*. 5 vols. Edinburgh: G. G. G. and J. Robinson, 1790.

Buck-Morss, Susan. *The Dialectics of Seeing: Walter Benjamin and the Arcades Project*. Cambridge, MA: MIT Press, 1989.

Bunn, David. 'Our Wattled Cot': Mercantile and Domestic Space in Thomas Pringle's African Landscapes. In W. J. T. Mitchell (ed.), *Landscape and Power*. Chicago: University of Chicago Press, 1994, pp. 127–73.

Burke, Edmund. *The Works of the Right Honourable Edmund Burke*. Revised edition, 12 vols. Boston: Little, Brown & Co., 1865–7.

The Correspondence of Edmund Burke. Ed. George H. Guttridge. Cambridge: Cambridge University Press, 1961.

Burney, Charles. Review of *Lyrical Ballads*. *The Monthly Review*, 2nd Series, 29 (June 1799), pp. 202–10.

General History of Music, From the Earliest Ages to the Present Period. 2 vols. Ed. Frank Mercer. London: G. T. Foulis, 1935.

Burns, Robert. *The Songs of Burns*. Ed. Donald A. Low. London: Routledge, 1993.

Carroll, Lewis. *The Penguin Complete Lewis Carroll.* Harmondsworth: Penguin, 1982.

Carver, Jonathan. *Travels through America, 1766–68.* Ed. Norman Gelb. New York: John Wiley, 1993.

Chandler, James. *Wordsworth's Second Nature: A Study of the Poetry and the Politics.* Chicago: University of Chicago Press, 1984.

'Wordsworth's Great Ode: Romanticism and the Progress of Poetry'. In James Chandler and Maureen N. McLane (eds.), *The Cambridge Companion to British Romantic Poetry.* Cambridge: Cambridge University Press, 2008, pp. 136–54.

Cioran, E. M. *History and Utopia.* Trans. Richard Howard. London: Quartet Books, 1996.

Coe, Charles Norton. *Wordsworth and the Literature of Travel.* New York: Bookman Associates, 1953.

Cohn, Norman. *The Pursuit of the Millennium: Revolutionary Millenarians and Mystical Anarchists of the Middle Ages.* London: Paladin, 1970.

Coleridge, Samuel Taylor. *Collected Letters of Samuel Taylor Coleridge, 1785–1834.* Ed. Earl Leslie Briggs. 6 vols. Oxford: Clarendon Press, 1956–71.

The Notebooks of Samuel Taylor Coleridge. 3 vols. Ed. Kathleen Coburn. London: Routledge & Kegan Paul, 1957.

The Collected Works of Samuel Taylor Coleridge, The Friend. 2 vols. Princeton: Princeton University Press, 1969.

The Collected Works of Samuel Taylor Coleridge, Marginalia. 3 vols. Ed. H. J. Jackson and George Whalley. Princeton: Princeton University Press, 1992.

Biographia Literaria. Ed. Nigel Leask. London: J. M. Dent, 1997.

Condillac, Etienne Bonnot de. *Essay on the Origin of Human Knowledge.* Trans. and ed. Hans Aarsleff. Cambridge: Cambridge University Press, 2001.

Connell, Philip. *Romanticism, Economics, and the Question of 'Culture'.* Oxford: Oxford University Press, 2001.

Cronin, Richard (ed.). *1798: The Year of the Lyrical Ballads.* Basingstoke: Macmillan, 1998.

Curley, Thomas M. *Samuel Johnson and the Age of Travel.* Athens: University of Georgia Press, 1976.

Daniels, Bruce C. *Puritans at Play: Leisure and Recreation in Colonial New England.* Basingstoke: Macmillan, 1995.

Davie, Donald. Syntax in the Blank Verse of Wordsworth's *Prelude*. In *Purity of Diction in English Verse and Articulate Energy.* London: Penguin, 1992, pp. 294–305.

Davies, Hugh Sykes. *Wordsworth and the Worth of Words.* Ed. John Kerrigan and Jonathan Wordsworth. Cambridge: Cambridge University Press, 1986.

Debord, Guy. Introduction to a Critique of Urban Geography. In *Situationist International Anthology.* Revised and expanded edition. Ed. and trans. Ken Knabb. Berkeley: Bureau of Public Secrets, 2006.

Psychogeographical Venice (1957). www.notbored.org/psychogeographical-venice.html.

Preface to the Fourth Italian Edition of *The Society of the Spectacle* (1979). www.notbored.org/debord-preface.html.

De Certeau, Michel. *The Practice of Everyday Life*. Trans. Steven Rendall. Berkeley: University of California Press, 1984.

Montaigne's 'Of Cannibals': The Savage 'I'. In *Heterologies: Discourse on the Other*. Trans. Brian Massumi. Minneapolis: University of Minnesota Press, 1986), pp. 67–79.

The Certeau Reader. Ed. Graham Ward. Oxford: Blackwell, 2000.

Deleuze, Gilles. *Difference and Repetition*. Trans. Paul Patton. London: Continuum, 2004.

de Man, Paul. Wordsworth and the Victorians. In *The Rhetoric of Romanticism*. New York: Columbia University Press, 1984.

De Quincey, Thomas. *The Collected Writings of Thomas De Quincey*. 14 vols. Ed. David Masson. Edinburgh: Adam and Charles Black, 1890.

Confessions of an English Opium-Eater and Other Writings. Second edition. Ed. Grevel Lindop. Oxford: Oxford University Press, 1996.

Derrida, Jacques. *The Archeology of the Frivolous: Reading Condillac*. Trans. John P. Leavey, Jr. Pittsburgh: Duquesne University Press, 1980.

Of Grammatology. Trans. Gayatri Chakrovorty Spivak. Corrected edition. Baltimore: Johns Hopkins University Press, 1997.

Specters of Marx. Trans. Peggy Kamuf. London and New York: Routledge, 2006.

Donelan, James H. *Poetry and the Romantic Musical Aesthetic*. Cambridge: Cambridge University Press, 2008.

Duffill, Mark. *Mungo Park, West African Explorer*. Edinburgh: NMS Publishing, 1999.

Empson, William. *Seven Types of Ambiguity*. London: Chatto & Windus, 1949.

The Structure of Complex Words. London: Chatto & Windus, 1951.

Erskine-Hill, Howard. *The Poetry of Opposition and Revolution: Dryden to Wordsworth*. Oxford: Clarendon Press, 1996.

Ferguson, Adam. *An Essay on the History of Civil Society*. Edinburgh: Millar & Cadell, 1767.

Ferguson, Frances. *Wordsworth: Language as Counter-Spirit*. New Haven: Yale University Press, 1977.

Ferris, David. *Theory and the Evasion of History*. Baltimore: Johns Hopkins University Press, 1993.

Foucault, Michel. Preface. In Gilles Deleuze and Félix Guattari. *Anti-Oedipus: Capitalism and Schizophrenia*. Trans. Robert Hurley, Mark Seem and Helen R. Lane. London: Athlone Press, 1984.

The Order of Things: An Archaeology of Human Knowledge. London and New York: Routledge, 2002.

Freud, Sigmund. The Uncanny. In *The Standard Edition of the Complete Psychological Works of Sigmund Freud*, vol. XVII (*1917–1919*). Ed. and trans. James Strachey. London: Hogarth Press, 1953, pp. 219–52.

The Complete Letters of Sigmund Freud to Wilhelm Fliess, 1887–1904. Ed. and trans. J. M. Masson. Cambridge, MA: Belknap Press, 1985.

Fry, Paul H. *Wordsworth and the Poetry of What We Are*. New Haven: Yale University Press, 2008.

Fulford, Tim. *Romantic Indians: Native Americans, British Literature, and Transatlantic Culture 1756–1830*. Oxford: Oxford University Press, 2006.

Funkenstein, Amos. *Theology and the Scientific Imagination: From the Middle Ages to the Seventeenth Century*. Princeton: Princeton University Press, 1986.

Gadamer, Hans-Georg. *Truth and Method*. Second revised edition. Trans. Joel Weinsheimer and Donald G. Marshall. London: Sheed & Ward, 1989.

Girard, René. *Violence and the Sacred*. Trans. Patrick Gregory. Baltimore: Johns Hopkins University Press, 1977.

Glen, Heather. *Vision and Disenchantment: Blake's Songs and Wordsworth's Lyrical Ballads*. Cambridge: Cambridge University Press, 1983.

Godwin, William. *An Enquiry Concerning Political Justice and Its Influences on General Virtue and Happiness*. 2 vols. London: G. G. J. and J. Robinson, 1793.

Goodman, Kevis. *Georgic Modernity and British Romanticism: Poetry and the Mediation of History*. Cambridge: Cambridge University Press, 2004.

'Uncertain Disease': Nostalgia, Pathologies of Motion, Practices of Reading. *SiR* 49 (2010), pp. 197–227.

Goody, Jack. *Renaissances: The One or the Many?* Cambridge: Cambridge University Press, 2010.

Graeber, David. *Towards an Anthropological Theory of Value: The False Coin of Our Own Dreams*. Basingstoke: Palgrave Macmillan, 2001.

Grassi, Ernesto. *Rhetoric as Philosophy: The Humanist Tradition*. University Park: Pennysylvania State University Press, 1980.

Gravil, Richard. *Wordsworth's Bardic Vocation, 1787–1842*. Basingstoke: Palgrave Macmillan, 2003.

Green, André. *The Fabric of Affect in the Psychoanalytic Discourse*. Trans. Alan Sheridan. London and New York: Routledge, 1999.

Greenblatt, Stephen. *Marvellous Possessions: The Wonder of the New World*. Oxford: Clarendon Press, 1992.

Gregg, Melissa, and Seigworth, Gregory J. (eds.). *The Affect Theory Reader*. Durham, NC: Duke University Press, 2010.

Haakonssen, Knud. *Natural Law and Moral Philosophy: From Grotius to the Scottish Enlightenment*. Cambridge: Cambridge University Press, 1996.

Hamilton, Paul. *Metaromanticism: Aesthetics, Literature, Theory*. Chicago: University of Chicago Press, 2003.

Haney, David P. *William Wordsworth and the Hermeneutics of Incarnation*. University Park: Pennsylvania State University Press, 1993.

Wordsworth and Levinas: Making a Habit of the Sublime. In Melvyn New with Robert Bernasconi and Richard A. Cohen (eds.), *In Proximity: Emmanuel Levinas and the Eighteenth Century*. Lubbock: Texas Technological University Press, 2001, pp. 395–451.

Harries, Karsten. *The Ethical Function in Architecture*. Cambridge, MA: MIT Press, 1998.

Harrison, Gary Lee. *Wordsworth's Vagrant Muse: Poetry, Poverty, and Power*. Detroit: Wayne State University Press, 1994.

Hartman, Geoffrey H. *Wordsworth's Poetry, 1787–1814*. New Haven: Yale University Press, 1964.

Toward Literary History. *Daedalus* 99, 2 (1970), pp. 355–83.

The Unremarkable Wordsworth. Minneapolis: University of Minnesota Press, 1987.

Reading: the Wordsworthian Enlightenment. In Helen Regueiro Elam and Frances Ferguson (eds.), *The Wordsworthian Enlightenment: Romantic Poetry and the Ecology of Reading*. Baltimore: Johns Hopkins University Press, 2005.

Hazlitt, William. *The Complete Works of William Hazlitt*. 21 vols. Ed. P. P. Howe. London: J. M. Dent, 1930–4.

The Selected Writings of William Hazlitt. 9 vols. Ed. Duncan Wu. London: Pickering & Chatto, 1998.

Hearne, Samuel. *A Journey from Prince of Wales Fort in Hudson's Bay to the Northern Ocean, 1769, 1770, 1771, 1772*. Ed. Richard Glover. Toronto: Macmillan, 1958.

Hegel, G. W. F. *Hegel's Aesthetics: Lectures on Fine Arts*. 2 vols. Trans. T. M. Knox. Oxford: Clarendon Press, 1975.

Heidegger, Martin. '. . . Poetically Man Dwells . . .'. In *Poetry, Language, Thought*. Trans. Albert Hofstadter. New York: Harper & Row, 1971, pp. 221–5.

Nietzsche. 4 vols. Trans. David Farrell Krell *et al*. London: Harper & Row, 1979.

Why Poets?. In *Off the Beaten Track*. Ed. and trans. Julian Young and Kenneth Haynes. Cambridge: Cambridge University Press, 2002, pp. 200–41.

Letter on Humanism. In *Basic Writings*. Ed. David Farrell Krell. London and New York: Routledge, 2011, pp. 141–82.

Building, Dwelling, Thinking. In *Basic Writings*. Ed. David Farrell Krell. London and New York: Routledge, 2011, pp. 239–56.

Henry, Michel. *Marx: A Philosophy of Human Reality*. Trans. Kathleen McLaughlin. Bloomington: University of Indiana Press, 1983.

Dessiner la musique: théorie pour l'art de Briesen. *Le Nouveau Commerce* 61 (1985), pp. 49–106.

Hickey, Alison. *Impure Conceits: Rhetoric and Ideology in Wordsworth's 'Excursion'*. Stanford: Stanford University Press, 1997.

Hobbes, Thomas. *Leviathan*. Ed. Richard Tuck. Cambridge: Cambridge University Press, 1996.

Horkheimer, Max and Theodor W. Adorno. *Dialectic of Enlightenment: Philosophical Fragments*. Ed. Gunzelin Schmid Noerr. Trans. Edmund Jephcott. Stanford: Stanford University Press, 2002.

Hubert, Henri and Mauss, Marcel. *Sacrifice: Its Nature and Function*. Trans. W. D. Halls. London: Cohen & West, 1964.

Hume, David. *A Treatise of Human Nature*. Ed. Ernest C. Mossner. Harmondsworth: Penguin, 1985.

Hunt, Lynn. *Inventing Human Rights: A History*. New York: W. W. Norton, 2007.

Husserl, Edmund. *Ideas: General Introduction to Pure Phenomenology*. Trans. Boyce Gibson. London: Routledge, 2012.

Jacobus, Mary. *Tradition and Experiment in Wordsworth's Lyrical Ballads (1798)*. Oxford: Clarendon Press, 1976.

Romanticism, Writing and Sexual Difference: Essays on The Prelude. Oxford: Oxford University Press, 1989.

Wordsworth and Winnicott. In *The Poetics of Psychoanalysis: In the Wake of Klein*. Oxford: Oxford University Press, 2005, pp. 148–69.

Romantic Things: A Tree, a Rock, a Cloud. Chicago: University of Chicago Press, 2012.

Jarvis, Simon. *Wordsworth's Philosophic Song*. Cambridge: Cambridge University Press, 2006.

Johnston, Kenneth K. *Wordsworth and The Recluse*. New Haven: Yale University Press, 1984.

Jones, Chris. *Radical Sensibility: Literature and Ideas in the 1790s*. London: Routledge, 1993.

Kames, Lord Henry Home. *Elements of Criticism*. Third edition, 3 vols. Edinburgh: printed for A. Millar, 1765.

Kant, Immanuel. *Critique of Pure Reason*. Trans. and ed. Paul Guyer and Allen W. Wood. Cambridge: Cambridge University Press, 1998.

Karatani, Kojin. *Transcritique: On Kant and Marx*. Trans. Sabu Kohso. Cambridge, MA: MIT Press, 2005.

Kaufman, Robert. Aura, Still. In Andrew Benjamin (ed.), *Walter Benjamin and Art*. London and New York: Continuum, 2005, pp. 121–47.

Lyric's Expression: Musicality, Conceptuality, Critical Agency. In David Cunningham and Nigel Mapp (eds.), *Adorno and Literature*. London and New York: Continuum, 2006, pp. 99–196.

Keate, George. *An Account of the Pelew Islands*. Ed. Karen L. Nero and Nicholas Thomas. London: Leicester University Press, 2002.

Keats, John. *Selected Letters of John Keats, Revised Edition*. Ed. Grant F. Scott. Cambridge, MA: Harvard University Press, 2002.

Kelley, Paul. Rousseau's *Discourse on the Origins of Inequality* and Wordsworth's *Salisbury Plain*. *Notes and Queries*, NS 24 (1977), p. 323.

Kerrigan, John. Wordsworth and the Sonnet: Building, Dwelling, Thinking. *Essays in Criticism* 35, 1 (1985), pp. 45–75.

Klancher, Jon P. *The Making of English Reading Audiences, 1790–1832*. Madison: University of Wisconsin Press, 1987.

Klein, Melanie. *Love, Guilt and Reparation and Other Works 1921–1945*. London: Vintage, 1998.

Lamb, Jonathan. *Preserving the Self in the South Seas, 1680–1840*. Chicago: University of Chicago Press, 2001.

The Evolution of Sympathy in the Long Eighteenth Century. London: Routledge, 2009.

Scurvy and the Terra Incognita. *Public Domain Review*, 6 May 2015. Available at http://publicdomainreview.org/2015/05/06/scurvy-and-the-terra-incognita/.

La Mettrie, Julien Offray de. *L'homme machine*. Leyden: Elie Luzac Fils, 1748.

Langan, Celeste. *Romantic Vagrancy: Wordsworth and the Simulation of Freedom*. Cambridge: Cambridge University Press, 1995.

Laugier, Marc-Antoine. *Essai sur l'architecture*. Paris, 1753.

Leask, Nigel. *Curiosity and the Aesthetics of Travel Writing, 1770–1840: 'From an Antique Land'*. Oxford: Oxford University Press, 2002.

Burns, Wordsworth and the Politics of Vernacular Poetry. In Peter de Bolla, Nigel Leask and David Simpson (eds.), *Land, Nation and Culture, 1740–1840: Thinking the Republic of Taste*. Basingstoke: Palgrave Macmillan, 2005, pp. 202–2.

Lefebvre, Henri. Preface to the Study of the Habitat of the 'Pavillon'. In *Key Writings*, ed. Stuart Elden, Elizabeth Lebas and Eleonore Kofman. New York: Continuum, 2003.

Levinas, Emmanuel. *Totality and Infinity*. Trans. Alphonso Lingis. The Hague: Martinus Nijhoff, 1979.

Uniqueness. In *Entre Nous: Thinking-of-the-Other*. Trans. Michael B. Smith and Barbara Harshav. London and New York: Continuum, 2006, pp. 162–8.

Levinson, Marjorie. *Wordsworth's Great Period Poems: Four Essays*. Cambridge: Cambridge University Press, 1986.

Lewis, Meriwether and Clark, William. *The Journals of Lewis and Clark*. Ed. Bernard DeVoto. Boston: Houghton Mifflin, 1953, reprinted 1981.

Liu, Alan. *Wordsworth and the Sense of History*. Stanford: Stanford University Press, 1989.

Locke, John. *Two Treatises on Government*. Ed. Peter Laslett. Cambridge: Cambridge University Press, 1988.

An Essay Concerning Human Understanding. Ed. Roger Woolhouse. London: Penguin, 2004.

Lowth, Robert. *Lectures on the Sacred Poetry of the Hebrews*. Facsimile edition, 2 vols. London: Routledge/Thoemmes Press, 1995.

Mackenzie, Henry. *The Man of Feeling*. Ed. Brian Vickers. Oxford: Oxford University Press, 1967.

Manning, Peter J. *Reading Romantics: Texts and Contexts*. Oxford: Oxford University Press, 1990.

Marshall, P. J. and Williams, G. *The Great Map of Mankind: British Perceptions of the World in the Age of Enlightenment*. London: Dent, 1982.

Marx, Karl. *Marx: Early Writings*. Trans. Rodney Livingstone and Gregor Benton. Harmondsworth: Penguin, 1975.

Grundrisse: Foundations of the Critique of Political Economy (Rough Draft). Trans. Martin Nicolaus. London: Penguin, 1993.

Marx, Karl and Engels, Friedrich. *Collected Works*. 50 vols. London: Lawrence and Wishart, 1975–2005.

McFarland, Thomas. *Romanticism and the Forms of Ruin: Wordsworth, Coleridge, and Modalities of Fragmentation*. Princeton: Princeton University Press, 1981.

McLane, Maureen N. *Romanticism and the Human Sciences: Poetry, Population, and the Discourse of the Species*. Cambridge: Cambridge University Press, 2000.

Balladeering, Ministrelsy, and the Making of British Romantic Poetry. Cambridge: Cambridge University Press, 2008.

Meek, Ronald L. *Social Science and the Ignoble Savage*. Cambridge: Cambridge University Press, 1976.

Menke, Christoph. *The Sovereignty of Art: Aesthetic Negativity in Adorno and Derrida*. Trans. Neil Solomon. Cambridge, MA: MIT Press, 1998.

Meschonnic, Henri. *Ethics and Politics of Translating*. Trans. and ed. Pier-Pascale Boulanger. Amsterdam and Philadelphia: John Benjamins, 2011.

Mill, John Stuart. *Autobiography of John Stuart Mill*. Oxford: Oxford University Press, 1940.

Millar, John. *The Origin of the Distinction of Ranks*. Reprint of 1806 edition. Bristol: Thoemmes Antiquarian Books, 1990.

Milton, John. *The Poems of John Milton*. Ed. John Carey and Alastair Fowler. London: Longmans, 1968.

Mitchell, Juliet. *Mad Men and Medusas: Reclaiming Hysteria and the Effects of Sibling Relations on the Human Condition*. London: Penguin, 2000.

Siblings: Sex and Violence. Cambridge: Polity Press, 2003.

Monboddo, Lord. *The Origins and Progress of Language*. 6 vols. Edinburgh: A. Kincaid and W. Creech, 1773.

Montesquieu, Baron de. *Spirit of the Laws*. Trans. Thomas Nugent. New York: Hafner, 1949.

Moorman, Mary. *William Wordsworth, a Biography: Early Years, 1770–1803*. Oxford: Clarendon Press, 1957.

Murrary, David. *Indian Giving: Economies of Power in Indian–White Exchanges*. Amherst: University of Massachusetts Press, 2000.

Nissen, Hans J., Damerow, Peter and Englund, Robert K. *Archaic Bookkeeping: Writing and Techniques of Economic Administration in the Ancient Near East*. Trans. Paul Larsen. Chicago: University of Chicago Press, 1993.

Novalis. *Philosophical Writings*. Trans. and ed. Margaret Mahony Stoljar. New York: State University of New York Press, 1997.

O'Donnell, Brennan. *The Passion of Meter: A Study of Wordsworth's Metrical Art*. Kent, OH: Kent State University Press, 1995.

Oliver, W. H. *Prophets and Millennialists: The Uses of Biblical Prophecy in England from the 1790s*. Auckland: Auckland University Press, 1978.

Pagden, Anthony. *European Encounters with the New World: From Renaissance to Romanticism*. New Haven: Yale University Press, 1993.

Paley, Morton D. *Apocalypse and Millennium in English Romantic Poetry*. Oxford: Clarendon Press, 1999.

Park, Mungo. *Travels in the Interior Districts of Africa Performed Under the Direction and Patronage of the African Association in the Years 1795, 1796, and 1797*. Second edition. London: W. Bulmer & Co., 1799.

Payne Knight, Richard. *The Progress of Civil Society: A Didactic Poem, In Six Books*. London: W. Bulmer & Co., 1796.

Phillips, Mark Salber. *Society and Sentiment: Genres of Historical Writing in Britain, 1740–1820*. Princeton: Princeton University Press, 2000.

Pinkard, Terry. *Hegel: A Biography*. Cambridge: Cambridge University Press, 2000.

Pocock, J. G. A. *Barbarism and Religion,* vol. IV, *Barbarians, Savages and Empires*. Cambridge: Cambridge University Press, 2005.

Pope, Alexander. *The Major Works*. Oxford: Oxford University Press, 2006.

Postone, Moishe. *Time, Labor, and Social Domination*. Cambridge: Cambridge University Press, 1993.

Pratt, Mary Louise. *Imperial Eyes: Travel Writing and Transculturation*. London and New York: Routledge, 1992.

Prynne, J. H. *Field Notes: 'The Solitary Reaper' and Others*. Cambridge: privately printed, 2007.

Huts. *Textual Practice* 22, 4 (2008), pp. 613–33.

Rancière, Jacques. *The Flesh of Words: The Politics of Writing*. Trans. Charlotte Mandell. Stanford: Stanford University Press, 2004.

Reider, John. *Wordsworth's Counterrevolutionary Turn: Community, Virtue, and Vision in the 1790s*. Newark: University of Delaware Press, 1997.

Ritson, Joseph. *A Select Collection of English Songs*. 3 vols. London: J. Johnson, 1783.

Robertson, William. *The History of America*, 2 vols. London: W. Strahan, T. Cadell, J. Balfour, 1777.

Roe, Nicholas. *Wordsworth and Coleridge: The Radical Years*. Oxford: Clarendon Press, 1988.

Rose, Gillian. *The Broken Middle: Out of Our Ancient Society*. Oxford: Blackwell, 1992.

Ruskin, John. *The Poetry of Architecture, or, The architecture of the nations of Europe considered in its association with natural scenery and national character: to which is added a chapter upon the propriety of combining works of art with the sublimity of nature*. Sunnyside, Orpington: George Allen, 1893.

Rousseau, Jean-Jacques. *The* Discourses *and Other Early Political Writings*. Trans. and ed. Victor Gourevitch. Cambridge: Cambridge University Press, 1997.

Russell, Corinna. A Defence of Tautology: Repetition and Difference in Wordsworth's Note to 'The Thorn'. *Paragraph* 28, 2 (2005), pp. 106–18.

Rykwert, Joseph. *On Adam's House in Paradise: The Idea of the Primitive Hut in Architectural History*. New York: Museum of Modern Art, 1972.

Said, Edward W. *Orientalism: Western Conceptions of the Orient*. 1978; London: Penguin, 1995.

Self, Will. Guy Debord's *The Society of the Spectacle. The Guardian*, 14 November 2013. www.theguardian.com/books/2013/nov/14/guy-debord-society-spectacle-will-self.

Shaftesbury, Anthony Ashley Cooper, Earl of. *Characteristics of Men, Manners, Opinions, Times*, ed. Lawrence E. Klein. Cambridge: Cambridge University Press, 1999.

Sharr, Adam. *Heidegger's Hut*. Cambridge, MA: MIT Press, 2006.

Shell, Marc. *The End of Kinship: 'Measure for Measure,' Incest, and the Ideal of Universal Siblinghood*. Stanford: Stanford University Press, 1988.

Shelley, Percy Bysshe. A Defence of Poetry. In *Shelley's Poetry and Prose*. Second edition. Ed. Donald H. Reiman and Neil Fraistat. New York: W. W. Norton, 2002, pp. 510–35.

Simpson, David. *Wordsworth and the Figurings of the Real*. Basingstoke: Macmillan, 1999; reprint of 1982 edition.

Wordsworth's Historical Imagination: The Poetry of Displacement. New York: Methuen, 1987.

Romanticism, Nationalism, and the Revolt against Theory. Chicago: University of Chicago Press, 1993.

'Wordsworth and Empire – Just Joking'. In Peter De Bolla, Nigel Leask and David Simpson (eds.), *Land, Nation and Culture: Thinking the Republic of Taste*. Basingstoke: Palgrave Macmillan, 2005, pp. 188–201.

Wordsworth, Commodification and Social Concern: The Poetics of Modernity. Cambridge: Cambridge University Press, 2009.

Siskin, Clifford. The Year of the System. In Richard Cronin (ed.), *1798: The Year of the Lyrical Ballads*. Basingstoke: Macmillan, 1998, pp. 9–27.

Skinner, Quentin. *Liberty before Liberalism*. Cambridge: Cambridge University Press, 1998.

Smith, Adam. *The Early Writings of Adam Smith*. Ed. J. R. Lindgren. New York: Kelley Reprint, 1967.

An Inquiry into the Nature and Causes of the Wealth of Nations. Ed. E. Cannan. Chicago: University of Chicago Press, 1976.

The Theory of Moral Sentiments. Ed. D. D. Raphael and A. L. Macfie. Oxford: Clarendon Press, 1976.

Lectures on Jurisprudence. Ed. R. L. Meek, D. D. Raphael and P. G. Stein. Oxford: Clarendon Press, 1978.

The Essential Adam Smith. Ed. Robert L. Heilbroner and Lawrence J. Malone. Oxford: Oxford University Press, 1986.

Smith, Bernard. *European Vision and the South Pacific*. Second edition. New Haven: Yale University Press, 1982.

Smith, Olivia. *The Politics of Language, 1791–1819*. Oxford: Clarendon Press, 1986.

Starobinski, Jean. *Jean-Jacques Rousseau: Transparency and Obstruction*. Trans. Arthur Goldhammer. Chicago: University of Chicago Press, 1988.

Steiner, George. *After Babel: Aspects of Language and Translation*. Third edition. Oxford: Oxford University Press, 1998.

Stewart, Dugald. *An Account of the Life and Writings of Adam Smith, LL.D*. New York: Kelley Reprint, 1966.

Stewart, Susan. Scandals of the Ballad. *Representations* 32 (1990), pp. 134–56.

Strauss, Leo. *Natural Right and History*. Chicago: University of Chicago Press, 1953.

Stukeley, William. *Stonehenge, a Temple Restor'd to the British Druids*. London, 1740.

Swift, Jonathan. *The Writings of Jonathan Swift*. Ed. Robert A. Greenberg and William B. Piper. New York: W. W. Norton, 1973.

Talbot, Ann. *'The Great Ocean of Knowledge': The Influence of Travel Literature on the Work of John Locke*. Leiden: Koninklijke Brill NV, 2010.

Taussig, Michael. *Mimesis and Alterity: A Particular History of the Senses*. New York: Routledge, 1993.

Thompson, E. P. *The Making of the English Working Class*. New York: Vintage Books, 1963.

Ticknor, George. *Life, Letters, and Journals of George Ticknor*. Ed. George S. Hillard. 2 vols. Boston: Osgood, 1876.

Valéry, Paul. *Rhumbs*. In *The Collected Works of Paul Valéry*, vol. 14. Princeton: Princeton University Press, 1970.

Vesely, Dalibor. *Architecture in the Age of Divided Representation: The Question of Creativity in the Shadow of Production*. Cambridge, MA: MIT Press, 2004.

Vico, Giambattista. *New Science*. Third edition. Trans. David Marsh. London: Penguin, 2001.

Vidler, Anthony. *The Architectural Uncanny: Essays in the Modern Unhomely*. Cambridge, MA: MIT Press, 1992.

Vigus, James. *Platonic Coleridge*. London: Legenda, 2009.

Vitruvius. *The Ten Books on Architecture*. Trans. Morris Hicky Morgan. New York: Dover, 1960.

Weber, Max. *The Protestant Ethic and the Spirit of Capitalism*. Trans. Talcott Parsons. London and New York: Routledge, 2001.

Weil, Simone. *Gravity and Grace*. Trans. Emma Crawford and Mario von der Ruhr. London: Routledge, 2002.

Wheeler, Michael. *The Lamp of Memory: Ruskin, Tradition and Architecture*. Manchester: Manchester University Press, 1992.

Wiley, Michael. *Romantic Geography: Wordsworth and Anglo-European Spaces*. Basingstoke: Macmillan, 1998.

Williams, Helen Maria. *Poems on Various Subjects*. London: G. and W. B. Whittaker, 1823.

Winnicott, D. W. *Playing and Reality*. London and New York: Routledge, 2005.

Woof, Robert (ed.). *William Wordsworth: The Critical Heritage*, vol. 1, *1793–1820*. London: Routledge, 2001.

Wordsworth, Dorothy. *The Journals of Dorothy Wordsworth*. 2 vols. Ed. Ernest de Selincourt. London: Macmillan, 1941.

Wordsworth, Jonathan. 'The Two-Part Prelude of 1799'. In *The Prelude, 1799, 1805, 1850*. Ed. Jonathan Wordsworth, M. H. Abrams and Stephen Gill. New York: Norton, 1979, pp. 567–85.

Wordsworth, William. *Two Addresses to the Freeholders of Westmoreland*. Kendal: printed by Airey and Bellingham, 1818.

The Prelude, or Growth of a Poet's Mind. Ed. Ernest de Selincourt. Oxford: Clarendon Press, 1926.

The Letters of William and Dorothy Wordsworth, Early Years 1787–1805. Ed. Ernest de Selincourt, revised Chester L. Shaver. Oxford: Clarendon Press, 1967.

The Letters of William and Dorothy Wordsworth, Middle Years. 2 vols. Ed. Ernest de Selincourt, revised Mary Moorman. Oxford: Clarendon Press, 1970.

The Prose Works of William Wordsworth. 3 vols. Ed. W. J. B. Owen and Jane Worthington Smyser. Oxford: Clarendon Press, 1974.

The Salisbury Plain Poems of William Wordsworth. Ed. Stephen Gill. Ithaca: Cornell University Press, 1975.

Home at Grasmere, Part First, Book First, of The Recluse. Ed. Beth Darlington. Ithaca: Cornell University Press, 1977.

The Poems. Ed. John O. Hayden. 2 vols. Harmondsworth: Penguin, 1977.

The Prelude, 1798–1799. Ed. Stephen Parrish. Ithaca: Cornell University Press, 1977.

Guide to the Lakes, The Fifth Edition (1835). Ed. Ernest de Selincourt. Oxford: Oxford University Press, 1977.

The Letters of William and Dorothy Wordsworth, Later Years. 4 vols. Ed. Ernest de Selincourt, revised Alan G. Hill. Oxford: Clarendon Press, 1979.

The Prelude, 1799, 1805, 1850. Ed. Jonathan Wordsworth, M. H. Abrams and Stephen Gill. New York: W. W. Norton, 1979.

The Ruined Cottage and The Pedlar. Ed. James Butler. Ithaca: Cornell University Press, 1979.

Poems, in Two Volumes, and Other Poems, 1800–1807. Ed. Jared Curtis. Ithaca: Cornell University Press, 1983.

Descriptive Sketches. Ed. Eric Birdsall. Ithaca: Cornell University Press, 1984.

An Evening Walk. Ed. James Averill. Ithaca: Cornell University Press, 1984.

The Fourteen-Book Prelude. Ed. W. J. B. Owen. Ithaca: Cornell University Press, 1985.

Peter Bell. Ed. John E. Jordan. Ithaca: Cornell University Press, 1985.

The Tuft of Primroses with Other Late Poems for The Recluse. Ed. Joseph F. Kishel. Ithaca: Cornell University Press, 1986.

The Excursion 1814. Facsimile edition. Oxford and New York: Woodstock Press, 1991.

The Thirteen-Book Prelude. 2 vols. Ed. Mark L. Reed. Ithaca: Cornell University Press, 1991.

Lyrical Ballads, and Other Poems, 1797–1800. Ed. James Butler and Karen Green. Ithaca: Cornell University Press, 1992.

Last Poems, 1821–1850. Ed. Jared Curtis. Ithaca: Cornell University Press, 1999.

The Major Works. Ed. Stephen Gill. Oxford: Oxford University Press, 2000.

Sonnet Series and Itinerary Poems, 1820–1845. Ed. Geoffrey Jackson. Ithaca: Cornell University Press, 2004.

The Excursion. Ed. Sally Bushell, James A. Butler and Michael C. Jaye. Ithaca: Cornell University Press, 2007.

Wordsworth, William and Coleridge, Samuel Taylor. *Wordsworth and Coleridge: Lyrical Ballads*. Ed. R. L. Brett and A. R. Jones. London and New York: Routledge.

Wright, George T. Hendiadys and *Hamlet. PMLA* 96, 2 (1981), pp. 168–93.

Wu, Duncan. *Wordsworth's Reading 1770–1799*. Cambridge: Cambridge University Press, 1993.

Wordsworth's Reading 1800–1815. Cambridge: Cambridge University Press, 1995.

Young, Arthur. *Travels During the Years 1787, 1788, and 1789; undertaken more particularly with a View of ascertaining the Cultivation, Wealth, Resources, and National Prosperity of the Kingdom of France*, second edition, 2 vols. London and Bury St Edmunds, 1794.

Young, Edward. *Conjectures on Original Composition. In a letter to the Author of Sir Charles Grandison*. London: A. Millar, and R. and J. Dodsley, 1759.

Žižek, Slavoj. *The Parallax View*. Cambridge, MA: MIT Press, 2006.

Index

CAMBRIDGE STUDIES IN ROMANTICISM

General Editor
James Chandler, *University of Chicago*

1. Romantic Correspondence: Women, Politics and the Fiction of Letters
   MARY A. FAVRET
2. British Romantic Writers and the East: Anxieties of Empire
   NIGEL LEASK
3. Poetry as an Occupation and an Art in Britain, 1760–1830
   PETER MURPHY
4. Edmund Burke's Aesthetic Ideology: Language, Gender and Political Economy in Revolution
   TOM FURNISS
5. In the Theatre of Romanticism: Coleridge, Nationalism, Women
   JULIE A. CARLSON
6. Keats, Narrative and Audience
   ANDREW BENNETT
7. Romance and Revolution: Shelley and the Politics of a Genre
   DAVID DUFF
8. Literature, Education, and Romanticism: Reading as Social Practice, 1780–1832
   ALAN RICHARDSON
9. Women Writing about Money: Women's Fiction in England, 1790–1820
   EDWARD COPELAND
10. Shelley and the Revolution in Taste: The Body and the Natural World
    TIMOTHY MORTON
11. William Cobbett: The Politics of Style
    LEONORA NATTRASS
12. The Rise of Supernatural Fiction, 1762–1800
    E. J. CLERY
13. Women Travel Writers and the Language of Aesthetics, 1716–1818
    ELIZABETH A. BOHLS
14. Napoleon and English Romanticism
    SIMON BAINBRIDGE

15. Romantic Vagrancy: Wordsworth and the Simulation of Freedom
CELESTE LANGAN

16. Wordsworth and the Geologists
JOHN WYATT

17. Wordsworth's Pope: A Study in Literary Historiography
ROBERT J. GRIFFIN

18. The Politics of Sensibility: Race, Gender and Commerce in the Sentimental Novel
MARKMAN ELLIS

19. Reading Daughters' Fictions, 1709–1834: Novels and Society from Manley to Edgeworth
CAROLINE GONDA

20. Romantic Identities: Varieties of Subjectivity, 1774–1830
ANDREA K. HENDERSON

21. Print Politics: The Press and Radical Opposition: in Early Nineteenth-Century England
KEVIN GILMARTIN

22. Reinventing Allegory
THERESA M. KELLEY

23. British Satire and the Politics of Style, 1789–1832
GARY DYER

24. The Romantic Reformation: Religious Politics in English Literature, 1789–1824
ROBERT M. RYAN

25. De Quincey's Romanticism: Canonical Minority and the Forms of Transmission
MARGARET RUSSETT

26. Coleridge on Dreaming: Romanticism, Dreams and the Medical Imagination
JENNIFER FORD

27. Romantic Imperialism: Universal Empire and the Culture of Modernity
SAREE MAKDISI

28. Ideology and Utopia in the Poetry of William Blake
NICHOLAS M. WILLIAMS

29. Sexual Politics and the Romantic Author
SONIA HOFKOSH

30. Lyric and Labour in the Romantic Tradition
ANNE JANOWITZ

31. Poetry and Politics in the Cockney School: Keats, Shelley, Hunt and their Circle
JEFFREY N. COX

32. Rousseau, Robespierre and English Romanticism
GREGORY DART

33. Contesting the Gothic: Fiction, Genre and Cultural Conflict, 1764–1832
JAMES WATT

34. Romanticism, Aesthetics, and Nationalism
DAVID ARAM KAISER

35. Romantic Poets and the Culture of Posterity
ANDREW BENNETT

36. The Crisis of Literature in the 1790s: Print Culture and the Public Sphere
PAUL KEEN

37. Romantic Atheism: Poetry and Freethought, 1780–1830
MARTIN PRIESTMAN

38. Romanticism and Slave Narratives: Transatlantic Testimonies
HELEN THOMAS

39. Imagination under Pressure, 1789–1832: Aesthetics, Politics, and Utility
JOHN WHALE

40. Romanticism and the Gothic: Genre, Reception, and Canon Formation, 1790–1820
MICHAEL GAMER

41. Romanticism and the Human Sciences: Poetry, Population, and the Discourse of the Species
MAUREEN N. MCLANE

42. The Poetics of Spice: Romantic Consumerism and the Exotic
TIMOTHY MORTON

43. British Fiction and the Production of Social Order, 1740–1830
MIRANDA J. BURGESS

44. Women Writers and the English Nation in the 1790s
ANGELA KEANE

45. Literary Magazines and British Romanticism
MARK PARKER

46. Women, Nationalism and the Romantic Stage: Theatre and Politics in Britain, 1780–1800
BETSY BOLTON

47. British Romanticism and the Science of the Mind
ALAN RICHARDSON

48. The Anti-Jacobin Novel: British Conservatism and the French Revolution
M. O. GRENBY

49. Romantic Austen: Sexual Politics and the Literary Canon
CLARA TUITE

50. Byron and Romanticism
JEROME MCGANN AND JAMES SODERHOLM

51. The Romantic National Tale and the Question of Ireland
INA FERRIS

52. Byron, Poetics and History
JANE STABLER

53. Religion, Toleration, and British Writing, 1790–1830
MARK CANUEL

54. Fatal Women of Romanticism
ADRIANA CRACIUN

55. Knowledge and Indifference in English Romantic Prose
TIM MILNES

56. Mary Wollstonecraft and the Feminist Imagination
BARBARA TAYLOR

57. Romanticism, Maternity and the Body Politic
JULIE KIPP

58. Romanticism and Animal Rights
DAVID PERKINS

59. Georgic Modernity and British Romanticism: Poetry and the Mediation of History
KEVIS GOODMAN

60. Literature, Science and Exploration in the Romantic Era: Bodies of Knowledge
TIMOTHY FULFORD, DEBBIE LEE, AND PETER J. KITSON

61. Romantic Colonization and British Anti-Slavery
DEIRDRE COLEMAN

79. Wordsworth, Commodification and Social Concern: The Poetics of Modernity
DAVID SIMPSON

80. Sentimental Masculinity and the Rise of History, 1790–1890
MIKE GOODE

81. Fracture and Fragmentation in British Romanticism
ALEXANDER REGIER

82. Romanticism and Music Culture in Britain, 1770–1840: Virtue and Virtuosity
GILLEN D'ARCY WOOD

83. The Truth about Romanticism: Pragmatism and Idealism in Keats, Shelley, Coleridge
TIM MILNES

84. Blake's Gifts: Poetry and the Politics of Exchange
SARAH HAGGARTY

85. Real Money and Romanticism
MATTHEW ROWLINSON

86. Sentimental Literature and Anglo-Scottish Identity, 1745–1820
JULIET SHIELDS

87. Romantic Tragedies: The Dark Employments of Wordsworth, Coleridge, and Shelley
REEVE PARKER

88. Blake, Sexuality and Bourgeois Politeness
SUSAN MATTHEWS

89. Idleness, Contemplation and the Aesthetic
RICHARD ADELMAN

90. Shelley's Visual Imagination
NANCY MOORE GOSLEE

91. A Cultural History of the Irish Novel, 1790–1829
CLAIRE CONNOLLY

92. Literature, Commerce, and the Spectacle of Modernity, 1750–1800
PAUL KEEN

93. Romanticism and Childhood: The Infantilization of British Literary Culture
ANN WEIRDA ROWLAND

94. Metropolitan Art and Literature, 1810–1840: Cockney Adventures
GREGORY DART

95. Wordsworth and the Enlightenment Idea of Pleasure
ROWAN BOYSON

96. John Clare and Community
JOHN GOODRIDGE

97. The Romantic Crowd
MARY FAIRCLOUGH

98. Romantic Women Writers, Revolution and Prophecy
ORIANNE SMITH

99. Britain, France and the Gothic, 1764–1820
ANGELA WRIGHT

100. Transfiguring the Arts and Sciences
JON KLANCHER

101. Shelley and the Apprehension of Life
ROSS WILSON

102. Poetics of Character: Transatlantic Encounters 1700–1900
SUSAN MANNING

103. Romanticism and Caricature
IAN HAYWOOD

104. The Late Poetry of the Lake Poets: Romanticism Revised
TIM FULFORD

105. Forging Romantic China: Sino-British Cultural Exchange 1760–1840
PETER J. KITSON

106. Coleridge and the Philosophy of Poetic Form
EWAN JAMES JONES

107. Romanticism in the Shadow of War: Literary Culture in the Napoleonic War Years
JEFFREY N. COX

108. Slavery and the Politics of Place: Representing the Colonial Caribbean, 1770–1833
ELIZABETH A. BOHLS

109. The Orient and the Young Romantics
ANDREW WARREN